Book A1

INFUSION LESSONS
Teaching Critical and Creative Thinking in Language Arts

Robert J. Swartz

Jacqueline Larisey

Mary Anne Kiser

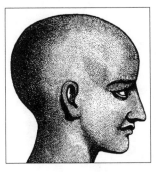

© 2000
CRITICAL THINKING BOOKS & SOFTWARE
www.criticalthinking.com
P.O. Box 448 • Pacific Grove • CA 93950-0448
Phone 800-458-4849 • FAX 831-393-3277
ISBN 0-89455-734-3
Printed in the United States of America

These lesson books are dedicated to all of the teachers with whom we have worked, whose creativity in the classroom has shown us how much can be done to help all of our students realize their full potential as thinkers and learners.

Robert Swartz received his B.A. and Ph.D. in philosophy from Harvard and studied as part of a Fulbright Scholarship at universities in Oxford and Cambridge in England. He is a faculty member at the University of Massachusetts at Boston. He is director of the National Center for Teaching Thinking. Through the Center, he provides staff development to educators across the country on restructuring curriculum by infusing critical and creative thinking into content area instruction. He has authored numerous articles and books on critical thinking and has acted as a testing consultant for the National Assessment of Educational Progress.

Jacqueline Larisey is currently a first grade teacher in Naperville, Illinois. She received her B.A. from Marycrest College in Davenport, Iowa and her Master of Education in Curriculum and Instruction from National Louis University in Evanston, Illinois. She has over 25 years of experience teaching primary students. She has shared her work in the field of infusing critical and creative thinking into content instruction as a consultant at district level inservice meetings as well as at state and national conferences.

Mary Anne Kiser received her B.S. in Elementary Education from the University of Missouri and her Master of Science in Education from Northwestern Illinois University. She is currently an elementary school principal in Naperville, Illinois. She has been a teacher at both the elementary and middle school levels. She has also been a district supervisor of staff development and is currently a consultant in cognitive coaching training for administrators.

ACKNOWLEDGMENTS

I have been working with teachers and school administrators since the early 1980s on ways to infuse critical and creative thinking into content instruction. My coauthors in this book, and in the other books in this series, stand out as among the most dedicated of these colleagues.

For her excellent and insightful contributions to the material contained in this book, I wish to thank Mary Anne Kiser, Principal of the Meadow Glens Elementary School, in Naperville, Illinois. Mary Anne has brought to this book an insight into the minds of young children and a sensitivity to the needs of teachers, developed over more than two decades of dedicated contact with both, that I have found in few other educators. Her authorship of many of the segments of this book and her help with its overall structure and content has revealed to me a person of deep sensitivity to the goals of a good education that must start, and start well, in the elementary grades.

I also wish to thank Jacqueline Larisey for her hard and dedicated work in producing the excellent lessons in this book. Her dedication to teaching all of her students to realize their full potential as good thinkers should be apparent in these lessons. In addition, I wish to thank the multitude of students whose clear and careful thoughts are recorded in these lessons. Jacqueline has great skill at bringing out the kinds of thinking you will see in these lessons. But it is her students' thoughts that we must, in the end, celebrate as a testament to what students, who might otherwise seem very ordinary, are capable of when prompted by lessons like these.

For help with the editing of the manuscript, my thanks go out to the editorial staff of Critical Thinking Books and Software.

Finally, I wish to acknowledge our indebtedness to the earlier books in this series, the lesson design handbooks on *Infusing Critical and Creative Thinking into Content Instruction*. In particular, I want to acknowledge the volume for elementary school classrooms which I coauthored with Sandra Parks as the source of most of the "thinking maps" and graphic organizers used throughout these lessons. It is through the use of this series of books that the lessons in this lesson book have been developed. Critical Thinking Books & Software has gladly made the teaching tools from the lesson design handbooks available for use in this lesson book series.

Robert Swartz
Newtonville, Massachusetts, May 2000

One of my goals as I begin each year with a new group of children is to develop a thinking classroom, a place where children are honored and respected as thinkers. Using the infusion model of teaching thinking has proven to be very successful in providing children with strategies that enrich their thinking by enabling them to think in different ways. The infusion model empowers children in the primary grades to think at levels that many adults mistakenly believe are beyond their realm of capabilities.

During the summer of 1999, when this book was finalized, the Chicago White Sox had a group of young athletes who were trying to establish themselves in the professional baseball arena. To promote their team, the White Sox organization developed the slogan These Kids Can Play! An adaptation of their slogan fits into my classroom and into any classroom where thinking is modeled, practiced, and encouraged. These Kids Can Think! In a thinking classroom, the teacher is the manager who believes in the ability of each player and coaches the team to the acquisition of good thinking strategies. Just as the White Sox management wants its players to master skills and have the confidence to use them in a variety of situations, I want my students to utilize thinking strategies successfully.

There are many people who supported me in this endeavor. My husband, Dan, has been my most loyal supporter, always celebrating the joys of learning with me. My children, Patrick and Courtney, gave me personal experiences with young thinkers as they grew and blossomed into

These lesson books are designed to provide teachers with lessons that infuse critical and creative thinking into content instruction that they can teach in their own classroom. Reproductive materials are provided in each lesson for this purpose.

During the past fifteen years, many schools in the United States have been working towards a revision of their curriculum in ways that put improving the quality of students' thinking as a central theme. At the same time, many states have revised their testing programs by putting a premium on thoughtful responses to open-ended questions, an ability which depends on these instructional changes. Yet a vast number of teachers and schools today are still not sure what this involves, how it translates into effective classroom practice, and even whether it is worth doing in the long run.

These lesson books are attempts to answer these questions. They collect together exemplary teacher-designed lessons based on standard topics in the curriculum or on much-used texts in schools across this country, that are designed to infuse instruction in critical and creative thinking skills into content instruction. These lesson books are a testament to what can be done within the standard curriculum when fine creative teachers put their best minds' work into their teaching. It is our belief that every teacher can teach this way. We have written these lessons to make them available and accessible to any teacher who wants to use them.

The beauty of these lessons is threefold. First, they are manageable within the standard school and classroom structure and do not presuppose any changes in the length of class periods, etc. Second, they combine and elaborate many sound practices, that teachers now use piecemeal in their own instruction, to produce a powerful and manageable instructional methodology. Third, they are exceptionally effective in meeting the goals of good instruction that have grown out of the reforms of the 1980s: deep content learning and careful, quality thinking.

The lessons in these books are presented so that they can be taught in any classroom that provides instruction in these lesson topics or uses the texts around which they revolve. The raw material needed to make these lessons work (except the basic texts that provide the contexts for many of these lessons) is all there in the lesson for teachers to use with their own students. They are scripted to provide guidance when they are taught. Student responses from the original classrooms in which they were developed are included to show what you can expect when you teach these lessons. They are designed so that they can be modified to suit students' special needs that may be idiosyncratic to the new classrooms in which the lessons will be taught. In short, we have tried to provide you with lessons that you can try out with your own students immediately and that show what quality instruction in thoughtful learning is like.

But these lesson books are designed to do more than just provide some lessons that teachers can teach and that have these enhanced goals. They are also designed to be used in conjunction with the lesson design handbooks, *Infusing the Teaching of Critical and Creative Thinking into Content Instruction*, as models for the creation of your own infusion lessons. What is in these lesson books will get you started immediately teaching quality infusion lessons, but by no means serve as complete programs in either language arts, social studies, or science. Such complete programs can be achieved only by your supplementing these lessons with your own, and the lesson design handbooks will help you do just that.

For now, though, we invite you to try the lessons we have included in this lesson book. We can guarantee that your students will find them challenging, that these lessons will bring out your students' natural abilities as thinkers, and that you will be able to help them to improve both their thinking and content understanding through these lessons. So—go to it! You have our support and dedicated encouragement.

Robert Swartz, Jacqueline Larisey, and Mary Anne Kiser, Co-Authors of this Series creative and critical thinking adults. My mother, Betty Donohue, has always believed in my ability to think and succeed. My teammates, Kathi Olson, Linda Pfeiffer, and Jayne Schmidt and the second grade team, Jeanne Sawyer, Barb Kling, Linda Poska, and Kathy Angelos helped me by providing encouragement, lesson ideas, and classrooms in which to test lessons. As we traveled the path of authorship, my friends and fellow authors at Meadow Glens, Mary Anne Kiser and Traci Whipple, gave me invaluable advice and insights as our books became dreams turned into realities. And finally, Robert Swartz introduced me to the infusion model and offered me a chance to share my enthusiasm for teaching thinking in the pages of this book. To all of these supporters, and to the students of Meadow Glens who have proven that young minds are so very capable, I extend my most grateful thank you!

Jacqueline Larisey
Naperville, Illinois, May 2000

One of the special joys of being an elementary school principal is observing the joy of learning in children and adults. Infusion lessons have, therefore, been the source of much joy in my professional life. For this, I am most grateful to the originator of the Infusion model, Robert Swartz, for opening up the possibilities for learning; to the teachers of Meadow Glens Elementary School, for the gifts of learning and love of learning that they give to our students; and to the students of Meadow Glens, for proving daily that thinking in depth comes in all sizes and with great promise. I wish all who read this book a similar experience of joy.

Mary Anne Kiser
Naperville, Illinois, May 2000

TABLE OF CONTENTS

LANGUAGE ARTS SKILLS MATRIX

Infusion Lessons

LANGUAGE ARTS SKILLS	DM: Duckling Decisions	DM: Jamaica's Find	PS: Wolf in My Bed!	PS: Rumpelstiltskin	CC: Bats	CC: City and Country	CL: Houses	CL: Nouns, Verbs, Adj.	PW: Do You See...?	PW: Parts of a Picture	SQ: The Bear and Crow	SQ: Writing	RC: Fox on the Losse!	UA: Petunia's Assump.	GP: Lots of Presents
READING															
Classifying information							■	■				■			
Drawing conclusions					■	■						■	■		
Finding supporting evidence	■	■										■	■		
Identifying main idea						■			■	■			■		
Making inferences															
Making predictions			■						■	■					
Reading for specific details	■	■	■	■	■	■					■			■	
Reading for general info.															
Sequencing											■	■			
Using references							■	■	■			■			
LITERARY ANALYSIS															
Analyzing characters	■	■		■	■	■								■	
Recognizing story parts			■						■	■	■				■
Recognizing literary genres											■	■			
Recognizing point of view	■	■			■	■									
WRITING															
Comparing/Contrasting					■										
Writing to explain	■		■							■				■	
Writing to describe		■						■							
Writing to persuade				■										■	
Writing poetry				■		■	■	■						■	

LANGUAGE ARTS SKILLS MATRIX

Infusion Lessons

LANGUAGE ARTS SKILLS	CM: Blizzards	RS: Whales	RS: Who Stole Diamonds?	CE: Why Those Stripes?	CE: Why is this Happening?	PR: To Help or Not?	PR: The Sweetest Fig	GN: Vowel Sounds	RA: How Beak Works	CR: The Talking Eggs
READING										
Classifying information		■				■		■		
Drawing conclusions	■			■	■		■	■	■	■
Finding supporting evidence			■		■		■	■		■
Identifying main idea	■									
Making inferences			■				■			
Making predictions						■				■
Reading for specific details			■			■	■			■
Reading for general info.		■		■	■					
Sequencing										
Using references		■						■	■	
LITERARY ANALYSIS										
Analyzing characters	■		■			■	■			■
Recognizing story parts										■
Recognizing literary genres			■							
Recognizing point of view						■				
WRITING										
Comparing/Contrasting										
Writing to explain	■				■	■				
Writing to describe										
Writing to persuade	■			■						
Writing poetry	■									

CHAPTER 1
WHAT IS INFUSION?

All of the lessons in these lesson books involve infusing instruction in specific thinking skills into standard content instruction. Many educators speak nowadays about infusing thinking skills into content instruction, in contrast to trying to teach thinking skills in separate educational programs. Not all of these references are to the kind of lessons that form the basis for the approach we call infusing the teaching of critical and creative thinking into content instruction. Infusion lessons have very special features that give them a special status in the array of classroom approaches to teaching thinking. These lessons blend together a cluster of well-researched instructional practices into what we feel is the most powerful way to instruct students so that they achieve a deep understanding of the content they are learning and develop habits of skillful thought that will serve them all of their lives. These special features include the following:

- Making strategies for skillful thinking explicit and guiding students to use them to think about the content they are learning.

- Involving students in collaborative thinking activities as they think about the content they are learning.

- Prompting students to engage in metacognitive reflection about their thinking.

- Teaching students directly to transfer and use the kinds of skillful thinking they are learning in a variety of other appropriate contexts.

The previously published lesson design handbooks on Infusing the Teaching of Critical and Creative Thinking into Content Instruction provide you with models, commentaries, and all the tools you need to design such lessons. These lesson books give you an array of lessons so that teachers can teach directly to develop skill in the kinds of instructional strategies that make Infusion lessons so effective.

The Ingredients in Effective Infusion Lessons

Infusion lessons are not just standard content-area lessons enhanced by such teaching tools as graphic organizers. Rather, Infusion lessons represent new ways of teaching the same content that shift the roles of the teacher and the student in a classroom to yield more active student learning and deeper content understanding.

When Infusion lessons are taught, the center of gravity changes in a school classroom. The classroom becomes more student-centered, and the teacher becomes more a facilitator for developing student understanding rather than solely a transmitter of information. The thinking structures that the students are learning become the support vehicles for their mustering relevant background information and engaging with the new material they are learning so that they achieve their own understanding of this material. Interaction with other students and with the teacher adjusts this understanding in the light of others' insights. At the same time, students develop the thinking skills and the disposition to use these skills for further learning.

What makes Infusion lessons "tick" in this way is the quartet of ingredients that are written into the well-crafted lesson plans in these books. Any teacher at any grade level can use these ingredients, suitably adjusted to the materials, concepts, and ideas being taught, to create meaningful Infusion lessons for his/her students. Let's look at these ingredients more closely.

Making Explicit What Goes into Skillful Thinking

Thinking Maps. In the lesson "Jamaica and the Dog," based on the book *Jamaica's Find*, just before the class reads about what Jamaica (a young child who has found a stuffed dog in the park) decides to do about the dog, the teacher writes the important questions that students must identify when thinking about decisions they have to make. By writing these questions down, the teacher is making explicit a verbal strategy for decision making. Students will use these questions as a guide as they "become" Jamaica themselves, and have to decide what to do. We call this a thinking map of skillful decision making (figure 1.1). The map defines a cluster of ideas about what is important to focus attention on—what questions are important to answer—in skillfully engaging in decision making.

SKILLFUL DECISION MAKING

1. What are some things I can do?

2. What will happen if I do these things?

3. Which are good things to do?

---

figure 1.1

Use of thinking maps like the one for decision making occurs in every Infusion lesson. However, it is the questions on these maps that are important, not necessarily the maps as shown in the figures. If you choose not to use these maps, making these questions explicit by writing them on the chalkboard and providing constant oral reinforcement of them is still of crucial importance. It is what guides the students to do well the kind of thinking they are practicing, and it is what they will internalize as they develop the habit of asking these questions in appropriate circumstances without having to be prompted by a teacher.

When students move beyond grade 2, more sophisticated thinking maps can be introduced like this one (see figure 1.2). Whatever the grade level, it will be question sequences like the ones contained in these thinking maps that play a key role in guiding students in their thinking.

SKILLFUL DECISION MAKING

1. What makes a decision necessary?

2. What are my options?

3. What are the likely consequences of each option?

4. How important are the consequences?

5. Which option is best in light of the consequences?

---

figure 1.2

Skillful Thinking. Some general comments about what it is to teach thinking, or to teach critical and creative thinking, are in order here and will give a broader context to these comments about the use of thinking maps in the lessons in this book. Thinking maps guide students in doing specific kinds of thinking skillfully. In effect, they represent strategies that students can learn that will make their thinking better. This means that our goal as teachers of thinking is teaching skillful thinking, and not, strictly speaking, just teaching thinking. When we blend this with our goals as teachers of content in the traditional subject areas, our goals are not just to get students thinking about the content they are learning, but to help them learn how to think carefully and skillfully.

To be more specific and focus again on decision making as an example, it would be misleading to say that we want to teach students decision making per se. We don't have to teach students to make decisions. They make decisions all the time. Rather, we want to teach them to make decisions carefully and skillfully—to think about everything that is important to think about prior to making decisions, and not just to make decisions "off the top of their heads." In our content-driven instruction, therefore, we want to teach students to think carefully and skillfully about the decisions of historical figures that they study and of characters in novels that they read. We want to teach students to think carefully and skillfully about what they eat and make use of what we teach them about nutrition in the process. We want them to think carefully and skillfully when they make decisions about how to manage their money, through which they make use of what we have taught them about the use of money in general. In all of these instances, we don't just want to encourage them to react to others' decisions or make their own the way they ordinarily do; that's a ticket to quick and hasty decision making, usually done without thinking much about either other options or the consequences of the choices they are considering.

This is where thinking maps come in. Thinking maps, like the one for skillful decision making, are ways of operationalizing what is involved in skillful thinking of specific sorts. In decision making, what the thinking map tells us is that there is a series of important questions to ask and answer before you make a decision. The thinking map also tells us what those questions are. In addition, it suggests a natural sequence in which to ask those questions.

That is why we like to think of these as thinking strategies, although these thinking maps should not be confused with algorithms that a person can memorize and that one must follow in only a certain order. You can ask these questions any time in a thinking process, and you can come back to ones that you've already considered. The numbering just suggests that there is a natural sequence that you might want to follow to do this kind of thinking in an organized and orderly way. The important thing, however, is that students focus attention on these questions, because they are what people often miss when they do their thinking in sloppy and careless ways that may lead to half-baked ideas, hasty choices, and trouble.

Skillful thinking, as represented in thinking maps like that in figure 1.1 is, of course, a matter of degree. Your thinking can be more or less skillful depending on the care with which you ask and answer these questions. In fact, maybe there are other questions that should be on this map that will fine tune this strategy immensely, like "How reliable is the information I am using to determine the consequences of my options?" Students can do this fine tuning as they learn more and more about the kinds of skillful thinking in this book. We present basic strategies for these kinds of thinking that you can use in the first introductory lessons that you teach. These basic strategies are incorporated in the thinking maps you find built into all of the lessons.

Kinds of Thinking Students Should Be Taught to Do Skillfully. So what are the kinds of thinking that are infused into content instruction in this book? Decision making is one of them, and represents a broad kind of thinking activity that people engage in every day of their lives. Problem solving (a type of thinking that is very much like decision making) is another broad and authentic type of thinking task that students engage in often, and that you can teach them to do skillfully through the use of a comparable thinking map.

In addition, however, there is a whole range of other more circumscribed types of thinking, many of which are part of broad thinking tasks like decision making and problem solving, that students also need to learn how to do skillfully if they are to become good thinkers. These fall into three main categories: generating ideas, clarifying ideas, and assessing the reasonableness of ideas. These categories, in fact, map right onto the earlier division of thinking found in Bloom's famous taxonomy. They are the three types of higher-order thinking Bloom isolated: synthesis, analysis, and evaluation.

In the work we have done on Infusion, however, these terms all designate categories of thinking skills and not, on their own, specific thinking skills. There is not just one way to analyze things, for example. So to focus on types of thinking that fall into these categories, that differ from each other in various ways, and for which different thinking maps represent strategies for doing them well, we have to focus our attention on such forms of thinking as parts-whole analysis, sequencing, comparing and contrasting, etc. That is the level at which thinking strategies are developed and taught in the lessons in this book and the basis for the chapter division.

The chart in figure 1.3 summarizes the scope and organization of the different types of thinking covered in these pages (see next page).

IMPORTANT TYPES OF THINKING
TO ENGAGE IN SKILLFULLY

SPECIFIC TYPES OF THINKING

I. SKILLS AT GENERATING IDEAS

1. Generating Possibilities

   A. Multiplicity of Ideas
   B. Varied Ideas
   C. New Ideas
   D. Detailed Ideas

2. Composition

   A. Analogy/Metaphor

II. SKILLS AT CLARIFYING IDEAS

1. Analyzing Ideas

   A. Compare/Contrast
   B. Classification/Definition
   C. Parts/Whole
   D. Sequencing

2. Analyzing Arguments

   A. Finding Reasons/Conclusions
   B. Uncovering Assumptions

III. SKILLS AT ASSESSING THE REASONABLENESS OF IDEAS

1. Assessing Basic Information

   A. Accuracy of Observation
   B. Reliability of Sources

2. Inference

   A. Use of Evidence

      1. Causal Explanation
      2. Prediction
      3. Generalization
      4. Reasoning by Analogy

   B. Deduction

      1. Conditional Reasoning (If...then...)

COMPLEX THINKING TASKS

1. Goal Oriented Processes

   A. Decision Making
   B. Problem Solving

figure 1.3

Graphic Organizers. The same general comment that we made about the thinking maps can be made about the graphic organizers that are used in each lesson. The graphic organizer used in grades 1 and 2 for skillful decision making is shown in figure 1.4. These are usually forerunners for more sophisticated graphic organizers that are introduced in grade 3 and higher (see figure 1.5) along with the more sophisticated thinking maps that can be used to guide student thinking when students reach that level of their education. The teachers who have developed these Infusion lessons have found the use of such diagrams extremely helpful. The organizers give students places to write down their ideas, and they are structured to reinforce the guidance we provide to take the students through the processes of thinking which they are learning. The graphic organizers in these lessons have been developed by teachers and students to accomplish this goal. In each lesson, we provide blank graphic organizers for you to use when teaching the lesson.

If you choose not to use the graphic organizers we reproduce for use in the lessons, we recommend that you use some other diagram (or work with the students to develop your own) that can serve the same purpose.

Thinking Language. In teaching Infusion lessons, it is important that you use the language of the thinking skill being taught as much as possible, as well as emphasizing the content being taught. In the prediction lesson based on the book *The Sweetest Fig*, in which the students try to predict what the main character Bibot will do once he discovers the magical qualities of the fig, it is natural to focus students' attention on the circumstances surrounding this decision in the book, and on Bibot's character. The teacher will also help students with the reading skills they need to get this information, so they won't be guessing about what she will do, but will be making well-founded predictions. This is more sophisticated than what many now do to prompt student predicting as they read—ask them to predict what will happen and then to read on to find out. Such activities miss what is crucially important about prediction—the need to support our predictions with reasons or evi-

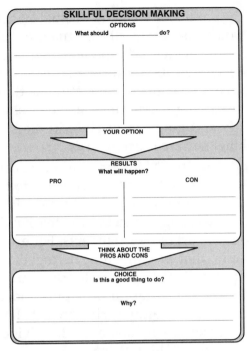

figure 1.4

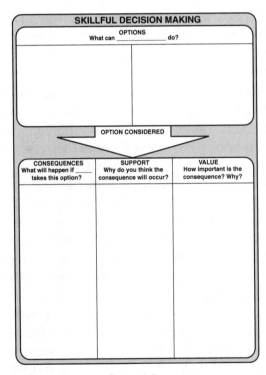

figure 1.5

dence to judge how likely they are to occur. This is not beyond the capabilities of our students, even in the 1st and 2nd grades. But it is equally important in teaching this lesson that you use the language of skillful prediction—including such terms as "prediction," "possible evidence that the prediction is likely," "actual evidence," etc. (Some teachers use the language of "clues" instead of "evidence," especially in first grade. Whatever the appropriate words, using explicit and accurate language to identify the thinking they are doing is crucial.) This helps students identify and guide themselves in the kind of thinking they are learning to do.

Collaborative Thinking. Various collaborative thinking strategies have proved effective in prompting more student involvement in what they are learning and in more extensive thinking on the part of more students. For example, we know that pairing students together and prompting them to ask each other questions yields more elaboration of details and more depth of understanding about what they are thinking and talking about. Such activities are usually called "Think-Pair-Share."

Other group activities, such as more elaborate cooperative learning engagements, have also proved to be learning-enhancers that produce more student involvement in what they are learning and improve the depth of their understanding.

Every Infusion lesson utilizes such collaborative thinking activities. For example, in the lesson "City Living and Country Living," based on the book *Town Mouse Country Mouse,* students "think-pair-share" the conclusions they drew about these two lifestyles after noting a number of their significant similarities and differences. When they do this, they prompt each other to clarify, elaborate, and defend their conclusions. The thinking that results throughout the class is deeper and more extensive than if students were asked to think about these matters on their own. In the lesson on generating possibilities, based on the book *Mr. Rabbit and the Lovely Present,* collaborative learning groups generate ideas about different presents that they could give. The result is a richer set of ideas than would have been generated if students did this activity on their own.

In Infusion lessons, as these examples illustrate, such group activities are usually employed in ways that involve students in doing the kinds of thinking that the lesson aims at helping students improve, e.g., compare/contrast, decision

making, determining the reliability of sources, etc. Collaborative thinking not only enhances content learning but also gives students a context in which to practice with the support of their peers the thinking strategies they are learning.

Collaborative thinking activities are also practiced in these lessons to give students an important message: teamwork in thinking through issues is not only acceptable, it is to be preferred over more individualized thinking tasks. It is always a good idea to bounce your ideas off someone else, and it is always a good idea to listen seriously to the ideas of others, even though they may not agree with you.

The primary function of these "collaborative thinking" activities is to enhance students' thinking by sharing their ideas in a group that is structured for collaboration, not competition. There is no reason why such groups cannot, at the same time, serve some of the broader functions of what has for some time been called "collaborative learning." Helping students develop skills in social interaction, mutual respect, teamwork, and in being spokespersons for others can all be incorporated into the goals of such group activities.

Metacognition. The main thinking-skill goal of Infusion lessons is to help students to internalize thinking strategies—mainly question and answer strategies—that make their thinking more skillful. This means that, for example, when the teacher is not around to say things like "What evidence is there for that possible cause?" the students remember to do this, take it seriously, and hence, prompt themselves to search for evidence. Metacognitive activities are key strategies in Infusion lessons that help students achieve this goal.

For example, in teaching the lesson "Jamaica and the Dog," you will be asking students not only to identify the kind of thinking they have done when deciding what Jamaica should do, but also to describe how they did it, assess whether this way of carrying out the thinking is a valuable way to do it, and plan how they will be doing it again the next time. These types of activities are not beyond students in grades 1 and 2, and you can present them with good modeling and prompts that are phrased in language they can easily grasp. When you teach the parts-whole lesson on picture books, you will be asking your students to think about how using the parts-whole strategy in this lesson helped them in creating their own picture book, and what they would think about next time they focused their attention on the parts of some whole object like they did in this lesson. This is metacognition as it should be practiced. Even in 1st and 2nd grade students can begin to learn to manage their own thinking.

Metacognition has been extensively researched as a mechanism for enabling people to take control of their own thinking by learning to monitor and guide themselves. When they guide themselves in doing certain kinds of thinking (such as decision making) in accordance with strategies that they certify as valuable, they are building the much-needed disposition for doing this kind of thinking a certain way onto their understanding of how to do it and onto their ability to translate this understanding into good practice. The earlier we start helping students to develop these dispositions, the better.

Many educators ignore the role of metacognition in good learning when they do what they think involves infusing thinking skills into their instruction. For example, teachers often have their students solve problems in class. They may even have their students follow a strategy and use a graphic organizer in solving these problems. However, if students do not reflect on how they solved the problems or if they do not develop a plan to guide themselves the next time they do have to solve the problems, they will not internalize the thinking strategy.

When students are guided by the teacher to guide themselves, however, the teacher has incorporated a powerful instructional tool in his or her lessons that can contribute to maximizing chances that students will guide themselves in good thinking when it is needed. Guided practice, combined with metacognitive reflection on the practice, enhances both students' abilities and their dispositions to engage these abilities when the need arises.

Teaching for Transfer. After students work on making judgments about what the evidence suggests about what Bibot will do in the prediction lesson based on the book *The Sweetest Fig*, and they reflect on how they did this and develop a plan to use when they do it again, the lesson "What Will Happen Next?" is not yet over. The teacher then reads the student another story and the student does the same kind of thinking again but in connection with what the main character in that story will do and about their situation—one that has nothing to do with Bibot in *The Sweetest Fig*.

The reason for this is fairly obvious. To develop the skill needed to do this kind of thinking well (in this case prediction), more practice is needed. This must be practice in which the teacher backs off from the kind of guidance provided in the initial lesson activity and prompts the students to guide themselves in the kind of thinking being taught. When you teach the lesson on what Bibot will do, students will try to figure out the most likely predictions based on evidence. But you will also follow up on this activity by asking the students to try to figure out what is likely to happen in other situations they read about or that you teach them about. You won't guide them in the same way this time, however. Rather, you will ask them to use the plan for skillful prediction they developed earlier and apply it and the graphic organizer to this situation as well.

For this type of activity to be effective, it should not occur immediately after the students have worked through the question of what Bibot will do. Too much practice too soon can be counterproductive. So, the teacher waits a few days or a week before getting to this. This is called "teaching for transfer." In this case, the goal of this component in the lesson is the transfer of the use of the strategy for skillful prediction to other appropriate contexts. Doing a number of such additional reinforcing examples is important until you notice that the students are starting to use this kind of thinking on their own.

Each lesson in this book contains at least two ideas for immediate transfer (close to the activity of the lesson) and for reinforcement later. Within these activities, there are examples similar to the main activity in the lesson ("near transfer") and additional examples to which the same kind of thinking applies but which are not like the original lesson activity ("far transfer"). For example, asking students to think about what another character will do in the same book they are reading is an example of near transfer. Asking students to think about the effects of wearing certain types of clothing in certain seasons is an example of far transfer.

If you have students keep a chart of types of contexts suitable for the kind of thinking you are teaching them, their sensitivity as to when to do this kind of thinking will be enhanced.

The Overall Structure of Infusion Lessons

We have developed a framework for planning and teaching Infusion lessons that makes it relatively easy to get all of these strategies into the lessons. This framework is used in all of the lessons in this book and involves a basic four-part structure outlined in figure 1.6:

INFUSION LESSONS

Introduction

Thinking Actively

Thinking about Thinking

Applying your Thinking

---

figure 1.6

A Four-Part Structure for Infusion Lessons

Lesson Structure. First, there is a lesson introduction in which the questioning strategy for the thinking skill is introduced explicitly, and in which you can ask the students to think about times when they do the kind of thinking involved in the lesson. The introduction is also where you introduce the content focus of the lesson. You can do this by reminding students of relevant background information they already have or by giving them introductory information about the content focus.

The second part of an Infusion lesson is the main thinking activity in the lesson. Students are asked to follow the thinking map and to do the kind of thinking involved in the lesson. It is in this context that such tools as graphic organizers can be introduced, that students can be broken into collaborative learning groups to think together, and that students can be prompted to gather information about what is needed in order to do the specific thinking skill well. It is in this part of the lesson that your classroom will become much more oriented towards active student learning than many classrooms are today. If you guide the students by following the thinking map, you will, nonetheless, retain control over the learning process.

The third part of each lesson is where you will prompt your students to engage in the forms of metacognitive reflection previously described. Here you can make use of oral questioning to guide the students. In so-doing you will be attempting to help your students think not only about the content material they have been learning, but also about the thinking processes they have used to learn the content.

Remember, one of the main purposes of this kind of instruction is to help your students get used to asking the questions that have been identified, and, indeed, guiding themselves in the kind of thinking you are teaching them in the lesson. When you are not around to provide this guidance, your students should have internalized these questions, and developed the habit of asking them. The metacognitive part of Infusion lessons is where you prompt students to think about their thinking so that they become familiar with what it involves, can monitor it themselves, and can ultimately guide themselves in it. The third segment of Infusion lessons—the thinking about thinking segment—is crucial if you expect this internalization to occur.

The final section of an Infusion lesson is for transfer activities. Students will apply the thinking skill learned to other contexts.

The lesson planning form included in this volume (found in the Appendix) is structured with these four basic parts to facilitate your planning new Infusion lessons.

Other Components of Infusion Lessons

Lesson Extensions. Additional segments called "Lesson Extensions" appear after the transfer section. For example, if students do a major piece of art or writing to follow-up their thinking, this is where a description of this activity appears. In the parts-whole lesson on picture books, for example, students are asked to create a picture book as a lesson extension. In the lesson on *Seven Blind Mice,* they are asked to draw pictures of the elephant with parts missing as a lesson extension. Similarly, if the lesson prompts more in-depth study by the students, this is where such study is outlined. In the lesson on *Seven Blind Mice,* again one of the lesson extensions is for the students to read more books about elephants and identify other parts not mentioned in the story *Seven Blind Mice.* Usually, lesson extensions occur after the whole four-segmented Infusion lesson is taught. In addition to content extensions, there may be very natural extensions of the lesson that stress other thinking skills.

Special Needs Modifications. An extensive section discusses various modifications that can be made in the lesson to accommodate the needs of special students. Many classrooms today are inclusion classrooms, and with the wide variety of students in a classroom, there are very specific things that can be done to make these lessons ones which can reach all students. The special needs modifications build on the framework presented for such modifications in Chapter 2 of this book.

Assessing Students' Thinking. The final section of an Infusion lesson contains ideas about how you might assess whether students have developed the thinking skills that you have taught. These ideas can be used for diagnostic assessment prior to a lesson, or for assessment just after a lesson is taught, or after the lesson and a number of the transfer activities have been undertaken. In fact, comparing all three may be instructive and guide you in judging how much instruction is needed in your classroom to give students a basic understanding of these thinking skills. We have incorporated a number of alternative assessment ideas in this section, as well as ideas for using standard modes of assessment.

Teaching Thinking to Young Learners Through Infusion Lessons

Some educators have said things to us like, "Teaching critical and creative thinking is not for young children. They can't do that kind of thinking. Maybe we can teach them to sort things and to compare and contrast them, but they need to learn the basics before they can really think." That has not been our experience. There is a wonderful openness in young minds. Their curiosity, sense of wonder, and developing sense of reality create in them natural dispositions to both creative and critical thinking. And those dispositions can be actualized in exciting—and eye-opening—ways by the right sort of teaching. But think further about this: if we can start to build those crucial habits of creative and critical thought when children first enter school, think of how they will soar as they move into the upper elementary, middle, and high school grades and are given opportunities to use these skills in thinking about what they will learn there! To us, that image is what education is all about.

If we use as our paradigm of instruction in thinking the way we teach children in grades 5 and 6, or even 3 and 4, our instruction in grades 1 and 2 will miss the mark and what those educators were saying will become a self-fulfilling prophesy. But if we build on the experiences of children in grades 1 and 2, use grade-appropriate material, and scale our language and thinking strategies more to their level, we can challenge them in ways that will bring out those riches of thought. The lessons in this book are a testament to this claim.

It is worthwhile, however, to flag some of the important modifications one must make in thinking skills instruction if we start with teaching at grades 3–6 as our paradigm. So how do these lessons differ?

First, of course, is the fact that grade 1 and 2 students are just learning to write and develop the motor coordination they need to write well. So for obvious practical reasons, graphic organizers that can be used in grade 3 and above need to be modified for use in grades 1 and 2. Larger space must be provided for writing, and writing can't be the primary way we expect students to respond with their thoughts. More oral interaction with the teacher writing on a large version of a graphic organizer is what you find in these lessons. More space is provided in the graphic organizers for students to draw pictures (in addition to or coupled with oral responses) instead of writing. And graphic organizers that are used successfully in grade 3 and above can be divided into two (as you find in many of the lessons), to give students tasks that challenge, but don't overwhelm, the more limited attention span students have in grades 1 and 2.

Similar comments can be made about students' reading abilities, especially in grade 1. More reading aloud and more emphasis on listening skills is called for in these lessons, in contrast to upper elementary lessons. But this does not mean that you should not attend to reading in these lessons. Do what you usually do with regard to reading skills and the children you teach in grades 1 and/or 2. You should exploit every opportunity you have to help them with their reading skills as long as it doesn't put too much of a cognitive strain on other components of the lessons you are teaching.

Then, of course, there is the language of the thinking skills that it is so important for students to learn to use, and the thinking maps that guide their thinking. Terminology that is sophisticated for young learners like "evidence," "consequences," "likelihood," etc. that appears in thinking maps used in the upper grades cannot be assumed to be understood by young students. This does not necessarily mean that that vocabulary should be abandoned and replaced by simpler "kid" language, though it could be (e.g. use "clues" for "evidence"). Rather, it can be used, but must be introduced carefully using language that young children more easily understand. You should not shrink from this. Your children will surprise you when they start talking about evidence, consequences, and how likely predictions are, even in 1st and 2nd grades! The trick is to introduce these words to them in ways that you know from your experi-

ence with these children is effective. Model their use out loud, connect them with words that they know, and reinforce their appropriate use. Remember, your students want to be like you, so your modelling, etc., can be a powerful tool that can prompt their using these words appropriately. You will see this illustrated again and again in these lessons, where you are asked to "talk students through" the process before they do it themselves.

Some things do have to be "simplified" if we use instruction in thinking in grades 3 and above as our paradigm. (Or, from another point of view, from grades 3 and above, what you teach your students can be further elaborated.) For example, the thinking map for skillful comparing and contrast in grades 3 and above includes having students thinking about the similarities and differences by identifying patterns. Initially, helping grade 1 and 2 students with pattern recognition is a job in itself. So it is not included as a focus in the compare contrast strategy used in these lessons. It can be introduced later when students have mastered the strategy for compare and contrast. On the other hand, asking students to think about the similarities and differences they have identified and draw some conclusion is something that grade 1 and 2 students can be challenged to do, and do well. So the strategy is not just the standard "find some similarities and differences" strategy so often used in schools today that fosters superficial comparing and contrasting without much thought. Getting students used to asking and answering the question "What do these similarities and differences show me about the things I've compared and contrasted?" is something 1st and 2nd grade students can easily get used to doing, and that fosters deeper and more insightful comparisons and contrasts. In the lessons, you will see a realistic set of thinking maps that all students in grades 1 and 2 can master in order to bring out their best critical and creative thinking.

Finally, there is the use of interesting grade appropriate material with these children. You, as their teacher, know the kinds of things they respond to in your classroom. Don't think that you have to use anything different from these standard materials and topics to teach your students in ways that both improve their thinking and, especially, get them going as good critical and creative thinkers. The lessons in this lesson book testify to what you can do when you take such ordinary materials and infuse instruction in critical and creative thinking into their use in your classroom. That's when your students will shine in ways that will make you—and them—proud of what they can do. Try these lessons and see for yourselves.

How The Infusion Lessons Are Presented

Scripting for the Teacher Who Will Teach These Lessons. We have presented this collection of Infusion lessons so that those of you who are not familiar with this type of lesson can have a text to follow as you go through them. These texts are, for the most part, expanded records of what the teachers who developed these lessons said to the students to guide them through the lessons. These scripted texts are all in bold print in the lessons.

We recommend that you stay as close to the scripted text as possible when you first do these lessons. That does not mean, however, that you have to repeat this text verbatim, although you may choose to. You can paraphrase, reword, etc., as it fits your own style and class dynamic. But we advise that you not leave out any of the ideas communicated to students in these scripted passages. They are all essential for these lessons to be maximally successful in your classroom.

Student Responses in These Lessons Actual student responses from when these lessons were taught are recorded in two places. They are in the lesson itself and they are also included in the samples at the end of the lesson—sample graphic organizers that student have produced or sample writing from students. When student responses appear in the text of the lesson, we put them in plain text and italicize them. When we put them at the end of the lesson, we identify them as "Sample Student Responses."

These responses should not be taken as the "correct answers" to the questions and tasks given students as these lessons progress. Rather, they are what they are—samples of how students in classes in which these lessons were taught responded. They should guide you in what to expect from your students, and what sort of response you may try to prompt with leading or direct questions when responses like these are not forthcoming. In a few places in these lessons we do suggest that you try to prompt responses pretty close to what we include as the student responses. In most cases, however, you should take these as guides, and not as the only type of acceptable answer.

Teacher Notes in These Lessons. There are various points in these lessons where teachers who are unfamiliar with some of the instructional tools and techniques used in these lessons may not be sure how to manage the class. We realize that teachers who use these lesson books will have a variety of different expertise with regard to these techniques and tools. So, we have tried to include notes on all of the important techniques you will need to manage these lesson well. These notes are structured to guide those who will be teaching them in practices that will increase the effectiveness of the lessons. They are included in the lessons as normal nonbolded, non-italicized text that speaks to the teacher.

Scripted text for teacher

Teacher notes

Possible student responses

Now we must consider possible solutions. Talk to your group and try to come up with two or three possible solutions, then we'll share. Allow time for discussing and sharing, supporting any groups that find this task difficult. As the groups share, record the suggested options on the group graphic organizer. POSSIBLE STUDENT RESPONSES: *Push out the wolf and lock the door. The three girls should run to Grandma's house. Trick the wolf by running out and then back into the house and locking the door. Get the wolf out by grabbing his hand and pulling him out. Kill the wolf. Sneak out and hide while the wolf is sleeping. Burn the wolf's tail to get him to leave. Say someone else is there in the house.*

Many of these teacher notes come from extensive experience in staff-development projects in which we have helped a large number of teachers learn how to conduct these lessons effectively. The notes reflect answers to the most frequently asked "What should I do here…?" questions in such contexts. Where there is a clear "best practice" we mention it; where there are a variety of things that can be done, we indicate that also.

Here is a portion of a lesson from the book which will show you what these three different components look like in an actual lesson. This is a problem-solving lesson based on the book *Lon Po Po*. The students are considering what possible solutions they have to the problem of there being a wolf in their bed:

Blanks for Your Use. Finally, we include blank graphic organizers tailored for these lessons that you can reproduce for your students when you teach the lesson. We also want to call your attention to the additional graphic organizers and thinking maps that are contained in the lesson-design handbook on *Infusing Critical and Creative Thinking into Elementary Instruction*, by Robert Swartz and Sandra Parks. These can be used in the design of your own Infusion lessons to supplement the ones in the lesson book.

Lesson Length. Because of the variation in the duration of class periods and the flexibility you must allow in teaching these lessons for student exploration, you may find yourselves in the position of having to break up some of these lessons and continuing them the next time you meet your students. If possible, do so at the juncture of one of the four parts, rather than in the middle of a part. But even if you break a lesson in the middle of a part, devices like the graphic organizers can help to provide continuity between one sitting and the next and make it easier for students to pick up where they left off.

Final Thoughts on Teaching Infusion Lessons

Remember, the goals of these lessons are to improve student thinking and enhance their content learning. We encourage you to build anything else into these lessons that will do this better for you. Infusion lessons, when done well, represent instruction at its best. We believe that teaching these lessons will be as enriching an experience for you as it will be for your students.

COMPONENTS OF INFUSION LESSONS

INTRODUCTION TO CONTENT AND PROCESS

Teacher's comments to introduce the content objectives

The lesson introduction should activate students' prior knowledge of the content and establish its relevance and importance.

Teacher's comments to introduce the thinking process and its significance

The lesson introduction should activate students' prior experience with the thinking skill/process, preview the thinking skill/process, and demonstrate the value and usefulness of performing the thinking skillfully. The introduction serves as an anticipatory set for the thinking process and should confirm the benefits of its skillful use.

THINKING ACTIVELY

Active thinking prompted by teacher questioning and graphic maps

The main activity in the lesson interweaves the explicit thinking skill/process with the content. This is what makes the content lesson an infused lesson. Teachers guide students through the thinking activity by using questions phrased in the language of the thinking skill/process and by using graphic organizers.

THINKING ABOUT THINKING

Distancing activities that help students think about the thinking process

Students are asked direct questions about their thinking that prompt them to reflect about what kind of thinking they did, how they did it, and how effective it was.

APPLYING THE THINKING

Transfer activities that involve student-prompted use of the skill in other examples

There are two broad categories of transfer activities: (1) near or far activities that immediately follow the substance of the lesson and (2) reinforcement of the thinking later in the school year. Both types of transfer involve less teacher prompting of the thinking process than in the Thinking Actively component of the lesson.

Immediate transfer
Near transfer
Application of the thinking process within the same class session, or soon thereafter, to content similar to that of the initial activity in the lesson. Decreased teacher prompting of the thinking is involved.
Far transfer
Application of the thinking process within the same class session, or shortly thereafter, to content different from that of the initial activity in the lesson. Decreased teacher prompting of the thinking is involved.

Reinforcement later
Application of the thinking process later in the school year to a variety of both near and far transfer contexts. Teacher prompting of the thinking is at a minimum.

Chapter 2
Special Learners and Infusion Lessons ——————

All learners are "special." All learners think, reason, and approach a task with a set of particular learning preferences and abilities. Effective teachers are well aware of these individual differences and are attuned to modifying and adjusting both content and lesson delivery to match student needs and learning styles. This is especially true (and challenging) for teaching students who had, in the past, been instructed in substantially separate classrooms and are now included in regular classrooms.

The power of Infusion lessons lies in the underlying premise that skillful thinking can be taught through explicit instruction. All students benefit from this direct, guided model, particularly those students for whom such strategic thinking is not yet automatic. When this instruction is done in the context of content instruction, content learning is enhanced.

Lesson content materials, instructional techniques, and teacher expectations can be routinely adjusted to match the learner. Infusion lessons, too, allow for these types of modifications to be made in order to ensure meaningful learning by all students.

In this chapter, modifications will be suggested to ignite your thinking for tailoring these, and future Infusion lessons, to match the diverse needs of your students. While it is impossible to build modifications for all varieties of special needs into each Infusion lesson, various suggestions have been included for commonly occurring needs in the classroom. Selecting from these ideas plus your own effective practices will ensure that Infusion lessons challenge all students' thinking.

It Begins With Planning

Anyone who has planned a unit of study recognizes the myriad decisions to be made: What concepts or skills are most vital to obtain deep understanding? What specific outcomes are to be expected of the students? What prerequisite skills or knowledge must students possess to be successful? What instructional strategies will result in meaningfully engaged students?

Infusion lessons, by design, aim at an understanding of both content and skill. At the completion of an Infusion lesson, students should have not only a deeper understanding of the content material, but also a conscious understanding of the thinking processes in which they have been engaged. For example, in the lessons "Picture Books" and "Writing," students develop an understanding of the importance of each aspect of a book and the qualities of effective writing necessary to the development of a story or piece of writing. They also acquire a method for analyzing relationships in part to whole thinking and the thinking skills involved in ranking, creating criteria, and making judgments regarding priorities.

Therefore, teachers should plan Infusion lessons as carefully as they plan any other lesson. Decisions should be made regarding prerequisite skills, learner outcomes, instructional materials, lesson delivery, and assessment of understanding to meet the diverse needs in their classrooms so that learning by all students takes place.

Figure 2.1 (next page) outlines the basic questions teachers must address in planning lessons which accomplish both thinking and content goals. At the end of this section , Figure 2 summarizes the most frequent modifications that have been made to meet the needs of special students, linked to the focal points for lesson planning identified in figure 2.1. These involve "frontloading," "streamlining," and "clarifying" as you diversify and expand the learning options in your classroom.

Frontload Skills and Knowledge

Frontloading Thinking. What does it mean to "draw a conclusion"? In a recent observation of an elementary class, when students were asked to "draw a conclusion," some of them

DUAL-GOAL FRAMEWORK FOR INFUSION LESSON PLANNING

	THINKING SKILLS	CONTENT UNDERSTANDING
PREREQUISITE KNOWLEDGE	What do students need to understand in order to manage the thinking task?	What background knowledge or experience will students need in order to understand the lesson content?
LEARNER OUTCOMES	What will students be able to do to manage the thinking task well?	What will the students know or understand when this lesson is completed?
INSTRUCTIONAL MATERIALS	Which materials best match students' abilities?	Which materials best match students' abilities?
ASSESSMENT	How will students demonstrate that they manage the thinking tasks well?	How will students demonstrate that they understand the content taught?

figure 2.1

responded by asking which color marker to use to "draw" it! Obviously, "drawing a conclusion" was not the artful endeavor they had anticipated.

For some students, the language of thinking and the steps in the thinking process are not yet developed. However, students can be taught these steps and the language, if they are given several clear, explicit experiences prior to applying these skills in an Infusion lesson.

So what *do* we do when we "conclude"? We must be able to identify salient features or clues from the information we already have, delete unnecessary information, identify patterns, and connect ideas. Then we must ask, What new idea(s), not already contained in the information we have identified, is (are) suggested or supported by that information? This is our conclusion. The process is similar in form to that which is done in predicting and generalizing, both examples of inferring. Therefore, the first task of the teacher is to identify these steps in order to plan experiences which will make them more obvious to students.

The steps involved in concluding or other types of thinking can be taught through consciously selected experiences using think-aloud. In the think-aloud, the teacher models his/her thinking using the language of thinking and the steps in the process. For example, an elementary teacher may select a language arts lesson to reinforce the process. "'Bake,' 'rake,' and 'take' all have long *a* sounds and end in silent *e*. I see a pattern. Let's see if it works again. What about the word 'fake'? I conclude from this evidence that a vowel followed by a consonant and silent *e* makes the long sound. How could I test my conclusion?"

In the preceding example, the steps in thinking were paired with the language for thinking. Yet, for some students, the language itself may require further definition. Terms such as "evidence," "conclusion," and "assumption," may require an introduction through relevant experiences and association with more commonly used terms. Many students, for example, may be familiar with detectives through solving mysteries with "evidence" or "clues." Yet, they may need additional everyday experiences to understand how evidence is used to support an idea or conclusion. While building on the students' experiences using think-aloud or stories, it is important to pair the language of thinking with the language of the student.

This type of preteaching is known as "frontloading." Frontloading arms the student with the necessary skills or knowledge he/she will need in order to successfully engage in the Infusion lesson.

Opportunities exist throughout the curriculum for "frontloading" the processes students will need to perform the thinking skills prior to an Infusion lesson. For example, in the lesson "Petunia's Assumptions," students may need prior experience in identifying assumptions. Similarly, in the lesson "Writing," the process of sequencing is related to students' prior knowledge of ordinal positions and patterning. By using common experience, such as steps in getting dressed in the morning or ranking favorite television shows, the distinction between the different purposes for sequencing can be stressed.

Helpful keys to "frontloading" in relation to thinking are as follows:

- Anticipating the kind of thinking students will be taught to do skillfully in a forthcoming Infusion lesson
- Consciously selecting simple or familiar content to model that kind of thinking
- Using the language of thinking
- Offering multiple examples prior to use in the Infusion lesson to familiarize students with the process and the language

When frontloading is used to anticipate an Infusion lesson, students can be helped to develop this understanding.

Frontloading Content. Similarly, students with limited background experience or little knowledge of the content of the Infusion lesson may benefit from "frontloading" content. Information can be provided in a variety of ways to match the students' abilities. For example, auditory learners and students who find reading difficult will benefit from a teacher reading aloud on the topic, books on tape, or partner-reading prior to the Infusion lesson.

Students may work with a strong partner to rehearse what they know about a topic prior to a large group discussion. Techniques such as "I Know," "I Think I Know," and "I Need to Know" or using a "KWL" (What I Know, Want to Know, and Have Learned) matrix access prior knowledge for the student. Videotapes or films that students can watch before a lesson are powerfully engaging tools to provide content knowledge or experience.

For example, in the lesson "Whales," students with difficulties may be helped by using any of the methods of accessing prior knowledge just described. The whole class can participate by reviewing what they know about whales in the introductory activity in this lesson. This activity brings a wealth of information to all students in the classroom in a way that keeps this information constantly before their eyes.

Provide special audio/visual materials to students who have limited background knowledge because of learning disabilities connected with reading and then ask them to discuss what they've seen with a partner. This can also bring them closer to the level of understanding other students have on an Infusion lesson topic. These techniques are all versions of frontloading content that are designed for special students.

Helpful keys to "frontloading" content are as follows:

- Anticipating background information students need in order to participate successfully in the Infusion lesson
- Selecting a method of accessing information in a manner which matches the students' ability and strength, (e.g., auditory/visual)

Streamlining Outcomes

What if someone were to say to you, "Tell everything you know about the Revolutionary War and how you acquired the knowledge." "Why?" you may ask. "What's worth knowing?" If you know the British wore red, is that critical? Would you explain how you accessed the information on the computer or would just listing your sources be sufficient?

In planning any lesson, teachers must make decisions regarding the essential skills and concepts students need to know as the result of the lesson. When planning instruction for students with limited cognitive ability or processing delays, teachers may take the "streamline" approach. The question becomes, "For what core knowledge and skill level should this student be held responsible?"

Streamlining Thinking Outcomes. It may be beneficial for some students to have the expected outcomes altered by reducing the cognitive demands. The teacher can gradually increase expectations with future Infusion lessons. However, most special needs students can achieve the same outcomes as the other students, though they may require some of the modifications described in this chapter to accomplish this.

One way to modify our expected outcomes for such students is to simplify the thinking map for the type of thinking being taught. For example, in the parts-whole lesson on picture books, the cognitive demand can be decreased by asking them to consider the function of single parts of picture books. Other students then continue with the last question on the thinking map by considering how the single parts work together to make the picture book what it is. They then share their results. In later parts-whole lessons, after special needs students have mastered the task, the teacher can ask them to consider how the parts of the whole item work together. Hence, the integrity of the thinking process is retained, though practice in using it is in two stages.

This process can be supported by a greater degree of guidance and teacher modeling. In initial lessons on specific thinking skills, teachers may make it clear to which questions from the thinking map these students should attend. As students contribute ideas, the teacher may paraphrase these students' responses in order to help clarify their thinking. The teacher may then choose to model the remainder of the thinking task by thinking aloud.

Streamlining Content Outcomes. Content outcomes can be similarly "streamlined" so that students are accountable for conclusions or generalizations, but are asked to provide a limited number of supporting details. In the compare/contrast lesson "Town Mouse and Country

Mouse," knowing that mice need food, clothing, and shelter no matter where they live and that people have these same needs, may be sufficient and important, without the need for them to support these conclusions with details from the similarities and differences they noticed.

The purpose of any Infusion lesson is to teach students to think skillfully about the content. The amount of content and the supports needed to guide thinking can be adapted to meet the needs of individual students. Helpful keys to "streamlining" are as follows:

- Diagnosing the degree of complexity and abstraction that students can be expected to achieve in their learning.

- Simplifying the goals, or the thinking tasks, for students to fit expectations for their achievements.

Clarifying by Adapting Instructional Materials

Anyone who has ever tried his or her hand at making household repairs, assembling a toy, or installing a computer knows that having the correct tool is essential and having the wrong tool spells frustration. Moreover, the tool must be designed not only to do the job, but also to be used easily.

Clarifying the Thinking Tools. In Infusion lessons, the graphic organizers serve as tools not only to provide a place to record essential information but also to guide students' thinking. However, if the tool is too complex or unwieldy for the learner, it can become confusing. Modifying the graphics for special learners is sometimes necessary. Something as simple as making larger versions of the graphic organizers with more writing space for students can enhance the usefulness of the graphic organizer for these students. The language of the graphic organizer can also be restated to be more suitable for certain learners. For example, if "function" is too confusing in Parts/Whole Relationships, then "use" may be more appropriate.

Graphic organizers can also be simplified by reducing the number of spaces provided for student responses. For example, on the decision-making or problem-solving graphic organizers,

the number of spaces for options can be reduced for students with processing and/or attention difficulties. At the same time, the teacher can be sure to provide an opportunity for such students to report on one or more of their options as part of the overall class effort. Parts of the graphic may be highlighted or color coded to help students who need more specific structure and guidance "keep track" of steps while recording information or during class discussion. Finally, icons summarizing the steps in the process can be added as a checklist for students who have processing and/or attention problems.

Since the graphics in Infusion lessons are designed to guide thinking, additional prompts to support learning could be interjected. For example, if students need an extra step to draw a conclusion, inserting questions or prompts that force students to look for patterns is appropriate. Similarly, if a stem added to the organizer would help guide thinking while students are acquiring the skill, its insertion may be appropriate for students less able to articulate abstract thinking. For example, the question on the parts-of-a-whole diagram, "What is the relationship between the parts and the whole?" could be guided by adding the frame, "The _____(parts) of the _____(object) help the _____(object) do _____."

The thinking maps used in each lesson can be similarly modified. It is a good practice for teachers to enlarge and post the thinking map in the classroom to serve as an easily accessible reference tool whenever the students engage in the thinking skill The teacher can highlight or check off the different steps in the strategy as students go through them. As an aid to memory, teachers can use icons or pictures to cue students to the steps in a thinking map, as suggested, for example in the parts/whole lesson "Parts of a Picture Book."

The thinking task itself can be made more experiential by adding manipulatives. To classify, see parts to whole relationships, and compare and contrast, students may need to actually move objects. For example, students may cut apart paragraphs to set pieces side by side. Students can sort information cards, pictures, or objects in order to make the thinking task clearer.

Clarifying Content Material. Content information can be clarified and targeted to a student's instructional level by providing for simpler text on the topic, reading aloud, pairing readings with peers, and providing audio or videotaped information.

For example, a primary teacher used a "trick" with first graders which is adaptable to any age group. Knowing that students often understand more than their reading ability will allow, she audiotaped the sources of information for her reliable sources lesson. All students, regardless of reading ability, had the content available to them to make the necessary judgments about reliability.

Graphic organizers, though wonderful thinking tools, can be stumbling blocks for students with fine motor, written expression, listening, and memory issues. Allowing such students to contribute orally as they work together in a group, with other students recording their remarks, and then providing all of the students with the final completed graphic organizer is one strategy that respects the needs of these students while sustaining their involvement in the group. Supplying the students with a copy of the teacher's completed diagram also assists students in actively participating in the thinking process without the distraction of the motor task.

Helpful keys to adapting materials are as follows:

- Identifying the students' needs
- Adjusting the thinking tools to highlight essential information
- Reducing the task demands so that maximum attention is focused on thinking and understanding

Diversifying Options for Lesson Delivery

Diversifying for Both Thinking Skill and Content Learning. An essential ingredient of Infusion lessons is collaborative thinking. The lessons lend themselves to teaching techniques which bring students together to build on each other's thoughts and strengths. For special learners, this can be a powerful means of engaging them in thinking and understanding content.

Cooperative, heterogeneous groups provide group members opportunities to model thinking, share information, elaborate on others' ideas, and share the workload. Since thinkers come with all types of capabilities, group activities allow the good reader to share his/her strength, yet allow the less able reader to share equally in the discussion; the efficient note-taker may log ideas while the others provide the ideas. By assigning group members "jobs," or Jigsawing, the teacher can value members' strengths and provide support for their challenges. Most of the Infusion lessons in this text include cooperative group opportunities, but the teacher should feel free to interject additional opportunities to support learning as well as to adjust material for the performance level of the groups.

Similarly, techniques such as Think-Pair-Share, Carousel Brainstorming, and Graffiti allow students to refine their thinking by seeing and hearing others' responses with the permission to combine others' ideas with their own. As with Brainstorming, "piggybacking" and elaborating on another's idea are not only fair, but encouraged. In Carousel Brainstorming and Graffiti, students pass their graphic organizer or brainstormed sheets from group to group, allowing others to read, discuss, add, and question. The classroom becomes a thinking room in which all are active participants.

There are times when homogeneous or like-ability and need groups also play a part in Infusion lessons. One teacher uses "red card–green card" to allow students to signal if they feel ready to go on (green) or feel the need for support (red). The students self-select to be part of a group receiving additional guidance. Similarly, reading material, graphic organizers, and transfer activities can be differentiated to match group needs. So, while all students within the class are generating possibilities about their state, different groups have access to content-related information with varying degrees of reading difficulty or varied formats, such as video or audiotapes.

Whatever the grouping strategy, the task demands for the special learner can be reduced. The student may dictate or audio-record responses instead of writing; the number of options to explore can be reduced (as we discussed when we considered streamlining); time can be extended; and checklists, symbols, or drawings can be substituted for lengthy written tasks.

While the Infusion lessons in this book are presented as coherent wholes, effective teachers recognize the need to break information into meaningful parts. The lessons, as well as the graphics, may need to be presented *in parts, over time, and with frequent summary statements* to guide students through the lesson parts to that final understanding. For example, one Infusion teacher created two problem-solving graphics, one for large-group conclusions, and a simpler one for small-group work.

Under the section "Thinking Actively," the teacher-authors of these Infusion lessons have attempted to scaffold questions to guide thinking. However, not every question can be predicted. Effective teachers recognize the need to restate a question in different form, phrase a question to include information students need to draw from in order to respond and, occasionally, to "backtrack" or summarize what has been said in order to redirect student thinking.

Just as the thinking *process* is the vital ingredient in Infusion lessons, so too is the *process* of lesson delivery, a key factor in students' successful participation. Diversifying teaching techniques opens the door to thinking for all students.

Helpful keys for diversification are as follows:

- Developing a repertoire of techniques that actively engage students in thinking
- Including a variety of tasks and resources of varied difficulty to match the abilities of the students

Expand the Possibilities in Determining Instructional Success

Throughout this chapter, "expanding the possibilities" has been the theme for constructing and delivering Infusion lessons. The possibilities are many, too, for accessing students' thinking and content understanding as an immediate result of the task in which they've been engaged. Of course, the ultimate indicator of gen-

eralization and internalization will come as the year unfolds and students demonstrate the thinking skills in contexts further removed from the original lesson, and successfully use the content concepts, principles, and information learned in the performance of other complex and challenging thinking tasks.

There are also alternatives for expressing understanding and demonstrating the level of skill development. While the written word and structured graphics of the text may convey that written responses are the norm, the truth is that Infusion teachers are as creative as they expect their students to be when suggesting alternatives for a written response. The list includes acting out/skits, role plays, demonstrations, orally promoting an idea, audiotaping a response, constructing a model, completing a "stem" or sentence frame, discussing with a peer or the teacher, drawing or webbing a response. It is common to reduce the amount of written tasks and extend the response time for special students.

Students with limited expressive language benefit from metacognitive guides which allow responses through a checklist, a rating, a picture, or a short answer. Students can place a happy, sad, or straight face on the graphic organizer to indicate the easy to difficult parts of the lesson for them. They might draw their own diagram of what they did and when they would do something similar again. Oral interaction with a teacher can replace the written metacognition log. Highlighting or "starring" the most beneficial aspects of their thinking on a thinking map shows that students are, indeed, thinking about their thinking.

Whatever adaptation is selected, it remains essential that assessment reflects the outcomes previously determined and that the expectations for *all* students is that they are capable of demonstrating skillful thinking.

Summary

Figure 2.2 is a graphic summary of the types of modifications for special learners that we have discussed in this chapter. Infusion lessons are lessons for all students. All can become more skillful thinkers through explicit instruction provided by effective Infusion teachers. The suggestions in this chapter on special students are designed as a beginning and give you permission to explore the possibilities of skillful thinking with all of your students.

We are thinkers, all, and we wish you a successful journey with Infusion!

MODIFICATIONS FOR SPECIAL LEARNERS

	THINKING SKILLS	CONTENT UNDERSTANDING
PREREQUISITE KNOWLEDGE	**Frontload:** • Introduce prerequisite • Use the basic language of thinking • Think aloud for students as a model	**Frontload:** • Provide content via oral reading, video, field trip, or experiential learning • Use Know/Think You Know/Need to Know • Pre-introduce skill/ knowledge to same-ability group • Pre-teach vocabulary • Rehearse with a partner
LEARNER OUTCOMES	**Streamline:** • Select which aspect of the thinking skill students should be able to explain • Limit the thinking task (reduce thinking "load")	**Streamline:** • Select core concepts appropriate for student (Reduce content "load")
INSTRUCTIONAL MATERIALS	**Clarify:** • Enlarge graphics • Simplify graphics (language or format) • Add prompting questions • Color-code or highlight • Use manipulatives • Provide frames or stems to guide thinking	**Clarify:** • Provide reading material at student's level • Use audiotaped information • Use videotapes • Provide copies of teacher's or student's completed graphic organizer • Do oral reading • Use group-created organizers • Highlight important information

figure 2.2

THINKING SKILLS AND CONTENT UNDERSTANDING		

LESSON DELIVERY	**Diversify Repertoire:**
	A. Collaboration
	  • Cooperative groups
	  • JIGSAW
	  • Carousel Brainstorming
	  • Think-Pair-Share
	  • Partner work
	  • Like-ability groups
	  • Graffiti
	B. Break lesson and graphic into meaningful parts
	C. Scaffold questions
	D. Frequently summarize
	E. Reduce task demands:
	  • Dictate instead of write
	  • Reduce number of tasks
	  • Select "jobs" for group members
	  • Use checklists, symbols, drawing instead of writing
	  • Use audio/video instead of reading content	

ASSESSMENT	**Expand the Possibilities:** • Record an audio tape • Construct a model • Draw a picture • Complete a stem • Use a metacognition checklist/rating guide/log • Allow time extensions for completion • Reduce amount of writing	**Expand the Possibilities:** • Record an audio tape • Construct a model • Draw a picture • Complete a stem • Allow time extensions for completion • Reduce amount of writing

figure 2.2 (Cont.)

Infusing Skillful Comparing and Contrasting into Language Arts

Teaching students skillful decision making in grades 1 and 2 involves helping them learn to ask and carefully answer the following questions about their decisions before they make them:

SKILLFUL DECISION MAKING

1. What are some things I can do?

2. What will happen if I do these things?

3. Which are good things to do?

---

figure 3.1

This "thinking map" is used to guide your students' thinking as they engage with the lesson content in the decision making lessons in this book.

When students learn and use this strategy for thinking about their prospective decisions, they don't just do the first thing that comes into their heads. They consider a number of options and then choose the best one by thinking about the positive and negative consequences that they project will result. When they go through this process they can explain why they think what they have decided to do is the best thing to do by providing specific supporting reasons for their choices.

These lessons also use various supporting classroom strategies such as using a graphic organizer, engaging in cooperative thinking, thinking about thinking, and receiving continued guided practice to supplement the use of the thinking map for decision making. These classroom strategies enhance both the thinking skill that the students are learning and their mastery of the lesson content.

The key graphic organizer for skillful decision making is in figure 3.2. This graphic organizer

helps students record a large number of options they generate either on their own or in student groups through brainstorming. For example, students may role-play characters who face a difficult decision. The graphic organizer prompts them to select one option to explore more fully by spelling out a range of consequences, both pro and con. The graphic organizer also has space for recording the judgments students make about whether, in light of the pros and cons, the option is a good one to consider, and why. Providing reasons to support thinking that an option is a good one is important in helping students get used to the need to support their ideas with reasons.

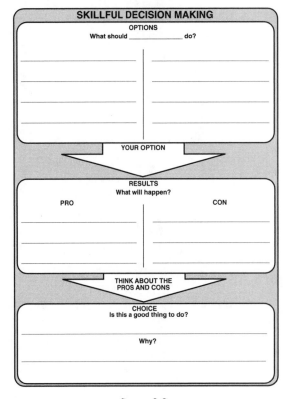

figure 3.2

A modification of this graphic organizer is used in one of the decision-making lessons. It eliminates the "Options" box, assuming that the teacher has already listed options on a chart or transparency at the front of the classroom. Then the students select one option to work on and use the whole page to explore it. This gives them more writing (and drawing) room on the graphic organizer (see figure 3.3) Reproducible blank organizers are found at the end of each chapter.

When a number of students or student groups explore a variety of different options in this way, they can compare their results to select what they think is the best choice. If they disagree, they can debate the issue in class.

For more in-depth information on teaching skillful decision making, please refer to Chapter 2 in the book *Infusing the Teaching of Critical and Creative Thinking into Elementary Instruction* by Robert Swartz and Sandra Parks. A computer disk containing the blank, reproducible graphic organizers used in this book is also available. Both book and disk are available through Critical Thinking Books & Software.

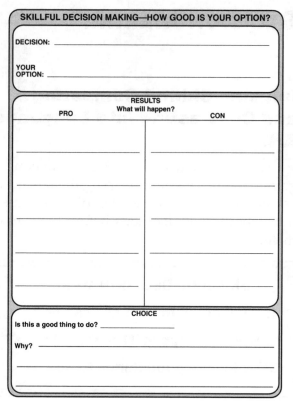

figure 3.3

DUCKLING DECISIONS
MAKE WAY FOR DUCKLINGS

Language Arts   **Grades 1–2**

OBJECTIVES

CONTENT

Students will learn how to interpret story characters in terms of their character traits and actions based on details in the story about what the characters say and do.

THINKING SKILL/PROCESS

Students will learn to think about options and the consequences of those options when they make decisions.

METHODS AND MATERIALS

CONTENT

Students will read the story *Make Way for Ducklings* by Robert McCloskey and explain the decisions the main characters, Mr. and Mrs. Mallard, must make as they raise their family of ducklings.

THINKING SKILL/PROCESS

An explicit thinking map, graphic organizers, and structured questioning emphasize options and consequences in decision making. Collaborative learning enhances thinking.

LESSON

INTRODUCTION TO CONTENT AND THINKING SKILL/PROCESS

• **Today we are going to think and talk about making decisions. How many of you have made some decisions today?** Ask for a show of hands. Most students raise their hands. **What are some of the decisions you've made today?** POSSIBLE STUDENT RESPONSES: *I decided what I was going to have for breakfast. I decided what I was going to wear this morning. I decided what I would choose to do when my work was finished. I decided what I would do at recess with my friend.* **We all make some decisions like this every day, don't we?** Most students agree.

• **Let's think about how we can think carefully about our decisions so that we can be sure we make good ones. I'd like to share with you a decision I made recently with my mother. My mother and I like to get together, but we do not live in the same community. In fact, we live 200 miles apart. I really enjoy going to see her, and my mother enjoys coming to see me. Because it is such a long distance, we wanted to think about how we could get together more often. When we thought of what we could do, we realized we had three choices. I could drive to my mother's house, she could drive to my house, or we could meet in a city halfway between our homes. Another word for choices is** *options.* **The first two options seemed to have some results that we did not like. If we chose either, one of us would be doing all the driving. And since the drive would be longer for the one driving, it would take more time and we would not get to spend as much time together. The third option, meeting halfway, seemed to make more sense to us. That is what we chose to do.**

• **It's amazing how many decisions I have to make every day. Many of the things I choose to do are small, easy-to-make decisions. For instance, I need to make a choice about what rubber stamps to use as I check papers, but it's not a major decision. Some of my decisions are more complicated, such as deciding how to arrange a visit with my mother. These are the decisions that make me think more.**

- **Now, think about some of the decisions that you have had to make that you think are really important.** Allow time for thinking. **Share those decisions with your partner and talk about why you had to make them.** Allow several minutes for students to share their decisions with the group.

- **When you were deciding, you may have thought of different choices, like I did. You could make one choice or you could make a different choice. Do you remember the words I used to talk about these different choices?** Some students usually remember that you used the words "options" or "choices." If they don't, tell them what the words are and what they mean. Write "Decision Making" on the board, and underneath, write "options/choices." Ask students to talk to their partners about the different options they had when they made their decisions. Then ask students for a few examples. Write down several clusters of options students give for their decisions under "options/choices." As you are writing down the examples, be sure to use the language of decision making. The terms "choice," "option," and "decide" are more clearly understood if modeled with the student's examples. **It is good to think of a lot of options. Having a lot of options will help us make good choices.**

- **Whenever you consider options as you make a decision, you should also consider what will happen if you choose the different options. We call these "results" or "consequences." When my mother and I decided that either of us making the long trip was not a good idea, it was because we thought of the consequences—that one of us would have to drive a long time and that we would not have as much time to get together as we would if we met halfway.** Write the terms "results" and "consequences" on the chalkboard connected by an arrow with the word "options." Next to these words, write "pro" and "con." **If something good would probably happen, we label the result a "pro," and if something would probably happen that is bad, it is labeled a "con." Do you remember some of the cons of driving all the way to see my mother?** Students usually remember that the fact that the trip would take a long time is a con. If they don't, remind them of this example. **Do you remember some of the pros I chose when I saw my mother?** Most students remember that the trip took half the time for each person. **Talk to your partner about the options you had. What were some of the results, pro or con?** Ask students to share the things they considered in making a choice and to label the consequences as either pro or con. When you ask for examples from the students, model the use of the terms by restating students' ideas using the decision-making terms.

- **After thinking about the consequences of the options, you are ready to make a choice. I picked the best option by thinking about all the consequences of the options. I usually ask: "Which option has the most pros and the least cons?" and "Are there some consequences that are very important ones to consider?" I ask this second question because they might count for more.** Discuss the options mentioned by the group for decisions they had to make. Ask students to point out some options that would have been bad to choose because of the consequences.

- **A thinking map like this can help us remember what to think about as we make choices.** Show the thinking map for decision making. It can be on a chart or the chalkboard so that it will be visible throughout the lesson for students to refer to as they practice this kind of thinking. Just showing it on a transparency will not be as effective. Ask students to read the questions aloud. **These are three important**

SKILLFUL DECISION MAKING

1. What are some things I can do?

2. What will happen if I do these things?

3. Which are good things to do?

questions we should ask ourselves when we need to make a decision. We should think of some things we could do. These are choices, or options. Then we should think about what would happen if we chose each of the options. That means we are thinking about the consequences and pros and cons of making each choice. Finally, we should think about which choices would be good to make. We can then make our decision about the best choice from that group of good choices. Go over the three questions that make up the map again, using examples from students to further explain.

THINKING ACTIVELY

- The book we will be reading today is *Make Way for Ducklings* by Robert McCloskey. In our reading, we will meet the main characters, a pair of ducks, and hear about the decision they must make. As we read, we will look for clues to help us learn things about the characters. This will help us put ourselves into the story. Later, I'm going to ask you to use the thinking map for decision making to make the decision as you think the pair of ducks would. Pass out copies of the book if available. Read aloud or have students read the story up to the point where the ducks are looking in Louisburg Square. **What is the decision Mr. and Mrs. Mallard are trying to make?** POSSIBLE STUDENT RESPONSE: *They want to find a place to live and raise their family.* **This is a very important decision to make. They are responsible for their family's happiness and safety.**

- We have read about the Mallards and their search for a home. **What do we know about Mr. and Mrs. Mallard that will help us understand why they have to make a decision?** Allow students to discuss the things they have noticed about the ducks. Students will probably make some connections between the duck parents and their own parents. POSSIBLE STUDENT RESPONSES: *They do not want to live where animals like foxes and turtles can hurt their babies. They like a place where they can get food for their babies, but if there are scary things, like bicycles, it won't be a good place to raise their babies. They don't like big buildings and would need water to live.* **Let's pretend we are Mr. and Mrs. Mallard. Imagine that you are a duck who is looking for just the right home for your ducklings. We will try to be very responsible as we follow our thinking map to make a good choice.**

- **We are going to use a special diagram called a "graphic organizer" to help us as we consider the options for the Mallards.** Show the Skillful Decision Making graphic organizer on a chart or an overhead transparency. It must be large enough for all of the students to read. **Remember, you are pretending to be Mr. and Mrs. Mallard. The decision is about where to raise your family. We know from the beginning of the story some of the things that are important to the ducks in choosing their home. In your groups, make a list of options for the duck family. Try to make a varied list so that you have a lot to choose from.** Allow time for group work, and then share ideas. The

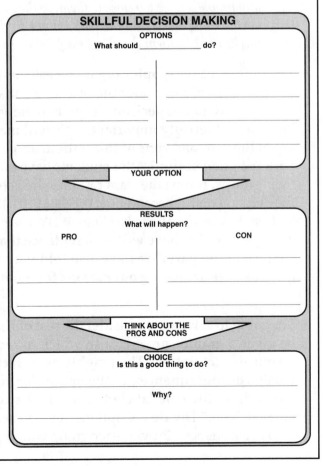

SKILLFUL DECISION MAKING

OPTIONS
What should _____ do?

YOUR OPTION

RESULTS
What will happen?

PRO   CON

THINK ABOUT THE
PROS AND CONS

CHOICE
Is this a good thing to do?

Why?

group lists can be made on paper or on dry erase boards. After the groups have generated a list, ask each group to report one of their options, then ask for any others that haven't been mentioned. Record the ideas on the class copy of the graphic organizer. This will allow everyone to see the entire list. POSSIBLE STUDENT RESPONSES: *in a quiet pond, under someone's deck, in someone's backyard, at a zoo, in a garden, on a river, in the park under a bench.*

- **What should we consider next, after we've come up with a lot of options like this, in order to help us make a choice?** Students usually remember that it is important to consider the results, consequences, or pros and cons. If they don't, refer them to the thinking map and ask them to read question 2. **Our graphic organizer is set up to consider one option at a time. Each option will need to be considered separately. The first arrow is the place to write the option that is being considered.** Point out the arrow on the graphic organizer to students. **Let's consider the option of living in the park under a bench. The pros and cons of choosing that option will go in the box below it.**

- **What would be a *good* thing about living under a bench in the park? Work in your groups again and try to come up with at least two good things that might happen if they live in the park under a bench.** Allow time for discussion. Then ask volunteers for one of their ideas until you have three or four. Write the ideas suggested in the box on the left side of the "Results" box. POSSIBLE STUDENT RESPONSES: *It is near to grass, so they could play in the grass. They would have food because people would see them and feed them. It might be near a pond, so they could go in the water. The bench is a top cover for them to protect them from rain and things that might fall on them.* **We have the pros recorded on the graphic organizer. Now think about things that might make living under a bench *not* such a good idea. These are the cons of the option.** Again, allow time for discussion, then ask volunteers for one of their ideas until you have three or four. Write the ideas suggested in the box on the right side of the "Results" box. POSSIBLE STUDENT RESPONSES: *Too many people will be too close to them, so they could get kicked or stepped on. Other animals, like dogs that people might bring into the park, might find them and chase them. The people that keep the park clean might not like them there and might shoo them away.*

- **The bottom of the graphic organizer asks us to think about and decide if this is a good thing to do. We should consider the pros and cons, making sure that we think about how important they are to the decision. They may be very important to choosing a home for the Mallards, or not terribly important. This will make a difference in the decision we make. Looking at the pros and cons of this option, do you think that making a nest under a bench at the park is a good option?** After students have engaged in some discussion of the pros and cons in their groups, record the class response in a sentence on the first line, and give the reasons for the decision on the second line. POSSIBLE STUDENT RESPONSES: CHOICE: *No, it is not a good place for them to raise their baby ducklings.* WHY: *The bench is a people place, not a duck place, and the ducks might get hurt.* **We have written a sentence that tells our decision about building a nest under a bench at the park. We have also told why we feel that way. When we answer this "why" question, we are giving our reasons for what we decide about whether it is a good option or not.**

- **I'm going to ask you to consider the rest of the options in your small groups. Each group will be given a graphic organizer on which to record one of our options, and to list the possible results of that option. The graphic organizer you will use has a larger space for recording results, or consequences, of the option for your group. If the consequence is good, you will record it on the side labeled "pro." If the consequence is a bad one, record it on the side labeled "con."** Divide the options among the groups and allow time for the groups to record their consequences. Provide each group with the modified version of the Skillful Decision Making graphic organizer called Skillful Decision Making—How Good Is Your Option? This version allows more space for recording. It is large enough that illustrations could be used if desired. When most of the groups have completed the results box, call them together to share their ideas. This can be done by pairing groups to share with each other or by sharing with the whole class.

- **We have thought of options, and we have considered the results, or the consequences of the options. It is time for your group to evaluate the option you are considering. You need to look at the work you have done. Are there any consequences that are more important to consider in making your choice? Is the option a good one, or are there some consequences that show that the Mallard family should not choose this home? Talk in your group and make a decision to tell the large group. Like the large graphic organizer, at the bottom of your sheet you will find a place to say whether or not your option is a good thing to do. You can write yes or no to answer the question, "Is this a good thing to do?" Write a sentence on the line to tell why you think that way.** After the groups have completed the task of choosing the best option and stating their reasons, allow time for the groups to share that information with the rest of the class. Mark on the original list (on the overhead or class chart) a "yes" by those options that were stated to be good choices and a "no" by those that were not.

- **We have gone over all of our options. We have marked the options that are good choices for a home with a "yes," and all the options that are not good choices with a "no." Talk to a neighbor, and choose the option that you think would be the best home for the Mallard family. Discuss with your neighbor why you think this option is better than the others.** When all options have been discussed, allow students to vote on the best choice for a home for the Mallard family.

- **Now we will read the rest of the story. Let's see if the decisions made by the Mallards are good choices.** Read the rest of the book with students, discussing the ducks' decisions as the story unfolds. In the discussion, students should bring out or be guided to realize that making their nest by the Charles River gave Mrs. Mallard a quiet place to sit on the eggs and be close to food and water, all good consequences. It was also a good place because they made a good friend in Michael the policeman. When the ducklings hatched, their parents were very proud of them and were careful to protect them from danger. The father went to see the rest of the river, but the mother chose to stay at the Charles River. That option was safer for the ducklings because they were still very little. The mother taught them to swim, dive, and walk in a line, and then took them to meet Mr. Mallard in the Public Gardens when she knew they had learned everything. Getting to the Public Gardens had some consequences that were not good. If Mrs. Mallard had crossed the street without Michael's help, the consequences could have been very

SKILLFUL DECISION MAKING—HOW GOOD IS YOUR OPTION?

DECISION: _____

YOUR OPTION: _____

RESULTS
What will happen?

PRO	CON

CHOICE

Is this a good thing to do? _____

Why? _____

serious. The duckling family could have all been killed by the cars. Waiting for Michael was a good option, because he helped them get across the street to the Public Garden where they decided to live. It had food, water, and a quiet place to sleep at night on the island. Use the terminology from the lesson where possible in the discussion. **Is the Mallards' decision a good one?** *Yes.* **Is it different from yours?** ANSWERS VARY. **Is one idea better than another?** ANSWERS VARY. **Did trying to solve the ducks' problem help you understand them better?** POSSIBLE STUDENT RESPONSES: *I liked trying to figure out where the ducks could live. Even though my answer wasn't the one in the book, I think it was a good one for the ducks. I really wanted them to decide on my option.* **It seems that doing this kind of thinking as you read helps you understand the story and its characters. If you were the author, perhaps you would have changed the ending so that the ducks decided on the option that you felt was the best. Still, we have put ourselves into the story to understand it, and we have made the story more interesting by the thinking that we did.**

THINKING ABOUT THINKING

- **When you were pretending to be Mr. and Mrs. Mallard, you were deciding, or making choices. You considered many options. Was it good to think about all these options before deciding on a home for the duck family? Why?** POSSIBLE STUDENT RESPONSES: *It was good to think of lots of options because then we didn't skip over any good ideas. It was fun to think of lots of places. If I were Mr. Mallard, I would have fun going around and looking at all the places I might pick.*

- **After we made a list of options, what did we do?** POSSIBLE STUDENT RESPONSES: *We thought about what would be good and bad about each option. Those were the pros and cons.* **Was it good to consider the consequences of each option? Why?** POSSIBLE STUDENT RESPONSES: *If we didn't, we might have made a bad choice and have been sorry. The ducklings could have gotten killed if the parents hadn't picked a good home.*

- **Was the thinking map helpful to you as you made your choices?** *Yes, because it helped me remember the next step.* **Were the graphic organizers helpful to you as you were thinking?** POSSIBLE STUDENT RESPONSES: *I liked the space to write what was good and bad. It was easier to decide if they should do that thing or not. I think that it is really good to think about whether the pros and cons were important ones. If it meant the ducks would die, then the option was really important to remember.*

- **What things would you tell someone if they were having trouble making a decision?** The students should include in their responses some of the points from the thinking map.

APPLYING YOUR THINKING

Immediate Transfer

- Using this decision plan, think about Peter Rabbit and his trip to Mr. McGregor's garden. Discuss with your group what options Peter had when he got to the garden. Use a graphic organizer to consider the pros and cons of his choice to go into the garden. Then go back and think of other options for Peter. Choose one to think about, and fill out another graphic organizer with the pros and cons of that option. Which option was a better one?

- Imagine that you are going to take a trip with your family. Choose a spot where you are going. Think about the options for getting there. What kind of transportation would be the best for your family to use? Fill out a graphic organizer to show the options you thought of. Discuss the options with a friend. Using a graphic organizer, consider the consequences of the options and their pros and cons, then show the pros and cons of the one you think will be the best choice. Write a letter to your family telling them about the decision-making process that you used and the choice of transportation that you made.

Reinforcement Later

- Goldilocks walked right into the bears' cottage. She made a decision without considering her options. Use our Decision Making thinking map and graphic organizer to show what she should have done before making her decision about whether to enter the bears' cottage. Draw and write about some other options she had.

- Your mother has given you permission to pack your own lunch. Think about the things we've learned about good nutrition. What things would you consider as you planned your lunch? Use our thinking map and graphic organizer for decision making to help you. The options should include several different menus. Draw the best choice and write a short sentence telling what things would be in your lunch.

WRITING EXTENSION

After students have completed the lesson, ask them to illustrate and write about what adventures the Mallard family would have had if they had made a different choice. The graphic organizer for decision making will guide them in their writing. To begin the story, present or have the class generate a story starter. Students who are not comfortable with writing can draw picture captions. Students should illustrate one of the alternate places the class determined to be a good home for the ducklings. Using the information from the graphic organizer, students write a caption for their picture explaining why it would be a good home for the ducks.

SUGGESTED SPECIAL NEEDS MODIFICATIONS

<u>Frontload:</u> For some students, engaging in a thinking strategy takes more time and teacher guidance through skillful questioning and modelling. The teacher's think aloud can serve as a model of such sequenced thinking. In this case the teacher might model thinking aloud about possibilities: *"What decision might I make?"* "Let me see. *How many possible ways* can I think of," etc., and/or about consequences: "What if I did _____? *What might happen?*" Questioning should be scaffolded in such a way as to direct students to such "what if" thinking.

Some students may need prior practice with generating many possibilities without thinking about whether or not they will work. If students can learn to suspend judgment until after they have investigated consequences of the options, they will be better able to make good decisions. Therefore, using multiple opportunities prior to the Infusion lesson to guide students in generating options without judging would be beneficial. Students could brainstorm suggestions about what to do with their friends in the playground, what a story character or historical figure might do on a particular occasion; or they could generate all the ways to use a geometric figure for some constructive or aesthetic purpose. Be explicit that the rules are to generate ideas without comment.

In addition, use the language of thinking to label student contributions: "That's an example of *flexible thinking*," "That's some *original thinking*," "You are *suspending your judgment* about whether that idea will work."

Students may require an introduction to the notions of "consequences" and "evaluating consequences." Using real life examples in the days prior to the lesson, teachers can guide students through the process of identifying and judging consequences. For example, using a think aloud, the teacher might discuss the consequences that were considered in making the decision to choose cookies rather than cake for a class treat. (Cake requires plates and forks, both taste good, the texture is different, etc.). During this process, it is important that the impact of the consequence be stressed over the mere number of pros or cons. This guides students in judging relative importance or value of each consequence.

Clarify: Color-coding the boxes to highlight different sections of the graphic organizer can help to clarify the different tasks involved in generating options, generating consequences, then rating the consequences. These terms can be explained by the teacher using words or phrases that students are more familiar with like "alternatives," "choices," "results," "what will happen," "importance," etc.

Diversify: Some students may need additional support, particularly if writing on a graphic organizer is expected. Picture responses or dictating to an adult may be necessary.

Cooperative groups also offer the opportunity to engage all students in the discussion and to utilize all students' strengths. By assigning the task of recorder to a proficient writer, the task load is reduced for the student who struggles with writing but who can engage in the discussion.

Expand the Possibilities: Assessments of written responses may be based upon the students' thinking first, and expressive skills second. Oral responses may also reveal thinking beyond students' ability to express themselves in writing. Pictures or responses recorded on tape may also reveal students' understanding.

ASSESSING STUDENT THINKING ABOUT POSSIBILITIES

To assess students' skills in decision making, present them with any of the suggested application items or a classroom/school situation in which a decision must be made. Students should be asked to write, draw, and discuss the steps they took in making a choice about what to do. Assess their skill at decision making by ascertaining whether they are thinking about a variety of options and also the pros and cons of the various options.

Sample Student Responses • Duckling Decisions

SKILLFUL DECISION MAKING

OPTIONS
What should _the Mallards_ **do?**

Live in someone's backyard.

Live at a zoo.

Live under someone's deck.

Live on a river.

Live in someone's swimming pool.

Live in a garden.

Live in a quiet pond.

Live under a bench at the park.

YOUR OPTION
under a bench
at the park

RESULTS
What will happen?

PRO

It is near to grass and food from people.

It might be near a pond.

The bench is a top cover for them.

CON

Too many people will be close to them.

There are no sides to the nest.

They could get kicked or stepped on.

THINK ABOUT THE
PROS AND CONS

CHOICE
Is this a good thing to do?

No, it is not a good place for them to raise their ducklings.

Why?

The bench is a people place, not a duck place.

Sample Student Responses • Duckling Decisions

SKILLFUL DECISION MAKING—HOW GOOD IS YOUR OPTION?

DECISION: _Where can the Mallards find a home?_

YOUR OPTION: _under the deck_

RESULTS
What will happen?

PRO	CON
It's a good hiding place from foxes.	It can be noisy and scary when people walk above you.
People could drop scraps to the ducks for food.	There can be poison nearby.
Spilled water can go through the cracks for them to drink.	People can throw rocks at the ducks.
People might be nice and make a pond.	There isn't much water.
	The deck could fall.

CHOICE

Is this a good thing to do? _No._

Why? _There is too much danger._

There is not enough food and water.

Sample Student Responses • Duckling Decisions

SKILLFUL DECISION MAKING—HOW GOOD IS YOUR OPTION?

DECISION: _Where can the Mallards find a home?_

YOUR OPTION: _Lake Michigan_

RESULTS
What will happen?

PRO	CON
They get fresh air.	They might sink into the water.
They have lots of room to swim.	The waves might blow the ducks away.
They can get lots of food.	They might get their wings stuck in the water.
They have lots of people to help them.	
They have lots of room for the ducks to fly.	

CHOICE

Is this a good thing to do? _Yes._

Why? _There are lots of people to help them, and they have the things they need for a home._

Sample Student Alternate Story Ending • Duckling Decisions

Story Starter:

Mr. and Mrs. Mallard flew and flew looking for a place to live. Finally they arrived at Lake Michigan. "Oh, my!" cried Mrs. Mallard. "Look at all of the water. Let's stop and look around." Mr. Mallard was getting hungry for a nice fish snack so he agreed. They landed on a beach. There were many people, but they were playing in the sand and there were no cars, so they felt safe. Mr. and Mrs. Mallard were very tired from flying so many miles from Boston Garden. They decided to make Lake Michigan their home.

First the Mallards looked for the right spot to build their nest. They found a place on top of a big sand dune. "This will be a perfect place to have babies," said Mrs. Mallard. They found some soft green grass and made a nest. Then the Mallards went back to the water to find some lunch. There were lots and lots of delicious fish. They were so busy eating that they did not notice the wind starting to blow. Suddenly the water started to have waves. A giant wave came up and went right on top of them! More big waves kept coming and coming. The water made the ducks dizzy. They did not know what to do. Some people noticed the ducks being hurt by the waves. They got in a motorboat and rescued them. Then a policeman came. He took the ducks to a place down the beach where the waves were not so big. "Stay away from waves and you will like living in Lake Michigan," said the policeman. The ducks quacked "Thank you!" "I think this will be a wonderful place for a family," said Mrs. Mallard. "Then we will stay here and raise our family," said Mr. Mallard. When the babies were born, the policeman and the people on the beach gave them treats. Mr. and Mrs. Mallard took their babies to the quiet place to swim and eat every day. Then they went back to their nest at night to sleep.

JAMAICA AND THE DOG
JAMAICA'S FIND

Language Arts   **Grades 1–2**

OBJECTIVES

CONTENT

Students will interpret story characters in terms of their character traits and actions and practice reading and/or listening skills.

THINKING SKILL/PROCESS

Students will learn to think about options and the consequences of those options in making decisions.

METHODS AND MATERIALS

CONTENT

The students will read or listen to *Jamaica's Find* by Juanita Havill. Students should use their comprehension skills as they listen to or read the story and study the illustrations in order to find and recognize clues to the main character's traits.

THINKING SKILL/PROCESS

A thinking map, a graphic organizer, and structured questioning emphasize options and consequences in decision making. Collaborative learning enhances the thinking.

LESSON

INTRODUCTION TO CONTENT AND THINKING SKILL/PROCESS

- **Have you ever made decisions about what to do? I am going to tell you about a time when I had to make a decision. It was summer, and I had a day free from all my chores and errands. I wanted to do something fun, and I thought about two choices: I could go swimming or I could go for a bike ride in the forest. I couldn't do both things. Now, think about a time when you had to decide about something and you weren't sure what was best. Take turns and tell your partner what you were thinking about doing.** Have students talk to their partners about the decisions they had to make. It may be necessary to prompt some pairs with questions or topics that will help them to think of times when they had a decision to make. **Let's hear some of the examples you shared with your partner.** Ask for three or four examples. POSSIBLE STUDENT RESPONSES: *I had to pick between joining soccer or t-ball. I got invited to my friend's house, and then my grandma said she would take me to the zoo. My friend wanted me to come outside and play, and I wanted to finish reading a book.*

- **What kind of thinking helped you figure out what to do?** POSSIBLE STUDENT RESPONSES: *Picking, choosing, deciding.* Write these words on the top of the chalkboard or a flip chart as a main heading. Tell the students that the words "decision making" mean the same thing as these words, and write "decision making" above the words.

- **The different things you were thinking of doing are called "choices" or "options."** Write these words on the chalkboard or chart under the main heading. **Let's hear one of the choices or options you were thinking about when you were trying to decide.** POSSIBLE STUDENT RESPONSES: *I could join soccer and just play t-ball with my friends. I could ask my friend if I could come over on another day. I could mark the place in my book.*

- **In order to pick the best thing to do, we usually think about what will happen if we do it. We** do this to figure out the good and bad things that might happen. These are usually called "results" or "consequences" of our options. Write "results" and "consequences" under options. Write "pro" and "con" under them. Explain that "pro" is used to describe the things that are good things, and "con" is used to describe the things that are bad, or things we do not want to happen. I knew that going for a bike ride would mean I could visit one of my favorite paths in a nearby forest. That's a pro. But I listened to the weather forecast which told me that the weather was going to be very hot and humid. It would be very hot riding my bike. That's a con.

- Pick one of your options when you needed to make a decision, and discuss with your partner what might have happened had you chosen it. Which of these consequences would you have wanted to happen, and which would you not have wanted to happen? As you are talking, use the word "pro" for the good things that would happen and use the word "con" for the bad things that would happen. Allow time for students to discuss the consequences of their options. As students are discussing their options, support them in using the terms by restating and modeling the use of "pro" and "con." Were there any consequences that really didn't make a difference? Sometimes the consequence is something that really doesn't matter. Use one of the student's examples to show an unimportant consequence. In my choosing between bike riding or swimming, I knew that the swimming pool was a little farther from my house than the bike trail. This was not that important to me, as I wasn't busy and had the day to myself.

- After we've thought about the consequences of our options and whether the consequences were important enough to consider, we can pick the best thing to do. Write "Choose the best thing to do" under "Consequences—pro and con." The best thing to do will be the option that has more important pros than cons. In making my decision, I found that swimming was the best choice for that day because it had more positive, or pro, consequences than going bike riding. Swimming would be cool on such a hot day, and I could also sit in the shade with a good book for part of the afternoon. The only con for swimming was that the pool was farther from home. That was not important to me, as it would just mean that I'd need to watch the clock so that I could get home in time for dinner. That was not important because I knew that I could easily watch the time.

- This thinking map shows what we need to think about when we make decisions. Show an enlarged copy of the primary thinking map for skillful decision making, going over the three questions: What are some things I can do? What will happen if I do these things? Which are good things to do? Post this on the wall of the classroom, on the chalkboard, or on a flip chart so that students can see it throughout the lesson.

> **SKILLFUL DECISION MAKING**
>
> 1. **What are some things I can do?**
>
> 2. **What will happen if I do these things?**
>
> 3. **Which are good things to do?**

- Now tell your partner what you decided to do. What did you think about in order to pick the best choice? Allow time for students to talk to their partner and then for the whole group to discuss choices. As students discuss the choices they made, refer to the thinking map questions to show the steps they used in their thinking.

- Decision making happens in many of the stories we read. As we read stories, we learn about characters who must make decisions. We should think about the choices they must make and what they should ask themselves as they decide. Doing this kind of thinking helps us to understand more about the characters and why they act as they do.

THINKING ACTIVELY

- **We are going to read the beginning of a story. This story has a young girl as the main character. She will need to make some decisions. We will think about what she should consider as she makes her decisions. As you listen to (or read) the story and study the illustrations, I'd like you to think about the girl and try to learn things about the kind of person she is. This will help you as you think about the decisions she must make.** If there are multiple copies of *Jamaica's Find* for students to read, pass them out, but read the story aloud to the students. Since this is a listening activity, review with students the things that they should do when they are listening. Tell them that they should keep their mind focused on the task, keep their eyes on the book to find picture clues, ask themselves questions as they hear the story, listen for answers to their questions, etc. Tell them also that they should think ahead about what may happen and revise their ideas about this as they get further into the story. Tell them that these skills are also part of a reader's work when reading a story by himself or herself. Read the story up to the point in the story where Jamaica finds the dog and the hat.

- **At this point in the story, let's review what we know. Tell me some things that have happened in the story so far.** POSSIBLE STUDENT RESPONSES: *The little girl, Jamaica, stopped to play at the park before she went home. Everyone else was gone, and she was all alone. When she went on the slide, she found a hat at the top and a stuffed dog at the bottom.* **Were there clues in the story to tell you how she felt about the stuffed dog that she found?** POSSIBLE STUDENT RESPONSES: *It was cuddly and worn from hugging. The picture shows her smiling at it.* **Are there any clues that make you think the hat is special?** POSSIBLE STUDENT RESPONSES: *No, it just says she found the hat. There is a lot about the dog, but not too much about the hat.* Having a student reread the section where Jamaica finds the hat and dog, or rereading the section to the class helps students see that the dog is more interesting to the girl than the hat. **What do you think she will do with the dog and the hat? Why?** ANSWERS VARY.

- **Let's read some more to see what Jamaica does next.** Read on to the point where Jamaica says. "I don't feel good." **Now we know more details. What can we say about Jamaica and her actions at this point in the story?** Students should retell the story, including details about taking the hat to the lost and found and putting the dog into her bicycle basket to take home. The reactions of Jamaica's family should also be brought out, including the comments from her mother about the dog probably belonging to some other little girl. **What decision has Jamaica made?** POSSIBLE STUDENT RESPONSE: *She turned the hat into the lost and found, but she kept the dog.* **What do you think that might tell you about Jamaica?** POSSIBLE STUDENT RESPONSES: *She didn't care about the hat, but she really liked the dog. She wasn't thinking about the person who lost the dog, she was only thinking about herself.* **Is there evidence in the illustrations to tell you more about Jamaica and her feelings?** POSSIBLE STUDENT RESPONSES: *She wasn't really selfish. Her face shows that she is upset. She doesn't like the way that she is feeling.*

- **Were there consequences that Jamaica did not think about when she brought the stuffed dog home?** *Yes.* **Were the consequences good or not so good?** POSSIBLE STUDENT RESPONSES: *They were not good consequences. She didn't like the way she felt. Her family said things that made her think she might have done the wrong thing.* **You are beginning to learn things about the character that will help you understand the things that she does. Her actions tell you things about her. So do the ways she looks in the pictures and the feelings the author tells you she is having. Careful listening and careful reading is helping us understand Jamaica.**

- **Do you think turning in the hat but keeping the dog was a good decision for Jamaica to make? Do you think Jamaica is beginning to feel bad about what she has done?** Students usually recognize that she is. If they hesitate about this, ask them why they think she says "I don't feel good" and what this shows about how she now feels about her decision to keep the dog.

- **If you think that maybe you've made a bad decision, is it okay to change your minds and make a different decision?** Students usually agree that this is okay. **So let's make believe we are Jamaica and we want to make a different decision about what to do about the dog. Let's think about this. What should we think about in order to make a better decision?** Students often hesitate, but some students usually remember the lesson introduction. If none do, refer them to the thinking map on the wall. POSSIBLE STUDENT RESPONSE: *We should think about what she could do, and then what the results might be to help us see the best choice for her to make.* Emphasize the use of the words "options," "consequences," and "best choice" when students respond by using them to summarize what the students say and writing them on the chalkboard.

- **We're going to use a graphic organizer to help us think. A graphic organizer is a diagram that gives us places to write down our ideas as we think about them. This one has places to write down the options we come up with, the consequences, and to state whether we think the option is a good one.** Show the Skillful Decision Making graphic organizer on an overhead projector or a flip chart. Point out the three basic areas on the graphic organizer for options, for results (or consequences), and for what they think about the option.

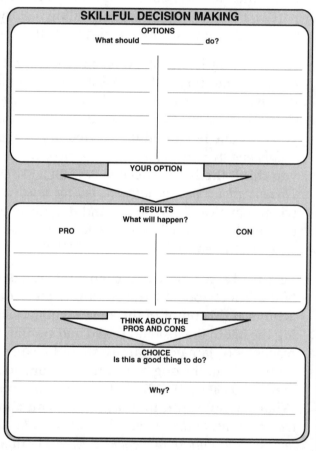

- **Let me state again what the situation is that Jamaica is in so that you can start to think like her. Jamaica has made one decision already. She has turned in the hat and kept the dog. But now her family is causing her to think about the decision she made. She is wondering what she should do with the dog. We're now going to start to help her by listing all the choices, or options, she has. What should she do with the dog? Work with your group to think of options for her. Try to think of at least three different things that she might do.** Break the class into groups of three or four students and allow time for discussion. **Now we'll record some of the options you've thought of in your groups on the organizer.** Ask for one option from each group and then ask if any of the groups have other options that haven't been mentioned. As students mention options, record them in the top section of the graphic organizer called "Options." POSSIBLE STUDENT RESPONSES: *Keep it. Find the owner. Look at the collar and call the owner. Take the dog back to the slide. Give it to the owner. Keep it until they find the owner. Put it in the Lost and Found. Make a poster to say you found it.*

- **Our next step is to think about the options and what the results will be if Jamaica chooses each one. We will list the good things that would happen on the "pro" side of the "Results"** box and the things we would not like to see happen on the side marked "con." Show this space to students, pointing out the pro and con sides.

- **We'll start with the option, "Keep it." What things would happen if Jamaica chose to keep the dog? Work in your groups again and try to come up with at least two pros and two cons.** Once again, give students about three or four minutes for this activity. Then ask them to share their ideas. As students share their ideas, record them on the appropriate side of the graphic organizer. Be sure to have students identify whether the consequence is pro or con and why they feel that way. POSSIBLE STUDENT RESPONSES: PRO: *You really like it and you will take care of it. The owner might not want it. It's too hard to find the owner.* CON: *The owner might cry. The owner will miss it. Somebody might say you took it. You might get into trouble.*

- **Now let's think about the importance of the results. If there is a pro or a con result that is not important, you need to keep that in mind when you decide if the option is a good one. Talk about this with your partners in your groups.** Give students two or three minutes to do this.

- **The bottom of the graphic organizer has a box for us to record our decision about the option. The first question asks, "Is this a good thing to do?" Based on the results that we have just recorded, and your discussion about which results are really important, is keeping the dog a good thing for Jamaica to do?** The class usually comes to a consensus that this is not a good option. If they do, ask for volunteers to say why they think this option is not good and formulate a statement that combines their ideas into a statement supporting their decision and write it under "Why?" on the graphic organizer. If there is a difference of opinion in the class, ask students from each side to explain why and then give students a chance to think about this question again. If there is still not a class consensus, take a vote and record the results on the graphic organizer.

- **We have considered one of the options. Now you will work with your groups to consider another of the options we have on the graphic organizer. I have a graphic organizer for each group to use to consider an option. Your graphic organizer has more space for you to show your work. On your graphic organizer, write the option your group is working on and the things that will happen if Jamaica chooses that option as the best one. You may also choose to draw your answer in the space instead of writing it.** Provide the groups with the Skillful Decision Making—How Good Is Your Option graphic organizer and assign each group one of the other options to work on. It has space for students to draw or to write their responses. Allow work time, and then ask students to look at the bottom portion of their sheet.

- **After making a list of the pros and cons of your option, it is important to decide if the option is a good one to consider. Talk in your groups about the pros and cons of the option,**

SKILLFUL DECISION MAKING—HOW GOOD IS YOUR OPTION?

DECISION: _____

YOUR OPTION: _____

RESULTS
What will happen?

PRO | CON

CHOICE

Is this a good thing to do? _____

Why? _____

and decide if you think this is something that would be good for Jamaica to do. Make sure that you think about the importance of the results. If there is a pro or a con result that is not important, you need to keep that in mind as you decide if the option is a good one. You can do that by putting a star next to the ones you think are really important. On the bottom of the graphic organizer, you have a spot to record the decision your group makes. Be sure to include a sentence that tells why you made your decision. After they have completed the task, ask the groups to share the results. Have students explain why each result is a pro or con, and why the option is or is not a good thing to do. As they share their decision, mark a "yes" or a "no" next to the option on the class graphic organizer.

- **Now we've considered all of the options and whether they are good choices. In your group, discuss and choose, from the good options, the option that would be the best. Talk together about why you think your choice is the best choice.** Give students time to discuss in small groups. They will then present to the class the option they chose and why they chose it. Make a record of how many groups choose which option. If there is a clear preference of the class, write "Class's Choice" on the board or flipchart and record that option.

- **We'll finish the story now to see what Jamaica does.** Read the rest of the story. Discuss the events of the story during and after the story to help students develop their understanding of the character and her actions. Jamaica changes her mind about keeping the dog after sitting with her mother and quietly thinking about what she had done. She turns the dog in to the lost and found at the park, then finds the real owner and makes a friend. **Did Jamaica make the choice you thought was the best one?** ANSWERS VARY. **Do you think Jamaica thought about some of the consequences we thought of when she decided to turn the dog into the lost and found?** POSSIBLE STUDENT RESPONSES *Yes, I think she thought about taking someone's dog.* **Do you think it was hard for her to change her mind?** ANSWERS VARY. **Could you tell how her feelings changed when she met Kristin, the real owner of the dog, and was able to help her get her Edgar dog back?** Students usually talk about how she was lonely for the dog after she turned it in and then how she was very happy and excited when she was able to tell Kristin where her Edgar dog was. When they do this, ask them what in the story or in the illustrations shows that she is lonely, and what shows that she is happy. **Our work has helped us to understand more about the character, Jamaica. We know what she is like and a little bit about the way that she thinks about things.**

THINKING ABOUT THINKING

- **Let's look back at the thinking that we have done. When you thought about Jamaica and the decision she had to make, you thought of the options she had. Was this helpful in making a choice?** POSSIBLE STUDENT RESPONSES: *Yes, it helped to think about the different things she could do. I liked that we could choose.* **Were the options important to think about? Why or why not?** POSSIBLE STUDENT RESPONSE: *You want to pick the right thing, so you should think about all the options.*

- **Was it good to think about the consequences of Jamaica's options? Why?** POSSIBLE STUDENT RESPONSES: *Some of the options had bad consequences. She shouldn't pick those.*

- **If Jamaica were here, what advice would you give her about making choices?** The students should include the things that they did as they considered the options and made a decision.

- **If you need to make a decision some time in the future, what words will help you remember the steps in good decision making? Make a list of these words.** Students should include on their lists the following words: *options, consequences, pro, con, choose.* Discuss with the class when they will use these words as they think about a decision they have to make.

APPLYING YOUR THINKING

Immediate Transfer

• Use the Skillful Decision Making thinking map to make a decision about what to do at recess tomorrow. Fill in a graphic organizer for skillful decision making to show the thinking you did. Be sure to consider the options and the consequences as you make your choice. Draw a picture of your choice and write about how your choice worked out. Was it a good choice?

• Put yourself in the place of Martin Luther King, Jr. when he was a small boy. Your friends are not allowed to play with you because you are black and they are white. What should you do to help them understand that the color of your skin should not be the reason for choosing friends? Use the steps in the Skillful Decision Making thinking map and the graphic organizer to help you make the best decision.

Reinforcement Later

• We have studied many animals. Use your plan for decision making to decide what animal would be a good one for our class to have in the classroom. Think about what animal would be happy in our room and what animal we would be able to take care of. Show your work on a graphic organizer.

• Dr. DeSoto, the mouse dentist, had a fox who wanted to be his patient. He needed to be very careful in deciding what to do. Put yourself in his place. Using careful thinking, follow the steps of the Skillful Decision Making thinking map as you fill in a graphic organizer to make the best choice for a small dentist. Act out the way that you would deal with this problem if you were the little mouse dentist.

WRITING EXTENSION

Have students pretend they are Jamaica. They will write a letter to their grandma or grandpa telling them about the decisions they've been making and how they made the best choice. They will tell their grandparents about how the decisions made them feel and what they have learned about what to do with special things that they find. They will also tell them about the way they thought as they were making decisions and how they used their thinking map. Students can also ask their grandparents to tell them about some decisions they have to make and how they will decide what to do. Students should use their graphic organizer and the template for narrative writing to guide them in their writing.

SUGGESTED SPECIAL NEEDS MODIFICATIONS

Frontload: For some students, engaging in a thinking strategy takes more time and teacher guidance through skillful questioning and modelling. The teacher's think aloud can serve as a model of such sequenced thinking. In this case, the teacher might model thinking aloud about possibilities: *"What decision might I make?"* "Let me see. *How many possible ways* can I think of,"* etc., and/or about consequences: "What if I did _____? *What might happen?"* Questioning should be scaffolded in such a way as to direct students to such "what if" thinking.

Some students may need prior practice with generating many possibilities without thinking about whether or not they will work. If students can learn to suspend judgment until after they have investigated consequences of the options, they will be better able to make good decisions.

Therefore, using multiple opportunities prior to the Infusion lesson to guide students in generating options without judging would be beneficial. Students could brainstorm suggestions about what to do with their friends in the playground, what a story character or historical figure might do on a particular occasion; or they could generate all the ways to use a geometric figure for some constructive or aesthetic purpose. Be explicit that the rules are to generate ideas without comment.

In addition, use the language of thinking to label student contributions: "That's an example of *flexible thinking*," "That's some *original thinking*," "You are *suspending your judgment* about whether that idea will work."

Students may require an introduction to the notions of "consequences" and "evaluating consequences." Using real life examples in the days prior to the lesson, teachers can guide students through the process of identifying and judging consequences. For example, using a think aloud, the teacher might discuss the consequences that were considered in making the decision to choose cookies rather than cake for a class treat. (Cake requires plates and forks, both taste good, the texture is different, etc.). During this process, it is important that the impact of the consequence is stressed over the mere number of pros or cons. This guides students in judging relative importance or value of each consequence.

<u>Clarify</u>: Color-coding the boxes to highlight different sections of the graphic organizer can help to clarify the different tasks involved in generating options, generating consequences, then rating the consequences. These terms can be explained by the teacher using words or phrases that students are more familiar with like "alternatives," "choices," "results," "what will happen," "importance," etc.

<u>Diversify</u>: Some students may need additional support , particularly if writing on a graphic is expected. Picture responses or dictating to an adult may be necessary.

Cooperative groups also offer the opportunity to engage all students in the discussion and to utilize all students' strengths. By assigning the task of recorder to a proficient writer, the task load is reduced for the student who struggles with writing but who can engage in the discussion.

<u>Expand the Possibilities</u>: Assessments of written responses may be based upon students' thinking first, and expressive skills second. Oral responses may also reveal thinking beyond students' ability to express themselves in writing. Pictures or responses recorded on tape may also reveal students' understanding.

ASSESSING STUDENT THINKING ABOUT POSSIBILITIES

To assess student thinking about decisions, ask them to identify each step of the thinking map plan as they solve an open-ended decision making problem. Any of the examples in the Application section of this lesson can be used for this purpose. Encourage students to use the language used in their previous decision-making lessons. This assessment can be done individually or in small groups. Students can use illustrations, write on graphic organizers, or verbalize the steps of the process.

Sample Student Responses • Jamaica's Find

SKILLFUL DECISION MAKING

OPTIONS
What should ___Jamaica___ do?

Keep it.	Give it to the owner.
Find the owner.	Keep it until they find the owner.
Look at the collar and call the owner.	Put it in the Lost and Found.
Take the dog back to the slide.	Make a poster to say you found it.

YOUR OPTION
Keep it.

RESULTS
What will happen?

PRO	CON
You really like it and you will take care of it.	The owner might cry.
The owner might not want it.	The owner will miss it a lot.
It's too hard to find the owner.	Somebody might say you took it.

THINK ABOUT THE PROS AND CONS

CHOICE
Is this a good thing to do?

No, it is not a good thing to do.

Why?

It is not good to keep something that is not yours even if you really like it.

Sample Student Responses • Jamaica's Find

SKILLFUL DECISION MAKING—HOW GOOD IS YOUR OPTION?

DECISION: _What should Jamaica do with the dog?_

YOUR OPTION: _Take the dog back to the slide._

RESULTS
What will happen?

PRO	CON
The boy or girl will get the dog back.	_Someone else will get the dog, not the owner._
Jamaica will feel good because she didn't keep something that wasn't hers.	_There might be rain and it will get wet._
She might meet the one who really owns it and they could be friends.	_A real animal might chew on it._
	The one who lost it might not know where they lost it.

CHOICE

Is this a good thing to do? _Yes._

Why? _It is good, but Jamaica should wait to make sure the right one gets the_

dog, not somebody else.

Sample Student Narrative Letter • Jamaica's Find

Tuesday morning

Dear Grandma,

   I have been making many decisions. It was hard to do. I found a nice doll that I wanted to keep but I thought about what would happen. If the girl that lost it couldn't find it again she would be very sad and lonely. I decided to give it back. The girl that lost it was at the park. I helped her find it! I was very proud of what I did. I think that it is important to think about what will happen before you make big decisions. Do you do that when you have a decision to make? I have a thinking map to help you if you want to use it. Write and tell me about how you make decisions.

Love,

Jamaica

SKILLFUL DECISION MAKING

1. What are some things I can do?

2. What will happen if I do these things?

3. Which are good things to do?

SKILLFUL DECISION MAKING

OPTIONS
What should _____ do?

_____ | _____
_____ | _____
_____ | _____
_____ | _____

YOUR OPTION

RESULTS
What will happen?

PRO | CON

_____ | _____
_____ | _____
_____ | _____

THINK ABOUT THE
PROS AND CONS

CHOICE
Is this a good thing to do?

_____

Why?

_____

SKILLFUL DECISION MAKING—HOW GOOD IS YOUR OPTION?

DECISION: _____

YOUR
OPTION: _____

RESULTS
What will happen?

PRO	CON
_____	_____
_____	_____
_____	_____
_____	_____
_____	_____

CHOICE

Is this a good thing to do? _____

Why? _____

_____

_____

CHAPTER 4
PROBLEM SOLVING

Infusing Skillful Problem Solving into Language Arts

Teaching students skillful problem solving in grades 1 and 2 involves helping them learn to ask and carefully answer the following questions about problems that they face before they try to solve them:

SKILLFUL PROBLEM SOLVING

1. **What is the problem?**

2. **What are possible solutions to the problem?**

3. **What would happen if we chose to solve the problem in that way?**

4. **What is the best solution to the problem?**

---

figure 4.1

This thinking map for skillful problem solving is used to guide your students' thinking explicitly as they engage with the content in the problem-solving lessons.

When students learn and use this strategy for determining the best way to solve problems that they face, they don't just choose the first thing that comes into their heads, but rather define the problem, consider a number of possible solutions, and then choose the best one by thinking about the consequences that they project will result, both positive and negative. When they go through this process, they can explain why they think what they have decided to do is the best choice by providing specific supporting reasons for the problem-solutions that they choose.

These lessons also employ various supporting classroom strategies such as using a graphic organizer, engaging in cooperative thinking, thinking about thinking, and continued guided practice to supplement the use of this thinking map. These classroom strategies enhance both the thinking skill that the students are learning and their mastery of the lesson content.

Two key graphic organizers for skillful problem solving are in figures 4.2 and 4.3.

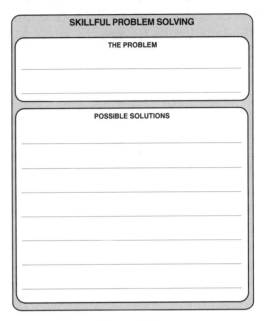

figure 4.2

The first graphic organizer (figure 4.2) helps students record a large number of possible solutions to a problem that they must define at the top of the diagram. The second graphic organizer (figure 4.3, see following page) provides students with space for an in-depth exploration of one possible solution to determine its pros and cons, as well as how important each of these is. One special feature of this graphic organizer is that it provides space for them to draw a picture of what the possible solution might look like. This visual representation can help them identify some of the major consequences of this possible solution. Students also have space on this graphic organizer to modify the solution they are considering to avoid the cons that they have identified.

When a number of students or student groups explore a variety of different possible solutions using these graphic organizers, they can compare results to determine the best solution. If students disagree, you can ask them to debate the issue in class.

For more in-depth information on teaching skillful problem solving, please refer to Chapter 3 in the book *Infusing the Teaching of Critical and Creative Thinking into Elementary Instruction*, by Robert Swartz and Sandra Parks. A computer disk containing the blank, reproducible graphic organizers used in this book is also available. Both book and disk are available through Critical Thinking Books & Software.

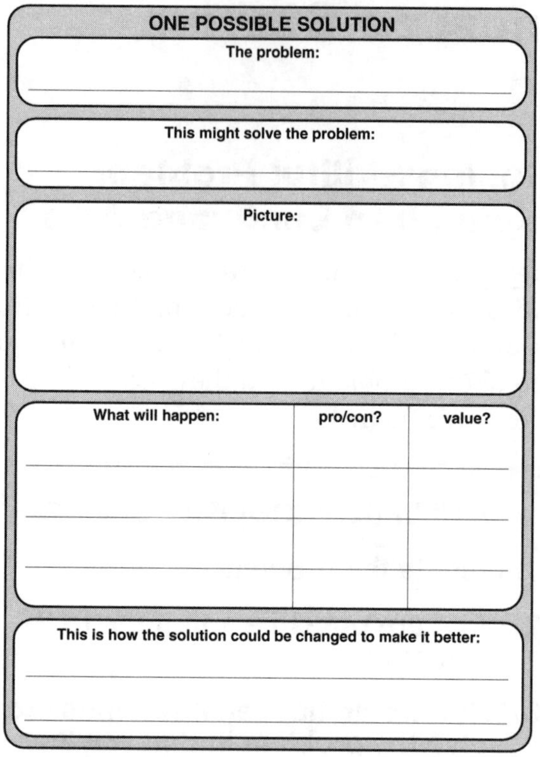

ONE POSSIBLE SOLUTION

The problem:

This might solve the problem:

Picture:

What will happen:	pro/con?	value?

This is how the solution could be changed to make it better:

figure 4.3

OH, NO, THERE'S A WOLF IN MY BED!
LON PO PO

Language Arts   **Grades 1–2**

OBJECTIVES

CONTENT
Students will analyze the plot of the story as they work to solve the problem presented. Using the details provided in the first part of the story, they will hypothesize a resolution to the problem.

THINKING SKILL/PROCESS
Students will learn to solve problems skillfully by identifying a problem, generating possible solutions, and selecting the best solution based on consequences.

METHODS AND MATERIALS

CONTENT
Students will listen to *Lon Po Po* by Ed Young. They will discuss the plot and the actions of the characters as they solve the problem presented in the story.

THINKING SKILL/PROCESS
An explicit thinking map, a graphic organizer, and structured questioning facilitate a thinking strategy for problem solving. Collaborative learning enhances the thinking.

LESSON

INTRODUCTION TO CONTENT AND THINKING SKILL/PROCESS

- Have any of you ever been in a situation where the people around you were crowding you so that you did not have enough room to work? What did you do so that you had enough room? Allow students to share their memories with a neighbor. Have a few share with the class. POSSIBLE STUDENT RESPONSES: *I moved to another place. I asked the people around me to move over. I moved my things into a neat pile so that I could work better.*

- You were trying to make things better so that you could do your project. When you were trying to make things better so that you could work, you were "problem solving." Write the words "Problem Solving" on the chalkboard or a chart. When we think that things aren't the way they should be, we know there is a problem. When we try to fix a situation, we are trying to solve the problem. We do a lot of problem solving. Can anyone tell us of other times when we have had to solve a problem? POSSIBLE STUDENT RESPONSES: *There was no one to play with. I didn't know if there was going to be a Brownie meeting. I didn't know how to do my homework.*

- When we try to solve problems, we need to think about them first. If we don't think first, then the way we solve our problems may not work the way that we would like. We are going to practice a way to problem solve that will help us think carefully and reach solutions that may be more successful. This thinking map for problem solving will guide us. Show the thinking map for problem solving. Display it on the wall of the classroom or on the chalkboard so that it can be seen through-

SKILLFUL PROBLEM SOLVING
1. What is the problem?
2. What are possible solutions to the problem?
3. What would happen if we chose to solve the problem in that way?
4. What is the best solution to the problem?

out the lesson. Discuss each of the steps. **The first question that needs to be answered is, "What is the problem?" In the case of the crowded work space, the problem was, How can we get the space that we need to do our work? It's always important to think about what the problem is first because then we can be very clear about what we want to do. The next question asks, "What are possible solutions to the problem?" We shared our ways to solve the problem. There were different ways it could have been solved. Once we are clear about what the problem is, it is a good idea to think of many possible solutions. Thinking of many different solutions will help us avoid missing a good way to solve the problem. The third question asks us to think about the possible solutions and what would happen if we chose to solve our problem in each of those ways. There could be good and bad things that happen as a result of the way we solve a problem. Finding these out will help us tell which solutions are good and which are bad. The last question asks, "What is the best solution to the problem?" After we have thought about the good and bad of each of the possible solutions, we will need to decide which is the best way to solve the problem.**

- **I'm going to share with you a time when I needed to solve a problem. I was planning to go to a party for one of my close friends. The party was in Chicago. Normally I would drive, but my car was making a funny sound. I was nervous about taking it to Chicago because I thought it might break down on the way. At first, all I could think about was the car and the sound it was making. Then I realized that I needed to think about what my problem really was. If I took a lot of time trying to get my car fixed, I would miss the party. Getting my car fixed was not the real problem—it was only part of the problem. The real problem was bigger than having to get my car fixed. The big problem was how I would get to the party. When we have a problem, we first need to think about what the problem really is. This is the beginning step in problem solving.** Refer to the first question on the think map. Write "The Problem" under "Problem Solving" and then write "How might I get to the party?" under it.

- **The next step in solving a problem is thinking of the possible solutions.** Show question 2 on the thinking map. **I thought of four ways to get to the party. I could call a taxi, I could call a nearby friend who was also going to the party to give me a ride, I could go on the train, or I could go on the bus.** Write the four possible solutions next on the chalkboard under the problem statement. Label them "Possible Solutions."

- **For each of these possible solutions, I needed to consider what would probably happen if I made that solution. These are called the *consequences* of the solution. This is step 3 on our thinking map. For each idea, or solution, I needed to decide what were its pros and cons. If the result of a possible action is something good, it is called a "pro." If it is not so good, it is called a "con." I also had to decide if it was important or not in solving my problem.** Refer to the list as you explain your next episode of thinking. **A taxi would cost quite a bit of money, but would get me to the party at the right time. Spending all that money was not good for me, so I called that consequence a "con." Getting to the party on time was a good thing, so I called that consequence a "pro." My friend would get me to the party, and would not charge me any money, both pros, but picking me up would be out of her way and might not fit into her schedule. That would be a con. I did not want to be a bother to my friend, so I considered that to be a very important consequence to consider. A train ride and a bus ride would cost less than a taxi. That would be a pro for either the bus or the train. But I also thought about a con for each—I would need to get from my house to the bus or train station and then from the Chicago station to the party. I did not have a way to get to the bus or the train station, so that was another very important consequence.** Record the consequences on the chalkboard under the problem as they are presented. Write "Pros" and "Cons" to the right of each and abbreviate each pro and con next to these words.

- My solutions all had important cons, so I saw that I needed to consider ways to change my solutions to make them better. I wanted to keep the best results and avoid the results that were not good. The last question on the thinking map for problem solving asks us to find the best solution. To pick the best solution, I wanted to make some changes. I decided that the best thing to do would be to call my friend who was also going to the party and ask for a ride. Since I didn't want her to rush to my house, I decided to take a taxi to her house. This was not too expensive for me, and it meant that her schedule would not need to be changed. Both consequences were good, or pros, and we had a great time at the party. I think I solved that problem pretty well. Do you think so? Students usually agree.

- In the stories we read there is often a problem to be solved. The action involved in solving the problem makes up the plot of the story. We can use this way of thinking as we read to choose a solution we think is best for solving the problem, and also to see whether the solution the author chooses is a good solution. Today we are going to read part of a story. Then we'll stop to consider a problem the characters must solve. We'll think about what the problem is, the ways the problem could be solved, and what will happen if the character does each thing. We will then consider ways to improve the possible solutions and choose the best action for the character to take in solving the problem. (Refer to the thinking map.)

THINKING ACTIVELY

- We will be reading a Chinese fairy tale called *Lon Po Po,* which was written in English by Ed Young. This story is a version of *Red Riding Hood.* What do we know about the plot in *Red Riding Hood?* Work in your groups to identify the problem and the solution in the story. Allow a short amount of time for the groups to state the problem and solution in the story of *Red Riding Hood* as a class. Have groups summarize the plot of *Red Riding Hood.* They should include the basic details of the wolf eating Grandmother and Red Riding Hood and the wood-cutter saving them. **There will be parts in this story that are very different from the *Red Riding Hood* that you know.** If multiple copies of *Lon Po Po* are available, pass them out. **Looking at the cover will give you a clue to the same problem Red Riding Hood had. What can you predict about the problem just by looking at the cover?** POSSIBLE STUDENT RESPONSES: *A wolf is going to try to eat somebody, just like in Red Riding Hood. They will have to get away from the wolf.* **Now I'm going to read the beginning of the story. Listen for the events that lead up to the problem in the story. Study the pictures as we read for more information. Pay attention to see why there is a problem, and what that problem is.** Read the beginning of the book to the class, sharing the pictures. Stop after the line, "The wolf did not answer."

- **What events have occurred so far in the story?** POSSIBLE STUDENT RESPONSES: *There is a mother and three children who live alone in the country. The mother left the three children alone overnight because she was going to visit the grandmother for her birthday. The grandmother is called PoPo. The mother told them to lock the door. The wolf saw the mother leave and went to the house. He tricked two of the children into letting him in. They thought it was their PoPo. The wolf blew out the candle so they couldn't see him.* **The children's mother has gone to see Po Po, but is that the problem?** *No.* **Was it part of *why* there was a problem?** *Yes.* **Was the wolf disguised as their grandmother *on the doorstep* the problem?** *No, but it was part of why there was a problem.* **What did Tao and Paotze do to cause a problem?** *They opened the door and let the wolf in.*

- **Tao and Paotze were tricked by the wolf into letting him in. But the children do not yet know that they have a problem because the wolf blew out the candle. Let's keep reading to see what the wolf, Shang, Tao, and Paotze do next.** Continue reading to "...but Shang had seen the wolf's hairy face."

• **Shang has just discovered there is a wolf in her bed! She had some clues when she felt his tail and claws. When she lit the candle, she saw him. We have found the problem in the story. Let's pretend we are Shang. We'll use our Problem Solving thinking map to help us. What should we ask first?** Most students will say that we have to ask what the problem is. **One way to figure out what the problem is is to ask if there is a danger. Is there? And if there is, what is it?** Students usually agree that there is a danger. POSSIBLE STUDENT RESPONSE: *Shang and her sisters are in danger of being eaten by the wolf.* **We know that the children are home alone and the wolf tricked them into letting him come into the house. You have identified a big danger for Shang and her sisters. Let's state the problem by completing the sentence "How might _____ ? What is the problem?** POSSIBLE STUDENT RESPONSES: *How might the children avoid being eaten by the wolf? How might the children escape from the wolf? How might the children kill the wolf?*

• **Let's think about whether some of these statements are about part of solving the problem, or about the whole problem. Suppose the children take the problem to be one of escaping from the wolf. What would happen if they couldn't escape?** POSSIBLE STUDENT RESPONSE: *The wolf might eat them.* **So if they spent all their time thinking about escaping, wouldn't that be like my spending all my time trying to get my car fixed? I would probably miss the party because I hadn't thought of my problem as being getting to the party. The children would probably be eaten because they hadn't thought about other ways of avoiding being eaten by the wolf. So what is a better way to state the problem that will give the children a better chance of surviving?** Students usually recognize that the broader problem can be stated as "How might the children avoid being eaten by the wolf?" because there are many possible ways to do this, not just one, like trying to escape.

• **We will use two graphic organizers to record our work and help us think. The first one has to do with the first two questions on the thinking map.** Display a copy of the Problem Solving graphic organizer on an overhead transparency, the chalkboard, or a flipchart. **We've been working on the first question, "What is the problem?" and you've come up with a good way to state it. I am going to write it in the space for "The Problem."** Write "How might the children avoid being eaten by the wolf?" in the space provided. **What is the second question we need to ask?** Students usually identify it as the question about possible solutions to the problem. If they have difficulty, refer them to that question on the thinking map. **Now we must consider possible solutions. Talk to your group and try to come up with two or three possible solutions, then we'll share.** Allow time for discussing and sharing, supporting any groups that find this task difficult. As the groups share, record the suggested options on the group graphic organizer. POSSIBLE STUDENT RESPONSES: *Push out the wolf and lock the door. Run to Grandma's house.*

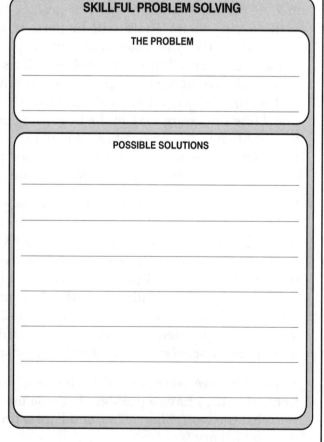

SKILLFUL PROBLEM SOLVING

THE PROBLEM

POSSIBLE SOLUTIONS

Trick the wolf by running out and then back into the house and locking the door. Get the wolf out by grabbing his hand and pulling him out. Kill the wolf. Sneak out and hide while the wolf is sleeping. Burn the wolf's tail to get him to leave. Say someone else is in the house.

- **In order to decide whether a possible solution to a problem is a good solution, what do we have to consider next?** Students usually say that we should consider the results of each possible solution, what would happen if we adopted each solution, or the pros and cons of each. **What would happen if Shang and her sisters did the things you suggested? I am going to give you and everyone in your group a second graphic organizer for problem solving called One Possible Solution to write your ideas about the solutions. In the top box, you will need to write the problem, "How might the children avoid being eaten by the wolf?"** Allow time for the students to copy the problem onto their graphic organizer. **Now your group should choose one possible solution to consider.** The possible solution could also be assigned by the teacher. You may want to write a copy of the problem and the problem solution to be considered on a sheet of paper for each of the groups. This will eliminate confusion about which group is working on which possible solution. **The next box has a space for you to write the solution you are considering. It says, "This might solve the problem."** In the box underneath this box, draw a picture of what would happen if the children choose that solution. Make sure you include in your picture things that you think will result from choosing this solution. Be sure to include all the important things that could happen. Remember, if the solution is likely to cause more problems than it solves, it may not be a good solution.** Allow work time. After 5–6 minutes, move the class to the next step.

ONE POSSIBLE SOLUTION
The problem:
This might solve the problem:
Picture:

What will happen:	pro/con?	value?

This is how the solution could be changed to make it better:

- **Now we will write about the pictures you drew. I will show you how to do this.** Ask one of the students for his or her picture. Model how to think about it aloud in front of the whole class. **Here is a picture of someone pushing the wolf out and locking the door. What consequences would there be if the children chose this solution? When we come up with a consequence, we can mark it as a pro or con, and we can decide if it is important. In this case, being important means that it will affect whether they avoid being eaten. I see that the wolf would be outside and away from the children. This is a pro. It is important because the house would be protection against the wolf. The wolf might come in the window. This is a con. It is important because then the wolf would be able to eat the children. The wolf is strong, and it would be hard to push him out the door. This is a con. It is important because there are only three small children to push against the wolf. The wolf might break down the door. This is a con. It is important because the wolf would be angry if he were pushed out and would try very hard to get back inside, and then, when he is inside, he could eat the chil-**

dren. As you do this, write the consequences on a large version of the One Possible Solution graphic organizer that you place below or next to the Skillful Problem Solving graphic organizer.

- **Now share your pictures in your group. As you take your turn sharing, mention one thing that will happen that you can see in your picture. Decide whether it is a pro or con, and whether it is important, and tell your group. Each student should write down all of the consequences mentioned by other members of the group. You will write the consequences in the box labeled "What will happen?" You may go around the group sharing consequences until you have no more consequences to mention.** Give the groups time for this exchange and writing. If a consequence is mentioned that is only shown in one group member's picture, the consequence can be marked with the child's initials to identify the source. When they are done, each group should share their pictures and the consequences with the whole class.

- **Each possible solution has some cons. Are there any ways that we could change the plan to make it better so that we can eliminate some of the cons? Let's go back to the solution that involves pushing the wolf out and locking the door.** POSSIBLE STUDENT RESPONSES: *They could be careful to lock the door. They could all push together to get him out. Three can be strong together.* **We can write these ideas down in the last box of the graphic organizer.** Write one of these modified solutions in the box at the bottom of the "One Possible Solution" graphic organizer. Then ask students to do this with their own. If a group feels that their solution is a good one just as it stands or that it is a solution that is unworkable, "No changes" can be written in the bottom space. Do not offer this as an option unless requested, as it is important to look for ways to improve the solutions.

- **You have thought of some interesting solutions to the children's problem. Where there was a need, you adjusted your plan to make it better. Let's think about these possible solutions now. Are there some plans that you think aren't going to be very good solutions because you can't eliminate the problems? Are there some plans that have been improved?** Ask each group to share their modifications with the rest of the class. For each solution, vote whether to keep or abandon it. Write the ones that the class decides to keep on the chalkboard or on a flipchart. Make it clear to the class that they are not voting yet for the best option, but only whether it is a good one that should be considered. **Now, which one do you think is the best solution and why?** Allow time for class discussion, then vote to determine the best solution. Circle the solution that the class decides is best.

- **We have tried to find a good solution to the problem in the story. We used our knowledge of the events at the beginning of the story to help us think of a solution. Now we will return to the story and see how the author solved the children's problem of avoiding being eaten by the wolf. As you listen to the story, think about the way that Shang and her sisters solve the problem.** Finish the story. **In your groups, describe the actions that Shang took in getting her sisters and herself away from the wolf so that they would not be eaten.** Allow time for the groups to process the actions taken by the children in the story, then discuss as a whole group.

- **Shang had a different way of solving the problem in the story. The author may have considered the solution we felt was best, but chose to have Shang solve the problem in a different way. Let's consider the solution used in the story. The children climbed the ginko tree and tricked the wolf into climbing into the basket to join them. Each time the wolf allowed them to pull him up in the basket, they dropped him until finally he was killed. What consequences might we have listed on our graphic organizer if this was our possible solution?** Allow time for the groups to discuss the consequences of the author's choice of solution. **What would you have recorded as a consequence for the author's solution? Would you say it is a**

pro or a con, important or not important? POSSIBLE STUDENT RESPONSES: CONSEQUENCE: *Wolves can't climb trees, so the children would be safe from being eaten. It is a pro and important because the whole problem is how to keep from being eaten.* CONSEQUENCE: *The children might have fallen out of the tree. It is a con and important because the children could have been hurt.* CONSEQUENCE: *The wolf is killed. It is a pro and important because the wolf will not be able to eat them.* CONSEQUENCE: *The wolf is dead and cannot eat them. It is a pro and important because it solves the problem of being eaten by the wolf.* **Looking at the pictures may help us see how the author eliminated some of the cons that we thought about. Notice how the children look in the tree. Are they holding on tightly? Are they on a branch that is large enough to hold them?** Support students as they examine the pictures to see that the children found a safe place in the tree.

- **How would the story have been different if one of our solutions had been used?** Have an open class discussion of two or three of the other solutions, encouraging students to tell two or three things that might change in the story. ANSWERS VARY.

- **Shang and her sisters had a big problem to solve in this story. As we read the story and discovered how they solved their problem, we saw how an author takes a problem and creates events to solve it. This is the *plot* of the story. Trying to predict the solution the author will put into a story to solve a problem makes reading fun. When we think about the events in the story, we better understand the way they work together to solve the problem.**

THINKING ABOUT THINKING

- **What do we call the kind of thinking we just did?** *Problem solving.*

- **What questions did we ask as we did our problem solving?** Students will mention the questions on the thinking map. If they struggle to remember, refer them to the thinking map. They should expand on the thinking map to include questions about revising and evaluating solutions.

- **Is the thinking map of skillful problem solving good for solving problems?** *Yes.* **Why?** *The questions help us think about what the problem really is and all the different ways to solve it. When we think about different ways, then we can pick the best one.*

- **How were the graphic organizers helpful?** *There was a place for each thing we had to think about. The one that we used in our group had places where we could draw what would happen. That helped us to think about the consequences of each possible solution.*

- **If you could talk to Shang, what advice would you give to her about solving problems?** POSSIBLE STUDENT RESPONSES: *I would tell her to think about what the problem is, and then to think of lots of ideas before choosing one way to solve the problem. I would tell her to think about the consequences so nothing bad happens.*

- **In this activity, you worked in groups. Did this help your thinking, or would you rather work on your own? Why?** Most students enjoy the support of their peers. If some students prefer to work on their own, question to see if there are points in the thinking process where having a group or a partner would be helpful.

APPLYING YOUR THINKING

Immediate Transfer

- **During our school day, we sometimes run into problems. Think about recess problems. Discuss a problem with your partner. Identify what the problem was. Use the graphic organizers** and the thinking map for problem solving to solve the problem. Draw a picture of the best solution. Write about your picture.

- There are many students in the classroom and the listening center has only four spots. What problem does this create? Use the thinking map and graphic organizers for solving problems to come up with the best solution to this problem.

Reinforcement Later

- Think about Gah-Ning in the story, *Where Is Gah-Ning?* by Robert Munsch. She really wants to go to Kapuskasing to shop in the mall. She came up with a solution, but it wasn't a safe one. See if you can solve her problem a better way. Use the thinking map and graphic organizers for problem solving to help you. Act out the best solution to Gah-Ning's problem.

- It is time for Thanksgiving break, and the animals and plants in our room will need to be cared for while we are not here. What can we do to solve this problem? Be sure to use the problem solving graphic organizers and the thinking map as you solve this problem.

WRITING EXTENSION

Have students explore the other possible solutions in story boxes. Each student or pair of students should choose one of the possible solutions to write and draw in the boxes. Tell students to put themselves in the author's place. They have written the beginning and the middle of the story. Now they are ready to solve the problem of how to get the wolf out of the house. Students will use one of the possible solutions on the graphic organizer to finish the tale. If they choose a solution that the class thought would be a good choice, the girls will be saved in their story. If they choose a solution that the class decided would not be a good choice, then the story will not have a happy ending, unless students are able to make some of the changes the class thought would improve it. Tell students to use story boxes to draw the way the story would look as the problem is solved. Students may begin their story boxes with the wolf in the bed and the girls realizing that it is not their beloved Po Po with them. Tell students that there must be enough details in their picture to show the story clearly.

SUGGESTED SPECIAL NEEDS MODIFICATIONS

<u>Frontload:</u> For some students, engaging in a thinking strategy takes more time and teacher guidance through skillful questioning and modelling. The teacher's think aloud can serve as a model of such sequenced thinking. In this case, the teacher might model thinking aloud about possibilities: *"How might I solve this problem?"* *"Let me see. How many possible ways can I think of,"* etc., and/or about consequences: "What if I did _____? *What might happen?"* Questioning should be scaffolded in such a way as to direct students to such "what if" thinking.

Some students may need prior practice with generating many possibilities without thinking about whether or not they will work. If students can learn to suspend judgment until after they have investigated consequences of the solutions, they will be better able to solve problems. Therefore, using multiple opportunities prior to the infusion lesson to guide students in generating solutions without judging would be beneficial. Students could brainstorm suggestions to improve the playground so everyone can play, ways a story character or historical figure could solve a problem or complete a task, or they could generate all the ways to use a geometric figure for some constructive or aesthetic purpose. Be explicit that the rules are to generate ideas without comment.

In addition, use the language of thinking to label student contributions: "That's an example of *flexible thinking,*" "That's some *original thinking,*" "You are *suspending your judgment* about whether that idea will work."

Similarly, students may need prior practice in the notion of evaluating or judging the relative importance of a pro or con. Using a think aloud or guiding the group in discussing everyday problems, the teacher can demonstrate the type of thinking used in judging. It is important that students see the impact of the consequence or option, rather that just a number of pros and cons. For example, the teacher might share that his solution to having forgotten his lunch meant that he shared a friend's lunch, which wasn't very tasty. The lack of taste wasn't very important. He was hungry and the food was nutritious. However, another friend offered him food to which he was allergic. That was a very important con because he would have gotten sick.

Clarify: Some students may benefit from repeated oral readings of the story. In books rich in vocabulary and illustrations, repeated read alouds allow students to develop a sense of the story before analyzing specific aspects.

Diversify: Problem solving can be a complicated thinking strategy. Some students may benefit from greater teacher guidance in exploring possible solutions. Instead of allowing each group to select an option, the teacher may wish to guide through additional examples with the whole group before asking them to work in groups. In addition, some small groups may benefit from additional teacher support. The options under consideration could also be limited to a select few or specifically assigned to particular groups of students based upon the level of complexity of the option.

Teacher guidance through the use of paraphrasing students' comments may help some students formulate precise problem statements and questions.

For some students, writing assignments connected with the graphic could be challenging. Assigning the task of writing to a proficient writer in the cooperative group allows all students to contribute ideas while reducing the task load for beginning writers. Students may also need the opportunity to explain their writing and pictures orally in order to demonstrate their understanding.

Expand the Possibilities: Assessments of written responses may be based upon students' thinking first, and expressive skills secondly. Oral responses may also reveal thinking beyond students' ability to express themselves in writing.

ASSESSING STUDENT THINKING ABOUT POSSIBILITIES

To assess students' ability to problem solve, select examples that challenge them to generate a wide range of possible solutions and combine their solutions to improve them. Any of the application examples can serve this purpose. Group work is acceptable and allows for assessing their thinking as they dialogue. As students become familiar with the problem-solving thinking process, they can move on to the original graphic organizer, using the back of the paper to draw their ideas. Observations should include data related to the types of questioning students are engaging in as they evaluate the possible solutions and consider changes that would improve them.

Sample Student Responses • There's a Wolf in My Bed!

SKILLFUL PROBLEM SOLVING

THE PROBLEM

How might the children avoid being eaten by the wolf?

POSSIBLE SOLUTIONS

Tell her sisters.

Push out the wolf and lock the door.

Run to Grandma's.

Trick the wolf. Run out, then run in and lock the door.

Get the wolf outside by grabbing his hand.

Sneak out while the wolf is sleeping.

Burn the wolf's tail to get him to leave.

Say someone else (like Dad) is there.

Sample Student Responses • There's a Wolf in My Bed!

ONE POSSIBLE SOLUTION

The problem:

How might the children avoid being eaten by the wolf?

This might solve the problem:

They could push out the wolf and lock the door.

Picture:

What will happen:	pro/con?	value?
The wolf would be outside and not be able to eat them.	pro	important
He might come in the window.	con	important
He is strong, and it will be hard to push him.	con	important
He might break the door down.	con	important

This is how the solution could be changed to make it better:

They could lock the windows so he can't get in. If they all push together

they can probably move him and get him out.

Sample Student Story Boxes • There's a Wolf in My Bed!

THE REST OF THE STORY
RUMPELSTILTSKIN'S DAUGHTER

Language Arts   **Grades 1–2**

OBJECTIVES

CONTENT

Students will analyze story characters in terms of their character traits and actions. They will look for details in the story to help them understand the characters and the choices the characters make.

THINKING SKILL/PROCESS

Students will learn to solve problems skillfully by determining what the problem is, generating possible solutions, and selecting the best solution after considering the consequences.

METHODS AND MATERIALS

CONTENT

Students will listen to the story *Rumpelstiltskin's Daughter* by Diane Stanley and discuss the characters and the actions they take to solve their problems.

THINKING SKILL/PROCESS

An explicit thinking map, graphic organizers, and structured questioning emphasize options and consequences in decision making. Collaborative learning enhances the thinking.

LESSON

INTRODUCTION TO CONTENT AND THINKING SKILL/PROCESS

- **Have you ever been in a situation where someone was reading to you but you could not see the pictures because of where you were sitting?** Ask for a show of hands. **What did you do so you could see?** Ask some of the students who raised their hands to explain what they did.

- **You were trying to make things better so that you could see. When we think something isn't working out the way it should, we know there is a problem. When we try to make the situation better, we are trying to solve the problem. We do a lot of problem solving. Can you think of any other times when you did some problem solving?** Allow time for thinking, then ask students to share their situations with a partner. Ask for two or three reports.

- **When I was at home last night, my family had a problem they needed to solve. My daughter, who is 17 years old, needed to borrow my car so that she could go to an appointment after school. Of course, I needed to be at school here today, so we had to solve the problem of both of us getting to school and my daughter getting to her appointment. The way that we solved the problem involved some careful thinking.**

- **When we try to solve problems, we should think carefully or things may not turn out as we planned. Let me tell you how we worked through my car problem. We decided the problem was how to get both of us to the different places we needed to be. Then we thought of possible solutions. We thought about her taking my car, my rushing home after school to drive her, her changing her appointment, and one of us taking a taxi. But then, when we thought about it, if she took my car, that created a problem of how I would get to work and then home again. And if I hurried home from school to get her to her appointment, that would mean I wouldn't have enough time to do my planning after school. A taxi was going to be very expensive. Then we found a solution by changing one of the possible solutions we were considering. That made it much better. My daughter did take the car, but she got up** early and drove me to school. She came and picked me up after her appointment, which gave me plenty of time to get my planning done. That was the best solution for us.

- Thinking carefully is the best way to solve problems. We are going to practice a way to problem solve that will help us think carefully in order to reach a good solution. If we don't think first, our solutions may not work the way we would like. This thinking map for problem solving will guide us. Show the thinking map for problem solving on a chart or the chalkboard so that it is visible throughout the lesson. Discuss each of the steps. **The first question that needs to be answered is, "What is the problem?"** When someone was reading to you but you couldn't see the pictures, the problem was how can you see the pictures. The next question asks, "What are possible solutions to the problem?" You shared the ways that you thought of to solve your problem. There were different ways it could be solved. The third question asks us to think about the possible solutions and what would happen if we chose to solve the problem in each of those ways. There could be good and bad things that happen as a result of the way that we solve a problem. The last question asks, "What is the best solution to the problem?" After we have thought about the good and bad consequences of each of the possible solutions, we need to decide which is the best way to solve the problem.

> ### SKILLFUL PROBLEM SOLVING
>
> 1. **What is the problem?**
>
> 2. **What are possible solutions to the problem?**
>
> 3. **What would happen if we chose to solve the problem in that way?**
>
> 4. **What is the best solution to the problem?**

- Today we will be using a story in our lesson. Often in stories, the main character has a problem. As we read, we can get clues about the character that help us understand how he or she solves the problem. In our lesson today, we will identify the problem the character has, and we will use our thinking map to try to solve the problem. **What do we do after we have decided what the problem is?** Ask for volunteers. Most students respond by saying that we'll think of possible solutions. If students are not quick to respond, refer them to the second question on the thinking map. **What will we do then?** POSSIBLE STUDENT RESPONSE: *We'll consider the consequences of each solution, and we'll choose the best solution for the character.* **Knowing how to problem-solve wisely will help us understand the problems we read about in stories. It will also help us decide whether the ways characters solve these problems are good ways to solve them.**

THINKING ACTIVELY

- **The name of the story for our lesson is** *Rumpelstiltskin's Daughter.* Show the book to the class. **This is a fairy tale that begins with the tale of Rumpelstiltskin.** It is advisable to read the original fairy tale a few days before this lesson. **Let's think back to that story and its events. In the beginning of that story the miller's daughter had a big problem. Who can recall the details from the beginning of that story? We need to know why she had a problem and what it was.** Students should retell the beginning of the story leading up to the problem created by the miller's boasting. POSSIBLE STUDENT RESPONSES: *Her father told the king she could spin straw into gold. The king was greedy and told her to spin all the straw into gold or she would be killed. She didn't know how to make the gold and she was going to be killed if she didn't make it.* Students may go to the second problem of avoiding giving away her first child. If this is the case, remind them of the beginning of the story and the first problem the miller's daughter had. **Yes, the miller told** the king that his daughter could spin straw into gold. His boasting caused a very serious problem for his daughter. She was taken to the castle and the king locked her into the rooms full of straw. **How did she solve her problem?** *She had the little man spin the straw into gold.* **What was the consequence of her solution?** *She had to give the little man a ring and a necklace, then she had to promise to give the man her first child.* **Giving the man some jewelry wasn't such a bad consequence, but giving up her first child was terrible! This consequence for having the man spin the gold was definitely a con. On the other hand, she was going to die the next day if she didn't get the straw spun into gold, so having the man spin the gold was a good consequence because she wasn't killed. This is a pro.**

- **These details in the story help us see the problem the miller's daughter had. We saw how she reacted to her problems by crying and feeling hopeless. Whatever she did would turn out bad, it seemed. When this happens, it is called a** *dilemma*, **and she really had one. But we can also understand why she agreed with what Rumpelstiltskin offered her: that he would spin the straw into gold in exchange for her first-born child. Sometimes a person has to accept the lesser of two bad things, and she felt that not being killed was so important to her that she would even give up her child to stay alive. Of course, we know that in the original version of the story, Rumpelstiltskin gave her another chance to save her child, but that comes later in the story and she didn't know that when she was trying to solve her problem.**

- **Now it's time to read the new fairy tale,** *Rumpelstiltskin's Daughter.* **As we read, pay close attention to the details of this story. They will help us understand the new main character and the problem** *she* **has. Then we will be able to understand why she chooses the solution to her problem. We can see if the problem solving she does results in her choosing the best solution.** Have students study the cover and the first pages for clues. They should identify the king and girl who must be Rumpelstiltskin's daughter. There are clues on the inside pages: two postcards, straw, some spun gold, coins, and a cigar ring. Students should predict what these items have to do with the story. After examining the clues, begin to read the story, discussing how the author changes the story from the original version of Rumpelstiltskin. The illustrations are very detailed, so be sure to allow time to study and enjoy them. They are important in that they help develop the story. The first stop in the story is after the king says, " Guards, take her to the tower and see what she can do with all that straw." You may want to put a post-it at this spot to help you remember.

- **Let's do a summary of this new story so far. Talk to the members of your group. Together, retell the story. Try to include the details that you think are important to us as we are helping to solve Rumpelstiltskin's daughter's problem.** Students should work in their groups to retell the story. They should tell the new version of Rumpelstiltskin, where the miller's daughter, named Meredith, actually escapes the tower and marries Rumpelstiltskin instead of the king. They have a daughter who grows up and is allowed to go into town with the gold that Rumpelstiltskin has spun. She takes it to the goldsmith who exchanges it for coins to buy things. It is the goldsmith who tells his friends about the girl and the gold. The king hears about it and remembers her mother who he locked into the tower to spin straw into gold. Because he is still greedy, he sends his guards to capture the daughter and bring her to the castle. The trip to the castle shows how poor the people of the kingdom are and how rich the king is in his golden castle.

- **Let's begin our problem solving here. We must first decide what problem Rumpelstiltskin's daughter is facing at the point in the story where we stopped. Talk in your groups about** *what* **her problem is. A good way to do this is to complete the sentence "How might she _____ ?"** Write this sentence frame on the chalkboard or on a flipchart. Ask students to share ideas in small groups and try to reach an agreement. Then ask each group to report. POSSIBLE STUDENT RESPONSES: *How might she escape from the tower? How might she spin all the straw into gold? How might she get out of the tower? How might she keep the king from keeping her in the tower forever?* Write these ways of stating the problem on the chalkboard or on a flipchart. Explain to students that we should choose only one problem to work on, that it should be an important one, and that it shouldn't be too narrow ("small") or too broad ("big"). Have a class discussion of the ways they state the problem, prompting students to see that stating the problem as one of getting out of the tower is important and allows for a lot of possible ways of escaping, while stating the problem as one related to converting the straw to gold is too narrow because it focuses on only one possible solution. **We will use a graphic organizer to help us with our ideas. We can record the problem at the top.** Display the graphic organizer for problem solving on a chart or on a transparency. Record the problem on the graphic organizer as stated by the group.

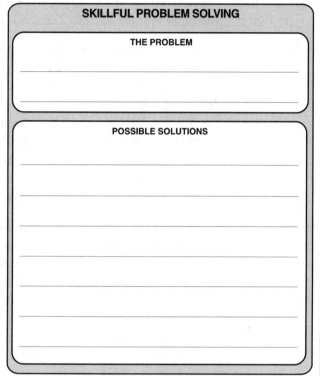

- **Once we've figured out what the important problem is that Rumpelstiltskin's daughter has to solve, what should we think about next?** Most students realize that thinking about possible solutions is the next step. If they don't, refer them to the thinking map. **Before we go on to the next step, I want to read to you a little more of the story. It will help us as we think of possible solutions.** Read the next page of the story. This page gives details of the room, the straw, and the thoughts the girl is having. **What are some things we know from the story that may help us as we think of a solution to the daughter's problem?** POSSIBLE STUDENT RESPONSES: *She can't spin straw into gold. She doesn't want to have her father come. The king is very greedy. The people in the kingdom are very poor.* **What can you tell about the daughter from the thinking she is doing?** POSSIBLE STUDENT RESPONSES: *She is smart. She knows that the king will just want to keep her father in the room forever spinning gold from straw. She doesn't just give up. She thinks a lot about what she knows until she has a plan.*

- **Now that you have thought about the details of the story that tell us about Rumpelstiltskin's daughter, you will work with your group to think of possible solutions to her problem.** Restate the problem as written on the graphic organizer to focus students on their task: How will she escape from the tower? **Try to think of a lot of solutions to this problem. Having several possibilities will help us find the best solution. It is also important to think about the things we have already learned in the story. These will help us in our thinking.** Allow time for group work. **It is time for us to share the ideas we have. We will list our ideas on the graphic organizer in the section labeled "Possible Solutions."** List the ideas students have on the graphic organizer. Continue to encourage students to be creative. POSSIBLE STUDENT RESPONSES: *Use a golden ladder that her father makes to climb down from the tower. Throw straw out of the window and then jump out of the window into the straw. Climb down a tall tree. Tie all the straw together to make a rope. Say she has to go to the bathroom and then run away. Make a magic carpet with* *the straw and fly off. Ask the king to let her go. Let her father come and get her. Hide in the straw and then run away when the door is opened.*

- **We have created a list of possible solutions. What do we need to do next to be good problem solvers?** POSSIBLE STUDENT RESPONSE: *We need to think about what will happen if the solutions are chosen.*

- **Let's work in groups again. I'm going to give everyone a special graphic organizer to work with. The graphic organizer you will use has room to consider one of the possible solutions from our class list of possible solutions.** Pass out the One Possible Solution graphic organizer to each student. **At the top, write the problem as we have stated it on the top of our class organizer.** Allow time for students to copy the problem onto their graphic organizer. **Now I will ask you to work on one of the possible solutions to see if it will work.** Assign one possible solution to each group. You may want to write a copy of the problem and the possible solution being considered on a sheet of paper for each of the groups. This will eliminate confusion about which group is working on which possible solution. **Write the possible solution on your graphic organizer in the section marked "This might solve the problem."** Then, in the box below, draw how it would look if Rumpelstiltskin's daughter chose it. This picture will show some of the consequences of choosing this solution. Be

ONE POSSIBLE SOLUTION
The problem:
This might solve the problem:
Picture:

What will happen:	pro/con?	value?

This is how the solution could be changed to make it better:

sure to include all the important things that would happen. Remember, if the solution is likely to cause more problems than it solves, it may not be a good solution. Allow 5–6 minutes for work time, then move the class to the next step. **Now we will write about the pictures you drew. I'm going to show you how to do this.** Ask one of the students for his/her picture. Model how to think about it aloud in front of the whole class. **Here is a picture of throwing the straw out the window and jumping into it. What consequences would there be if Rumpelstiltskin's daughter chose this solution? We can mark each of our possible consequences pro or con, and we can decide if it is important. In this case, being important means that it will affect whether she gets out of the tower and away from the king. I see that** *she will have a soft place to land.* **This is a pro. It is important because she will get hurt if she doesn't have a soft place to land.** *The straw might fall in with the crocodiles.* **This is a con. It is important because the crocodiles could eat her when she jumps into the straw.** *The crocodiles might eat the straw.* **This is a con. It is important because she needs a soft place to land when she jumps.** *Someone might see her or the straw.* **This is a con. It is important because she wants to get out without getting caught.** As you do this, write the consequences on a large version of the One Possible Solution graphic organizer that you place below or next to the Skillful Problem Solving graphic organizer.

- **Now share your pictures in your group. As you take your turn sharing, mention one thing that will happen that you can see in your picture. Decide whether it is a pro or con, and** whether it is important, and tell your group. Each student should write all of the consequences mentioned by the other members of the group on their graphic organizer. You will write the consequences in the box labeled "What will happen?" You may go around the group sharing consequences until you have no more consequences to mention. Give the groups time for this exchange and writing. If a consequence is mentioned that is shown only in one group member's picture, the consequence can be marked with the student's initials to identify the source. When they are done, each group should share their pictures and the consequences with the whole class.

- **Each possible solution has some cons. Are there any ways we could change this plan to make it better so that we can eliminate some of the cons? Let's go back to the solution that involves throwing straw down and jumping into it.** POSSIBLE STUDENT RESPONSES: *She could be careful to throw the straw over the water so it lands on the ground. She could crawl out of the straw so no one sees her. She could try to escape in the middle of the night so no one sees the straw or her.* **We can write these ideas down on the set of lines on the graphic organizer.** Write one of these modified solutions in the box at the bottom of the One Possible Solution graphic organizer. Then ask students to do this with their own. If a group feels that their solution is a good one just as it stands or that it is a solution that is unworkable, "No changes" can be written in the bottom space. Do not offer this as an option unless requested, as it is important to look for ways to improve the solutions.

- **You have thought of some interesting solutions to Rumpelstiltskin's daughter's problem. Where there was a need, you adjusted your plan to make it better. Let's think about these possible solutions now. Are there some that you think aren't going to be very good solutions because you can't eliminate the problems? Are there some that have been improved to be better plans?** Ask each group to share their modifications with the rest of the class. For each solution, vote whether to keep or abandon it. Allow time for class discussion, then vote to determine the best solution.

- **It is time for us to finish the fairy tale and see how the author had Rumpelstiltskin's daughter solve her problem. Listen for details, and see if Rumpelstiltskin's daughter uses good problem solving.** Read the rest of the story. Discuss how the author's solution, tricking the king into sharing his wealth with the people of the kingdom, compares to the class solution. **Did the daughter think about the consequences of her solution?** POSSIBLE STUDENT RESPONSE: *She thought that she could make the people of the kingdom happy.* **Did she keep her father safe from the greedy king?** POSSIBLE STUDENT RESPONSE: *Yes, because she got things for the king that weren't really gold but were gold-colored. That meant that Rumpelstiltskin didn't have to come and save her.* **What was her solution to avoid marrying the king?** POSSIBLE STUDENT RESPONSE: *She said she could be prime minister instead of his wife.* **Was this a good solution?** ANSWERS VARY. **Do you think Rumpelstiltskin's daughter was a good problem solver?** ANSWERS VARY. It is not likely that students will come up with the same solutions as the author. This is not a problem, since the author chose the way to write the story based on his perception of a good solution. The class decision is merely a different viewpoint.

- **The details of a story give us clues to the ways that the character will solve a problem. In this book, what were some of the details that helped us understand why the character chose to solve her problem as she did?** Students should bring out the actions of Rumpelstiltskin's daughter throughout the story that showed her to be kind, smart, and considerate of others' needs. **The details of this story show us the kind of people the characters are. As a result of knowing about the characters, we are better able to understand the ways that they solve their problems.**

THINKING ABOUT THINKING

- **What do we call the kind of thinking we have been doing?** *Problem solving.*

- **What questions did we ask as we did our problem solving?** Students should include the questions used in the thinking map. You might use the thinking map as a guide for students who are having trouble reviewing the steps taken.

- **Are the thinking map and the graphic organizers helpful in solving problems?** POSSIBLE STUDENT RESPONSES: *The map helps us so we don't make mistakes when we solve problems. We can do a better job solving problems. The graphic organizers are good to use so we can see how the solutions might work. Then we can fix them.*

- **Do you like working on solving problems in a group or would you rather work alone? What is good about the way you chose?** Students usually say that they like working with their friends and talking about the ideas they have to solve problems. They often say they think better when they can talk to someone. There will be some students who do not like group work. Ask them to think about what they might do instead that would be more helpful to them.

- **When you have a problem to solve, what will you do to solve it? Will you use the graphic organizers from our lesson?** ANSWERS VARY. Students usually will go over the things they like about the graphic organizers, such as the boxes for each step and the places for drawing to help their thinking.

APPLYING YOUR THINKING

Immediate Transfer

- **We have read the story,** *No Roses for Harry* **by Gene Zion. Harry does not like his new sweater. He solved his problem after trying several plans. What if you had his problem? What would you do if your grandmother made you a sweater that you didn't like? Remember, she is your grandmother and she loves you! Use the Problem Solving thinking map and graphic organizers to make sure that you choose the best solution. Write a story that uses the solution you decided was best. Be sure to illustrate your story.**

- **In the story** *Franklin in the Dark*, **what problem does Franklin have with dark places? How might he solve this problem? Use the Problem Solving thinking map and graphic organizers, find a solution to Franklin's problem that you think will work. Draw a picture of your answer and write about it.**

- **You are ready to plant your garden, but you know that there are many animals that will eat your plants. How can you solve this problem? Be sure to use the thinking map and graphic organizers for problem solving to make sure you choose the best solution. Draw a picture of your solution.**

Reinforcement Later

- **We are studying construction. What problems would we have to solve if we wanted to build a bookcase for our classroom? Choose one of the problems to solve using the thinking map and graphic organizers for problem solving and come up with a solution you think will work.**

- **You are in the middle of your work, and the student next to you has started to make noises and do things that are bothering you and making it hard to think. How can you solve this** problem? Use the Problem Solving thinking map and graphic organizers to help you find a solution that doesn't have consequences that are on the "con" side. Share your ideas in the form of a skit so that others can benefit from your thinking through this problem.

WRITING EXTENSION (GRADE 2)

Students will write a letter persuading Hope to try one of the possible solutions that students thought of while in groups. They will use the One Possible Solution graphic organizer to help them explain why she should use this solution to help solve the problem of her being able to escape from the king. The writing template for persuasive writing should be visible to students as they write.

WRITING EXTENSION (GRADES 1–2)

Students will choose one of the main characters, Hope or the king, to write an acrostic poem. They will follow the directions for writing acrostic poetry, which can be found in the Appendix. This writing extension can be done individually, in groups, or as a class.

SUGGESTED SPECIAL NEEDS MODIFICATIONS

Frontload: For some students, engaging in a thinking strategy takes more time and teacher guidance through skillful questioning and modelling. The teacher's think aloud can serve as a model of such sequenced thinking. In this case the teacher might model thinking aloud about possibilities: *"How might I solve this problem?"* "Let me see. *How many possible ways* can I think of," etc., and/or about consequences: "What if I did _____? *What might happen?"* Questioning should be scaffolded in such a way as to direct students to such "what if" thinking.

Some students may need prior practice with generating many possibilities without thinking about whether or not they will work. If students can learn to suspend judgment until after they have investigated consequences of the solutions, they will be better able to solve problems. Therefore, using multiple opportunities prior to the Infusion lesson to guide students in generating solutions without judging would be beneficial. Students could brainstorm suggestions to improve the playground so everyone can play, ways a story character or historical figure could solve a problem or complete a task, or they could generate all the ways to use a geometric figure for some constructive or aesthetic purpose. Be explicit that the rules are to generate ideas without comment.

In addition, use the language of thinking to label student contributions: "That's an example of *flexible thinking,"* "That's some *original thinking,"* "You are *suspending your judgment* about whether that idea will work."

Similarly, students may need prior practice evaluating or judging the relative importance of a pro or con. Using a think aloud or guiding the group in discussing everyday problems, the teacher can demonstrate the type thinking used in judging. It is important that students see the impact of the consequence or option rather that just a number of pros and cons. For example, the teacher might share that his solution to having forgotten his lunch meant that he shared a friend's lunch, which wasn't very tasty. The lack of taste wasn't very important. He was hungry and the food was nutritious. However, another friend offered him food to which he was allergic. That was a very important con because he would have gotten sick.

Clarify: Some students may benefit from repeated oral readings of the story. In books rich in vocabulary and illustrations, repeated read alouds allow student to develop a sense of the story before analyzing specific aspects.

Diversify: Problem solving can be a complicated thinking strategy. Some student may benefit from greater teacher guidance in exploring possible solutions. Instead of allowing each group to select an option, the teacher may wish to guide students through additional examples as a class before asking them to work in groups. In addition, some small groups may benefit from additional teacher support. The options under consideration could also be limited to a select few or specifically assigned to particular groups of students based upon the level of complexity of the option.

Teacher guidance through the use of paraphrasing students' comments may help some students formulate precise problem statements and questions.

For some students, writing assignments connected with the graphic organizer could be challenging. Assigning the task of writing to a proficient writer in the cooperative group allows all students to contribute ideas while reducing the task load for beginning writers. Students may also need the opportunity to explain their writing and pictures orally in order to demonstrate their understanding.

Expand the Possibilities: Assessments of written responses may be based upon students' thinking first, and expressive skills second. Oral responses may also reveal thinking beyond students' ability to express themselves in writing.

ASSESSING STUDENT THINKING ABOUT PROBLEM SOLVING

To assess students' ability to problem solve, select examples that challenge them to generate a wide range of possible solutions and to combine their solutions to improve them. Any of the application examples will serve this purpose. Group work is acceptable and allows for assessing their thinking as they dialogue. As students become familiar with the problem-solving process, they can be transferred back to the primary graphic organizer, using the back of the paper to draw their ideas. Observations should include data related to the types of questioning students are engaging in as they evaluate the possible solutions and consider changes that would improve them.

Sample Student Responses • Rumpelstiltskin's Daughter

SKILLFUL PROBLEM SOLVING

THE PROBLEM

How might she escape from the tower?

POSSIBLE SOLUTIONS

Use a golden ladder that her father makes to climb down from the tower.

Let her father come and get her.

Tie all of the straw together to make a rope.

Say she has to go to the bathroom and then run away.

Throw straw into the moat and then jump down into it.

Make a magic carpet with the straw and fly off. Take some of the king's gold for the poor people.

Ask the king to let her go. Then they can trick the king and take his gold to the people.

Climb down a tall tree.

Hide in the straw and then run away when the door is opened.

Sample Student Responses • Rumpelstiltskin's Daughter

ONE POSSIBLE SOLUTION

The problem:

How can Rumpelstiltskin's daughter escape from the tower?

This might solve the problem:

She could throw straw into the moat and then jump down into it.

Picture:

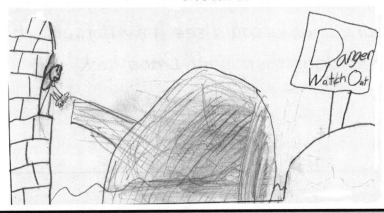

What will happen:	pro/con?	value?
She will have a soft place to land.	pro	important
The straw might fall in with the crocodiles.	con	important
Someone might see her on the straw.	con	important
The crocodiles might eat the straw.	con	important

This is how the solution could be changed to make it better:

She could be careful to throw the straw over the water so it lands on the ground. She could crawl out of the straw so no one sees her. She could try to escape in the middle of the night so no one sees the straw or her.

Sample Student Persuasive Writing • Grade 2 • Rumpelstiltskin's Daughter

Dear Hope,

I am sorry that you were put into the tower with the straw just like your mother, and I have a way for you to escape. I think that you should call your father to come and help you. He could make a straw ladder and then the two of you could crawl down it, just like when your mother was stuck there. After you get out you should get all of the people together to talk to the king about sharing the gold. Maybe you could even lock him in a barn and he could see how it feels. This plan will work if everyone does their part. Good luck!

Sincerely,

Sample Student Poetry • Grade 1 • Rumpelstiltskin's Daughter

Rumpelstiltskin's Daughter

Had to trick the king who liked gold

Ordered him to give things to the poor people

Pretended to know how to make gold

Ended up the Prime Minister

SKILLFUL PROBLEM SOLVING

1. What is the problem?

2. What are possible solutions to the problem?

3. What would happen if we chose to solve the problem in that way?

4. What is the best solution to the problem?

SKILLFUL PROBLEM SOLVING

THE PROBLEM

POSSIBLE SOLUTIONS

ONE POSSIBLE SOLUTION

The problem:

_____

This might solve the problem:

_____

Picture:

What will happen:	pro/con?	value?

This is how the solution could be changed to make it better:

_____

CHAPTER 5
COMPARING AND CONTRASTING

Infusing Skillful Comparing and Contrasting into Language Arts

There are two types of comparing and contrasting that can be done skillfully: open comparing and contrasting and focused comparing and contrasting. Teaching students either of these in grades 1 and 2 involves helping them learn to ask and carefully answer the following questions:

COMPARE AND CONTRAST

1. **How are they similar?**

2. **How are they different?**

3. **What does this show?**

---

first-grade thinking map, figure 5.1

OPEN COMPARE AND CONTRAST

1. **How are they similar?**

2. **How are they different?**

3. **What similarities and differences are important?**

4. **What interpretation or conclusion is suggested?**

---

second-grade thinking map, figure 5.2

The questions used in the thinking maps will guide your students' thinking explicitly as they engage in the compare and contrast lesson.

In open and focused thinking, comparing and contrasting does not stop with merely noting some similarities and differences between two or more things (which often results in superficiality and lack of depth). Students are also asked to think about which of the similarities and differences they have noted are important. By doing this, students gain insight and draw conclusions about what they are comparing and contrasting. Open comparing and contrasting is done by starting with a broad range of similarities and differences and then narrowing them down. Focused comparing and contrasting always has a specific purpose that is identified and focuses attention from the start on specific similarities and differences that are relevant to the purpose (see figure 5.3).

FOCUSED COMPARE AND CONTRAST

1. **What is our purpose for comparing and contrasting?**

2. **What kinds of similarities and differences are important to the purpose of our comparing and contrasting?**

3. **What similarities fall into these categories?**

4. **What differences fall into these categories?**

5. **What does this show?**

---

figure 5.3

In these lessons, various supporting classroom strategies, such as using a graphic organizer, engaging in cooperative thinking, thinking about thinking, and using continued guided practice will supplement the use of these thinking maps. These classroom strategies further enhance both the thinking skill that the students are learning and their mastery of the lesson content.

The key graphic organizers for comparing and contrasting in grades 1 and 2 are in figures 5.4 and 5.5 (see following page).

In both graphic organizers, students can write the similarities and differences they uncover in the space provided. They are also asked to think about and record what kinds of similarities (Fo-

---

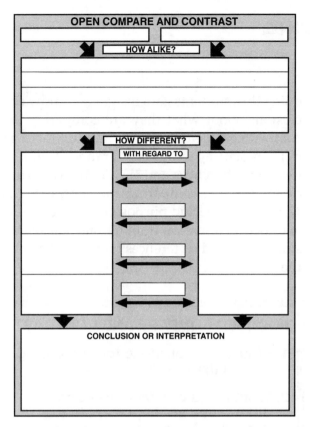

figure 5.4

figure 5.5

cused CC only) and differences (both) they are recording; and then articulate a conclusion about what they are comparing and contrasting, based on the similarities and differences they have recorded. These graphic organizers take students well beyond merely listing similarities and differences (like devices such as Venn diagrams promote) and instead guide them to thinking about what they have discovered about the similarities and differences they have identified. Reproducible blank graphic organizers are found at the end of each chapter.

For more in-depth information on teaching skillful comparing and contrasting, please refer to Chapter 4 in the book *Infusing the Teaching of Critical and Creative Thinking into Elementary Instruction,* by Robert Swartz and Sandra Parks. A computer disk containing the blank, reproducible graphic organizers used in this book is also available. Both book and disk are available through Critical Thinking Books & Software.

BATS
STELLALUNA

Language Arts   **Grades 1–2**

OBJECTIVES

CONTENT

Students will develop their comprehension skills as they read, searching for details in text and in illustrations that will identify bats as part of the mammal family of animals. Previous lessons will have already established the basic characteristics of birds and mammals.

THINKING SKILL/PROCESS

Students will learn to compare and contrast effectively by determining similarities and differences and by drawing a conclusion based on the similarities and differences.

METHODS AND MATERIALS

CONTENT

Students will examine the text and illustrations of the factually based book *Stellaluna* by Janell Cannon. This will not be a first-read situation, as the activity requires students to focus on a specific task. They will have read the story on a previous day.

THINKING SKILL/PROCESS

Comparing and contrasting is guided by structured questioning and a graphic organizer which highlights points for careful attention in using the thinking skill.

LESSON

INTRODUCTION TO CONTENT AND THINKING SKILL/PROCESS

- I'd like us to think back to our study of dinosaurs. We looked at the different ways they moved, the differences in their teeth, food, body size, and shape. We found many differences, but we also found there were many ways the dinosaurs were alike. Do you remember that? Talk to your partner about the ways that meat-eating dinosaurs and plant-eating dinosaurs were alike and different. Allow share time, then have several students share their responses with the rest of the class. POSSIBLE STUDENT RESPONSES: *They lived long ago. They are extinct. They lived in the same places. They laid eggs. Meat-eating dinosaurs had sharp teeth, and plant eating dinosaurs had flat teeth. The plant eaters had to have ways to protect themselves from enemies. The biggest dinosaurs were plant eaters.*

- Finding ways that things are alike and different helps us to better understand those things. By looking at the ways dinosaurs were alike and different, we came up with statements that helped us better understand dinosaurs. The statements that we made based on our study of the ways they were alike and different are called "conclusions." Conclusions don't repeat the similarities and differences—they tell what the similarities and differences show. They are new statements about information we now know about dinosaurs. One conclusion that we came to when we compared dinosaurs was that meat eaters were built to move faster than plant eaters. How else did looking at similarities and differences in dinosaurs help us to better understand what they were like? POSSIBLE STUDENT RESPONSES: *We could see how meat eaters and plant eaters have teeth to let them eat the food they like. We could see how plant-eating dinosaurs had different things on their bodies, like armor and bony plates, to protect them from meat-eating dinosaurs that moved fast.*

- Similarities are the way things are the same. Differences are how they are different. When we use similarities and differences to draw conclusions, we call it "comparing and contrasting." Write these terms on the chalkboard or a chart: comparing—alike, contrasting—different, conclusion—what does it show?

- Here is a thinking map for comparing and contrasting that tells us to first look for ways two things are the same. Display the thinking map for comparing and contrasting on a chart or the chalkboard where it will be visible to students during the lesson. The thinking maps for first and second grade differ, though the first and second steps are the same. Read the first step, "How are they similar?" **Then we look for ways they are different.** Read "How are they different?" **Step three** (for first graders) **says, "What does this show?"** That means, what can we conclude about the two things that we are looking at because we have seen the ways that they are alike and different. Step three (for second graders) says, "What similarities and differences are important?" Finally, in step four, we ask what this shows about the things we are comparing and contrasting. "What interpretation or conclusion is suggested?" When you answer the question in step four you are explaining what new things we have learned from the similarities and differences.

> **COMPARE AND CONTRAST**
>
> 1. How are they similar?
> 2. How are they different?
> 3. What does this show?

first-grade thinking map

> **OPEN COMPARE AND CONTRAST**
>
> 1. How are they similar?
> 2. How are they different?
> 3. What similarities and differences are important?
> 4. What interpretation or conclusion is suggested?

second-grade thinking map

- In this lesson, we will reread the story, *Stellaluna*. Bats are often misunderstood. Some people think that they are birds. What would make someone think this? POSSIBLE STUDENT RESPONSE: *Bats can fly so people think they are birds.* This story is fiction, but it is based on factual information. We will look for facts about bats and birds within the story that we can use to compare and contrast them. We are going to use comparing and contrasting to understand more clearly why bats are mammals and not birds. Ask students to review what the characteristics of mammals are. If they are having difficulty, ask leading questions like "What do we know about mammal skin covering?" "How are mammal babies born?" "How do mammals feed their young?" Ask students to name some mammals and explain why they are mammals.

- We will follow the thinking map as we look for similarities and differences between birds and bats, and we will write a conclusion that shows what we have learned about bats. Our conclusion will be a statement of what we learn about bats based on the information that we gather from our thinking about the similarities and differences.

THINKING ACTIVELY

- In the book *Stellaluna* by Janell Cameron, we learned about a young fruit bat who lived with a family of birds. The story showed us many ways that the bat, Stellaluna, was similar to the young birds. It also showed us many ways that they were different. We can compare and contrast Stellaluna to the young birds. This will help us to understand more about why

a bat is part of the mammal family, not the bird family. Pass out a book to each group, or if there are enough copies, to each student. Students should be working in groups. This lesson will move back and forth between small and large group activities.

• **As we reread** *Stellaluna,* **our purpose will be to find the similarities and differences between the fruit bat and the baby birds. We will be thinking about the information given in the text and in the illustrations, looking for ways that bats and birds are similar and different. To help us come back to the information we find, we will mark the places where we find similarities and differences with sticky notes. When we find a similarity in the words or in a picture, we will mark it with a sticky note labeled "S." When we find a difference, we will mark it with a sticky note labeled "D."** Have a supply of small sticky notes available. Read the book again. As students find similarities and differences, have them mark the spot with the appropriately lettered sticky note.

• **You have used many sticky notes to mark the similarities and differences between the fruit bat and the young birds. You have answered the first and second questions on the thinking map for comparing and contrasting.**

• **We'll use a graphic organizer to put the similarities and differences together. This will help us in our thinking.** A group graphic organizer for comparing and contrasting should be displayed on a chart, the chalkboard, or an overhead transparency. **We can write "Stellaluna—fruit bats" and "birds" in the top boxes to identify what we are comparing.** Write the words "Stellaluna—fruit bats" and "birds" in the top boxes. **The next section has a place for us to answer the question, "How alike?" We will record our similarities here. Could someone tell us one similarity?** POSSIBLE STUDENT RESPONSE: *They both have wings.* **Yes, that is a similarity. We can write it in the box.** Write their example as a model on the class graphic organizer. **What are some other similarities? I want you to work together in your groups to write the similarities on the copies of the graphic organizer. Look for the "S" notes you left in the book. Record the similarities. Try to write at least three similarities. Write the similarities in short, simple sentences.** Pass out one copy of the graphic organizer to each group. **Use the large box at the top to write the ways that fruit bats and birds are alike as I did on the class graphic organizer.** Allow work time for the groups to find and record their similarities. Some groups may need help doing this. At the end of the work time, ask one student from each group to share one statement that his or her group recorded in the similarities box. Record these statements on the class copy of the graphic organizer. Explore these responses by questioning for clarity and extension. Ask students to refer back to the text or illustrations to support their statements of the similarities. Allow groups to share more than once if they have similarities

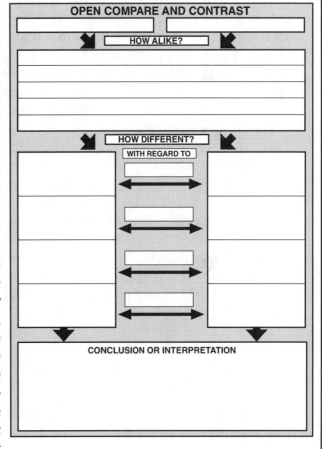

OPEN COMPARE AND CONTRAST

HOW ALIKE?

HOW DIFFERENT?

WITH REGARD TO

CONCLUSION OR INTERPRETATION

that have not been mentioned after all the groups share. POSSIBLE STUDENT RESPONSES: *They have wings*. EVIDENCE: *You can see them in the pictures, and they talk about them. They were telling how they were learning how to fly. They can fly*. EVIDENCE: *That is in the middle part of the story. They have to grow up before they fly*. EVIDENCE: *That was what they said in the beginning part of the story. Their feet have toes or claws*. EVIDENCE: *The pictures show that they have little claws to hang upside down. They both sleep and wake up*. EVIDENCE: *That is what they said when they were talking about the birds and Stellaluna growing up. They are both the same color, brown*. EVIDENCE: *We can see in the pictures that they have colors that are about the same. They are soft*. EVIDENCE: *We can see it in the pictures*.

- **You have gathered onto your graphic organizer some of the ways that fruit bats and birds are alike. The differences should be recorded next. For each difference, we will put what the fruit bat has or does on the bat side of the graphic organizer, and what the bird has or does on the bird side. There is an arrow between the boxes. The arrow has a place above it to label the difference. For example, one difference is that bats hang by their feet and birds sit on branches.** Record these differences in the boxes on the class graphic organizer. **What term would describe this difference?** POSSIBLE STUDENT RESPONSES: *Perching, ways to sit in trees*. **This term would be written above the arrow. With your group, find the places in your book that you marked for differences. Record these differences on your graphic organizer, and label each difference in the box above the arrow that separates the differences between fruit bats and birds.** Support the groups with their work, particularly the labeling of the differences. After allowing small group work time, ask for groups to share. Record their responses on the class copy of the graphic organizer. As with the similarities, ask questions to clarify and identify sources of the statements. After the answers have been shared, allow time for any groups that would like to add to their own organizer to do so, and tell then that this is all right. POSSIBLE STUDENT RESPONSES: *Bats hang by their feet. Birds sit on branches* (perching). EVIDENCE: *They show this in the pictures and they talked about it when the birds and Stellaluna were growing up. Bats have a nose and a mouth. Birds have beaks* (body parts). *Bats don't have tail feathers. Birds have tail feathers* (body parts). EVIDENCE: *The pictures show how they look. Bats have fur. Birds have feathers* (body coverings). EVIDENCE: *You can see this in the pictures. Bat wings are covered with skin. Bird wings are covered with feathers* (wings/body coverings). EVIDENCE: *Some of the pictures that show Stellaluna up close show her wings, and the pictures of the birds show theirs* (wings/body coverings). *Bat wings are attached to their sides. Bird wings are attached at one spot* (wings/body parts). EVIDENCE: *We saw this in the pictures. The mother bird fed the birds bugs and the fruit bats showed Stellaluna where to find fruit. Fruit bats eat fruit. Birds eat bugs* (food). EVIDENCE: *The story tells what they like to eat and what tastes bad to them. Bats have ears that show. Bird don't have ears that show* (ears, body parts). EVIDENCE: *We can see the bat ears in the pictures. Bats can see in the dark. Birds cannot see in the dark* (sight). *Stellaluna found out she could see to fly in the dark, but the birds could not. They had to have Stellaluna rescue them*.

- **(ALTERNATIVE FOR SECOND GRADE:) The third step asks us what similarities and differences seem significant. As we filled in the graphic organizer for comparing and contrasting, we may have noticed some things that are not really important to us in learning more about why fruit bats are mammals and not birds. It's time to study the similarities and differences we've recorded on our graphic organizers. Some of the things we've recorded may be true but are not important. For example, they are both brown animals but so are many other animals. Do you think that the color of animals is important to the reason they are in a particular animal group?** Students should discuss and agree that color is not a vital piece of information for the conclusions we are looking for. **We want to base our understanding of fruit bats and birds on things that *are* important to our understanding of bats as mammals. We should not use the** information about colors of the animals as we make our conclusion. **Draw a line through that statement to remind us that it is true but not important to us and the thinking we are doing. Are there any similarities that are not really important?** Discuss the similarities and differences in terms of importance. If there are items that are judged to be unimportant, draw a line through them. Usually students will eliminate similarities like "They are soft."

- (FINAL STEP FOR FIRST AND SECOND GRADE:) **We will continue in our comparison of bats and birds by moving to the final step.** For first grade: **This step asks us to decide what the information shows us that we did not already know.** For second grade: **This step asks what conclusion is suggested by the significant or important similarities and differences.**

- **It is time for us to think about the information we have collected to make conclusions. Using your graphic organizer, think about what you have learned about bats and birds as a result of this activity. What does this tell you about fruit bats as part of the mammal group of animals?** Do a whole group discussion to allow for a variety of answers and to allow students to model thinking for each other. It may be necessary to do a think aloud in order for students to understand this final step. After group reflection time, ask each group to write a statement in the bottom box, or as a group, compose a statement for everyone to write. POSSIBLE STUDENT RESPONSES: *Even though bats can fly they are not birds. They are mammals because they have the body parts that mammals have. Bats fly in a way that is different from birds because they do not have bird wings and bird bodies. Even though two animals look alike, they may be made differently and do different things.*

- **Are there other things that we could find out about bats that would show us that bats are truly members of the mammal family? What things do we know about mammals that this book did not confirm about bats?** Students usually refer to classroom charts of mammal and bird characteristics. They will point out that they did not find out about kinds of bones, how the young are born (eggs/born alive), and feeding the young milk. **We can do more research in other books and on the Internet to find the answers to those questions. Although this book had many facts about bats, it is a fictional story. Using this as a beginning source has shown us that fruit bats do not have the characteristics that would say that they belong to the bird family. Our comparisons have shown that although there are some similarities, the differences tell us that bats are mammals and not birds. To find out more details about bats, we should check more sources.**

THINKING ABOUT THINKING

- **We've been using a compare and contrast strategy to think about fruit bats and birds. As a result of this activity, we've been able to learn something important about them. What did you do to compare the two animals?** Allow students to review the process, calling attention to the thinking map as students remember the steps they took in comparing and contrasting.

- **What steps did we take to go beyond just looking for similarities and differences?** POSSIBLE STUDENT RESPONSES: *We thought about what kind of difference it is. We wrote about what we did at the end of the comparing and contrasting. Our sentences helped us remember the things on the graphic organizer.*

- **Is this strategy of comparing and contrasting a helpful way to think about and to understand things?** POSSIBLE STUDENT RESPONSE: *Yes, because if you know about something and it's a lot like something else, then you can learn about the new thing.*

- **Was it helpful for you to use the graphic organizer as we compared and contrasted fruit bats? How?** POSSIBLE STUDENT RESPONSES: *We got a lot of ideas this way. We had a chance to write down our ideas to help us remember them.*

- **If you need to learn by comparing and contrasting in the future, what will you do?** Students should tell you the steps of the thinking strategy in their own words.

- **Would comparing and contrasting help us better understand other animals, such as tigers and lions, or raccoons and opossums?** Students usually think that comparing and contrasting is a fun way to learn about and understand animals. They like looking for ways that the animals are alike and different.

APPLYING YOUR THINKING

Immediate Transfer

- You have learned a new recess game. You want to teach it to some of your friends. Describe how you would use comparing and contrasting to teach them to play the new game. What recess game would you compare the new game to? Use a comparing and contrasting graphic organizer and thinking map to compare the two games.

- When moving to a new school, a student might use comparing and contrasting to help him or her understand their new surroundings. Act out a scene with someone else. Pretend one of you is new and the other is explaining the new school. Use a graphic organizer and thinking map for comparing and contrasting to help you plan what you will say in your skit.

Reinforcement Later

- The Pilgrims came to a new land that was very different from England. Pretend you are one of the Pilgrims. You are writing a letter to a friend back in England. The *Mayflower* will take the letter back for you. Tell your friend about your new home, using comparing and contrasting. Don't forget to use the graphic for comparing and contrasting to plan your writing. The thinking map will also help you as you plan.

- Compare and contrast an adding sentence and a subtracting sentence. How are they alike and different? What does this tell you about the two ways to use numbers? Do your thinking with the help of a Compare and Contrast thinking map and graphic organizer.

- Compare and contrast a penguin and a child. Follow the thinking map for comparing and contrasting. Use the information about penguins from our studies of water animals as you gather information. The comparing and contrasting graphic organizer will help you organize your thinking to understand more about the ways they are alike and different. Draw a picture of the penguin and you. Then use your graphic organizer to tell a group of students about the ways you and a penguin are alike and different, and what conclusions you can make.

RESEARCH EXTENSION (GRADE 2)

Ask students to go further and gather information from school libraries, computer programs, and the Internet about bats. Have them report on what they found and where they got the information. They should continue to use the information gathered from the comparing and contrasting lesson as they search for more support to show that bats are mammals.

WRITING EXTENSION (GRADE 1)

Have students make a book that shares the important things they learned about fruit bats and birds. Illustrations should show the important details of their text. Be sure students include a page that discusses the conclusions from the comparing and contrasting lesson.

WRITING EXTENSION (GRADE 2)

Have students use the information collected on their graphic organizer to write a paragraph comparing and contrasting fruit bats and birds. They should use the expository paragraph template to assist them (see Appendix).

ART EXTENSION

Using the illustrations from Stellaluna and other sources, have groups of students draw a series of pictures of a bat and a bird. The groups' pictures should show the ways that bats and birds are similar and different. Sentence captions should be written to go with the pictures.

SUGGESTED SPECIAL NEEDS MODIFICATIONS

<u>Frontload:</u> Some young learners, particularly those with language delays, may still be unclear on the concepts of "same" and "different." Prior to this lesson, these students may benefit from practice in sorting like objects and discussing what makes them "similar" or the "same" followed by another activity with unlike objects and discussion.

The Open Compare/Contrast strategy also requires that students have some facility with categorizing. Being able to categorize will help students be more skillful in labelling the attribute arrows. Sorting "games" can be helpful in practicing this skill. "Nose, foot, hand are all body parts. Desk, chair, sofa are all…?"

Generating a conclusion may prove challenging to students. You can support students in building this skill by using daily experiences and content examples to guide their thinking through use of think alouds. For example, you can point out a pattern of similarities and demonstrate how these were used in making his/her conclusion. "I see a pattern …Because of this, I conclude…" It is important that you model the language as well as the thinking in order for students to make the connections.

<u>Clarify</u>: Terminology such as, "similar," "contrast," and "significant" may be unfamiliar to students. While it is important to use these terms, it may be necessary to consistently pair them with more familiar terms, such as, "same," "different," or "important."

<u>Diversify</u>: The story may be read aloud to support those students who have difficulty with the text.

The number of similarities and differences can be reduced so that students can attend to the process of comparing and contrasting the more salient features.

By combining pairs of students or cooperative groups, you can capitalize on each student's strengths. The proficient writer can record responses so that all may contribute to the thinking. Students may also respond orally and thus reduce the additional task of writing for some students. It is important that thinking take precedence over task demands.

Combining ideas to generate labels for the attribute arrows or formulating a conclusion may require greater teacher guidance for some students. The teacher may wish to support students by paraphrasing their responses in order to provide clear models. ("You noticed that the bats land in trees and birds sit in trees. You are telling me that the animals 'perch.'") Instead of allowing students to work in groups, you may wish to guide this process for a longer period of time before allowing group work.

Expand the Possibilities: Assessments of written responses may be based upon students' thinking first, and expressive skills secondly. Oral responses may also reveal thinking beyond students' ability to express themselves in writing.

ASSESSING STUDENT THINKING ABOUT POSSIBILITIES

To assess students' skill at comparing and contrasting, you can use any of the suggested application activities. Use the thinking map as a guide to look for key stages in their thinking. When students are working, have them use a graphic organizer and then write and draw about what they learned. Questioning students about the steps of the process will help in assessing the mental steps they take.

Sample Student Responses • Bats

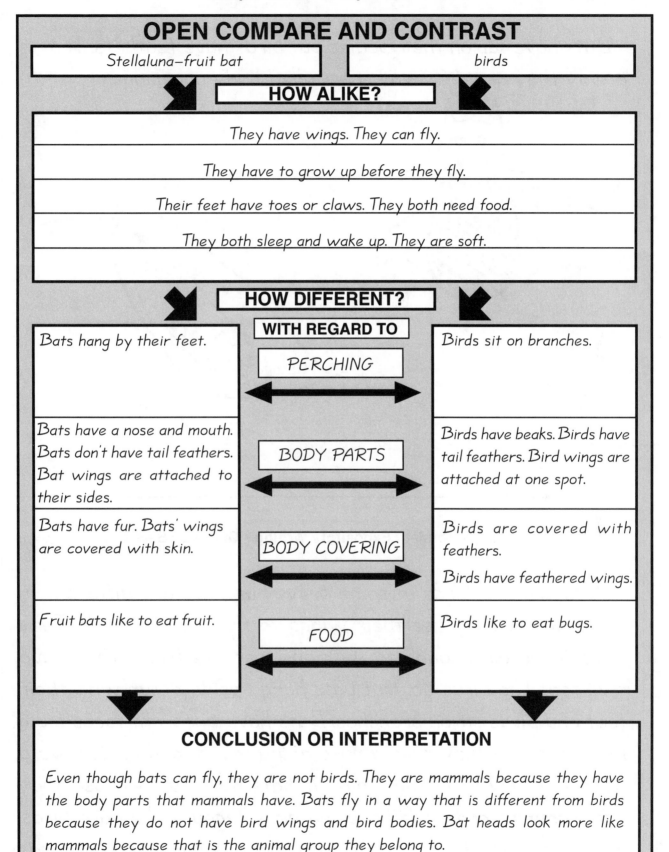

OPEN COMPARE AND CONTRAST

Stellaluna–fruit bat	birds

HOW ALIKE?

They have wings. They can fly.

They have to grow up before they fly.

Their feet have toes or claws. They both need food.

They both sleep and wake up. They are soft.

HOW DIFFERENT?

WITH REGARD TO

	PERCHING	
Bats hang by their feet.		Birds sit on branches.

	BODY PARTS	
Bats have a nose and mouth. Bats don't have tail feathers. Bat wings are attached to their sides.		Birds have beaks. Birds have tail feathers. Bird wings are attached at one spot.

	BODY COVERING	
Bats have fur. Bats' wings are covered with skin.		Birds are covered with feathers. Birds have feathered wings.

	FOOD	
Fruit bats like to eat fruit.		Birds like to eat bugs.

CONCLUSION OR INTERPRETATION

Even though bats can fly, they are not birds. They are mammals because they have the body parts that mammals have. Bats fly in a way that is different from birds because they do not have bird wings and bird bodies. Bat heads look more like mammals because that is the animal group they belong to.

Sample Student Picture/Caption • Grade 1 • Bats

Bats have fur on their bodies but birds have feathers. That is a way they are different. It is called body coverings.

Sample Student Expository Writing • Grade 2 • Bats

Bats are like birds in some ways but they are different in other ways. They use their wings to fly just like birds. They have to be old enough to fly alone just like birds. They have two feet like birds do. But bats hang upside down with their feet and birds sit on branches. Bats have different faces from birds because they have a nose and a mouth and birds have a beak. A really important thing is bats have fur because they are mammals and birds have feathers because they are birds. The most important thing to remember is bats can't be birds because they have mammal body parts and are really mammals.

CITY LIVING AND COUNTRY LIVING
TOWN MOUSE COUNTRY MOUSE

Language Arts   **Grades 1–2**

OBJECTIVES

CONTENT

Students will identify details in a story that show the different perspectives of characters coming from different home environments. Students will learn that lifestyles vary from one location to another but that basic needs are the same.

THINKING SKILL/PROCESS

Students will compare and contrast effectively by determining the purpose of the comparison and contrast, the kinds of similarities and differences relevant to the purpose, and by drawing a conclusion from the similarities and differences they uncover.

METHODS AND MATERIALS

CONTENT

The teacher will read aloud *Town Mouse Country Mouse* by Jan Brett. This should not be a first reading. Students will use the story and illustrations to compare the characters in the story as they attempt to exchange homes.

THINKING SKILL/PROCESS

Focused Comparing and Contrasting is guided by structured questioning and a graphic organizer. Collaborative learning and think-pair-share techniques are used to help clarify ideas and work to a conclusion or interpretation based on the information gathered.

LESSON

INTRODUCTION TO CONTENT AND THINKING SKILL/PROCESS

- Recently I was working on a project at home. I wanted to add a tree to my yard. Because I know that trees are very different, I needed to be careful to choose the tree that would look best among the other plants. A very good way to learn about things is comparing and contrasting. When I compared different kinds of trees, I was able to choose the one that would best fit in my yard. Finding the tree that would best fit in my yard was the purpose I had as I studied the trees. I thought about what things would be important to know about the tree that I chose for my yard. I focused on just those things that would help me make up my mind. The things that I considered as I looked at trees included their size, how fast they grow, how easy they are to care for, and the general shape of the tree. I looked at the ways they were similar and the ways they were different with these factors in mind. Looking at trees in this way helped me to understand the trees, and I could draw a conclusion about which tree would best fit in my yard.

- Using similarities (the ways things are alike) and differences (the ways things are different) and then coming up with a conclusion helps us to understand things better. This is called "comparing and contrasting." Write the words "Comparing and Contrasting," "Alike—similarities," and "Different—differences" on the chalkboard or a chart. They will be the beginning of the list of terms for this lesson. A *conclusion* is a new statement of what we understand about something after we think and learn things about it. When we studied subtraction, we compared it to addition. We looked at the ways they were alike and the ways they were different. We could make the *conclusion* that subtraction was the opposite of addition. In this way we were able to understand subtraction more easily. My decision about which tree to buy was based on the conclusion I made about which tree would best fit into my yard. Add the word "Conclusion" to the list of terms.

- In our daily lives there are times when we need to use the comparing and contrasting thinking strategy. For example, if you are buying a new bike, you probably will look at the different kinds of bikes to see how they are alike and how they are different. What things would you want to consider when you buy a new bike? Talk to your partner. Try to think of three things that you would want to know about the bike. Allow time for the pairs to generate a list of factors. Share the factors with the class. POSSIBLE STUDENT RESPONSES: *the size, the color, the kind of tires, the number of gears.* This information will help you when you are ready to choose the bike that is best for you. You will understand more about the bikes by comparing and contrasting them with the important factors in mind. This understanding will help you to draw a conclusion about which bike is the best for you based on the new knowledge you have about the kinds of bikes that are for sale.

- Try to think of times when you have looked for ways that things are similar and different to help you understand them. Did you have a specific purpose, or reason, for comparing and contrasting? Why did you need to compare and contrast? Talk to your partner and share one of these times. After time for paired sharing, ask a couple of students to share with the whole group. POSSIBLE STUDENT RESPONSES: *Comparing two different shirts to choose the one that was best to buy, comparing books at the library to pick the ones to check out, comparing a new computer game to an old one to learn how to win.* In the discussion, use the words from the terms list with the students' examples. As the students share, encourage them to tell about the purpose they had for making the comparison.

- Here is a thinking map that will help us use this kind of comparing and contrasting. This thinking is called *focused comparing and contrasting* because it always begins with a purpose. Show the thinking map for focused compare and contrast on a chart or chalkboard. It should be displayed in a way that allows students to refer to it during the lesson. Read through the questions with the class. **First, we should know our purpose for comparing and contrasting.** Read "What is our purpose for comparing and contrasting?" **Next we must decide what kinds of similarities and differences are important to our purpose.** Read "What kinds of similarities and differences are important to the purpose of our comparing and contrasting?" **The third step is to look for and find similarities that fit into these categories.** Read "What similarities fall into these categories?" **The fourth step is to find the differences that fit into these categories.** Read "What differences fall into these categories?" **Finally, we should look at all of the information to see what we now know because of the comparing and contrasting we have done. In other words, "What does this show?"**

> **FOCUSED COMPARE AND CONTRAST**
>
> 1. **What is our purpose for comparing and contrasting?**
>
> 2. **What kinds of similarities and differences are important to the purpose of our comparing and contrasting?**
>
> 3. **What similarities fall into these categories?**
>
> 4. **What differences fall into these categories?**
>
> 5. **What does this show?**

THINKING ACTIVELY

- Today we are going to read a story with four main characters. The story is called *Town Mouse Country Mouse* by Jan Brett. We have read this story before, so we know that two of the mice are from the country, and two live in the city. In the story, they will trade places. We are going to compare the lifestyles of the two sets of mice to see what we can learn about the similarities and differences of mice who live in different locations. We want to know how they live their lives. This will help us to understand the characters better. Authors often use animals to show how people lead their lives. That means that the thinking we do as we study the mice and the ways they live in this story will also help us to understand more about how humans live.

- Before we begin the story, I'd like you to think about what you know about mice that live in town. Talk to your partner about what you know about how town mice live. Provide discussion time. Allow a few to share their ideas with the group. Students should be familiar with the story, having already read it, so they should have several ideas to share. POSSIBLE STUDENT RESPONSES: *They live in holes. They are afraid of cats. They sneak into the house at night.* **Now talk about country mice with your partner. Share what you know about how they live.** Provide another discussion time. Again allow a few to share. POSSIBLE STUDENT RESPONSES: *They live in the forest and fields. They eat berries. Owls eat them.* **These ideas can start to help us to think of ways that town mice and country mice are alike and how they might be different. This will help us in our task of comparing and contrasting the mice in the story.**

- After we read the story we will be recording the ways that the characters are alike and different in the story on a graphic organizer. Show the graphic organizer for focused comparing and contrasting on a chart or on an overhead transparency. **The top boxes will be the places to record the names of the mice. We can write "Town Mice" in one box and "Country Mice" in the other box. We will write our purpose in the next box. Our purpose will be to learn about how where the mice live makes a difference in how they live—what is called their** *lifestyle.* **After we've made our comparison and contrast, we will see if the conclusion we come to helps us understand more about the ways that people live.** Write "To learn about how where the mice live makes a difference in the lifestyle of the mice" in the "Purpose" box at the top of the graphic organizer.

- **The next box asks us to decide on the factors we will look at. That means we must decide on the things that are important to us to think about in comparing and contrasting the mice** for this purpose. **What things do you think we should think about as we find ways that the mice were alike and different in the way they lived their lives? Talk to your group about the things we should watch for in the story.** Allow time for the groups to share their ideas, then share as a class. Record the ideas on a chalkboard or chart. POSSIBLE STUDENT RESPONSES: *The clothes they wear, their homes, the food they eat, their friends and enemies, the furniture they have in their houses, the things they like to do, whether or not they are happy.* **In our studies of people and the ways that they live, we have identified the four basic needs. Many of the answers that you have given would fit into the basic needs of food, clothing, love or security, and shelter. We can use these as our main factors. You also mentioned that they like to do different things, and whether or not they were happy. When you were talking about the things they liked to do and their happiness, it reminded me of our lessons on feelings. Let's use feelings as another factor. Let's write these in the "Factors" box on the graphic organizer. We will also write the factors in two other places. They will go next to the section where we record the ways the mice are similar and next to the section where we record the ways the mice are different.** Write the factors "food, clothing, shelter, love, and feelings" in the boxes at the top for factors and in the boxes down the left-hand side of the graphic organizer next to the similarities and differences.

- **It is time to read the story, and as we read we will take time to stop and enjoy the illustrations again.** Read and discuss the story with the class. As students see similarities and differences in the mice, ask them to be sure to remember them so that they can share them when their group works on completing the graphic organizer after the story.

- **The story has shown us many things about the two mouse pairs. Let's go to the graphic organizer to see what we have learned so that we can answer the questions about similarities and differences on the thinking map. We should begin with the similarities. Together with your partner, I'd like you to think of ways that the town mice are similar to the country mice. Your similarities should go along with the factors we have listed. You will be thinking of the similarities that have something to do with food, clothing, shelter, love, and feelings.** Reread the factors on the chart to students to remind them of their focus. **On your slates/paper make a list of the similarities with regard to each factor that you saw and heard in the story.** Individual dry erase slates are good to use in making the lists, but if they are not available, paper can be used. Allow time for students to work in pairs. If prompting is needed, suggest they work on these one by one, starting with food. Suggest that they think about what they ate, where they got their food, and where they ate it. You may also ask them about the feelings the mice had during various parts of the story. Ask students to share their responses when they are ready by volunteering. Have them share only one response per team. When students share the similarities, record their responses on the class graphic organizer. As a similarity is suggested, guide students to make explicit the connection between the story and the factors listed on the graphic organizer. POSSIBLE STUDENT RESPONSES: *They both searched for and ate food (food). They both wished for a vacation (feelings). They both were excited to go away (feelings). They both were tired of their homes (shelter). They both found things that were different and scary (love, security). They both wanted to go home (shelter). They both decided the safest place to live was their own home (love, security). They both wore clothes (clothing). They were married (love, security). They helped each other (love, security).*

- **As we created our list of similarities, you said that the mice had all their basic needs met. Let's look at the differences now. To help us in thinking about the differences, I'd like you to keep thinking about the four basic needs plus feelings. Talk with your partner to see how the mice were different, especially in meeting their basic needs. Use your slates/paper again to make a list of differences.** Allow share time, then record the ideas they bring back to the group in the boxes on the graphic for differences. Accept only one idea per student who volunteers. On the arrows, record the type of difference they are referring to. POSSIBLE STUDENT

RESPONSES: *The town mice found their food in the house pantry. The country mice found their food in the meadows and forests (food). The town mice wore nice fancy clothes. The country mice wore clothes that were nice but not made of fancy materials (clothing). The town mice lived in a wall in the house. The country mice lived in a tree stump (shelter). The town mice were careful not to go near the cat and the mousetraps. The country mice were careful to stay out of the rain and not go near the larger animals of the forest (shelter or security). The town mice were excited to go to the country. The county mice were excited to go to the town (feelings).*

- **Now we need to look at our similarities and differences to see what we have learned from comparing and contrasting the town mice and the country mice. If we look back to our purpose, we will see that we wanted to learn how the mice lived. We used the four basic needs and feelings as the factors we wanted to consider. Our job now is to decide what the information we now have shows. When we do that we will be drawing a conclusion from what we've learned about their similarities and differences. What can you say about the mice and their feelings? What can you say about the mice and their needs?** POSSIBLE STUDENT RESPONSES: *Mice have the same sorts of feelings, and it doesn't seem to matter whether they come from the city or the country. The city mice and country mice both liked their homes much better than the places they visited. It didn't matter to the mice whether they lived in the city or country because they each were happier in their homes than in the new place they visited. They all needed the same basic things. They had food, clothing, shelter, and love or security. They didn't have the same food, clothing, and shelter but they had them.* Record students' ideas on a chart or the chalkboard to refer to in making a statement of the conclusion. **These are all statements that can be put into the bottom box on the graphic organizer as a conclusion. But let's try to combine some of these into one interesting conclusion.** Work with students to combine their ideas into an interesting conclusion statement connected with the purpose of the comparison and contrast. Don't formulate it for them, but prompt them by asking questions like "What can we say about the way the mice lived and felt that is connected with whether they lived in the country or city?" or "Did the mice meet their basic needs the same ways in the city and country? How?" POSSIBLE STUDENT RESPONSES: *The mice all have the same feelings and basic needs but they do different things to meet their basic needs depending on whether they are from the city or the country. They get so used to it that when they change, they don't like it.*

- **Do you think that there is a connection we can make to people around the world and the feelings they have and the ways they meet their basic needs?** Allow for a class discussion of ideas, encouraging students to utilize prior knowledge from their families, travels, and studies. Record their statements on a chart or chalkboard. POSSIBLE STUDENT RESPONSES: *People everywhere have basic needs. What they eat and wear depends on where they live. What their houses look like depends on where they live, too. People all over the world have families, and they help each other. People all over the world have feelings. People get used to where they live and when they move, they sometimes don't like it.* **So what can we say about people that is like what we said about the town and country mice?** POSSIBLE STUDENT RESPONSES: *People all over the world have feelings and the same basic needs, but some of their needs get met in different ways because of where they live.*

- **Think about the book we just read, now. Is there some special way that the author wrote the book that helped us to make this connection with the way people live? Work with your partners again and discuss this.** Work with students to help them focus attention on how the mice are portrayed both in the story and in the illustrations. If students have trouble with this, ask them leading questions like "Do mice talk?" "Do mice wear clothes?" etc. Then ask for volunteers to respond. POSSIBLE STUDENT RESPONSES: *The mice in the story pictures are made to look like people. The author makes the mice talk and say things like people say. The mice do things that* *people do.* **When authors do this it is called** *personification.* **Can you think of other stories that you've read in which the animals look and talk like people?** ANSWERS VARY. **You might want to look back at some of those books and ask: "What connection does the author want us to make with people?"**

THINKING ABOUT THINKING

- **The thinking we have done in this lesson has helped us to compare and contrast the mice and the way they lived. We used this way of thinking to help us understand the characters in the story. Our discussion of the similarities and differences also helped us to relate the story to our lives. We all have similar feelings no matter where we live. And there are many ways that our basic needs can be met, just as with the mice. What were the questions we asked as we compared and contrasted the mice in the story?** The students should repeat the questions from the thinking map for focused compare and contrast.

- **How was thinking by comparing and contrasting different from just looking for ways that two things are alike and different?** POSSIBLE STUDENT RESPONSES: *Comparing and contrasting made us look at the kinds of differences we found. We had to have a conclusion at the end. We needed to see which things were important to think about because of the purpose of the comparison and contrast.*

- **Was the graphic organizer helpful to you in this thinking process? How?** POSSIBLE STUDENT RESPONSES: *It helped us remember our ideas because we wrote them down. We could look at all the ideas to figure out what we learned for the conclusion.*

- **Do you think this is a valuable way to look at two things? Why or why not?** ANSWERS VARY. Most students agree that this helps them think more about what they are comparing and contrasting.

APPLYING YOUR THINKING

Immediate Transfer

- Some people live in rural locations, while others live in urban settings. Compare the two different places, using a comparing and contrasting thinking map and graphic organizer. Choose the place you would like to have for your home. This will be the conclusion of your work. Plan an advertisement to convince people it is the best place to live.

- Use comparing and contrasting to help choose which transportation you would use for your family to go on a trip. First choose a location for your vacation, then use the thinking map and a graphic organizer for comparing and contrasting to help you choose between going on a train or flying in an airplane. Once you have a conclusion about the best way to go, write a letter to your parents suggesting the way you think would be best to travel. Be sure to use the information from the graphic to support your choice.

Reinforcement Later

- We have read the story *The Empty Pot* by Demi. To help us understand the main character, Ping, we can compare him to the other children in the story. How are they alike and different? Use the thinking map and graphic organizer for focused compare and contrast to help you. What does this tell you about Ping? That will be your conclusion.

- Compare and contrast a fiction book and a nonfiction book in order to find out when you would use each and what you would use them for. Use the comparing and contrasting thinking map and then record the similarities and differences on the graphic organizer. What conclusions would you make about the uses of the two kinds of books?

WRITING EXTENSION

Students will use the information they have learned about the similarities and differences in mice to write an acrostic poem. They will use the Comparing and Contrasting graphic organizer to help them remember what they have learned from their comparisons. They will use the template for writing acrostic poems to help them put their ideas down in the form of acrostic poetry (see template in Appendix).

SUGGESTED SPECIAL NEEDS MODIFICATIONS

Frontload: Some young learners, in particular those with language delays, may still be unclear on the concepts of "same" and "different." For these students, prior practice with sorting like objects together with a discussion of the ways they are alike, followed by similar activities with unlike objects may be necessary to clarify these concepts.

Forming a conclusion based upon information may also be challenging for students. You can guide this type of thinking by using everyday examples with students and modelling their thinking though a think aloud. For example, you may notice a pattern of similarities (students being absent, playground disagreements, story character actions and feelings) and point out these similarities as he/she states the conclusion. "I notice that there is a pattern…I conclude that…because of the pattern I see." It is important that the thinking terms (conclusion) be used in the examples in order for students to make the thinking-language connection.

Clarify: Terms such as "similar," "contrast," and "significant" may be unfamiliar to students. While it is important to use these terms, it may be necessary to consistently pair them with more familiar terms, such as "same," "different," and "important."

Diversify: You may limit the similarities and/or differences to only a few for some students. In general, limiting the number of ideas within each area of the graphic organizer because of time constraints can help the student focus on the process as they skillfully compare and contrast.

Students who need help with their writing should be challenged to write on their graphic organizers along with the other students. Oral interaction with these students can help them articulate what they have written. Pairing students to capitalize on the strengths of each learner allows the ideas of the nonproficient writer to be captured by the partner.

Expand the Possibilities: Assessments of written responses may be based upon students' thinking first, and expressive skills secondly. Oral responses may also reveal thinking beyond students' ability to express themselves in writing.

ASSESSING STUDENT THINKING ABOUT COMPARING AND CONTRASTING

To assess students' ability to compare and contrast, ask them to use a graphic organizer to compare and contrast two items. The examples in the application section of this lesson, or similar examples, are ideal for this type of assessment. After they fill in the graphic organizer, have them write a paragraph explaining the similarities and differences and what they have learned from comparing, or have them discuss their thinking with you. Ask students to describe how they went through the steps of the comparing and contrasting process.

Sample Student Responses • City Living, Country Living

FOCUSED COMPARE AND CONTRAST

Town Mice	Country Mice

PURPOSE: To learn about the ways that town mice and country mice live, and how where they live might make a difference to their lifestyle (how they live).

FACTORS TO CONSIDER:

food, shelter, clothing, love (protection), feelings

FACTORS CONSIDERED IN THIS ACTIVITY:	HOW ALIKE?
Food	They search and find food to eat.
Shelter	They were tired of their homes. They wanted to go back to their own home.
Clothing	They both wear clothing.
Love (Security)	They find things that are scary. They decide the safest place is their own home. They are married and help each other.
Feelings	They both wished for a vacation. They were both excited to go away. They were happy, sad, scared.

HOW DIFFERENT?

Food	food from the pantry	food from forests and meadows
Shelter	a hole in a wall in a house	a tree stump
Clothing	clothes made from fancy materials	clothes made from plain materials, like old sacks
Love (Security)	stayed away from cat and mousetraps	stayed out of rain and stayed away from the larger animals in the forest
Feelings	excited to go to the country	excited to go to the town

CONCLUSION OR INTERPRETATION:

The mice all have the same feelings and basic needs but they do different things to meet their basic needs depending on whether they are from the city or the country, and they get used to how they live no matter where it is.

Sample Student Writing (Grade 1) • City Living, Country Living

Makes his home in different places

Owls or cats can be his enemy

Up and down it runs every day

Staying with its family

Eating berries or cheese

Sample Student Writing (Grade 2) • City Living, Country Living

Making nests in trees

Or living in houses and hiding

Under things to

Stay safe from

Enemies.

OPEN COMPARE AND CONTRAST

1. How are they similar?

2. How are they different?

3. What similarities and differences are important?

4. What interpretation or conclusion is suggested?

COMPARE AND CONTRAST

1. How are they similar?

2. How are they different?

3. What does this show?

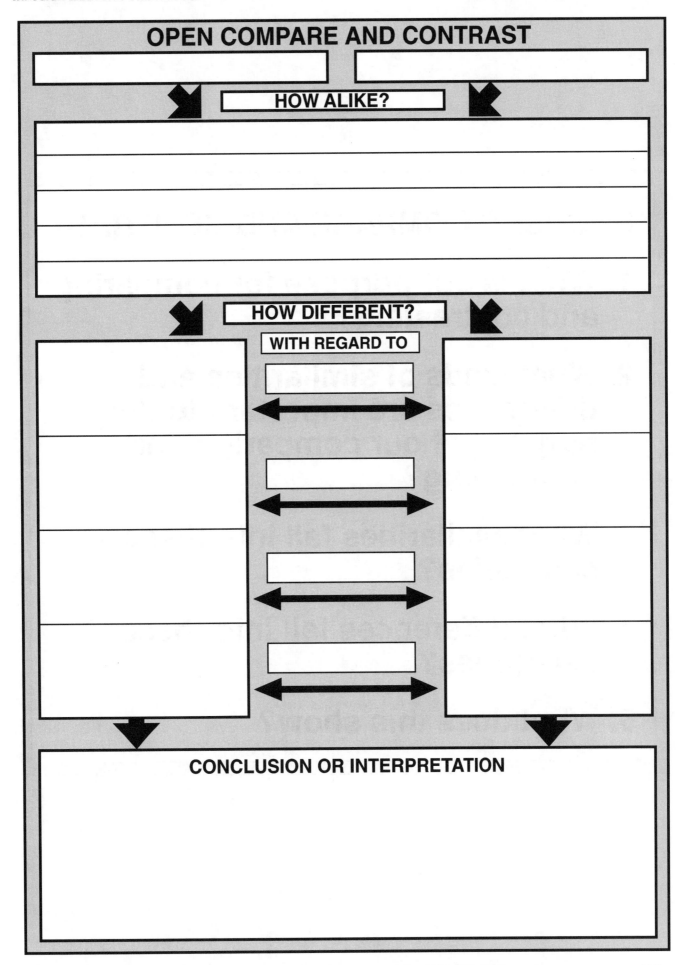

OPEN COMPARE AND CONTRAST

HOW ALIKE?

HOW DIFFERENT?

WITH REGARD TO

CONCLUSION OR INTERPRETATION

FOCUSED COMPARE AND CONTRAST

1. What is our purpose for comparing and contrasting?

2. What kinds of similarities and differences are important to the purpose of our comparing and contrasting?

3. What similarities fall into these categories?

4. What differences fall into these categories?

5. What does this show?

FOCUSED COMPARE AND CONTRAST

PURPOSE:

FACTORS TO CONSIDER:

FACTORS CONSIDERED IN THIS ACTIVITY:

HOW ALIKE?

HOW DIFFERENT?

CONCLUSION OR INTERPRETATION:

CHAPTER 6
CLASSIFICATION

Infusing Skillful Classification into Language Arts

In the lessons on classification, students are taught to do two types of classification skillfully—bottom-up classification and top-down classification. Teaching students these skills involves helping them learn to ask and carefully answer the following questions.

BOTTOM-UP CLASSIFICATION

1. **What characteristics do the given items have?**

2. **What ways of classifying items can be based on these characteristics?**

3. **What purpose do we have for classifying the items?**

4. **What way of classifying the items best serves this purpose?**

5. **Which items fall under each classification?**

---

figure 6.1

TOP-DOWN CLASSIFICATION

1. **What are the defining characteristics of the categories under which I want to classify things?**

2. **Which items have these characteristics?**

3. **How do I classify these items into the given categories?**

---

figure 6.2

In the classification lessons in this chapter, each of these thinking maps is used to guide your students' thinking explicitly as they engage with the lesson content.

Bottom-up classification is a thinking process that involves sorting individual things by common characteristics and then developing a classification system for the groups that result. If someone sorts a group of animals by their connection with humans, they may end up with a subgroup that they can call—and hence classify—as "pets." Other animals not already in this group but who share this characteristic can then be placed there as well. In doing bottom-up classification skillfully, students think about what purpose such groupings and classifications might serve and who would be interested in having information classified in this way. For example, a pet store owner might want to specialize in animals that make good pets for humans (like cats and dogs), hence sorting and classifying animals in this way may well serve his or her purpose. Bottom-up classification is especially important to do skillfully when there are a lot of items that are undifferentiated and need to be sorted out. Since they can be sorted in any number of ways, keeping in mind the purpose of sorting them will help to select the best way to do it.

Top-down classification is simply the last few steps in this process. When there is already a classification system that we are working with—for example, types of clothing, like shirts, trousers, socks, etc.—and we have to place individual things, like items from the laundry, into these groups, then we are doing top-down classification. Skillful top-down classification involves making explicit the defining characteristics for each category, identifying those characteristics in the individual things we're sorting, and then classifying them according to these defining characteristics. So, for example, finding something that is stretchy and can be pulled over the foot, leads us to classify it as a sock because we know that's the defining characteristic of a sock.

These lessons also make use of various supporting classroom strategies such as using graphic organizers, engaging in cooperative thinking, thinking about thinking, and continued guided practice to supplement the thinking map. These classroom strategies enhance both the thinking skill that the students are learning and their mastery of the lesson content.

The key graphic organizers for bottom-up classification are shown in figures 6.3 and 6.4.

The key graphic organizers for top-down classification are shown in figures 6.5 and 6.6 (see following page).

In the Ways to Classify Things graphic organizer (6.3) for bottom-up classification, students write the groupings they come up with on the horizontal lines down the left side and then determine what type of classification these groupings involve and record them above the vertical lines. Students then take one possible classification, for example, "Helpful Animals," and write it in the middle circle on the accompanying Classification Web (6.4). Students record different subcategories in the branching boxes, and, in the outer branches, record even further subcategories. For example, "Helpful Animals" might be branched into "Food-Providing Animals," "Work-Providing Animals," etc. The subcategory "Food-Providing Animals" might be branched into "hens, cows, and pigs." An alternative, encouraged in the lesson on bottom-up classification, is to have students do a freehand diagram expressing these relationships.

In the Top-Down Classification—Defining the Categories graphic organizer (6.5), students record the items to be classified. For example, they would write "Foods" in the "Type of Item to be Classified" box at the top of the graphic organizer. Types of food are written in the three "Category" boxes below; for example, fruit, fish, and nuts. Students define characteristics for each category in the "Defining Characteristics" box; for example, the defining characteristics of fish could be that it was once alive, is a meat, breathes through gills, and lives in the sea. Now students move to the Top-Down Classification—Classifying Items graphic organizer (6.6). Tuna may be on the graphic organizer under "Item To Be Classified." Its characteristics would include that it is a meat, lives in the sea, breathes through gills, etc. These characteristics should be written in the "Characteristics" box on the graphic organizer. These characteristics should be matched with the defining characteristics on the Defining the Categories graphic organizer, the correct category selected (tuna), and the name of that category written in the "How Classified" box on the Classifying Items graphic organizer. Once classified, the item is placed under the correct category in the "Items" box of the first graphic

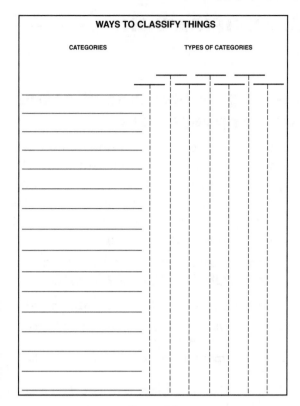

figure 6.3

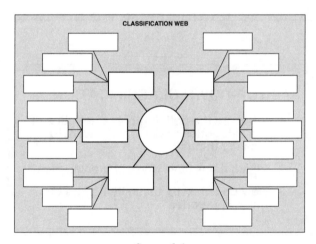

figure 6.4

organizer. The crucial step here is making the characteristics of an item to be classified explicit in the Classifying Items graphic organizer and then matching these characteristics with the characteristics students' identify in the Defining the Categories graphic organizer. This step is often missing in simpler classification activities.

Reproducible blank graphic organizers are found at the end of each chapter.

For more in-depth information on teaching skillful classification, please refer to Chapter 5 in the book *Infusing the Teaching of Critical and*

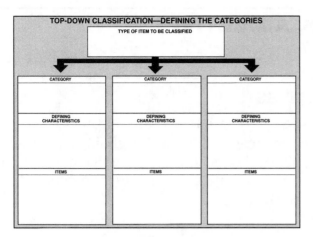

figure 6.5

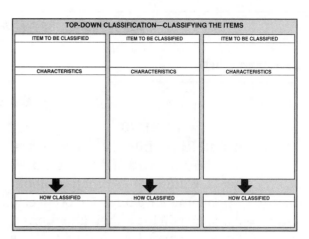

figure 6.6

Creative Thinking into Elementary Instruction, by Robert Swartz and Sandra Parks. A computer disk containing the blank, reproducible graphic organizers used in this book is also available. Both book and disk are available through Critical Thinking Books & Software.

NOUNS, VERBS, ADJECTIVES

Language Arts   **Grades 1–2**

OBJECTIVES

CONTENT

Students will learn different ways to classify words and recognize that different classifications yield different information about them (e.g., phonemic structure, part of speech, length, etc.). They will focus their attention on the classification of words according to parts of speech.

THINKING SKILL/PROCESS

Students will identify defining characteristics of classes and recognize that the purpose for classification determines the defining characteristics.

METHODS AND MATERIALS

CONTENT

Students will work together in collaborative learning groups. Each group will receive a set of words with which to make a variety of classifications. They will then classify the words according to parts of speech.

THINKING SKILL/PROCESS

In this bottom-up classification activity, students discover the different ways to classify words through guided questions and directions. Groups of students will create concept maps to illustrate classification. A thinking map and graphic organizers for bottom-up classification will guide student thinking.

LESSON

INTRODUCTION TO CONTENT AND THINKING SKILL/PROCESS

- **I'd like you to study the set of pictures in our pocket chart.** On a pocket chart, display a set of pictures showing groceries. **I have not placed these in any particular groups or order. As you are looking at them, try to find a way to group them according to particular attributes, or characteristics. For example, we could group some of the groceries together because they are breakfast foods. The characteristic that makes them belong in that group would be that they are eaten for breakfast. Or we could make a group of green foods. The characteristic, or attribute, that makes them belong in that group would be that they are green. What other ways could we group these groceries? What characteristics do the groceries have that allows us to group them in these ways?** Ask students to pair up and try to come up with two different ways that the groceries could be grouped. Ask them to share their ideas by mentioning one of them and identifying the characteristics that allowed them to group this way. POSSIBLE STUDENT RESPONSES: *We could group them by their size, by their weight, by their color, by the kind of food, by which ones are good for a party, by where they get put away at home, by which ones are for baking, by which ones are snacks, by which ones are favorites.*

- **The purpose that you have for grouping things makes a difference in the characteristics that you use as you make your groups. When I go shopping for groceries, I must come home and put them away. I want to be able to find them easily when I need them for a meal, so I don't jumble them all together. I might group together the breakfast foods, or the foods I use for snacks, for example, and keep them each in their own place. I might even put a label on the** cabinet to remind family members what is in there, like "snacks." Then, when someone is looking for a snack, they can find one easily. **When we group things like this and give them a name, we are doing what is called "classification."** Write the word "Classification" on the chalkboard. Under it, write "Your purpose tells you how to classify." **Think about the ways we thought of for classifying groceries. What purpose might you have for classifying the food? How would the reason, or purpose, for classifying affect which characteristic you choose to use for your groupings?** POSSIBLE STUDENT RESPONSES: *If I were putting them away, I would group them so that the things that go in the same place were in the same bag. If I were deciding on food for a party, I would group them to show which things I want for the party and which ones I don't. If I were going on a camping trip, I would put in a group the things I would eat out in the woods.*

- **Groceries are just one thing that can be sorted. In our world, there are many things that can be put into groups for a purpose, or reason. When I am working in the garage, I put things in places according to what I use them for. My yard tools go in one place, my tools for cleaning the car go in another place, and the sports items that the family uses go in yet another place. Think of a time when you needed to sort or classify things. Tell your partner what it was that you sorted. Also tell your partner why you were classifying and the characteristics you used to classify the things.** After allowing some discussion time, ask for three or four volunteers to report one example. POSSIBLE STUDENT RESPONSES: *clothes—by season; toys—by where I play with them; toys—which ones I was going to give away and which ones I wanted to keep; puzzle pieces—which ones were on the edge, which ones were going to go together in the puzzle; books—by the authors.* **When we classify things, it is important to do it well. Otherwise we might not accomplish our purpose. If we did not do a good job in classifying where we put the groceries, some of the foods may have spoiled because they were not properly stored. We might not be able to find things in our rooms or homes when we need them. With your partner, discuss what might go wrong if you didn't classify well the items you just mentioned.** After giving students two or three minutes discussion time, ask a few students to share their ideas.

- **In this lesson, we're going to learn how to group and classify things carefully by thinking about what we are doing. We will examine some things to be classified and then determine the best way to do it. Here is a thinking map that will help us as we work.** Show the primary thinking map for bottom-up classification. Go over the questions, using previous examples to further explain each step.

- **In our reading and writing, we have learned many words. Our lesson today will help us**

BOTTOM-UP CLASSIFICATION
1. **What characteristics do the given items have?**
2. **What ways of classifying items can be based on these characteristics?**
3. **What purpose do we have for classifying the items?**
4. **What way of classifying the items best serves this purpose?**
5. **Which items fall under each classification?**

classify some of these words. **Different ways of classifying the words will tell us different things about them. There will be different purposes for the different types of classification.**

THINKING ACTIVELY

- **In this classification activity, I'm going to ask you to work in groups and not just with partners. We will follow the thinking map as we do the activity. Each group has been given an envelope. In the envelope you will find a set of word cards and some blank cards.** The words you choose for this activity should be a variety of nouns, verbs, and adjectives. They should also be chosen so that they can be put into a number of different groups, such as by the number of letters, double letters, words for things to wear, etc. To help model the grouping, you might want to have a set of the words on a pocket chart or a transparency to manipulate on the overhead. **Spread the cards out on the table (or floor) so that they can be read by everyone in your group. Take a minute to read each card. Question one on the thinking map asks what the characteristics of the items are. Without moving any of the cards, look for characteristics that are shared by some of the words and could be used for classifying. For this first try at classifying, think about just the letters in the words. Are there any words that belong together because of the letters that they have?** Allow time for students to think through some possible types of groupings. Ask two groups to share theirs, and move the words to model how they can be grouped. As you group them, use blank cards to label, for example, "Words that start with *A*" "Words that have double letters," etc., and show the class what you are doing.

- **Question two on the thinking map asks us how we can classify the items based on their characteristics. With your team, discuss some other common characteristics that could be used to group the words. Place the words that share those characteristics into piles. It is not necessary for all the words to be in groups right now. Use blank cards to label the piles just like I did. You might also use the phrase, "Words that..." for your labels.** After a few minutes, ask each group to show the class a sample grouping, their label, and which words are included in the group. Then tell them to rearrange the words into another grouping. Ask each group to report on some of the other classifications they have come up with for their words. **You've found out that there are different ways to classify your words. We can keep a list of the ways that we classified the words on this graphic organizer for Ways to Classify.** Ask each group to report one or two of the ways they classified their words. As the groups report, write the categories down the left side of an enlarged copy of the Ways to Classify graphic organizer that has been placed

WAYS TO CLASSIFY THINGS

CATEGORIES   TYPES OF CATEGORIES

on the board, a chart, or a transparency. When all groups have shared, allow time for students to move around and see the groupings of other teams. POSSIBLE STUDENT RESPONSES: *Words that have four letters, words that have six letters, words that end with "e," words that don't end with "e," words with a double letter, words with one syllable, words with two syllables, words with a long vowel, words with a short vowel.*

- **On the left side of our graphic organizer, we have a list of different ways to classify the words that you have identified. Some of these categories describe the same feature of the words. For example, words that end with "e" and words that don't end with "e" both describe the ending letter/sound of the word. We can show these two ways to classify by giving them another label called "Ending letter/sound." How can we group the other categories on the list to organize them better?** Write "Ending letter/sound" on one of the horizontal lines at the top of the diagram. Connect the appropriate subcategories from the list on the left to the vertical line under "Ending letter/sound." Use multicolored markers or chalk to show the connections more clearly. POSSIBLE STUDENT RESPONSES: *Number of letters, number of syllables, kind of vowel sound, ending letter.*

- **We have many categories for the ways that words are constructed and the letters and sounds that they use. These are good ways to classify words and there are purposes, or reasons, for using these ways of classifying. Work in your groups again and see if you can come up with a purpose for one of the ways we have classified these words.** Assign a way of classifying the words to each group. After a few minutes, ask for responses from a few of the groups. POSSIBLE STUDENT RESPONSES: *We might want to find a word with a special vowel sound or ending letter for a poem we are writing. We might want a word with a certain number of syllables for a song.*

- **There's a second way that we can classify words. Let's look at the words now and think about what the words *mean*. For example, we could have a category of things to do in school.** Write "Words about things to do in school" as a category on the left side of the graphic organizer. Make a grouping of words that would fit into this category (ask, sing, listen, move, follow) and write them on the chalkboard or on a transparency under this heading. **What other groups could you make? Work with your groups to put words together according to their meaning.** Allow the groups time to look for ways to group according to meaning. After the groups have had time to work, have them share their ideas and add them to the left side of the graphic organizer. POSSIBLE STUDENT RESPONSES: *Words for things to do at school, words that are about things to wear, words for places to live, animal names, food names, words for places to go to, words about things to do with your feet, words about things to do with your mind, words about things to do with your mouth, words about things to do with your hands, words that tell about colors, words that tell about how things feel, words that tell about how things look.* **As you were sharing ways to group the words this time, I noticed that we could group some of these categories together. The words that tell about color and how things feel and look are all words that *describe* things. Some people call these words "adjectives."** Write the category label "adjective—words that describe" on the top line of the Ways to Classify graphic organizer.

- **What other categories might be grouped together?** Allow students time to discuss this, and then work together as a class to generate the broad categories of *words for things* and *words about what we do*. Write these on the two other horizontal lines at the top of the graphic organizer. Introduce the terms "nouns" and "verbs" for these types of categories and write the terms above the appropriate description. **Let's use these three general types of categories—nouns, verbs, and adjectives—to group the words on the cards. I have some large sheets of paper that we can use to web the words. The centers of the webs will be nouns, verbs, or adjectives. Then we can add the different, smaller groups coming out from those centers.** Work as a class to build the webs, using the word groupings that students made as part of the noun, verb, and adjective webs. Have the chart paper in a place where everyone in the class can view the webs and assist in the placement of words. This may be on the floor, in an open space, or on a wall.

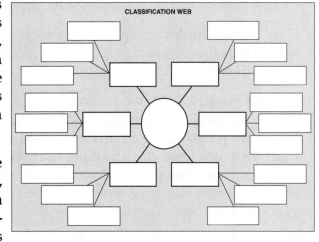

CLASSIFICATION WEB

- **We have classified the words into three groups. These groups were labeled nouns, verbs, and adjectives. The third question on the thinking map asks what might be a purpose for classifying words this way.** Students will usually recognize that these categories are helpful because we use these words in different ways in sentences to say different things. If they have trouble with this, show them some sentences and ask them to identify the kinds of words they see using the category labels.

- **Let's think about why we classify words for this purpose. Using words in sentences according to their meaning helps us communicate with others. When we speak or write, we put together nouns, verbs, and adjectives to share our ideas and tell people things. For this reason, they are called "Parts of Speech." They are parts of the language, or speech, that we use when we communicate. There are also other categories of words, but for now we will just be looking at these three. The last question on the thinking map asks us to decide which items fall under each classification. When we are talking about people or things, we use the words that name them, such as ball, man, or street. When we want to tell about an action, we use a verb, perhaps run, read, think, or eat. And if we want to describe something, we would use a word such as pretty, scary, blue, or terrific. Take a few minutes and work with your partner. See if you can take words from each of the webs and put them together to make a sentence. You may fill in words that are not on the chart, but each sentence should have a noun, a verb, and an adjective from our webs.** Model this activity for students with several sentences. Allow time for the student pairs to share sentences orally with each other. ANSWERS VARY.

- **Let's check back to our thinking map to remember the thinking we've done so far. The first question asked us what things we noticed about the items. We noticed that they were used in different ways. The second question asked about what classifications could be made using the things we noticed. What were the ways of classifying words that we chose to use?** *Nouns, verbs, and adjectives.* **What purpose did we have for classifying the words? That's question three on the thinking map.** *We were grouping according to how the words were used in sentences.* **The final question asked us which items fell into each category. How did we show this?** *We made a web and put the words in the right places.* **As you read and write, you will learn many more words that fall into these three groups. You will also learn about more groups for the ways that words are used. Today's lesson was a good start in thinking about the different kinds of words we have in our language.**

THINKING ABOUT THINKING

- **I want you to think back to the things we did as we classified words. What did you do first, second, etc.?** POSSIBLE STUDENT RESPONSES: *We looked for things (characteristics) that would be reasons to put the words together. We gave the groups labels, then we put groups together with other groups that were using the same characteristic, like beginning sound, or number of letters. We then put the words into groups that showed how the words would be used in sentences.*

- **How did the thinking map help you as you were working?** Students usually repeat the steps as they remember what they did as they practiced classifying. They may discuss how the steps helped them make different groups before they went with one final set of classifications.

- **For this classification, we worked from the bottom up. That means we looked at all the things we wanted to group and created a variety of categories. Then we picked one that suited our purpose. The opposite of this kind of classification is called "top-down classification." In a top-down classification, the categories are provided for you. How would this be different from what we did?** POSSIBLE STUDENT RESPONSES: *There are more kinds of groups when we do bottom-up classifying because you don't all begin doing the same thing. We got to change our groups over and over as we made new labels.*

- **Did classifying words this way help you understand the way they are used?** POSSIBLE STU-

DENT RESPONSE: *I think it will be helpful for me when I am writing stories and I want to think of a word that is an adjective or a noun or a verb.*

APPLYING YOUR THINKING

Immediate Transfer

- Look at one of the stories you have written. Make a list of the words that are not nouns, verbs, and adjectives. Do a bottom-up classification of these words.

- Suppose you were the owner of a pet store. Make a list of all of the pets that might be in your store. How would you organize the pets in your store so that your customers can find the pets they want to buy? Use the thinking map to find the best way of classify the animals.

Reinforcement Later

- We have been studying animals that live in or near the water. Create a way of classifying these animals into smaller groups. Use a Classification Web to show your categories. What are the defining characteristics of the groups?

- We have studied transportation. Design a way to classify the different modes of transportation. What was your purpose? Explain why you chose the categories.

CONTENT EXTENSION

Have students create one sentence from the class webs. This will help them make the connection that putting words together can make meaningful statements. The sentence/picture sheets can be displayed near the webs or put into a class book.

Provide each group with a large sheet of bulletin board paper. Have groups draw a different classification web of words. They may use the parts of speech classification or some other type of category. Word cards can be glued on the web, and illustrations can be added to show meaning. Word cards from the original lesson can be used and additional cards can be provided to add other appropriate words to the categories. You may also want to help them draw a freehand graphic to illustrate their classification scheme.

WRITING EXTENSION

After this lesson, students will be able to write a framed definition poem to solidify the terms presented in the lesson. Use the frame for a definition poem as presented in the Appendix. The poem frame could be similar to the one presented in the sample at the end of the lesson. The framed sections should be developed with the students as a class activity. Each student then fills in the rest of the poem independently or in pairs. The framed sections are underlined so that the teacher can identify them.

SUGGESTED SPECIAL NEEDS MODIFICATIONS

Frontload: Some students may need a refresher in sorting by attribute. The teacher may wish to provide concrete objects to sort by color, shape, etc. prior to this lesson. Practice may also be part of a mathematics lesson in which students sort geometric shapes.

Clarify: The term "characteristics" may be unfamiliar to some students. The term should be used as the teacher explains the qualities of the objects that cause them to be grouped together.

For example, "Cereal, toast, juice and eggs are grouped together because they are breakfast foods. The characteristic they share is that they are all food we eat for breakfast. Can you think of another food that has this characteristic?" Provide students several guided examples so that the term "characteristic" becomes more clear to them.

Diversify: Students may find sorting a wide unspecified group of words overwhelming. A smaller selection of familiar words from the larger group will be less demanding. Similarly, limit the number of categories on the graphic organizer.

Special needs students are often aided by working in cooperative groups. Establish an atmosphere in which all answers are initially accepted in such groups.

Expand the Possibilities: Assessments of written responses may be based upon students' thinking first, and expressive skills second. Oral responses or a freehand drawing linking the objects classified in a mind-map may also reveal thinking beyond students' ability to express themselves in writing.

ASSESSING STUDENT THINKING ABOUT CLASSIFICATION

To assess students' skill in classification, question them about the process they followed in any of the transfer activities, their purpose in choosing the types of categories they used, and their choice of classification. Encourage students to use the language of the strategy (e.g., characteristics, classify, label, groups, classification, purpose).

Sample Student Responses • Nouns, Verbs, Adjectives

WAYS TO CLASSIFY THINGS

CATEGORIES	TYPES OF CATEGORIES				
	adjectives—describing		verbs—actions	nouns—names	
	#of letters	vowel sound	ending letter	#of syllables	
words that have four letters—					
words that have six letters—					
words that end with an "e"—					
words that don't end with an "e"—					
words with a double letter—					
words with one syllable—					
words with two syllables—					
words with a long vowel—					
words with a short vowel—					
words that are names of places—					
words that are things to do in school—					
animal names—					
food names—					
words that tell about size—					
words that tell about emotions—					
things to do with your mouth—					
things to do with your feet—					
things to do with your hands—					

Possible Word List • Nouns, Verbs, Adjectives

house	slow	goose	brave	town
fancy	sleep	puppy	milk	farm
jumps	mother	run	candy	beach
necklace	wonderful	soft	dive	huge
read	sing	skip	trade	
whale	bus	hop	funny	
listen	bike	wiggle	toe	
terrific	wet	chilly	leg	
small	street	quick	belly	
scatter	fast	shirt	plane	
pumpkin	grow	cookie	truck	
purple	baby	take	finger	
kitten	scary	count	yellow	
large	move	sister	bee	
ask	wear	dress	tiger	
school	long	coat	pickle	
follow	puppet	tap	church	
sweater	dance	pretty	park	
favorite	hot	important	bedroom	
try	hard	think	moon	

Sample Student Responses • Nouns, Verbs, Adjectives

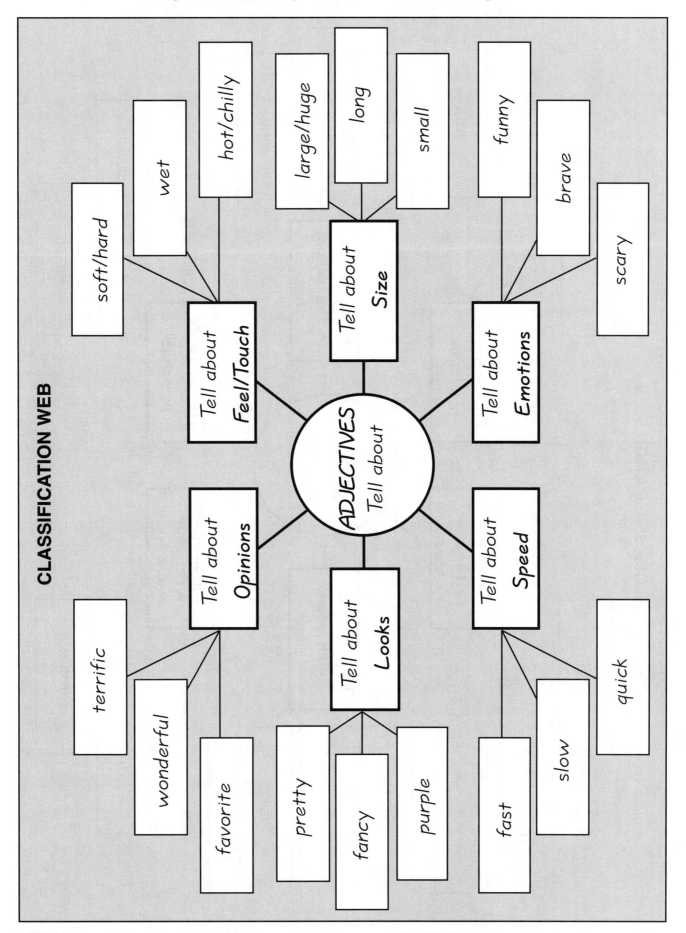

CLASSIFICATION WEB

ADJECTIVES
Tell about

Tell about *Size*
- large/huge
- long
- small

Tell about *Feel/Touch*
- soft/hard
- wet
- hot/chilly

Tell about *Emotions*
- funny
- brave
- scary

Tell about *Opinions*
- terrific
- wonderful
- favorite

Tell about *Looks*
- pretty
- fancy
- purple

Tell about *Speed*
- fast
- slow
- quick

Sample Student Responses • Nouns, Verbs, Adjectives

CLASSIFICATION WEB

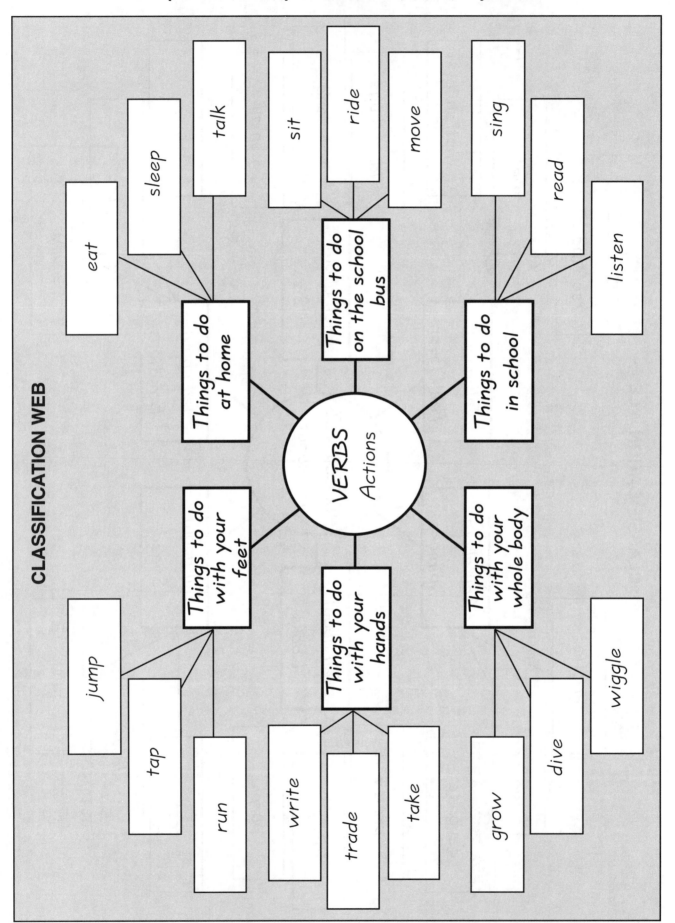

Sample Student Responses • Nouns, Verbs, Adjectives

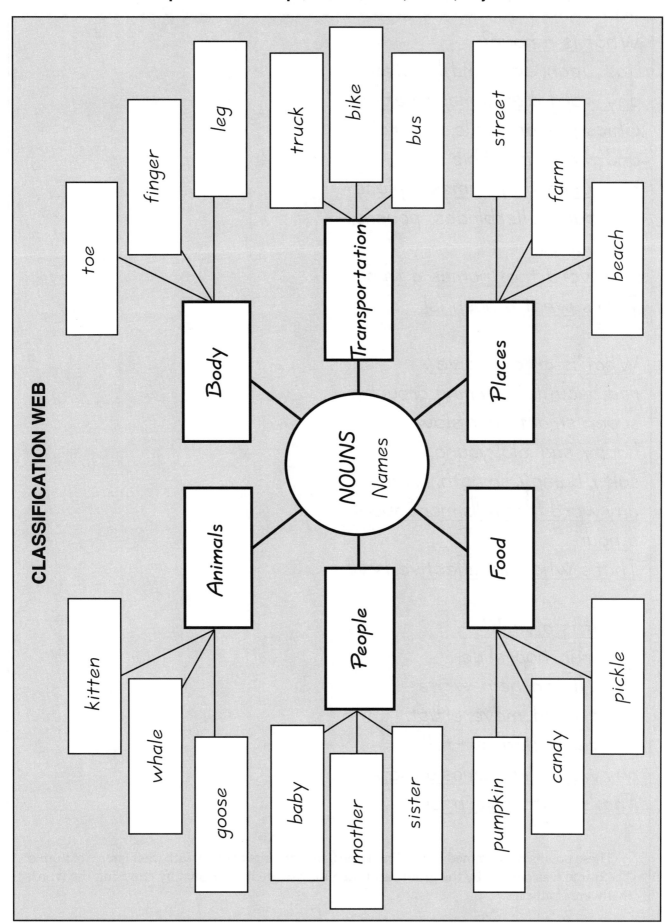

CLASSIFICATION WEB

Sample Student Definition Poems (Grade 2) • Noun, Verbs, Adjectives

What is a noun?
Joe, Jean, Sam, and Kristen
any word that names a person
Chicago, Naperville, Australia,
and the North Pole
any word that names a place
baseball, rollerblades, pencils,
and books
any word that names a thing
That's what a noun is!

What is an adjective?
red, beautiful, sleeping, grouchy,
super, smart, fast, slow,
happy, sad, old, young,
salty, bumpy, smooth, rough,
any word that tells more about
a noun
That's what an adjective is!

What is a verb?
skip, run, hop, slide,
read, listen, help, write,
shine, bend, move, erupt,
freeze, melt, grow, fall
any word that names an action,
That's what a verb is!

(These poems were framed (underlined lines) for students to fill in with their choice of nouns.
The frame was created by the group, and then they made it their own by choosing the words
that were examples.)

HOUSES, HOUSES, AND MORE HOUSES
A HOUSE IS A HOUSE FOR ME

Language Arts   **Grades 1–2**

OBJECTIVES

CONTENT

Students will explore the ways that the author defines the term "house" as they read *A House Is a House for Me.*

THINKING SKILL/PROCESS

Students will learn to classify individual things by determining whether their characteristics match the defining characteristics of specific classes.

METHODS AND MATERIALS

CONTENT

Students will have previously read *A House Is a House for Me* by Mary Ann Hoberman. They will work together to examine the text and illustrations. Prior study of different kinds of houses people live in is desirable.

THINKING SKILL/PROCESS

Students will be guided by specific questions and directions to engage in top-down classification. Students will use two graphic organizers: one for defining the categories, the other for classifying specific items. Students will construct a classification web and write a class book to illustrate their classification of the items in the lesson.

LESSON

INTRODUCTION TO CONTENT AND THINKING SKILL/PROCESS

- **I'd like you to study the set of pictures I have placed in our pocket chart.** In a pocket chart, display a set of twelve to fifteen pictures showing a variety of plants that could be grown in a yard or garden. **I have not grouped the plants in any particular group or order. As you are looking at the pictures, try to find ways to group them.** Allow think time, then ask the students to share ways that the plants could be grouped. Move the pictures in the pocket chart to create the groups. Make labeling the categories a class effort. POSSIBLE STUDENT RESPONSES: *trees, vegetable plants, fruit trees, bushes, flowers, grasses.*

- **The thinking that you are doing now is called "classifying." That means that you are thinking about grouping things together because they are similar in certain ways.** Write the term, "Classify" on the chalkboard or a chart. **There are lots of ways that you can group and classify things. I'm going to give you a specific purpose for grouping the plants. Let's see if this purpose will change the way that you group, or classify, the plants. A friend of mine would like to do some planting at her house. She wants to put some of these plants in her front yard and others in her back yard. Here are some important details you will need to know. Her front yard is much smaller than her back yard, and looks out over a lake. She enjoys seeing the lake from her front windows. It is a beautiful view. In her back yard, she likes to sit in the shade on her patio and listen to the many birds. She also likes to work in her back yard garden.**

- **The things I've told you about my friend's yard will help us classify the plants. We will know where each plant would work best. I have some cards that we will use to label the groups, or categories. The cards say, "front yard plants," "backyard plants," and "either yard** plants." **Some of the plants belong in the front yard, some in the back yard, and some of the plants could go in either yard.** Put the cards in the pocket chart so that the plant pictures can be arranged underneath.

- **We need to remember the details that I told you about the front and back yards so that you can think about what plants would work well in each yard. There are certain things that must be true of the plant for it to be planted in the front yard. I said that the front yard is small and that my friend likes to look out her front window and see the lake. What kind of plants would be good for my friend to plant in her front yard?** POSSIBLE STUDENT RESPONSES: *Ones that are pretty to look at and small enough to allow your friend to have a good view of the lake.* Place a card with the words, "pretty to look at" and "allows a good view of the lake (not too big)" in the pocket chart next to the card for the front yard. **We call these the "defining characteristics" for the front yard plants. They tell us which plants my friend would like in her front yard.** Write the term, "defining characteristic" on the chart or chalkboard. **In order for a plant to fit into this group, it must have the defining characteristics that we list for the group. In this case, it must be pretty to look at and small enough to allow a good view of the lake.**

- **I said that my friend likes to sit in the shade on her patio and listen to the birds in the back yard. She likes to garden there, too. What plants could be in her back yard?** POSSIBLE STUDENT RESPONSES: *Ones that make shade, or can be a home for birds, or belong in a garden.* **The defining characteristics for the back yard are "provide a home for birds," "provide shade," and "garden plants." These plants will give my friend all the things she needs to enjoy being in her back yard.** Place a card with the words, "provide a home for birds," "provide shade," and "garden plants" next to the card for the back yard. **The third category has as its defining characteristics "plants that fit in either the front yard or the back yard."** Place another card with those words next to the card for "either yard."

- **This kind of classification is called "top-down classification" because we are setting the categories up first, and then filling them with items that fit the characteristics. We can look at each plant to see its characteristics. We then match the plant to the category in which it fits. I am going to pass out plant pictures to each group. The group will discuss the plants characteristics and match them to the defining characteristics of the categories.** Allow time for groups to check their plants against the characteristics of the categories to find the correct spot. As a class, place them under the correct label on the pocket chart.

- **We have decided on the classification of the plants for my friend's yard. Can you think of other plants that would also fit into one of the categories? The new plants will fit into a category if they match the defining characteristics of the category, or group.** Allow time for discussion and then add a plant from each group to one of the categories, using cards to write the names. Have the group explain how their plant fits into the category. ANSWERS VARY.

- **This thinking map shows what you have done as you classified the plants. It will help you as you classify items from the top down.** Show the thinking map for top-down classification and go over the three questions, relating them to the classifying of plants.

TOP-DOWN CLASSIFICATION

1. **What are the defining characteristics of the categories under which I want to classify things?**

2. **Which items have these characteristics?**

3. **How do I classify these items into the given categories?**

THINKING ACTIVELY

- **We have been reading about and studying houses. There are many different types of houses used by people around the world. In your groups, I'd like you to talk about some of the different kinds of houses we have studied.** Remind students of any pertinent information or activities from their previous study of houses that will prompt them to think of the various types of housing. For example, showing them pictures of different kinds of houses that humans live in (a ranch house in the USA, an igloo, a tent) can be enough to remind them of others. Also remind them that the kind of house is often determined by the location, available building materials, and needs of the people living in it. You can ask helpful questions like "Why do you think a tent is light in weight?"

- **One of the books we read was** *A House Is a House for Me,* **by Mary Ann Hoberman. In the book, the author tells us about many kinds of houses, but she also tries to help us understand what makes something a house.** Write on the chalkboard or on a flipchart "What is a *house*?" **Maybe if we classify the different kinds of houses the author shows us, we can figure out what they all have in common.**

- **Mary Ann Hoberman, the author, tells us about three sorts of houses. Let me show you some pictures to see if you can identify the houses by what lives in them.** Show students pictures of two animal houses, two people houses, and two "houses" for things (like a garage). Students usually have no trouble identifying these types of houses. However, if they do, prompt them by asking them to complete the sentence orally "The kinds of things that live or stay in these houses are _____." When they have identified them, write these three categories on a chart or chalkboard. **This is a very broad classification of the houses in the book. That means that these three groups are very large. They are large because we only have one defining characteristic for each group. That defining characteristic would be "places where animals live," or "places where people live," and "places where things stay."** Point to the appropriate category as the defining characteristic is read. **As we reread the book, pay attention to the many different kinds of houses Hoberman includes in her book and think about which kind of house each is.** Reread the story to or with students. Take time as the text is read to make sure students have time to process the different ideas. You might do his by pausing and asking focus questions like "Who lives in this kind of house?"

- **Now let's think about what the book lists as houses for animals. We will be working on those houses first. One kind of house in the book is a kennel. The story said, "A kennel is a house for a dog." When I think about what is special about this kind of house, I think about the fact that it is a house made by people for a dog to live in. We can classify and label this type of house as a "Person-made animal house." There are other houses that would fit into the category "Person-made animal houses." What would be the defining characteristics of this type of house?** Most students respond by saying that it is a place where animals live and that is made by people. **Yes, we can say that person-made animal houses have two defining characteristics: they are "houses *made by people*" and "houses *where animals live.*" We have answered the first question on our thinking map for Top-Down Classification.** Refer back to the thinking map to show students the question "What are the defining characteristics of the categories under which I want to classify things?"

- **We have labeled and identified the defining characteristics of one of the groups of animal houses. Now let's work together to pick out other categories, or different kinds, of animal houses that are described in the book. We will give each category a label, just as we labeled the first category, "Person-made animal house." The first step will be to find animal houses** in the book that belong in different categories. Let's take a minute to find some of the other kinds of animal houses. I will record the animal house categories on a chart as you find them in the book. Try to find one or two examples of each different kind of animal house you identify. Work as a class for this part of the lesson. Students should look in their books for animal houses. Have them read the sections that name the houses. Or, if there is no actual text that does so, identify them through the illustrations. Have them put a sticky note on the page the example appears with the name of the kind of animal house that they have found. Guide students in this part of the lesson as necessary by pointing out particular animal houses that would belong in different categories, though let them think about how to classify them. Tell them that once they have identified a different kind of animal house and labelled it, they should think about what the defining characteristics are of that type of house. After a few minutes, ask volunteers to tell about one type of house that they found and to show where it is in the book. Write the labels and defining characteristics on the chart under the words "category" and "defining characteristics." (If necessary, modeling can be done with another think aloud. For example, you might say "I see that there is a mudhole on this page. The author says that it is a house for a mosquito. It seems to me that this is a house made by rain and dirt mixing together. I guess I could call it an 'animal house made in nature.' The defining characteristics of an animal house made by nature would be that it is made by nature and it is a place where animals live.") POSSIBLE STUDENT RESPONSES: *Animal-made animal houses (Defining characteristics: Places that animals live in that they make themselves), Nature-made animal houses (Defining characteristics: Places that animals live in and that already exist in nature).*

- **We have created labels and identified the defining characteristics for three animal-house categories. The labels and the defining characteristics for the three animal-house categories can be recorded on this graphic organizer for top-down classification.** Show students a blown-up version of the Top-Down Classification—Defining the Categories graphic organizer with the words "Animal Houses" written in the top box. It should have three categories. The classification labels and defining characteristics should be written in the appropriate spaces, but the space for items left blank.

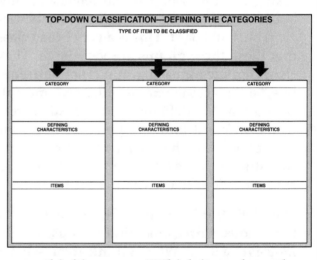

- **Our task now moves to the second question on our thinking map, "Which items have these characteristics?" We are working with animal houses, so that means we have to find the animal houses in the book. The third question on the thinking map asks, "How do I classify these items into the given categories?" As we find the animal houses, we will look at their defining characteristics so that we can put them into their correct categories. For example, the kennel has the defining characteristics of the category "person-made house," so it belongs in that group. After we have done this, we will write the type of house under the correct category in the "Items" box.**

- **Each group will be given a list of animal homes to find in the book. You will also be given another graphic organizer on which to write the name of the house, the characteristics it has, and how it is classified. For example, if you were given the anthill house, you would write "anthill" in the "Item To Be Classified" box. Then you would look for the anthill in the book. That way you could use the picture in the book to help you see all of its characteristics.**

Next you would write the characteristics in the box. Last, you would classify the type of house using one of the categories from our first graphic organizer, Top-Down Classification—Defining the Categories. Model this on a transparency of the Top-Down Classification—Classifying The Items graphic organizer. Put "anthill" in the "Item to be Classified" section. **What do we know about anthills that would tell us what category they belong in?** POSSIBLE STUDENT RESPONSES: *Ants make their own houses. They dig and carry dirt around to make the house.* In the characteristics section, write "Ants dig and carry little pieces of dirt to make their own house." **These characteristics fit with the defining characteristics of which group?** *Animal-made houses.* **Yes, that seems to be a fit, so your group would write "animal-made houses" in the box for "How Classified."**

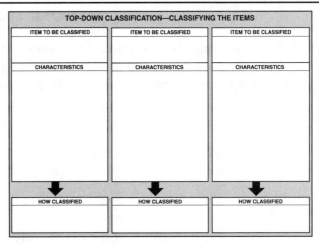

- **Now it is time for you to classify some of the other houses in your groups.** The items listed should be divided so that the groups have different "houses" to classify. There are twenty-nine other houses for animals in the book, so putting students in groups of three would allow each group to have at least three items to classify. (A list of the houses is included at the end of this lesson). The graphic organizer for the groups is an adaptation of the class graphic organizer that provides space for three items to be classified. Allow time for students to work. If there are groups that finish early, have them use extra graphic organizers to add some houses that are not mentioned in the book but that fit the defining characteristics of one of the groups. When they have finished, the groups should share their work and the thinking that they did to classify the houses.

- **The categories we have been working with can be extended by adding more houses. Let's do some brainstorming to see if we can think of other houses.** Share the work done by any of the groups who finished the first classification task early, then work with the class to add to the lists of items in the different categories. Use a different colored marker or chalk to identify and separate the ideas of the author from ideas of the class. As the class is working, continue to check to see that the item matches the defining characteristics of the category.

- **Can we use the information we have gathered and organized so far to help us determine the defining characteristics of a house? What do we know about houses from this activity?** Students' discussion should be guided to help them identify the defining characteristics of houses as places that humans and animals live in, or that cover and provide protection.

- **Now we've come up with the defining characteristics of a house: A house is a place to live in or a place that covers and provides protection. Let's test this definition on a couple of the other items from the book. Ms. Hoberman said that "a book is a house for a story." How does this fit with our definition?** POSSIBLE STUDENT RESPONSES: *A story is in a book, and the covers protect it. Since it is written down in the book, the story is protected from being forgotten.* **What about "a rose is a house for a smell?"** *The smell is inside the rose, and all the petals and leaves keep the smell so it has a place to "live."*

THINKING ABOUT THINKING

- **What questions were important to answer as you did this kind of thinking?** Students should mention the questions that are on the thinking map for classifying top-down. Help them recognize that there are two stages to this process: identifying the defining characteristics of the category and putting items into the category based on the characteristics of the item and the defining characteristics of the category into which it is placed.

- **Is this a helpful way to classify things? Why?** Most students say that it is because they can be sure that the category they put things in is the right category.

- **Why do you think this way of classifying things is called "Top-Down Classification?"** Most students recognize that in this kind of classification you start with categories that are given and put items under them. (If you have already done an activity using Bottom-Up Classification, ask students what the difference is between these. They should recognize that in bottom-up classification you start with the items and build "up" to their classification, whereas in Top-Down Classification, you start with the categories and then look at the items that fall under them.

- **How does classifying houses help you understand the meaning of the term "house"?** POSSIBLE STUDENT RESPONSES: *It shows what a house is. I can see the characteristics of a house, so I know what is needed for something to be a house.*

- **In this activity, you worked in groups. Is this a good way to do classification?** Most students say that they like to work in groups because they get ideas from other students Their teammates help them check to see if the item fits in the category.

- **You used a graphic organizer to record the thinking you did in this lesson. How did this help you as you grouped the houses? How did it help you as you worked to make a definition of the term "house"?** Students usually state that they could keep track of which houses they thought about by using the graphic organizer. It helped them to understand houses because everything could be seen all together.

APPLYING YOUR THINKING

Immediate Transfer

- **The number of categories in a classification depends on the purpose and the defining characteristics of the groups. Let's do the same thing we did for "animal houses" for "houses for people" and "houses for things." As we look at the graphic organizers for houses for people and houses for things, we'll find each has just two categories.** Show chart-sized graphic organizers for "houses for people" and "houses for things." The groups will be working on the same graphic organizer sheet they used in the animal-house classification, though redrawn so that it has only two blank category boxes. The "houses for things" categories will be "houses made by men" and "houses made by nature." The people categories are "places to live in" and "coverings." Using a chart-sized copy of the houses to be classified as people houses and copies of the book *A House Is a House for Me*, work as a group to generate labels and defining characteristics for the two categories. Write these on a chart copy of the Defining the Categories graphic organizer. Repeat for "house for things," using another chart-sized copy of the Defining the Categories graphic organizer. **Now we have identified the categories and their defining characteristics. Each of our small groups will have a list of houses to fit into the categories. You will use copies of the Items to be Classified graphic organizer to help you place each house** in the right category. Once your group has decided on the category, you may record the house on our charts. Pass out a list of 5–6 houses to classify and copies of the Items to be Classified graphic organizer. Support students as they think through this second round of classification. If groups finish early, provide extra graphic organizers for the students to add houses not mentioned in the book. Share results when all groups have completed their tasks.

- Specify different categories of modes of transportation (e.g., "Land Vehicles"). Ask students to use top-down classification to put items (either from a predetermined list or from a list that they generate) into the categories in which they belong and to be prepared to explain why they belong where they were put.

Reinforcement Later

- Keep a record of the food you eat in one day. Classify the items on your list according to the food groups. Use the thinking map and graphic organizers for top-down classification to help you with your thinking. What does this tell you about the way that you eat? Are there any things you should change in your eating habits?

- In our Earth Days studies, we have read the book *The Great Kapok Tree*, by Lynne Cherry. Use the book to classify the animals according to the level of vegetation where they live in the rain forest.

WRITING EXTENSION

To demonstrate what students have learned, have them write a class book about houses. Each student will make a different house for the book, which will be organized into chapters titled after the classification labels used in the lesson. Provide students with pre-formatted pages for the book. A page might say, "A (blank) is a house for a (blank), but a house is a house for me." The page could be shaped like a house, and the door could be opened to reveal a small picture of their example taped to the back to fill the doorway. It may be necessary to sign up students for the houses they want to illustrate so that the pages are different. The houses in the class book can be a combination of the ideas from the original book and the ideas from the class.

SUGGESTED SPECIAL NEEDS MODIFICATIONS

<u>Frontload</u>: Some students may also benefit from a refresher in sorting by attribute. This can be done across subject areas as students sort and classify geometric shapes, complete word sorts, or list story characters by similar traits.

<u>Clarify</u>: Terminology may need to be simplified or paired with a synonym for some students. For example, "classifying" can also be described as "sorting by things in common."

<u>Diversify</u>: Assigning the task of writing to a proficient writer in the cooperative group allows all students to contribute ideas while reducing the task load for beginning writers.

<u>Expand the Possibilities</u>: Assessments of written responses may be based upon students' thinking first, and expressive skills second. Oral responses may also reveal thinking beyond students' ability to express themselves in writing.

ASSESSING STUDENT THINKING ABOUT POSSIBILITIES

Using the activities in the application section of this lesson to assess students' skill in classification allows students to display their knowledge in a variety of ways. They can be asked to use the graphic organizers or to draw their own. It is important that students show their thinking by explaining their work and using the terms of the classification strategy in their explanation.

Houses for Animals, from *A House Is a House for Me*

anthill

beehive

mole hole

mouse hole

spider web

bird nest

coop (chicken)

sty (pig)

fold (sheep)

barn (cow, horse)

kennel (dog)

hutch (rabbit)

shed (mule)

rug (bug)

dog (flea)

boy (flea)

mudhole (mosquitoes)

puddle (mosquitoes)

ocean (whales)

sea (whales)

lake (fish, snake)

tree (monkeys)

river (hippos)

the open (lions)

shell (shellfish, oysters, lobsters, clams, snail, turtle)

eggshell (chick)

pouch (kangaroo joey)

cage (hamster)

stall (donkey)

Sample Student Responses • Houses, Houses, and More Houses

TOP-DOWN CLASSIFICATION—DEFINING THE CATEGORIES

TYPE OF ITEM TO BE CLASSIFIED

ANIMAL HOUSES

CATEGORY

nature-made animal houses

DEFINING CHARACTERISTICS

a place in nature where an animal lives

ITEMS

puddle (mosquito)
ocean (whales)
pouch (kangaroo)
tree (monkeys)
river (hippos)
shell (turtle)

CATEGORY

person-made animal houses

DEFINING CHARACTERISTICS

a structure made by people for an animal to live in

ITEMS

coop (chicken)
sty (pig)
fold (sheep)
barn (cow)
kennel (dog)
hutch (rabbit)
shed (mule)

CATEGORY

animal-made animal houses

DEFINING CHARACTERISTICS

a structure made by an animal to live in

ITEMS

anthill
beehive
mole hole
spider web
bird nest

Sample Student Responses • Houses, Houses, and More Houses

TOP-DOWN CLASSIFICATION—CLASSIFYING THE ITEMS

ITEM TO BE CLASSIFIED	ITEM TO BE CLASSIFIED	ITEM TO BE CLASSIFIED
coop	mudhole	turtle shell
CHARACTERISTICS	**CHARACTERISTICS**	**CHARACTERISTICS**
A coop is a house that is made for chickens to live in. Farmers make it.	Rain comes down and mixes with dirt. That makes a mudhole that animals live in.	A turtle is born with a shell. It lives in its own body covering.
HOW CLASSIFIED	**HOW CLASSIFIED**	**HOW CLASSIFIED**
Person-made animal home	Nature-made home	Nature-made home

Houses for Immediate Transfer Activities • Houses, Houses, Houses

Houses for People

igloo	snow fort	shoe
teepee	cardboard box	boot
pueblo	beach umbrella	hat
wigwam	table	Band-Aid
tent	glove	coat
castle	stocking	

Houses for Things

box	barrel	rose
teapot	bottle	garage
person	pot	hangar
carton	sandwich	dock (slip)
bag	cookie jar	terminal
mitt	bread box	peach
basket	mirror	pumpkin
tic tac toe	pocket	nutshell
bowl	pen	pod
pin cushion	trash can	husk
tube		
toothbrush		

Sample Student Writing Using a Sentence Frame • Houses, Houses, and More Houses

Each of the sentences would be on its own page and would be accompanied by a picture.

A <u>brain</u> is a house for <u>ideas</u> and a house is a house for me!

A <u>bowl</u> is a house for <u>soup</u> and a house is a house for me!

A <u>mouth</u> is a house for <u>teeth</u> and a house is a house for me!

A <u>skyscraper</u> is a house for <u>offices</u> and a house is a house for

me!

BOTTOM-UP CLASSIFICATION

1. What characteristics do the given items have?

2. What ways of classifying items can be based on these characteristics?

3. What purpose do we have for classifying the items?

4. What way of classifying the items best serves this purpose?

5. Which items fall under each classification?

WAYS TO CLASSIFY THINGS

CATEGORIES

TYPES OF CATEGORIES

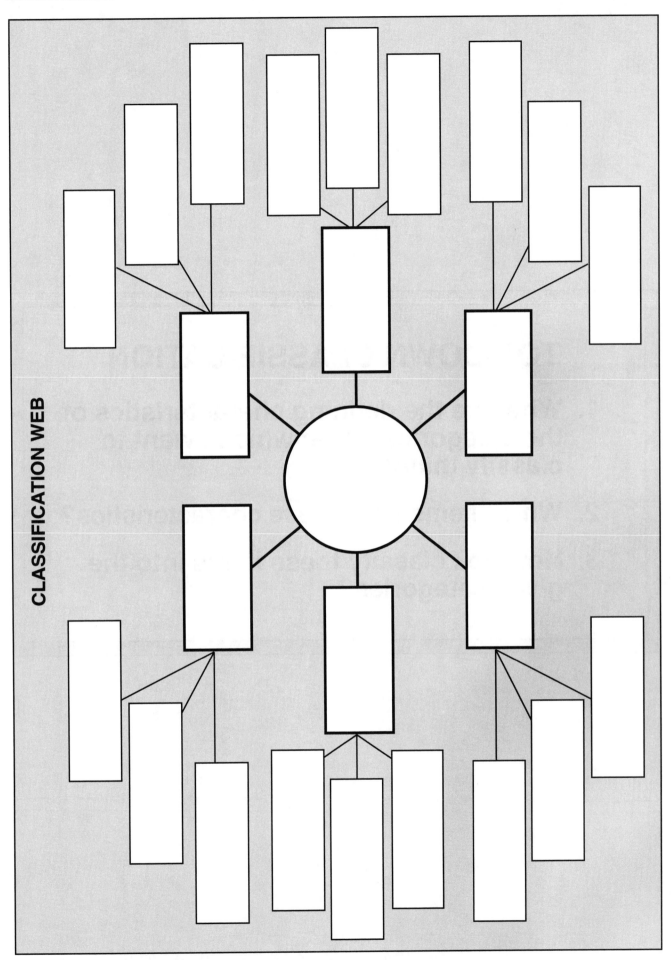

CLASSIFICATION WEB

TOP-DOWN CLASSIFICATION

1. **What are the defining characteristics of the categories under which I want to classify things?**

2. **Which items have these characteristics?**

3. **How do I classify these items into the given categories?**

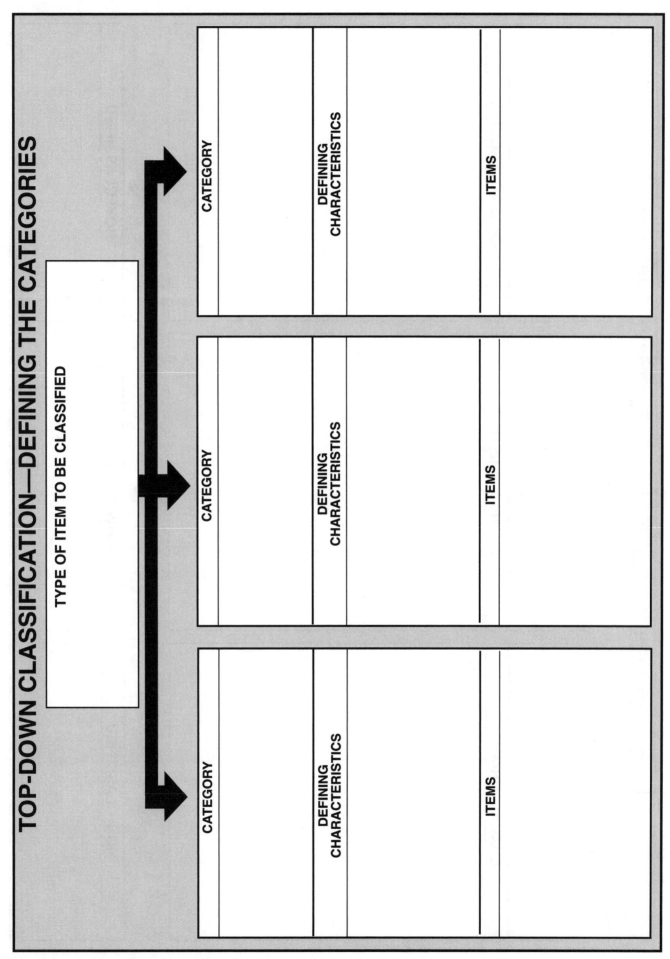

TOP-DOWN CLASSIFICATION—DEFINING THE CATEGORIES

TYPE OF ITEM TO BE CLASSIFIED

CATEGORY

DEFINING CHARACTERISTICS

ITEMS

CATEGORY

DEFINING CHARACTERISTICS

ITEMS

CATEGORY

DEFINING CHARACTERISTICS

ITEMS

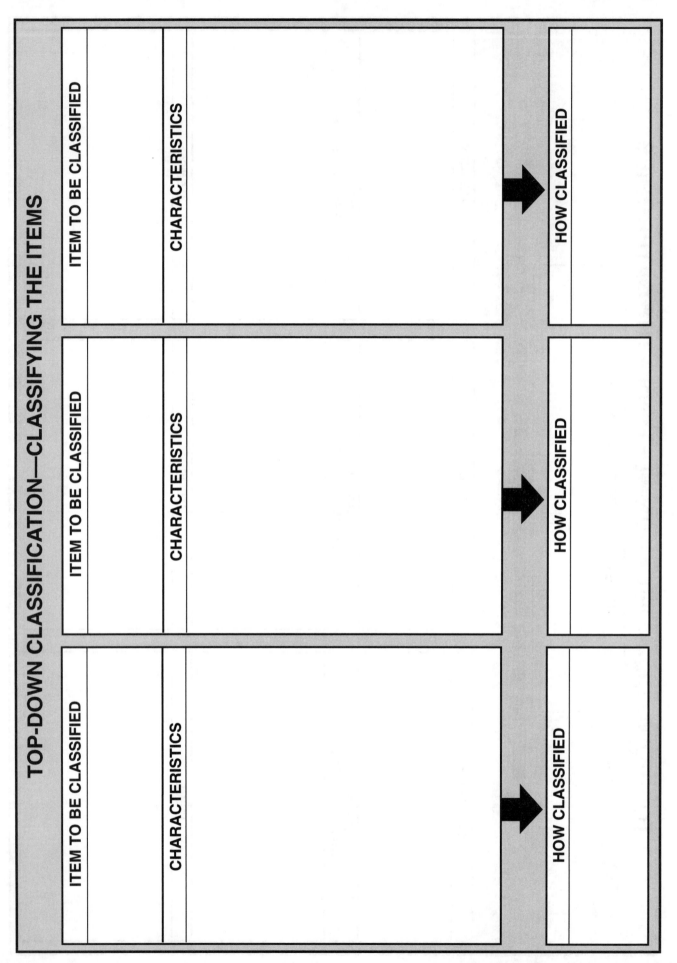

TOP-DOWN CLASSIFICATION—CLASSIFYING THE ITEMS

ITEM TO BE CLASSIFIED

CHARACTERISTICS

HOW CLASSIFIED

ITEM TO BE CLASSIFIED

CHARACTERISTICS

HOW CLASSIFIED

ITEM TO BE CLASSIFIED

CHARACTERISTICS

HOW CLASSIFIED

CHAPTER 7
PARTS-WHOLE RELATIONSHIPS

Infusing Determining Parts-Whole Relationships into Language Arts

Teaching students how to skillfully determine parts-whole relationships in grades 1 and 2 involves helping them learn to ask and carefully answer the following questions about whole items and the parts from which they are made:

DETERMINING PARTS-WHOLE RELATIONSHIPS

1. **What smaller things make up the whole?**

2. **For each part, what would happen if it were missing?**

3. **What is the function of each part?**

4. **How do the parts work together to make the whole what it is or operate as it does?**

---

figure 7.1

In the lessons on parts of a whole, this thinking map is used to guide your students' thinking explicitly as they engage with the lesson content.

When students learn and use this strategy for thinking about the relationship between parts and the whole they are part of, they don't stop simply by listing parts. They must also determine the function of the parts in the whole by considering what would happen if specific parts were missing. They then draw conclusions based on how the parts work together to make the whole operate as it does. This yields a deep understanding of the thing they are analyzing. For example, they will not simply tell you that one of the parts of a song is its words. They will also articulate the function of the words—to tell a story that can be sung along with the music—and be able to illustrate this by reference to what happens when the song is sung.

In these lessons, the use of this thinking map is supplemented with various supporting class-room strategies such as using graphic organizers, engaging in cooperative thinking, thinking about thinking, and continued guided practice. These classroom strategies enhance both the thinking skill that the students are learning and their mastery of the lesson content.

The key graphic organizers for determining parts-whole relationships are in figures 7.2 and 7.3 (see following page). Reproducible blank graphic organizers are found at the end of each chapter.

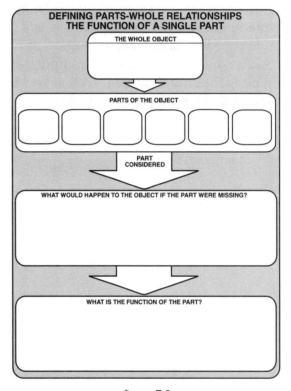

figure 7.2

In the first graphic organizer, shown in figure 7.2, students write the names of a large number of parts of an object in the boxes at the top of the diagram. Students then focus on one of the parts and write it down in the "Part Considered" arrow. In the following box, students write what they think will happen if the part were missing. In the last box, students write a clear statement of the function of the part, based on what they think would happen if the part were missing. The second graphic organizer, shown in figure 7.3, should be made into a large chart and used at the front of the room to record what individual students or student groups develop on their single-part graphics, and then to compose a paragraph answering the last question on the thinking map, "How do the parts work together to make the whole object operate as it does?" Such statements show deep learning, when students don't simply say things like "The parts all work together" but mention the parts, what they do, and how what they do leads to another part doing what it does. Reproducible blank graphic organizers are found at the end of each chapter.

For more in-depth information on teaching skillful parts-whole analysis, please refer to Chapter 6 in the book *Infusing Critical and Creative thinking into Elementary Instruction*, by Robert Swartz and Sandra Parks. A computer disk containing the graphic organizers that are in the lessons in this book is also available.

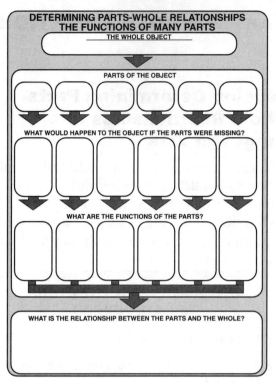

figure 7.3

DO YOU SEE WHAT I SEE?
SEVEN BLIND MICE

Language Arts

Grades 1–2

OBJECTIVES

CONTENT

Students will practice reading comprehension skills as they read the book *Seven Blind Mice*. They will explore the plot to see how the author was able to show the moral of the story.

THINKING SKILL/PROCESS

Students will identify the significant parts of a whole by identifying the parts and determining their functions.

METHODS AND MATERIALS

CONTENT

Students will read *Seven Blind Mice* by Ed Young and study the illustrations to gather details and information on the parts of an elephant.

THINKING SKILL/PROCESS

A thinking map, a graphic organizer, and structured questioning prompt students to determine the parts of a whole and how the parts function with regard to the whole. Collaborative learning and group discussion enhance student learning.

LESSON

INTRODUCTION TO CONTENT AND THINKING SKILL/PROCESS

- **I have a puzzle I'd like us to put together. I am going to give each group a few puzzle pieces.** Use a simple picture, perhaps an old calendar print, to create a very simple puzzle. Cut the picture into the number of pieces that will provide each group with one or two pieces. Pieces of tape should be placed on the backs of the pieces so that the puzzle can be constructed on the wall where it can be viewed by the group. This could also be done by copying the picture to a transparency and showing it on an overhead for easier viewing by the group. Pass out the pieces to the groups. **What will we need to do to complete the puzzle?** Students will discuss the steps that will be necessary for all the groups to find where their pieces fit in the puzzle. Once they have discussed the process of constructing a puzzle, allow the groups to bring up their pieces and fill in the puzzle. **When you work to put a puzzle together, you find the special place for each puzzle piece. When it is complete, all the pieces blend together to make one picture. The parts, or the pieces, make one whole picture when the puzzle is solved. As you were working, you also fit together to make a good team!** Write the words "parts" and "whole" on a chart or the chalkboard.

- **Can you think of some other things that are made up of smaller parts that combine to make up a whole?** POSSIBLE STUDENT RESPONSES: *School bus, car, bike, skateboard, computer, pencil, watch, yo-yo, telephone, book, desk.*

- **Pick one of these things and work with your group to list the parts. List as many as you can.** After a few minutes, ask some of the groups to share one thing and a few of its parts. Write the name of the object on the chart, and list the parts mentioned underneath. POSSIBLE STUDENT RESPONSES: *Bike (tires, seat, handlebar, brakes, basket, horn, chain, spokes), yo-yo (string, finger loop, two round sides, middle bar).*

- We can list the parts of a whole object, but to understand how important each part is to the whole, it is necessary to consider its *function*. Write the word "function" under the other words on the chart. **The word *function* means what it adds to the whole and what it does for the whole. For example, the function of the eraser on a pencil is to allow the user to erase something written. The word *function* will be used often today as we learn about parts and wholes.**

- It is very important to think about parts and wholes and how the parts function to help the whole. If we find that something will not work, we can look to see if one of the parts is not functioning, or doing what it is supposed to do. If we can find the part that is not working in the way it should, it will be easier to fix. For example, if a bike does not stop, what part might need to be fixed? POSSIBLE STUDENT RESPONSE: *The brakes.*

- **Here is a thinking map that will help when you are learning about the parts and what they add to the whole.** Show the thinking map for parts of a whole on a chart or the blackboard. The thinking map must be in a place where it can be viewed by the students throughout the lesson. Go over the four steps in determining the parts-whole relationship.

DETERMINING PARTS-WHOLE RELATIONSHIPS
1. **What smaller things make up the whole?**
2. **For each part, what would happen if it were missing?**
3. **What is the function of each part?**
4. **How do the parts work together to make the whole what it is or operate as it does?**

- **Let's consider a bike as we look at the thinking map. The first question asks, "What smaller things make up the whole?" We listed** the parts on the chart. **The second question asks, "For each part, what would happen if it were missing?" If the handlebars were missing, what would happen?** POSSIBLE STUDENT RESPONSES: *We couldn't steer the bike. There would be no place to put our hands. We would probably fall over.* **The third question asks, "What is the function of each part?" The function of the handlebars is to give us a place to hold on to with our hands and to steer the bike in the right direction. The last question asks, "How do the parts work together to make the whole do, or operate, as it does?" If we were to go through all of the other parts, we would be able to take all of the information we have gathered from our thinking to see how the parts work together to make the whole do what it is supposed to do, in this case provide a means of transportation for people.**

THINKING ACTIVELY

- **We are going to read a book about a puzzle that some mice solve. At the beginning of the story, they know that it is a strange Something, but because they are blind they cannot see the whole thing.** You may need to review the concept of blindness. **The mice take turns learning about the parts by touching or feeling them and deciding the job each part does in working with the whole. They think about the function of the parts. When they put them together they find a whole thing that is known and understood. The name of the book is *Seven Blind Mice*. It was written by Ed Young.** Read the book with students. Take time to discuss the many things that students find interesting. For example, students enjoy seeing that the color of the part always matches the color of the blind mouse that is exploring. The color is significant in that the author is showing the connection between the mouse and his thinking about the Something he is touching.

- **I'd like you to think about the mice, the part that each one felt, and the name the mouse gave** to the big Something. Share this list with your partner. Try to retell the story in the same order that the author wrote it. Allow time for the pairs to retell the story. To involve both students in each pair, identify one student to start the story. After a minute, ring a bell to have the other student take over from the point where the first child stopped. Continue the signalling until all of the pairs have finished their retelling. Have students return to the large group and retell the story by calling on different students to tell parts of the story. The retelling should include the beginning when the mice find the strange Something and run home. Then each of the mice take turns finding out what the Something is. The first mouse feels a foot and thinks it is a pillar. The second mouse feels the trunk and thinks it is a snake. The third mouse feels a tusk and thinks it is a spear. The fourth mouse feels the forehead and thinks it is a cliff. The fifth mouse feels an ear and thinks it is a fan. The sixth mouse feels the tail and thinks it is a rope. The mice all argue about what the Something is until the seventh mouse, the last one, goes out and feels all over the Something. He puts all of the parts together and recognizes the Something is an elephant. **The first six mice looked at only one part of the whole. It was the seventh mouse who finally put all the parts together by examining the whole, and he found it to be an elephant. As we read the story, did you agree that the parts felt by the first six mice did sort of feel like the things they thought of?** Most students will agree that the parts really do resemble the various items the mice declared the Something to be.

- **The moral of the story was written at the end. A moral is the lesson the author wants us to learn. Let's reread those sentences that give us the moral.** Reread the moral, "The Mouse Moral: Knowing in part may make a fine tale, but wisdom comes from seeing the whole." **Each mouse could tell a fine tale, or story, about what he thought the Something was. The moral says that wisdom comes from seeing the whole. Which mouse was the wisest, and why?** POSSIBLE STUDENT RESPONSES: *The last one, the seventh one, the white one. He looked and felt all of the elephant before he said what it was. Then he knew because he had felt all of the parts. He could put all of the parts together.*

- **We will come back to this moral later in our lesson, but first let's be like the seventh mouse and look at all of the parts of an elephant. We all know about elephants, so we will be using the things we know as we work. Did you also use the things you already knew about elephants when you read the story? Did you know what the Something was before the seventh mouse came into the story?** Students will discuss the points where they knew that it was an elephant. **You used the knowledge you had to make a good prediction about the Something.** In the story, the mice did not have the information you have. Using the things you already know about a topic, can be a big help when you are reading. This is called using *prior knowledge,* meaning knowledge from before. That's something important to do whenever you read.

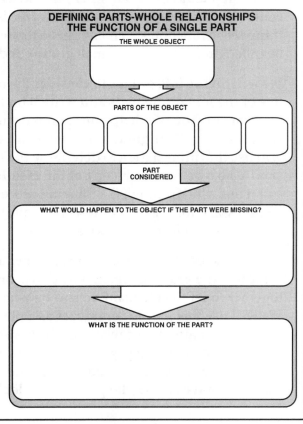

- **Let's make a list of the parts each mouse found and what he called it. We'll use a graphic organizer for parts-whole relationships to help us.** Show a copy of the graphic organizer for parts/

whole relationships on an overhead transparency. Later in the lesson, blank overlays will be used to consider different parts. Using an overlay will allow you to continue exploring other parts of the whole picture book with the class on the original graphic organizer. Record the parts on the graphic organizer in the spaces for "parts of the object" as students list them. Under each part, also record the name each mouse gave to the part he examined. For example, list "leg," and under the word put the word "pillar."

- **Knowing the parts of the elephant and what they do for the whole elephant can help us understand the animal. We can also use the information we know about elephants to help us determine the functions of the parts of the whole elephant. Each part that the mice found has a special function. To see the importance of the part, we should think about what would happen if that part were missing. Let's think about the leg of the elephant.** Use an overlay so that two parts can be considered, one at a time. Write the word "leg" in the arrow labeled "part considered." **What would happen to the elephant if the leg were missing?** Allow time for student pairs to share, then invite some students to respond. Record the responses on the graphic organizer. They should include the ideas of not being able to stand and move. **If the elephant were not able to stand or move as a result of having his legs missing, we could say that the function of the part, the leg, is to support the elephant and to help it move.** This statement can be recorded in the box at the bottom of the graphic organizer. Modeling a function statement is helpful for students.

- **Now think about another part, the trunk. What did the mouse call the trunk?** *A snake.* **Let's consider the trunk of the elephant to determine its function. What would happen to the elephant if its trunk were missing?** Allow time for pair sharing, then again have several students respond. Record their responses on another overlay of the graphic. POSSIBLE STUDENT RESPONSES: *It couldn't drink or eat. It couldn't pick up things. It couldn't smell. It couldn't give itself a bath.*

- **If the elephant could not smell, drink, or pick up food and things without the trunk, we could say that the function of the trunk is to help the elephant smell, drink, and pick up things.** The function statement can be modeled by the teacher a second time, or the class could be called on to respond in small groups and then share the statements with the class.

- **We will divide into groups to consider the other parts of the elephant. Each group will choose one of the remaining parts and write it on the group's graphic organizer in the "Part Considered" arrow. You will help your group decide what would happen to the elephant if that part were missing. Your group's answer will be recorded by one of the members, and he or she will use this information to determine the function of the part. The statement of the function should also be written by one of the members of the group.** Allow the groups time to choose a part and work through the thinking process as they complete their graphic organizer. It may be necessary for a group to research a part. Having several sources of information about elephants available is a good idea.

- **We have used the information we know and information from the books on elephants to complete the graphic organizers. Our work lets us see how the parts of an elephant work together to let the elephant do and be what an elephant is. Let's share the work we've done. We will use this graphic organizer as a place to record everyone's work in one place.** Show a copy of the parts-whole relationships graphic for showing multiple parts on a chart or transparency (see following page). **This graphic has room to show all of the work the groups have done.** Using the graphic organizer, record all of the parts and their functions as the groups share. **We have shown the parts of an elephant and their functions. We could say we are as** wise as the seventh mouse because we worked to understand the whole.

- The moral of the story said that seeing, or understanding the whole, makes a person wiser. How could this apply to things that you learn? Let's think about reading a story. What if someone read only a part of the story. What could we say about their understanding of the whole story? POSSIBLE STUDENT RESPONSES: *They wouldn't really know what was going on. They wouldn't know the end if they only read the beginning, and they wouldn't know the beginning if they only read the end. The things the characters did would not make sense because they wouldn't know why they were doing them.* **Reading the whole story certainly makes us wiser about the story. We need to know all of the parts to understand the whole thing. Sometimes we may feel like one of the six mice who did not see the whole Something because we missed a part. And so, as good readers do, we go back to read again and find out about the part we don't understand. Then we can be sure we understand the whole story.**

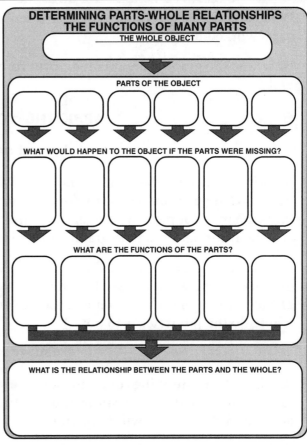

If we look at the last pages, we can read and see that all of the mice learned from the seventh mouse because they explored the whole thing and then agreed that the Something most definitely was an elephant!

THINKING ABOUT THINKING

- **We have been looking at parts in order to understand the whole. We looked at the parts of an elephant in order to understand it. Did thinking about the parts of an elephant help you to understand more about how an elephant lives?** POSSIBLE STUDENT RESPONSES: *It made me think about all the things that an elephant needs to live. I think I want to know more about how they move their trunk to understand it even better. It was cool to think about missing parts and what would happen to the elephant without something.*

- **When we do this kind of thinking, we are using the parts and our understanding of what they do to help us understand more about the whole. What was our first step in using this strategy to learn more about elephants?** POSSIBLE STUDENT RESPONSE: *We thought about the parts of the elephant.*

- **After you listed the parts, what did you think about to determine the function of each part?** POSSIBLE STUDENT RESPONSES: *We thought about what would happen if the part were missing. Then we could figure out what the part does for the elephant.*

- **What would you do if you did not know what would happen if a part were missing? How could you find out?** POSSIBLE STUDENT RESPONSES: *Maybe we could try it, or imagine it. Maybe we could look at something else that is sort of like it to see what the part does on the other thing.*

- **What was the last question you answered?** Student will relay that they considered how the parts worked together.

- **How was the graphic organizer helpful for you as you did this kind of thinking?** ANSWERS VARY.

APPLYING YOUR THINKING

Immediate Transfer

- Identify an animal that you are familiar with. What are its parts and what are their functions? What parts are necessary for the animal to survive? Use a graphic organizer and the thinking map for parts-whole relationships to help you. Draw an illustration of the animal. Use the information on the graphic organizer to write a report about the animal.

- Look around the classroom. Choose an object, and list its parts. Using the thinking map and graphic organizer for parts-whole relationships, list the parts of the object and the functions of the parts to the whole. Demonstrate to another student how the parts work to make the whole do the job it needs to do.

Reinforcement Later

- You have been studying communities. Use what you know about parts-whole relationships to explain a job in the community and its function in regard to the whole. The thinking map and graphic organizer will help you.

- Explain the parts of a mathematical sentence. It can be an addition sentence or a subtraction sentence. Look at all parts, and decide what their functions are. Use a graphic organizer and the thinking map for parts-whole relationships to help you as you work. Make a booklet about the mathematical sentence to explain the parts and how they work together as a whole.

- Schools are built with a special purpose in mind. They are meant to be a place for many people to come together and learn. Using the thinking map and graphic organizer for parts-whole relationships, describe the parts of a school building and their functions. Just include the parts of the building, not the people who work there. Divide the parts among the people in your group, then combine your work into a class book.

ART EXTENSION (GRADE 1)

Ask students to illustrate the thinking done in this lesson by drawing an elephant missing a part. In the picture, students will show the consequences of not having the part. They will also write about the picture and what it shows.

SCIENCE EXTENSION (GRADE 2)

Assign groups to search for further information on elephants, especially parts that they haven't yet thought about. The groups could divide the job, each looking at a source and reporting back to the whole orally or with pictures and written reports. This structure is similar to the parts-whole lesson just completed. Possible sources: *Zoo Books*, computer programs, library books, the Internet, encyclopedias.

SUGGESTED SPECIAL NEEDS MODIFICATION

<u>Frontload</u>: Some students may need work on the idea of "function" prior to the lesson. Use more common language in explaining function: "It is what the part does," for example. Have students explore simple items around the classroom like chairs, pencils, etc. until they can tell you what each part does.

<u>Clarify</u>: Generating a statement of "function" and "relationship" may be difficult for students. Teacher guidance with paraphrasing of students' answers may be needed to form a clear idea. During the lesson, use clarifying phrases such as, "what the part does" and "how the parts work together."

<u>Diversify</u>: Students are often aided by working in cooperative groups. However, some students, even with partner support, may have difficulty formulating function-relationship summaries. This may require greater teacher guidance with the teacher paraphrasing students' ideas to create a clear statement. A sentence frame like "The part ____ makes the part ____ do ____ by doing _____ itself" may help students in formulating relationship statements.

Cooperative groups are also an excellent way to utilize students' strengths. Assigning the task of writing to a proficient writer in the cooperative group allows all students to contribute ideas while reducing the task load for beginning writers. Specific "parts" may also be assigned to specific groups of students in order to match the task with the students' knowledge base.

<u>Expand the Possibilities</u>: Assessments of written responses may be based upon the students' thinking first, and expressive skills second. Oral responses, or a freehand drawing of a part doing what its function is, may also reveal thinking beyond students' ability to express themselves in writing.

ASSESSING STUDENT THINKING ABOUT POSSIBILITIES

To assess student thinking about parts and wholes, give them a problem about an item that is familiar to them. Explain that it doesn't work. Ask the students to figure out what part is causing the problem. This can be an oral assessment done individually or in small groups. The students should identify the steps in the thinking map as they work through the problem. Any of the application examples in this lesson can also serve as a vehicle for assessing student thinking about parts-whole relationships.

Sample Student Responses • Do You See What I See?

DEFINING PARTS-WHOLE RELATIONSHIPS
THE FUNCTION OF A SINGLE PART

THE WHOLE OBJECT

Elephant
(the big Something)

PARTS OF THE OBJECT

| *legs*
(pillars) | *trunk*
(snake) | *tusk*
(spear) | *head*
(cliff) | *ear*
(fan) | *tail*
(rope) |

PART CONSIDERED
legs

WHAT WOULD HAPPEN TO THE OBJECT IF THE PART WERE MISSING?

The legs hold up the elephant. They make it so it can stand. If it didn't have legs, it couldn't walk or move around. Then it couldn't get food and water.

WHAT IS THE FUNCTION OF THE PART?

The elephant has four legs that hold him up when he stands. They hold up the body and head of the elephant. The elephant can use his legs to walk in the jungle. The legs are good for running, too.

Sample Student Responses • Do You See What I See?

DETERMINING PARTS-WHOLE RELATIONSHIPS
THE FUNCTIONS OF MANY PARTS

THE WHOLE OBJECT
Elephant

PARTS OF THE OBJECT

legs	*trunk*	*tusk*	*head*	*ear*	*tail*

WHAT WOULD HAPPEN TO THE OBJECT IF THE PARTS WERE MISSING?

It couldn't stand or move.	*It couldn't smell, drink, or pick up things.*	*It couldn't dig for food. It would be missing a weapon.*	*It wouldn't have a brain, eyes, ears, and trunk.*	*It couldn't hear things or cool itself off.*	*It would get bitten by lots of bugs and flies.*

WHAT ARE THE FUNCTIONS OF THE PARTS?

standing and moving	*smelling, drinking, and picking up things*	*digging to get food and as a weapon*	*thinking and it is a place for its face*	*for hearing and cooling off the elephant*	*swishing away flies and bugs*

WHAT IS THE RELATIONSHIP BETWEEN THE PARTS AND THE WHOLE?

The elephant uses all the parts of its body to help it live. Missing any one of the parts would make it hard for the elephant to live. Each part is important. The legs are used for moving. It can walk to its food with its legs. The trunk is used for smelling, drinking, and picking up things, like its food. The tusks help it eat and fight. The head is the place for the elephant's brain, face and ears, and mouth. It puts food in its mouth with its trunk. The ears cool off the elephant and help it hear. The tail helps to keep away bugs.

PARTS OF A PICTURE BOOK

Language Arts   **Grades 1–2**

OBJECTIVES

CONTENT

Students will learn that picture books have specific parts that help us enjoy reading and learning from them.

THINKING SKILL/PROCESS

Students will identify the significant parts of a whole by identifying parts and determining their functions.

METHODS AND MATERIALS

CONTENT

Students will work in groups to examine a variety of picture books. They will already be familiar with picture books, recognizing them as stories told in text and illustrations.

THINKING SKILL/PROCESS

A thinking map, a graphic organizer, and structured questioning prompt students to describe the various component parts of a whole and how these parts function with regard to the whole. Collaborative learning groups enhance student thinking.

LESSON

INTRODUCTION TO CONTENT AND THINKING SKILL/PROCESS

• **Building sets or construction sets are favorite toys for many of us. These sets allow us to choose pieces that go together to make something. Perhaps it is a building or a machine. Each part helps to make that thing.** A sample of something made with a type of building set could be used here as a physical model. **The parts are important. You can see how if I took certain parts away, the whole thing wouldn't be able to stand. There are things that we use in school that we don't build ourselves. These also have parts. Everyday at school we use pencils. Let's look at a pencil and see what parts it has. Work with your group to make a list of all of the parts of a pencil.** Make sure that each group has a complete pencil to examine. The lists can be made on paper or on individual dry erase slates. After a few minutes, ask groups to share, listing the parts on the board under the word "pencil." POSSIBLE STUDENT RESPONSES: *wood, eraser, metal ring, lead, paint, point.*

• **These small parts go together to make the pencil work. To understand how the parts are important to the whole, we need to think about what they do as a part of the whole. We call this the "function" of the part.** Write the term, "function of parts" on the chalkboard next to the word "pencil." **For example, what does the wood do on a pencil? To find out the function of the wood, we can think about what would happen if it were missing. Think about what would happen if the wood of the pencil were missing. Discuss this with your group.** Allow discussion time in groups, then share ideas as a whole. POSSIBLE STUDENT RESPONSES: *I would get my fingers all dirty when I wrote. The lead would break.* **From the things you have said would happen if the wood were missing from a pencil, we can determine that the *function* of the wood is to protect the lead from breaking and smearing and to make it easier for the writer to write.** Write a summary of the function of the wood under the term "function of parts" and next to the word "wood."

• It is important to think about the parts of a whole to better understand the whole thing. Understanding each part's function helps us understand how things work. If a flashlight doesn't light when turned on, we can think about the parts that make it light and be better able to fix it. What part would be the first thing we would check? POSSIBLE STUDENT RESPONSE: *The batteries.* We know that batteries provide the energy for the flashlight. That is their function. So we would check them to see if they are providing power for the flashlight. What else might we check? POSSIBLE STUDENT RESPONSE: *The light bulb.* Why? POSSIBLE STUDENT RESPONSE: *Because its function is to light up.*

• Here is a thinking map to guide you when you are looking at the parts to understand a whole thing. Show a copy of the thinking map for determining parts-whole relationships on a chart or on the chalkboard. It will need to be visible to the students during the lesson to guide their thinking. Go over the four questions, referring to the previous examples as needed.

DETERMINING PARTS-WHOLE RELATIONSHIPS

1. What smaller things make up the whole?

2. For each part, what would happen if it were missing?

3. What is the function of each part?

4. How do the parts work together to make the whole what it is or operate as it does?

THINKING ACTIVELY

• We've been reading many picture books in school. Which have been favorites for you? Talk with a neighbor about one or two of your favorites. Allow time for sharing. Think about why you like those books. Did you like the pictures? The story? The characters? As a class, discuss the things they liked about their favorite books.

• Let's use our thinking map for parts of a whole and think about the parts of a picture book. Looking at the parts and their functions in relation to the whole can help us understand how a picture book can be something we enjoy reading and how it can teach us things as well.

• A graphic organizer will help us keep track of the information we gather about the parts and what they do for the whole. Show the graphic organizer for determining parts-whole relationships on an overhead transparency. Later in the lesson, you will be using blank overlays for the bottom section of this graphic organizer to allow for more than one student answer. The top box has been filled in with the words "picture book." This is the whole object that we are working with today. Now, we are ready to answer the first question on the thinking map. We will decide what smaller things make up the whole picture book. I have some picture books for us to examine. Looking at the books will help us

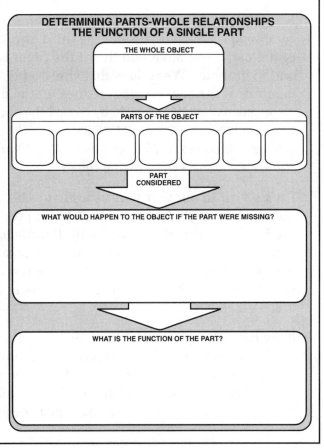

identify the parts. It will also help us determine the functions of the parts. Pass out a pile of books to each group. Allow time for students to explore and comment on the books in their group.

- **In each of your groups, I'd like you to make a list of the parts of the books. Work together to make one list. Look carefully at the books to include as many parts as possible.** Have students make a list of the parts of a picture book on paper or dry erase slates. Encourage them to explore the books to be sure they've noticed as many of the parts as they can. After work time, have the groups share items from their lists with the class. Get one item per group and then go back and ask if there is anything else anyone wants to mention. Make a class list of the parts identified on the chalkboard. Recording the list on a chalkboard before writing it on the graphic organizer allows you and the class to "fine tune" the labels for the parts. When everyone is satisfied with the list, it is time to record it on the graphic organizer in the section "Parts of the Object." POSSIBLE STUDENT RESPONSES: *Cover, book jacket, illustrations (pictures), text (story), title page, pages, binding, blank page at the end, spine, book title.*

- **One of the parts of a picture book that you identified is its cover. The second question on the thinking map for determining how the parts work as a whole asks us, "What would happen if it were missing?" What would happen to the picture book if the cover were missing? In your groups, talk about how you would answer this question.** After share time, allow students to share with the large group by telling one of the things that they came up with. POSSIBLE STUDENT RESPONSES: *The book would get ripped. The pages would get wrinkled and dirty. We couldn't see what the title of the book is. The pages would flop around.* Record these ideas on an overlay of the graphic organizer transparency. Using an overlay will allow you to continue exploring other parts of the whole picture book with the class on the original graphic organizer. In the "Part Considered" arrow, write "cover." In the box underneath, write the things suggested by the students that would happen if this part were missing.

- **Now that we know what would happen if the cover were missing, we can decide what its function is. This will answer the third question on the thinking map, "What is the function of the part?" We have said that if the cover were missing...** (state students' ideas as recorded on the graphic). **What does that show us that the cover does for the book? Remember, the *function* of the cover is what it does for the book.** Involve the group in a discussion, and once a consensus has been reached, record the statement of the function in the bottom box of the graphic. POSSIBLE STUDENT RESPONSES: *The cover protects the book and holds the pages flat when you are not reading it. The cover shows the title and keeps the pages from getting wrinkled and dirty. It also keeps the pages from getting ripped.*

- **Let's go on to another part of a picture book. The binding is another part. We will think about what would happen if the binding were missing so we can understand the function of the binding, just like we did with the cover. Share your ideas in your groups.** Allow a few minutes for the students to share ideas in small groups, and then ask them to share these ideas with the class, just as before. Write the responses on a new overlay. POSSIBLE STUDENT RESPONSES: *The book would fall apart. The pages would fall out. The pages would get lost. The pages would get all mixed up.*

- **Now just as we did with the cover, we can use this information to decide on the function of the binding.** Reread the ideas recorded, then allow students time to discuss the function of the binding. Ask them to share these ideas, then come to a consensus. Record the function on the overlay. POSSIBLE STUDENT RESPONSES: *The binding holds the book and the pages together and keeps the pages in order. Then it can be read and understood by people.*

- We will continue our task of looking at the other parts of a picture book by dividing the other parts among the groups. Do the same thing with your new part that we did with the two parts we have considered so far. Assign one part to each group. If there are more parts than groups, assign some groups two parts. Give each group a copy of the graphic organizer to complete. If students are comfortable, the graphic organizer can be on a transparency for sharing later with the class, or it can be on a large chart. Walk students through the steps, having them all write the part they are considering on the arrow, then all recording what would happen if the part were missing, and finally, recording the function of the part. Each group should share their work with the class. This can be done by your designating a reporter for the group. The graphic organizers could be hung for later viewing. As a group shares, the information should be transferred to a second graphic organizer for parts-whole relationships, the one designed for looking at multiple parts of a whole.

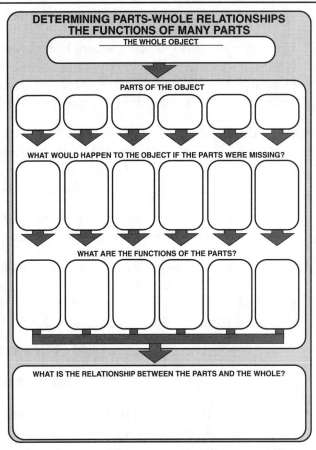

DETERMINING PARTS-WHOLE RELATIONSHIPS
THE FUNCTIONS OF MANY PARTS

THE WHOLE OBJECT

PARTS OF THE OBJECT

WHAT WOULD HAPPEN TO THE OBJECT IF THE PARTS WERE MISSING?

WHAT ARE THE FUNCTIONS OF THE PARTS?

WHAT IS THE RELATIONSHIP BETWEEN THE PARTS AND THE WHOLE?

- The work we have done to examine the parts of a picture book has helped us understand why the books are made as they are. Our graphic organizers show the information we have gotten from examining the parts. We know more about the title page, the binding, the cover, the pictures, and the other parts. Point to the separate graphic organizers made by the groups and the large graphic organizer showing all the parts and their functions. This information helps us to know more about the whole picture book. We can use what we know about the parts to explain why all the parts of a picture book are important in making the picture book an enjoyable choice for reading and a good way to learn about things. This is the last question on the thinking map. How do the parts work together to make a picture book that we can learn from and enjoy reading? Talk as a whole group to generate sentences that tell about the whole book and its parts. Each supporting sentence should mention one of the parts and its function. Guide students by referring to the graphic organizer sections that tell the functions of the parts. POSSIBLE STUDENT RESPONSES: *All of the parts of a picture book help make it one that we like to read. The words make up the story. The pictures show us important things in the story that the words describe and help us see what it is like. The pages are the places for those words and pictures to be so that we can easily see them and read them. The cover and the binding keep the story clean, keep the pages in the right order, and make them lie flat when we are not reading them. The spine shows us the title of the book when it is on the shelf. The cover and the book jacket show the title, the name of the author, the name of the illustrator, and give us picture clues about the story so that we can know what we are going to be reading and get interested. They are the first things we see, so they need to make us want to read the book. These all work together to help us understand what is happening in the story in a way that is fun.*

- The thinking you have done, studying the parts of a picture book, has given you a better understanding of how we learn as we read picture books. Your answers show that you can use the information we have about the parts of a picture book to continue learning each time you read a book!

THINKING ABOUT THINKING

- **Let's stop thinking about picture books for a moment and use our thinking map to review what we've done today.** Go over the questions as students respond to the following questions. **How did you know what the parts of a picture book are?** POSSIBLE STUDENT RESPONSE: *We looked at picture books in our groups and made a list.*

- **What did we do with the list?** POSSIBLE STUDENT RESPONSE: *We listed the parts of a picture book on the graphic organizer.* **What did we think about next?** POSSIBLE STUDENT RESPONSE: *We thought about what would happen if a part were missing.* **Why did we do that?** POSSIBLE STUDENT RESPONSE: *So we could figure out the function of that part.*

- **There was one last big job we did in our thinking. What was the final thinking task we did?** POSSIBLE STUDENT RESPONSE: *We thought about how the parts work together to make a picture book.*

- **Pretend you are explaining to a friend how to look at the parts of an object and how to understand what they do for the whole object that they are parts of. What would you say to them? Model this with a friend.** Allow the students to pair and discuss the thinking process. The steps listed on the thinking map should be included in their answers.

APPLYING YOUR THINKING

Immediate Transfer

- **Look at this picture of a wagon. It is a good way to transport things from one place to another.** Show a picture of a simple wagon. **What are its parts? What would happen if a part were missing? What are the functions of the parts of a wagon and how do they make the wagon do what it does? Use a graphic organizer to show your thinking.**

- **We have made many graphs in our math studies. Look at some of the graphs on display in our room. List the parts of a graph on a graphic organizer for parts-whole relationships and determine their functions in relation to the whole graph.**

Reinforcement Later

- **List the parts of an addition sentence. Use a graphic organizer to determine their functions within the whole sentence.**

- **We have just read (title of story). Use the thinking map for parts-whole relationships to identify the main parts of the story and their functions in the story. How did the parts of the story work together to help us understand and enjoy the whole story?**

- **Our hands are very important to us. Examine your hand. Use a graphic organizer to determine the parts of your hand and their functions. How do they all work together to make the hand work for you? Discuss ways in which a person would need to change the things they do if a part of their hand were missing.**

- **Choose one mode of transportation. Draw a picture of your choice on paper. Discuss the functions of the parts. If you want, you can create a toy vehicle at home. I'll give you a copy of the thinking map and graphic organizer to take home with you. Then you can explain the parts and functions of your creation by writing about it or by telling about it to the class.**

ART/WRITING EXTENSION

Have students use the information gathered about picture books to make their own. The graphic organizer will guide the student to include the important parts of a picture book as they create a story, illustrate it, design a cover, and publish it for others to read. These books should be displayed in the classroom and, if possible, in the school library. They also could be the reason for a shared reading time with another class.

SUGGESTED SPECIAL NEEDS MODIFICATIONS

Frontload: Prior to the lesson, some students may need work on the idea of "function." Use more common language in explaining function: "It is what the part *does*," for example. Have students explore simple items around the classroom like chairs, pencils, etc., until they can tell you what each part does.

Streamlining Outcomes: Reducing the number of questions on the thinking map will reduce the cognitive demand for some students in this lesson. For example, eliminate question four about how the parts work together. Then, in the application activities, when these students have mastered this more limited task, question four can be added.

Clarify: Generating a statement of "function" and "relationship" may be difficult for students. Teacher guidance with paraphrasing of students' answers may be needed to form a clear idea. During the lesson, clarify phrases such as, "what the part does" and "how the parts work together."

Diversify: Students are often aided by working in cooperative groups. However, some students, even with partner support, may have difficulty formulating function-relationship summaries. This may require greater teacher guidance with the teacher paraphrasing students' ideas to create a clear statement. A sentence frame like "The part _____ makes the part _____ do _____ by doing _____ itself" may help students in formulating relationship statements.

Cooperative groups are also an excellent way to utilize students' strengths. Assigning the task of writing to a proficient writer in the cooperative group allows all students to contribute ideas while reducing the task load for beginning writers. Specific "parts" may also be assigned to specific groups of students in order to match the task with the students' knowledge base.

Expand the Possibilities: Assessments of written responses may be based upon students' thinking first, and expressive skills second. Oral responses or a freehand drawing of a part doing what its function is may also reveal thinking beyond students' ability to express themselves in writing.

ASSESSING STUDENT THINKING ABOUT PARTS-WHOLE RELATIONSHIPS

To assess student thinking about parts and wholes, present a problem using an item that is familiar to them, such as a pencil box or a lunch box. Explain that it is not working because of a broken part. Ask the student to figure out what part is causing the problem. Have the student solve the problem orally, listening for the steps in the process as delineated in the thinking map. Any of the application examples can be used as vehicles for assessment of this thinking skill as well.

Sample Student Responses • Parts of a Picture

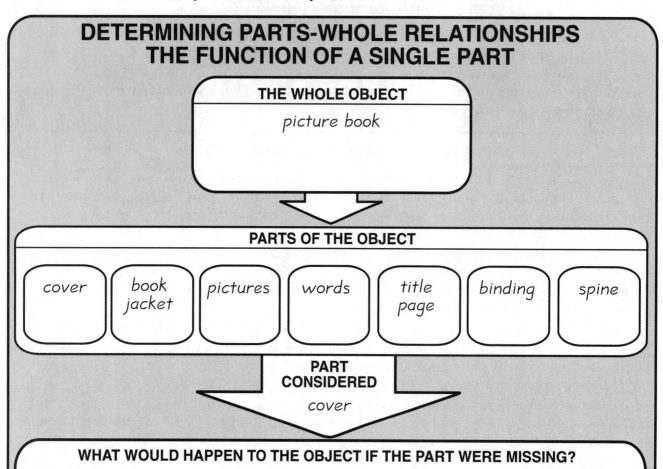

DETERMINING PARTS-WHOLE RELATIONSHIPS
THE FUNCTION OF A SINGLE PART

THE WHOLE OBJECT

picture book

PARTS OF THE OBJECT

| cover | book jacket | pictures | words | title page | binding | spine |

PART CONSIDERED

cover

WHAT WOULD HAPPEN TO THE OBJECT IF THE PART WERE MISSING?

The pages of the book might get ripped, wrinkled, and dirty. It wouldn't look as nice, so people might not want to read it.

WHAT IS THE FUNCTION OF THE PART?

The cover protects the book from getting ripped, wrinkled, and dirty. It looks nice so that people will want to read the book.

Sample Student Responses • Parts of a Picture

DETERMINING PARTS-WHOLE RELATIONSHIPS
THE FUNCTIONS OF MANY PARTS

THE WHOLE OBJECT
a picture book

PARTS OF THE OBJECT

| cover | book jacket | pictures | words | pages | binding | spine |

WHAT WOULD HAPPEN TO THE OBJECT IF THE PARTS WERE MISSING?

| The book would get ripped. The pages would get dirty. People would not pick up the book to read. | The book would look plain without pictures. We wouldn't think it was good. | The story wouldn't be as much fun. We wouldn't know as much about the story. | There would be nothing to read. We would not understand the story. | We couldn't see any pictures or words. | The book would fall apart. The pages would fall out and get lost. | We wouldn't know what book it is when it is on a shelf. |

WHAT IS THE FUNCTION OF THE PARTS?

| The cover protects the book. It keeps it looking nice so people will read it. | The book jacket has fancy pictures to make you want to read it. | The pictures help tell the story and make it fun to read. | The words tell the story. They help us understand what is happening. | The pages are the places for the words and the pictures of the story. | The binding holds the book together. Then it can be read by people. | The spine has a place to write the title of the book. When it is on a shelf you can find it. |

WHAT IS THE RELATIONSHIP BETWEEN THE PARTS AND THE WHOLE?

All of the parts of a picture book help make it nice to read. The words make up the story. The pictures show us what the words describe. The pages provide places for the words and pictures. The cover keeps the pages clean. The binding keeps the pages together so they don't fall out. The spine shows us the title of the book when it is on the shelf. The book jacket has fancy pictures to make you want to read it. They are the first things we see, so they need to make us want to read the book. These all work together to help us enjoy and understand what is happening in the story.

DETERMINING PARTS-WHOLE RELATIONSHIPS

1. What smaller things make up the whole?

2. For each part, what would happen if it were missing?

3. What is the function of each part?

4. How do the parts work together to make the whole what it is or operate as it does?

DETERMINING PARTS-WHOLE RELATIONSHIPS
THE FUNCTION OF A SINGLE PART

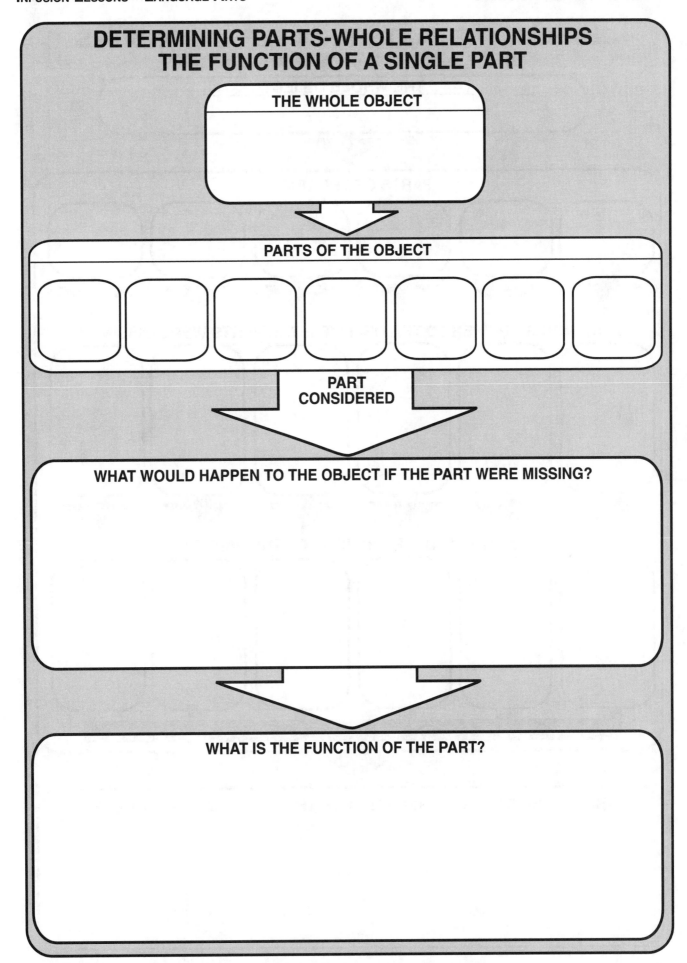

THE WHOLE OBJECT

PARTS OF THE OBJECT

PART CONSIDERED

WHAT WOULD HAPPEN TO THE OBJECT IF THE PART WERE MISSING?

WHAT IS THE FUNCTION OF THE PART?

DETERMINING PARTS-WHOLE RELATIONSHIPS
THE FUNCTIONS OF MANY PARTS

THE WHOLE OBJECT

PARTS OF THE OBJECT

WHAT WOULD HAPPEN TO THE OBJECT IF THE PARTS WERE MISSING?

WHAT ARE THE FUNCTIONS OF THE PARTS?

WHAT IS THE RELATIONSHIP BETWEEN THE PARTS AND THE WHOLE?

CHAPTER 8
SEQUENCING

Infusing Skillful Sequencing into Language Arts

Teaching students to sequence skillfully in grades 1 and 2 involves helping them learn to engage in two types of sequencing, simple sequencing and ranking, by asking and carefully answering the following questions:

SEQUENCING

1. Why do you want to put them in order?

2. What is the best way to order them?

3. What do you have to find out about them in order to know where they fit?

4. Where does each item fit?

---

figure 8.1

SEQUENCING BY RANK

1. What is the purpose of the ranking?

2. What should you find out in order to rank things for this purpose?

3 How do these things rank from highest to lowest and why?

---

figure 8.2

In the sequencing lessons in this chapter, these "thinking maps" are used to guide your students' thinking explicitly as they engage with the lesson content.

When students learn and use these strategies for sequencing and ranking, they don't just put things in some order, but rather consider the purpose for the ordering, determine what criteria they must look at to determine where something falls in the order being established, and then ascertain to what degree the things being ordered meet these criteria. For example, when

the task is to organize books in some sequences for the classroom resource library so that students will be able to find what they are looking for easily, ordering them alphabetically by topic and then alphabetically by author within the topics may serve this purpose well. Then it is a matter of finding out what the books are about and who the authors are in order to place them in the right sequence. Some other sequence may serve some other purpose.

When ranking the books they have read, students should be clear about why they are ranking them (for example, to determine which book provides the most reliable information on a topic), establish criteria that they will look for to decide this (reputation of the author, etc.), and then determine to what extent the books meet these criteria.

Thinking through how to sequence and rank things enables students to think skillfully, rather than just "off the top of their heads." In these lessons, using graphic organizers, engaging in cooperative thinking, thinking about thinking, and continued guided practice are all strategies used to supplement and reinforce the use of the thinking maps. These classroom strategies enhance both the development of the thinking skill that the students are learning and their mastery of the lesson content.

The key graphic organizers for sequencing are shown in figures 8.3 and 8.4 (see following page). The key graphic organizer for ranking is shown in figure 8.5 (see following page).

These graphic organizers help students record all of the ingredients that go into the thinking tasks of sequencing and ranking. They write down the purpose of the sequencing or ranking after they record what they will be sequencing or ranking, determine to what criteria they should attend, and then locate items in a sequence, explaining why they are so located by referring to the degree to which the items satisfy the established criteria. As such, these are handy tools to move a good sequencing or ranking lesson along. Reproducible graphic organizers are found at the end of each chapter.

For more in-depth information on teaching skillful sequencing, please refer to Chapter 7 in the book *Infusing the Teaching of Critical and Creative Thinking into Elementary Instruction*, by Robert Swartz and Sandra Parks. A computer disk containing the blank, reproducible graphic organizers used in this book is also available. Both book and disk are available through Critical Thinking Books & Software.

figure 8.3

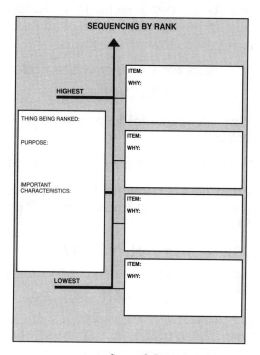

figure 8.5

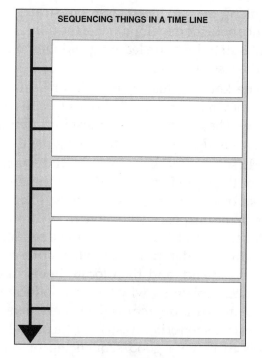

figure 8.4

FABLES
THE BEAR AND THE CROW

Language Arts

Grades 1–2

OBJECTIVES

CONTENT

Students will develop skills in recognizing plot development in a story. They will learn how to use details from the story to summarize the story and put the events into chronological order.

THINKING SKILL/PROCESS

Students will learn how to put things in order based on the purpose of the ordering and the criteria of the purpose.

METHODS AND MATERIALS

CONTENT

Students will work together in collaborative learning groups, using the book *Fables* by Arnold Lobel. Students should have prior experience in summarizing sections of a story using pictures or words.

THINKING SKILL/PROCESS

A thinking map will guide the teacher's directions in describing the task for the sequencing. Structured questioning facilitates the thinking process of sequencing for a purpose. A graphic organizer designed to fit drawings or print is used for the lesson.

LESSON

INTRODUCTION TO CONTENT AND THINKING SKILL/PROCESS

- **In our lives there are many things that we put in a particular order. We can order books by size, from smallest to largest. We can order rocks by weight, lightest to heaviest. We can order ropes by length, shortest to longest. With your partner, think of other kinds of orders.** Allow time for discussion with partners, and have several examples shared with the class.

- **When things are put in order, it means that they are sequenced.** Write the terms "order" and "sequence" on a chart or the chalkboard. **We are sequencing when we follow a pattern of things we do in the morning to get ready for school. We are following a sequence when we come to school and do our lessons in a regular pattern. When we make cookies, we follow a sequence of directions.**

- **Today we are going to practice putting things into a time order. We will begin by making a list of things that are organized by time sequence.** Write "Examples of Time Order" on the board. Ask for examples to put on the board. POSSIBLE STUDENT RESPONSES: *grades in school, the helper schedule, days of the week, the seasons, the order that we get our things ready to go home.*

- **Why is it important to put things in the right sequence? Discuss this in your groups.** Allow time for groups to discuss the reasons for sequencing. Share some of the reasons students give as a class. POSSIBLE STUDENT RESPONSES: *You have to learn the things in one grade before you can go on to the next. People need to know when they are coming to help in our room. When we go home, we will forget things if we don't plan and do all the things to get ready to go.*

- **I have a thinking map that will help you put things in order, or sequence them.** On a chart or chalkboard, show the Sequencing thinking map. **There are four questions we should answer** as we sequence. The first question asks "Why do you want to put them in order?" In the case of the helper schedule, we need to put the helpers in order so that they will know what day to come and help. We don't want all of them to come on one day or none of them to come on another day. The second question asks, "What is the best way to order them?" What would be the best way to sequence the helpers? POSSIBLE STUDENT RESPONSES: *The best way to sequence them is to use a calendar. The days are all in a sequence, and you*

<table>
<tr><td colspan="2">SEQUENCING</td></tr>
<tr><td>1.</td><td>Why do you want to put them in order?</td></tr>
<tr><td>2.</td><td>What is the best way to order them?</td></tr>
<tr><td>3.</td><td>What do you have to find out about them in order to know where they fit?</td></tr>
<tr><td>4.</td><td>Where does each item fit?</td></tr>
</table>

just have to add the names of the helpers. If there are the same helpers each week, you can make a chart of who helps on Monday, Tuesday, and all of the other days. **Those are good ideas. Now, let's look at the third question. It asks, "What do you have to find out about them in order to know where they fit?" For our helpers, we need to know who can come on each of the days. If the helper has another job on Tuesdays, we would not want to schedule them for that day. The fourth question asks us, "Where does each item fit?" When we look at the helpers, the days they can help, and the calendar, we need to put everything together so that we know and the helpers know who will help on each day.**

• As we read stories, we usually find that they are also usually written in a time sequence. The plot moves from event to event, beginning to end, in an order that makes the story enjoyable and understandable. Although not all stories are told in exactly the sequence that the events happened, the plots of many stories follow the sequence of events as they happened in time. This helps us to understand the story plot and how the events of the story follow each other.

THINKING ACTIVELY

• In this lesson, we are going to use a fable to practice our skills of sequencing the plot of a story as well as our skills of listening and summarizing. The story that we will use is from the book *Fables*, by Arnold Lobel. It is called, "The Bear and the Crow." Fables are stories that teach lessons. At the end of the story, there is a moral, a statement that says something that might be helpful for us to remember as we go about our lives. I will read you the moral at the end of the story, just as it was planned by the author. But the rest of the story will not be in order. There will be five sections of the story. One section will be the beginning, one section will be the end, and the rest will be in the middle. Each time I read a section, I will give you time to write (or draw) a short summary of what happened in that section on a piece of paper. The directions at this point may vary. The story has been split in two ways: in five sections and in three sections. Depending on the needs of students, the activity can be done using either of the divisions. For demonstration purposes, the rest of the lesson will be based on the five-section version of the story. It can be adapted easily to a three-section version.

• The first graphic organizer we will use helps us organize how and why we are sequencing. Show the How to Sequence Things graphic organizer on a chart or overhead transparency. The graphic organizer has a place for us to put the answers to the questions on the thinking map. The first question talks about purpose. The purpose of our sequencing is to put the events of a story, or its plot, into an order that makes sense. We will write this in the section labeled "Purpose." As the discussion develops, uncover each section on a transparency of the graphic organizer. In the space marked purpose write, "to put the events of a story into an order that makes sense." **The second question asks us to decide on the best way to order the items. How do you think we should order the events of the story?** POSSIBLE STUDENT RESPONSE: *We can put them in the order they happen in the story so they make sense when we read it.* **The way to do that is to use a time line. A time line begins at one point, just as a story does, and continues to another point where it ends, in this case, at the end of the story. We will write "time line" in the section called "Type of Sequence Used." The third question asks us what we need to find out about the items to know where they fit. What will you be listening for so that you will know where to place the parts of the story on the time line?** The students should talk about recognizing the beginning of the story where the characters and action are introduced, the middle of the story where events happen to the character, and the end of the story, where the problem is solved. **We can write this in the section labeled "what we need to know."** In the section labeled "what we need to know" write the criteria suggested by the students. "Beginning? (Characters and plot introduced) Middle? (Events happen to the character) Ending? (Problem is solved). Pass out a graphic organizer to each student.

- **I have given each of you a graphic organizer. You will also need five summary papers for this lesson. Each paper will be a place for you to write (or draw) a summary of the section I read to you.** Pass out five blank summary strips to each student. The papers on which the students will record their section summaries should be sized to fit into the time line graphic organizer. As an alternative, students who are not strong writers can draw the summaries.

- **The graphic organizer also has places for you to order the events of the story so that they match the actual sequence of the story. As we work, you will place the pieces in the order in which they seem to belong.** Demonstrate how the summary strips will fit into the sections of the graphic organizer. **However, we will not do any gluing until we have heard all of the sections as well as the moral of the story. This will allow us to check to** make sure the sections of the story follow the sequence of the plot.

- **We are ready to begin listening to the story sections. Here is a section of the story. Listen**

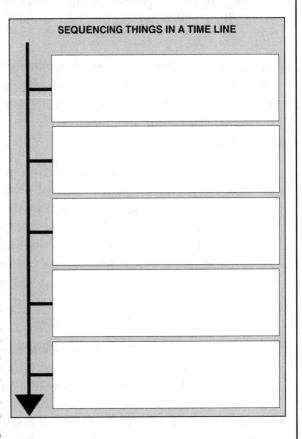

HOW TO SEQUENCE THINGS

PURPOSE:

TYPE OF SEQUENCE USED:

WHAT WE NEED TO KNOW:

SEQUENCING THINGS IN A TIME LINE

carefully to what the author is telling us. Read the section of the story that begins, "The Bear hurried home." Read with expression and with a pace that allows students to create a scenario in their minds. **As you were listening, were you thinking about where in the story this part belongs? On one of your strips of paper, write what happened in this part of the story.** Those who are drawing will draw the part of the story. **Then put the paper on the time line where you think it might belong.** Allow time for the students to put a summary statement on one strip and place it on the graphic organizer. Have the students share with a neighbor what reasons they have for their placement. The first section read should be identified as a middle section of the story. **What clues do you have that this section goes in the middle?** POSSIBLE STUDENT RESPONSES: *The bear hurried home. We don't know where he's been, so it's probably not the beginning. He does silly things, changing his clothes and wearing bags and sheets and frying pans, and we don't know why. It says he meets the crow again, so there was something that happened before.* Continue by reading another section. This time read the section that begins "The bear was on his way to town." Have students record a summary and place the strip on the graphic as they did with the first one.

- **As you heard another section, what were you thinking? Did you try to place it before or after the section you've already heard? Talk to a neighbor about the things that were clues to the placement of this section on our story time line.** Allow time for students to share their placement of the section and their reasons for the placement. They should be using their prediction skills as they work, planning for what they anticipate will be in the missing pieces based on the clues they hear in the story. **What clues were in this section to help you choose the place it belongs in the sequence of the story?** POSSIBLE STUDENT RESPONSES: *It tells what the bear is doing. It tells what he looks like, so it sounds like it is telling us about the character and the beginning of the story.*

- **We have heard two sections of the story. With two pieces to work with you were able to start framing a sequence. It is important for you to practice good listening skills in this activity. Why?** POSSIBLE STUDENT RESPONSES: *We have to hear the clues that tell us where the part fits into the story. We have to put down on the paper what happened in each part, so we have to listen and remember.*

- **We will go on now to another section of the story. Be sure to practice good listening!** Read another part of the story, and then follow the same format, allowing students time put down on a paper what happened in that section and putting the paper in the time line spot where they see it fitting in the story. Then continue until all of the parts have been completed. POSSIBLE STUDENT RESPONSES: The section beginning "This year," said the crow...: *This goes right before the bear goes home to dress funny. Now we know why he did that.* The section beginning "Crow, you did not tell the truth!": *This comes right after the bear gets embarrassed and goes home. He finds out the crow tricked him.* The section beginning "Forgive me for listening...": *This comes near the beginning because the bear meets the crow. The crow talks about how the bear is not dressed right.*

- **Now let's shift and think about what the story tells us. Here is the moral of the story: "When the need is strong, there are those who will believe anything." Who do you think really needed to believe something?** POSSIBLE STUDENT RESPONSE: *The bear.* **Why do you think that?** POSSIBLE STUDENT RESPONSE: *He wanted everyone to think he was the best dressed bear.* **Does the moral go with the story as you have it sequenced?** Answers usually are that it does match the way they have sequenced the story. **I'd like you to go back now and check your summary strips. Are they in the right order?** Allow students time to read just their sequences. **When you decide that they are just the way the story happened, retell the story to your partner in the order you placed the strips on your story time line. Check with your partner to see if you** agree on the sequence the story should follow. As students retell the story, they should be following the sequence in which they have the papers arranged on their time line. Working with a partner allows them to adjust where necessary.

- **You have practiced good listening skills as you heard the story of the bear and the crow. You have used your knowledge of the way that story plots develop and your skills of sequencing to arrange the story in the order that the author, Arnold Lobel, wrote the story. Listen as I read you the story, this time in the correct sequence.** Read the story. After discussing the story and its moral, have students complete the task by gluing the papers onto the time line.

THINKING ABOUT THINKING

- **What did you think about when you put the papers onto the story time line?** *I thought about where in the story each part fits.*

- **Let's compare what we did to the steps listed on the thinking map for putting things in order. What did we think about?** POSSIBLE STUDENT RESPONSES: *First, we decided why we wanted to put the events in order. We decided that we wanted to put them in order so the story would make sense. Next, we decided that the best way to order the events was by putting them in the order in which the author put them. Then, we had to find all the events and put them in the correct time order. We used the time line graphic organizer to help us see where all the events fit into place.*

- **Is it a good idea to think about the purpose of the sequencing and what we need to look for in order to make a good sequence before we do any sequencing?** Students usually agree that this is a good idea. They say that it helps them make the correct sequence.

APPLYING YOUR THINKING

Immediate Transfer

- **Use the story *The Mouse At the Seashore* to do another lesson that follows the same format. The story is included at the end of this lesson.**

- **Sequence the things you did yesterday from the last school bell until it was dinner time at your house. Use the sequencing thinking map to help you. You may write or draw the events of your day. A time line graphic organizer will help you to show your work.**

- **In the story *Little Polar Bear*, by Hans de Beer, the little polar bear has quite an adventure. Using the thinking map for sequencing and a time line graphic organizer, sequence the events in the story to show the order in which they happened to the bear. Retell the story to a friend using your time line for help.**

Reinforcement Later

- *A New Coat for Anna*, **by Harriet Ziefert, shows the sequence of making a coat. Use the sequencing thinking map and a graphic organizer to retell the steps in making Anna's coat. Explain why the sequence was so very important in the making of the coat.**

- **The caterpillar's life is interesting because of the changes it goes through. Use the thinking map for sequencing and a time line to show the sequence that a caterpillar follows on its journey to becoming a butterfly.**

SUGGESTED SPECIAL NEEDS MODIFICATIONS

Frontloading: For some students, understanding the purpose for sequencing in a certain way is a difficult concept. Teachers might need to begin with concrete situations to help develop the concept. You can explain the idea of purpose by using the word in the context of situations they are familiar with that don't involve sequencing. For example, you could say "The *purpose* I had in wearing a heavy coat today is to keep me warm when I am outside because it is cold. That's *why* I wore it." Then you could extend the idea of purpose to sequencing by saying something like "The *purpose* I had in ordering the books whose names begin with A, then those that begin with B next, and so forth, is so that you can find them easily. That's *why* I put them in that *sequence*."

You may also need to familiarize some students with the basic idea of sequencing. One idea is to visually model sequencing by using concrete objects or pictures to illustrate "first," "second," "next," etc.

Students may also benefit from a review of story elements. Using a familiar story (i.e., "Little Red Riding Hood"), reconstruct the story labelling the story events and elements (problem, solution, resolution).

Diversify: In this lesson format, students who need help with their writing are allowed to use pictures. Oral interaction with these students can be used to allow them to share their ideas verbally.

Special needs students are often aided by working in cooperative groups. Assigning the task of writing to a proficient writer in the cooperative group allows all students to contribute ideas while reducing the task load for beginning writers.

For young students, "summarizing" may take the form of "retelling." Often, students in the early stages of literacy development are not yet able to delete nonessential details in their retellings. With teacher paraphrasing and guidance, the essential events can be captured.

Expand the Possibilities: Assessments of written responses may be based upon students' thinking first, and expressive skills second. Oral responses or drawings may also reveal thinking beyond students' ability to express themselves in writing.

ASSESSING STUDENT THINKING ABOUT POSSIBILITIES

The transfer examples can be used for assessing students' skill levels by including a writing component that asks them to explain the steps of the different kinds of sequencing. The assessment can also occur as students present the work they've done and explain the steps they went through to complete the task. Use questions to encourage them to justify the decisions made during the process.

Source Material • The Bear and the Crow • 5 sections

The Bear was on his way to town, He was dressed in his finest coat and vest. He was wearing his best derby hat and his shiniest shoes. "How grand I look," said the Bear to himself. "The townsfolk will be impressed. My clothes are at the height of fashion."

"Forgive me for listening," said a Crow, who was sitting on the branch of a tree, "but I must disagree. Your clothes are not at the height of fashion. I have just flown in from town. I can tell you exactly how the gentlemen are dressed there."

"Do tell me!" cried the Bear. "I am so eager to wear the most proper attire!"

"This year," said the Crow, "the gentlemen are not wearing hats. They all have frying pans on their heads. They are not wearing coats and vests. They are covering themselves with bed sheets. They are not wearing shoes. They are putting paper bags on their feet."

"Oh, dear," cried the Bear. "My clothes are completely wrong!"

The Bear hurried home. He took off his coat and vest and hat and shoes. He put a frying pan on his head. He wrapped himself in a bed sheet. He stuffed his feet into large paper bags and rushed off toward the town.

When the Bear arrived on Main Street, the people giggled and smirked and pointed their fingers.

"What a ridiculous Bear!" they said.

The embarrassed Bear turned around and ran home. On the way he met the crow again.

"Crow, you did not tell the truth!" cried the Bear.

"I told you many things," said the Crow, as he flew out of the tree, "but never once did I tell you that I was telling the truth!"

Even though the Crow was high in the sky, the Bear could still hear the shrill sound of his cackling laughter.

Moral: When the need is strong, there are those who will believe anything.

Source Material • The Bear and the Crow • 3 sections

The Bear was on his way to town, He was dressed in his finest coat and vest. He was wearing his best derby hat and his shiniest shoes. "How grand I look," said the Bear to himself. "The townsfolk will be impressed. My clothes are at the height of fashion."

"Forgive me for listening," said a Crow, who was sitting on the branch of a tree, "but I must disagree. Your clothes are not at the height of fashion. I have just flown in from town. I can tell you exactly how the gentlemen are dressed there."

"Do tell me!" cried the Bear. "I am so eager to wear the most proper attire!"

"This year," said the Crow, "the gentlemen are not wearing hats. They all have frying pans on their heads. They are not wearing coats and vests. They are covering themselves with bed sheets. They are not wearing shoes. They are putting paper bags on their feet."

"Oh, dear," cried the Bear. "My clothes are completely wrong!"

The Bear hurried home. He took off his coat and vest and hat and shoes. He put a frying pan on his head. He wrapped himself in a bed sheet. He stuffed his feet into large paper bags and rushed off toward the town.

When the Bear arrived on Main Street, the people giggled and smirked and pointed their fingers.

"What a ridiculous Bear!" they said.

The embarrassed Bear turned around and ran home. On the way he met the crow again.

"Crow, you did not tell the truth!" cried the Bear.

"I told you many things," said the Crow, as he flew out of the tree, "but never once did I tell you that I was telling the truth!"

Even though the Crow was high in the sky, the Bear could still hear the shrill sound of his cackling laughter.

Moral: When the need is strong, there are those who will believe anything.

Source Material for Immediate Transfer

The following is a story that could be used for immediate transfer. The lesson could be another listening lesson, or it could be changed to a reading lesson by arranging the parts of the story so that they are out of sequence on the page that is given to the students. As in the original lesson, the students should summarize the parts of the story on strips of paper and then arrange them in the correct order. When they have completed the sequencing task, the story can be read to them in the correct order for checking, or it can be distributed to them for reading and self-checking.

The Mouse at the Seashore

A Mouse told his mother and father that he was going on a trip to the seashore.

"We are very alarmed!" they cried. "The world is full of terrors. You must not go!"

"I have made my decision," said the Mouse firmly. "I have never seen the ocean, and it is high time that I did. Nothing can make me change my mind."

"Then we cannot stop you," said Mother and Father Mouse, "but do be careful!"

The next day, in the first light of dawn, the Mouse began his journey. Even before the morning had ended, the Mouse came to know trouble and fear.

A Cat jumped out from behind a tree.

"I will eat you for lunch," he said.

It was a narrow escape for the Mouse. He ran for his life, but he left a part of his tail in the mouth of the Cat.

By afternoon the Mouse had been attacked by birds and dogs. He had lost his way several times. He was bruised and bloodied. He was tired and frightened.

At evening the Mouse slowly climbed the last hill and saw the seashore spreading out before him. He watched the waves rolling onto the beach, one after another. All the colors of the sunset filled the sky.

"How beautiful!" cried the Mouse. "I wish that Mother and Father were here to see this with me!"

The moon and the stars began to appear over the ocean. The Mouse sat silently on the top of the hill. He was overwhelmed by a feeling of deep peace and contentment.

Moral: All the miles of a hard road are worth a moment of true happiness.

Sample Student Responses • The Bear and the Crow

HOW TO SEQUENCE THINGS

PURPOSE:

To put the events of a story into an order that makes sense

TYPE OF SEQUENCE USED:

We can use a time line.

WHAT WE NEED TO KNOW:

Beginning? Meet characters and find out about the plot.

Middle? Things happen to the character.

End? The problem is solved.

Sample Student Responses • The Bear and the Crow

SEQUENCING THINGS IN A TIME LINE

The bear is going to town all dressed up so everyone can see him.

A crow tells him that he is dressed all wrong. Bear wants to know the right way to dress.

The crow tells the bear that everyone is wearing frying pans, bed sheets, and paper bags.

The bear goes home and changes to dress the way the crow said. When he goes to town, everyone laughs at him.

The bear went home embarrassed. He sees the crow, and the crow says he never said he was telling the truth.

WRITING

Language Arts   **Grades 1–2**

OBJECTIVES

CONTENT

Students will gather data to rank the stories they have written and, using the same grouping, rank the books they have checked out to read from the school library.

THINKING SKILL/PROCESS

Students will learn how to prioritize by selecting criteria for ranking, identifying things that meet those criteria, and explaining how items are ranked according to those criteria.

METHODS AND MATERIALS

CONTENT

Students will gather data to show the number of each type of book that has been written in the class and create a graph to show students' favorite type of book to write. They will gather separate data that will indicate the number of books of each type checked out from the library that week and the favorite kind of books to read.

THINKING SKILL/PROCESS

An explicit thinking map, graphic organizers, and structured questioning facilitate a thinking strategy for ranking items accurately for a specific purpose. Collaborative learning enhances the learning.

INTRODUCTION TO CONTENT AND THINKING SKILL/PROCESS

- **There are lots of ways to put things in order. The alphabet puts the letters in order and can be used to put words in order. The numbers come in a special order and so do the months of the year. Work in your groups to think of other things that are organized in a kind of order.** Allow time for students to think and discuss the sequencing that they know about. Share a few of the ideas with the whole class.

- **When things are put in order, it means that they are sequenced.** Write the terms "order" and "sequence" on the chalkboard or a chart. **We are sequencing when we make a schedule of things that we will do each day. We are following a sequence when we join a team and go to the practices and games. When we make cookies with the family, we follow a sequence of directions. Today we are going to study putting things into a special kind of order. We are going to rank things. Ranking means putting things in order by how much of a specific quality they have or by how well they serve a specific purpose. When I am looking for a new picture to hang on my wall, I may find several that I like. I think about the place that I will be hanging the picture, the colors that I think will be good there, and the amount of space that is available for the picture. I then buy the picture according to those specific characteristics .** On a chart or the chalkboard write "Thing To Be Ranked" and "Purpose—Why?" Underneath, write "pictures" and "to find the best picture for the room." **When you are asked to tell someone what your favorite toy, your favorite color, or your favorite television show is, you are ranking.** Write the three items in the column under "Thing to Be Ranked." **Why would someone want to know what your favorite toy is?** POSSIBLE STUDENT RESPONSES: *They might want to play with you. They want to know because they are your friend. They want to buy you a present.* **Why might you rank colors and television shows?** POSSIBLE STUDENT RESPONSES: Color— *They are going to get you a new shirt. They are going to give you a pencil. They are sharing crayons with* *you. They are making you a picture.* Television—*They want to know if you like the same shows. They are going to invite you over to watch television.*

- **Sometimes ranking is something you do quickly without a lot of thinking. But you should know why you are ranking. If there is a specific reason, you might change the way that you rank things. Let's try ranking colors.** Put a basic color chart on the chalkboard. **I want you to rank the colors according to your favorite color of shirt. Just write down the top three colors. Write your favorite, your second favorite, and your third favorite.** Allow time for students to write and compare their answers on a sheet of paper. **Now I want you to turn over your paper. We are going to rank colors again. This time I want you to rank your favorite color of dogs. Just write your three favorite colors of dogs.** Allow time for students to write and then compare their answers. **What did you notice about ranking colors?** POSSIBLE STUDENT RESPONSES: *The way that we ranked the colors changed. I like different colors of shirts than I do dog colors. There isn't even a purple dog and that is what my favorite shirt color is.* **Knowing the purpose for ranking seems to be something important. Here is a thinking map that will help you when you are ranking. It will help us to be careful thinkers when we rank things.** Display the thinking map for ranking on a chart or a chalkboard. It should be in a place where the students can read and refer to it during the lesson. **When you are ranking, you should know why you are ranking. This is the purpose of the ranking.** Read question one. **Question two asks "What should you find out in order to rank things for this purpose?" When you were thinking about your favorite shirt color you probably thought about all of the shirts you have at home or maybe you thought about the shirt you saw at the store last week. The last question asks how you decided to rank them and why you chose that order.** Read question three. **You may have said your favorite color was black because your dog is black and he is a great-looking dog.**

THINKING ACTIVELY

- **We have written many books during our writing workshop time this year. It would be interesting to see which books are our favorite kinds to write. We can rank the different books using our thinking map and graphic organizer for ranking.**

- **The graphic organizer for ranking has a place for us to record the answers to the thinking map questions.** Display a copy of the Sequencing By Rank graphic organizer on the overhead or a chart. **What is the thing being ranked?** *The books we write.* Fill in the chart as the class

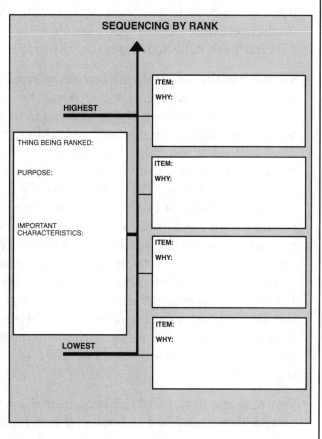

SEQUENCING BY RANK

1. **What is the purpose of the ranking?**

2. **What should you find out in order to rank things for this purpose?**

3 **How do these things rank from highest to lowest and why?**

SEQUENCING BY RANK

HIGHEST

ITEM:
WHY:

THING BEING RANKED:

PURPOSE:

IMPORTANT CHARACTERISTICS:

ITEM:
WHY:

ITEM:
WHY:

LOWEST

ITEM:
WHY:

responds. **What is the purpose for doing this?** *We want to see which books are our favorite kinds to write.* **Those two sections go with the first question on the thinking map.**

- **The next section asks us to write down the important characteristics. This means we have to decide what information we want to have so that we can do the ranking. That is the second question on the thinking map. What should we find out? How will we find it out? We will need to gather information about the books we have written that will tell us which books are our favorite kinds to write. Discuss with your partner how we could do this.** Share ideas with the class. POSSIBLE STUDENT RESPONSES: *We can ask everyone what their favorite is and put it on a graph. We can look at all the books on the shelf to see what kinds of books we have written.*

- **The ideas you have for gathering the information are good ones. We can find out information from a graph we make by asking students which books are their favorite kinds to write. We can also find out information by counting the different kinds of books we have written and making a graph with that information. On our graphic organizer, we should write the two important characteristics we are looking at for our ranking. You said you want to ask everyone to tell their favorite kind of book to write and put it on a graph. From the graph, we will be able to count the tally for each kind of book. That will answer the question, "How many votes did each kind get on our graph?"** Record the statement under "Important Characteristics." **Some of you think counting the books would give us important information, so let's write, "How many of each kind have been written?"** Record the second statement under "Important Characteristics."

- **I've noticed in talking with you during writing workshop that there are some general categories of books. I'll list the categories for you to use in making the graph and in grouping the books to count.** List the kinds of books students have been writing. A possible list might be books about me (biographies), books about my family and friends, make-believe books (fiction), and reports (nonfiction). Assign some groups the task of counting and categorizing books on the shelf, others to creating a graph, and others to collecting the data for the graph. When the data has been collected, the rest of the graphic organizer should be completed.

- **We have gathered all the information. Now we should combine the information and put it on our graphic organizer for ranking. We know that our books are being ranked and we know that the purpose of the ranking is to discover which books are our favorite kinds to write. What characteristics are we looking at to make the ranking?** *How many of each kind have been written and how many votes each kind got on the graph.* **The book counters have shown us their tallies and the numbers put the types of books into a ranking.** Refer to the tally list made by the book counters. **This ranking is only part of the information we gathered. To decide on our favorite kind of book to write we also must look at the information on the graph. This shows which kind of book each person in the class voted to be their favorite. We can put the two sets of numbers together to see which type of book ranks at the top. With your partner, add the number of votes given to nonfiction books with the number of nonfiction books written. Now add the numbers for fiction books, biographies, and books about families and friends.** The class should look at the data together and make decisions on the ranking based on the data. As they rank the items, place them in the diagram, using the number totals from the data collection in explaining why the item received the ranking. This information should be placed in an ordered sequence from most to least in the boxes down the right side of the graphic organizer.

- **Our ranking shows that fictional, or make-believe, books are our favorites to write. They received 9 votes and had 15 books written for a total of 24 points. The second book type in our** ranking had 17 books written and 6 votes for a total of 23 points. The third favorite seems to be books about family and friends with a total of 18 points, and the least favorite books to write seem to be nonfiction books with a total of 12 points. **Does the ranking give us information about our writing?** Students will have a variety of answers about what the ranking shows, but generally they will be commenting on how their opinions fit into the ranking.

- **We have spent time examining the kinds of stories you like to write. As we worked, some people wanted to know which books were our favorites to read. We can also rank these books. It would be interesting to see how the two rankings compare. Let's take a new graphic organizer for ranking and see what we can learn about our favorite books to read.** Display a new Sequencing By Rank graphic organizer. **Check with the thinking map to remember what we do first.** Have one student read the first question to the class. **What is the thing being ranked?** *The books we read.* **What is our purpose?** *To see what kinds of books we like to read.* Have someone read the second question on the thinking map. **What important characteristics should we consider?** Students usually realize that they can do similar kinds of data collection that they did for the first ranking, except that instead of counting how many books of a certain kind there are, they will have to find out how many of each kind of book have been taken out of the library. Guided questioning will help students to see that they will be able to compare the books they read with the books they write by using the same groupings of book types. To help them develop a data collection plan, ask them what someone does when there is a book in a library that they would like to read. They will usually respond that you take it out of the library. Then you can help them develop a plan for finding out how many of each kind of book have been taken out of the library. If they don't yet know that a record is kept when someone checks out a book, tell them.

- **As we work through the second ranking, we will use the same labels for the book types. We will again divide the tasks so that we can collect the data more quickly. Some of you will ask the students in our class what their favorite kind of book is to read. Others will construct the graph to show that information. Another group will tally the books that were checked out of the library this week to see what books we have just chosen to read. When all of the work has been completed, we will combine the information and rank the books on our graphic organizer.** As in the first ranking, divide the tasks among students and assist them in the collection of the data. When all information has been gathered, the class should again combine the numbers to find the rankings of the types of books they like to read.

- **It seems that the numbers show a different ranking this time. Nonfiction books have moved from the bottom of the ranking to the top. Why do you think that the rankings changed the second time?** Students will have a variety of answers, most alluding to the idea that we asked a different question. When they were asked about writing, they said one thing, and when they were asked about reading, they said another thing. **We can rank book types in different ways. When we changed the purpose for ranking, we ranked the books in different orders.**

- **The next time you are ready to write a book, you may want to consider the information we have from our two rankings. Will this information help you in deciding what kind of book you will write?** POSSIBLE STUDENT RESPONSES: *I am going to try to write something new. I keep writing the same kind of story. I want to write a nonfiction book because that is what the people in our room like to read. Then more people will want to read my book. I am going to read more biographies so that I can do a better job when I write about the things I do.* **Some of you may change the kinds of books you write and others may change the kinds of books you read. Either way, it seems that we have learned some interesting things about ourselves as we practiced ranking.**

THINKING ABOUT THINKING

- **Let's look back at the thinking we've done. What questions were important for you to answer as you practiced ranking as a way of sequencing?** The students should refer to the steps of the thinking map for ranking.

- **Do you think that this was an accurate way to rank things?** Most students will agree that this was an accurate way to rank. **Why?** Students will refer to making decisions about what they needed to know and to the ways that they collected the information.

- **What advice would you offer someone who needed to rank something?** Answers vary. Often the students will say not to guess but to have a plan. Many students will say to get help because the work goes faster when people work together.

APPLYING YOUR THINKING

Immediate Transfer

- The school has a variety of things to do at recess. There are many students using the playground at the same time. We need to gather information about how the playground is being used. Use the thinking map and graphic organizer for sequencing by rank to rank the areas of the playground by size. Then rank the areas of the playground by the numbers of students using them during a recess period. How do these rankings compare? What can you say about the information you've found?

- We are studying houses. Study the neighborhood around our school. What kinds of houses are in our neighborhood. Rank the houses according to the style of house. What can you learn from this ranking?

Reinforcement Later

- We have learned the characteristics of a fairy tale. For each fairy tale we have filled in our chart to show which characteristics were in the story. Rank the stories we have read to show which are the best examples of fairy tales. The best examples of fairy tales would be the ones with the most characteristics from our chart. The thinking map and graphic organizer for sequencing by ranking will help you.

- Use a time line to show how you spend a Saturday. Rank the things according to which are the most important to you and which take up the most time. Are there any changes in your day that would give you more time to do the things that are the most important?

SUGGESTED SPECIAL NEEDS MODIFICATIONS

<u>Frontload</u>: For some students, verbalizing purposes and characteristics that define purpose can be difficult. The "characteristics" are similar to developing a criteria for determining what constitutes "best," for example. Students may benefit from prior experience with this type of thinking using everyday examples. The teacher may think aloud his/her criteria for making choices: "I wonder which color marker I should use. Let's see. It must be dark enough so everyone can see it on the chart and it should be different from the last color so we can see I'm starting something new. Based on these characteristics (criteria), I'll choose black."

For some learners, especially those with specific types of language delays, concepts such as "first," "second," etc. can be challenging. Students may benefit from physically arranging objects or themselves in these positions while using this terminology.

Clarify: It is important to stress with students that "criteria" is a broader concept than just frequency (number of times we do something), quantity (number of objects or votes) or unsubstantiated preferences. As stated in the Frontload section above, think aloud examples using several forms of criteria may be necessary.

Diversify: Cooperative groups in which the proficient writer has the assigned job of "scribe" would allow students with difficulty writing to participate in the thinking while reducing the task demands.

This lesson may be divided into two sessions in order to focus thinking on the task at hand.

Expand the Possibilities: Assessments of written responses may be based upon students' thinking first, and expressive skills second. Oral responses or drawings may also reveal thinking beyond students' ability to express themselves in writing.

ASSESSING STUDENT THINKING ABOUT RANKING

The transfer examples can be used for assessing students' skill levels by including a writing component that asks them to explain the steps of the ranking. The assessment can also occur as students present the work they've done and explain the steps they went through to complete the task. Use questions to encourage them to justify the decisions made during the process.

Sample Student Responses • Writing

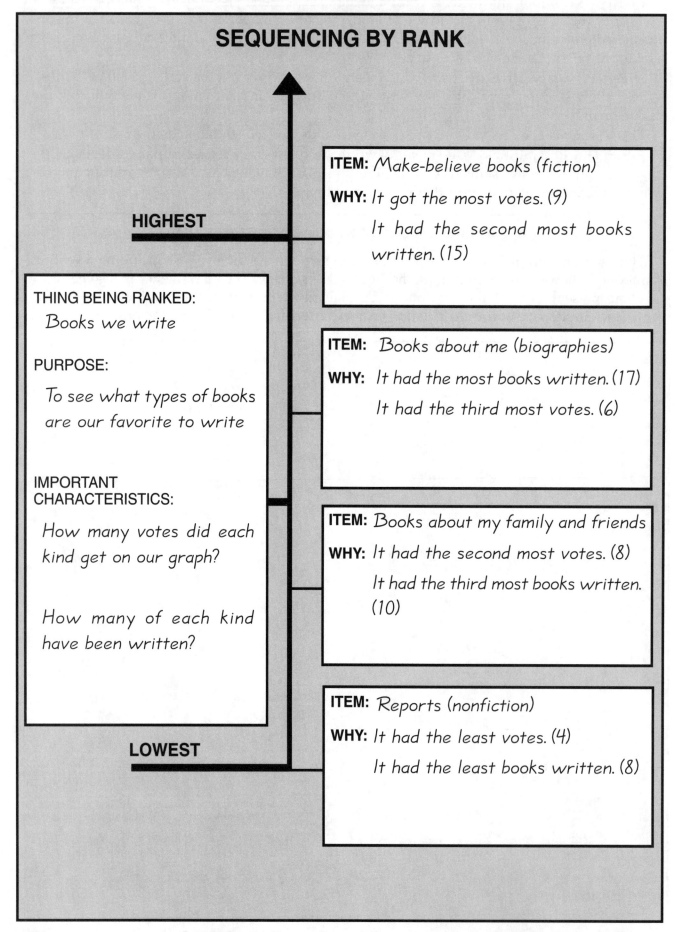

SEQUENCING BY RANK

HIGHEST

ITEM: *Make-believe books (fiction)*

WHY: *It got the most votes. (9)*

It had the second most books written. (15)

THING BEING RANKED:

Books we write

PURPOSE:

To see what types of books are our favorite to write

IMPORTANT CHARACTERISTICS:

How many votes did each kind get on our graph?

How many of each kind have been written?

ITEM: *Books about me (biographies)*

WHY: *It had the most books written. (17)*

It had the third most votes. (6)

ITEM: *Books about my family and friends*

WHY: *It had the second most votes. (8)*

It had the third most books written. (10)

LOWEST

ITEM: *Reports (nonfiction)*

WHY: *It had the least votes. (4)*

It had the least books written. (8)

Sample Student Responses • Writing

SEQUENCING BY RANK

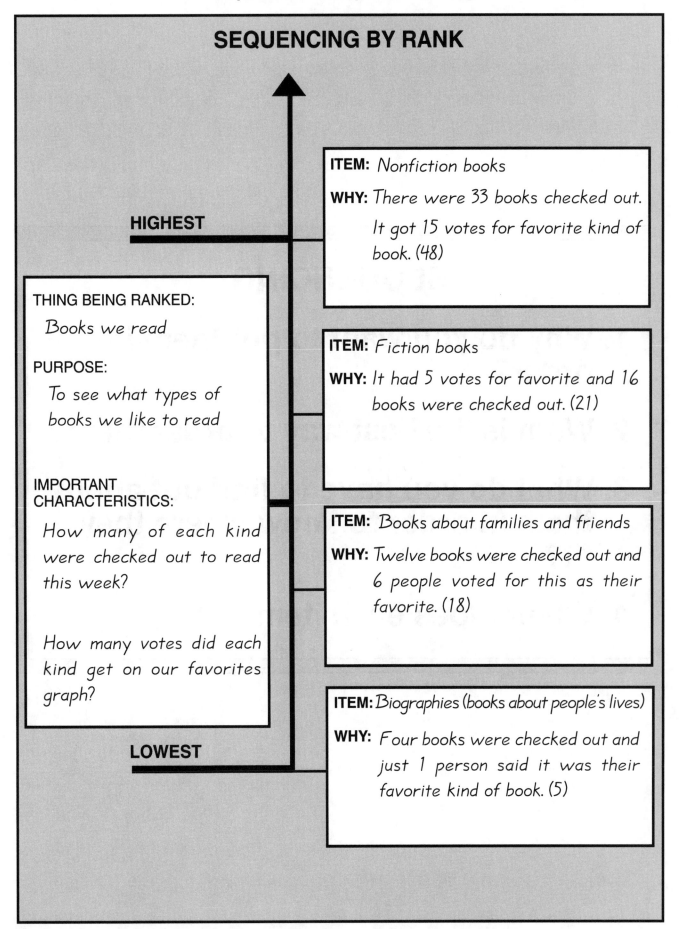

HIGHEST

THING BEING RANKED:

Books we read

PURPOSE:

To see what types of books we like to read

IMPORTANT CHARACTERISTICS:

How many of each kind were checked out to read this week?

How many votes did each kind get on our favorites graph?

LOWEST

ITEM: Nonfiction books

WHY: There were 33 books checked out. It got 15 votes for favorite kind of book. (48)

ITEM: Fiction books

WHY: It had 5 votes for favorite and 16 books were checked out. (21)

ITEM: Books about families and friends

WHY: Twelve books were checked out and 6 people voted for this as their favorite. (18)

ITEM: Biographies (books about people's lives)

WHY: Four books were checked out and just 1 person said it was their favorite kind of book. (5)

SEQUENCING

1. Why do you want to put them in order?

2. What is the best way to order them?

3. What do you have to find out about them in order to know where they fit?

4. Where does each item fit?

HOW TO SEQUENCE THINGS

PURPOSE:

_____

_____

TYPE OF SEQUENCE USED:

_____

_____

WHAT WE NEED TO KNOW:

_____

_____

_____

_____

_____

_____

SEQUENCING THINGS IN A TIME LINE

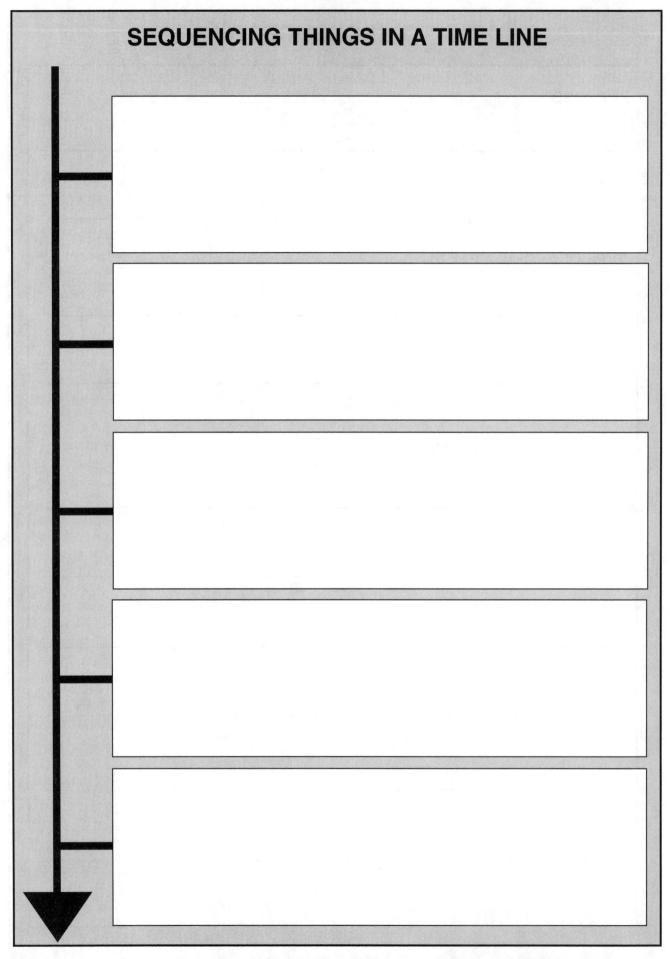

SEQUENCING BY RANK

1. What is the purpose of the ranking?

2. What should you find out in order to rank things for this purpose?

3 How do these things rank from highest to lowest and why?

SEQUENCING BY RANK

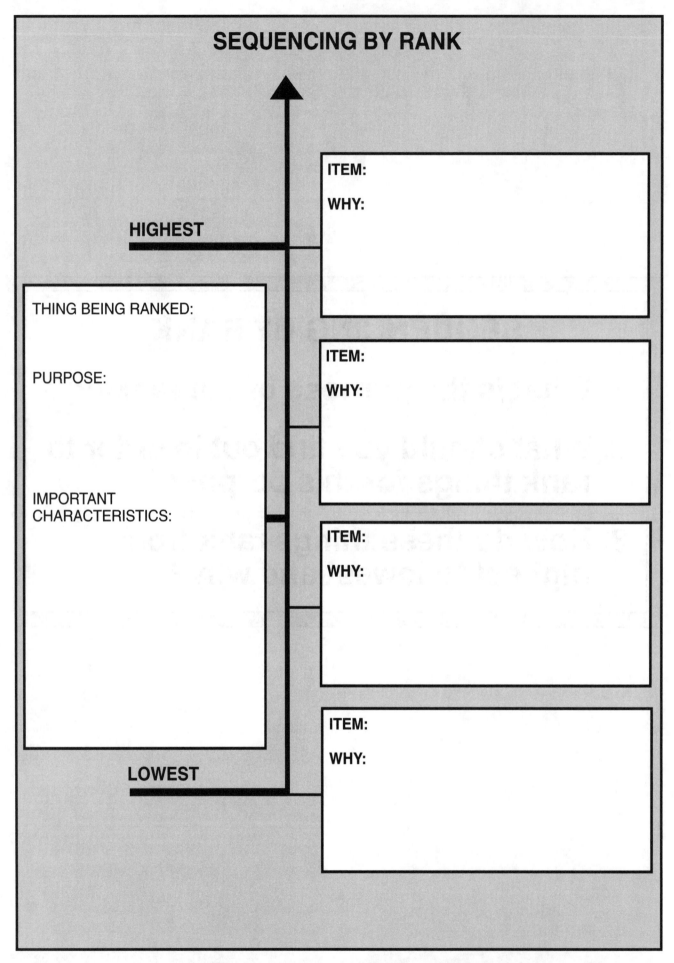

HIGHEST

LOWEST

THING BEING RANKED:

PURPOSE:

IMPORTANT
CHARACTERISTICS:

ITEM:

WHY:

ITEM:

WHY:

ITEM:

WHY:

ITEM:

WHY:

CHAPTER 9
FINDING REASONS AND CONCLUSIONS

Infusing Finding Reasons and Conclusions into Language Arts

Teaching students how to find conclusions and supporting reasons in grades 1 and 2 involves teaching students to analyze arguments by asking and answering the following questions:

> **FINDING REASONS AND CONCLUSIONS**
>
> 1. **What are you being asked to conclude about what you should accept or do?**
>
> 2. **What reasons are provided to convince you to accept or do that?**

figure 9.1

When these questions are made explicit, what results is what you find in figure 9.1—a thinking map for skillful argument analysis. In the lessons in this chapter, this thinking map is used to guide your students' thinking explicitly as they engage with the lesson content.

When students learn and use this strategy for locating and articulating conclusions that people come to and the reasons they offer to support their conclusions, they first look for the author's conclusion and then attend to indicator words like "because" and "therefore" to locate the reasons offered to support this conclusion. This strategy helps students find the "main idea" of a passage (often a conclusion) and the supporting details (often the reasons offered in support of the main idea), as well as locate conclusions and reasons given in more direct persuasive writing.

These lessons also supplement the use of the thinking map for reasons and conclusions with various supporting classroom strategies such as using graphic organizers, engaging in cooperative thinking, thinking about thinking, and continued guided practice. These classroom strategies enhance both the thinking skill that the stu-

dents are learning and their mastery of the lesson content.

The key graphic organizer for finding reasons and conclusions is in figure 9.2.

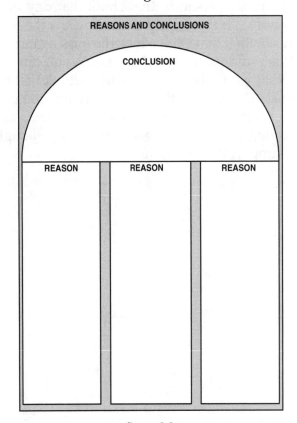

figure 9.2

This graphic organizer provides a place for students to write down what they identify as the conclusion of the argumentative passage they are given, and then, in the supporting columns, the reasons they think are offered. These columns can be divided to provide room for more than three reasons. It is always a good idea, when possible, to give students at least two arguments offered from opposing viewpoints, as is done in the lessons in this book, and to ask them not to decide if one is a good argument before they consider the other. This fosters their open-mindedness.

To supplement what is a purely analytical task, students can also be asked to evaluate whether the reasons given in any specific argument that they have identified are good reasons, or whether they are strong enough to support the conclusion. This should be done orally in class with students referring to specific examples to help students start to think about when they need better reasons than they have to be able to support a conclusion. You can describe a situation in which something is missing from the classroom and someone saw an unfamiliar person in the school that day, and then ask: "Is that a good reason to draw the conclusion that that person took the missing item?" When students realize that it is not, you can ask "What would be good reasons to think that he took it?" Then, in the lesson activity, you can refer back to this example when students are judging whether the reasons are strong enough to support the conclusion.

When opposing arguments are analyzed by the class, you can have half the class or half the student groups explore one argument and the other half explore the other, and then report back to class. If they disagree, they can debate the issue in class. Reproducible blank graphic organizers are found at the end of each chapter.

For more in-depth information on teaching skillful decision making, please refer to Chapter 8 in the book *Infusing the Teaching of Critical and Creative Thinking into Elementary Instruction*, by Robert Swartz and Sandra Parks. A computer disk containing the blank, reproducible graphic organizers used in this book is also available. Both book and disk are available through Critical Thinking Books & Software.

FOX ON THE LOOSE!
FLOSSIE AND THE FOX

Language Arts   **Grades 1–2**

OBJECTIVES

CONTENT

Students will read to discover and evaluate conclusions and the supporting reasons provided by characters in a story.

THINKING SKILL/PROCESS

Students will learn to recognize conclusions and the supporting reasons offered for these conclusions.

METHODS AND MATERIALS

CONTENT

Students will read *Flossie and the Fox* by Patricia C. McKissack.

THINKING SKILL/PROCESS

Detecting reasons and conclusions is guided by structured questioning and by the use of a graphic organizer that highlights the conclusion and its supporting reasons for an argument.

LESSON

INTRODUCTION TO CONTENT AND THINKING SKILL/PROCESS

- Today we are going to practice a kind of thinking called *finding reasons and conclusions*. Recently I received an advertisement about a vacuum. The ad gave many *reasons* why I should buy the vacuum. It said that the vacuum was very easy to use. It has tremendous power to pick up dirt from my floors, and has many extra pieces that would make cleaning so much easier for me and for anyone else who owns that vacuum. The ad was encouraging me to buy this vacuum. Many *reasons* were given to *convince* me that this would be a good thing to do.

- My friend also tried to *convince* me to do something, but it wasn't buying a vacuum. She wanted me to take a class on making pottery with her. She told me how much fun it would be, and how we could make gifts for our family and friends. She said it would be a good way to relax while learning something new.

- There are labels we can use to identify and understand what was being said in these situations. What the person or ad was trying to convince me to do or believe was a *conclusion* they wanted me to accept based on the *reasons* given. The reasons are presented to convince a person to accept or to believe an idea or position as a true statement. The ad was trying to convince me and anyone else who read it to buy a new vacuum. My friend was trying to convince me that I should take a pottery class. Write the words "reasons" and "conclusions" on the chalkboard or on a flipchart to help students recall them and become familiar with their meanings.

- **Has anyone ever tried to convince you of something by giving you reasons to believe or accept what he is saying? Talk to your partner about one of these times.** Allow share time. Ask for a few examples. Have the students state exactly what the other person was trying to convince them of and the reasons that were given. Identify the reasons and conclusions using the terms to support the students in making the meaning connection.

- Looking for reasons that are given to support the conclusions is important. We can see if the reasons are good and support the conclusion. If they do, then we can believe or act according to the conclusion. If they are not good reasons, or if they are not enough to support the conclusion, then we shouldn't accept it for the reasons given. I thought that the reasons my friend was offering to take the pottery class were good ones so I did take it. But I didn't think that the reasons for my buying the vacuum cleaner were good enough because I didn't need a new vacuum cleaner—I already had one that worked fine. Sometimes there is more information needed to make the reasons good ones that will convince you of the conclusion. Discuss with your partner the reasons you were given for the conclusion the person was trying to convince you of. Were they good supporting reasons? Why? If not, why not? Allow share time, then ask for one or two class examples.

- The thinking map for finding reasons and conclusions has two main questions. Show the thinking map for finding reasons and conclusions on a chart or on the chalkboard. It should be visible to the students during the lesson. The first question asks us what the author or person is trying to convince us to do or believe. It says, "What are you being asked to conclude about what you should accept or do?" In the

> **FINDING REASONS AND CONCLUSIONS**
>
> 1. **What are you being asked to conclude about what you should accept or do?**
>
> 2. **What reasons are provided to convince you to accept or do that?**

case of the vacuum ad, they wanted me to conclude that I should buy that vacuum. The second guiding question asks us to think about the reasons that are given for doing what they want. "What reasons are provided to convince you to accept or do that?" The reasons for buying the vacuum were all of the special features and the ability of the machine to make my cleaning a much easier task.

- People sometimes use clue words when they are giving reasons and conclusions. If they are telling the reasons first, they sometimes use the word "so" or the word "therefore." Here's an example: It is raining, *so* you need your umbrella to walk to the store. Or I could say, "It is raining, *therefore* you need your umbrella to walk to the store. What is it I want to convince you of? *To take an umbrella when I walk to the store.* What is the reason I gave you? *It is raining.* In your groups, practice using the words "so" and "therefore" to state reasons and conclusions. You can use the examples you shared earlier. Allow practice time. A chart with the examples you have used may be helpful, since students can reread the sentences to clarify their thinking. You should highlight the words "so," "therefore," and "because."

- If the conclusion is given first, different signal words are used. Consider this example: I am trying to convince you to read a new book. I might say, "I think you should read this new book *because* it's very exciting and has a surprise ending." What was the signal word? *Because* In this case, the conclusion, I want you to read the book, comes first, and the reasons, that it is exciting and has a surprise ending, come last. Using the same examples of your own, practice this with your partner. Use the signal word "because." Share 3 or 4 statements after they have had a chance to practice.

THINKING ACTIVELY

- Here is a graphic organizer that can help us when we are working with reasons and conclusions. Show the graphic organizer for reasons and conclusions by using a transparency, or by drawing it on the chalkboard or on a flipchart. The conclusion the person is trying to convince you of goes in the top section. The reasons being offered as to why you should believe or do what the person says go in the bottom spaces. The graphic organizer has this shape to help you remember that the reasons support the conclusion. Let's try a sample on the graphic organizer. Pretend you are in the car with your family, ready to go to the store. You are talking to your little brother, trying to convince him to put on his seat belt. Look at the thinking map's first question. What conclusion do you want your little brother to accept? Students will easily identify the conclusion as that your brother should put his seat belt on in the car. If they have difficulty, you can ask "What are you trying to convince him of about his seat belt? Write the conclusion on the graphic organizer in the dome. **The second question on the thinking map asks for reasons. What reasons do you think would support this belief that seat belts should be worn?** POSSIBLE STUDENT RESPONSES: *If there is a car accident he won't get tossed out of the car. Seat belts keep people from getting hurt. If the police see you they can give your mom or dad a ticket.* Write the reasons on the graphic organizer. **Are**

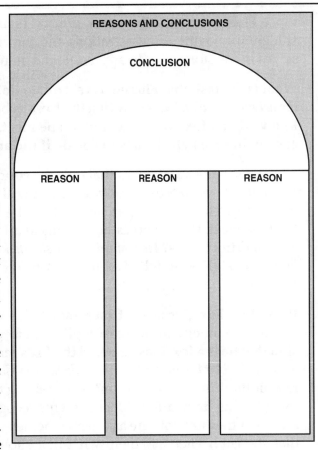

these good reasons for your little brother wearing his seat belt? Do you think that there is anything else you might find out that would show that maybe he shouldn't, like the information that I had about my vacuum cleaner? Most students agree that there isn't anything else that you could find out that would be relevant here, and that these are good reasons to support the conclusion that your little brother should wear his seatbelt.

- **Often we can find reasons and conclusions in the stories we read. One character may try to convince another character of something, or the writer may try to convince you, the reader, of something. Today we will read a book with reasons and conclusions in the story. Imagine that you are a little girl sent on an errand by your mother. The path takes you through the forest. What problems or dangers might you encounter?** POSSIBLE STUDENT RESPONSES: *A wild animal, getting lost, eating poison plants* **What stories have you read that have a little girl going through the forest to do an errand?** *Little Red Riding Hood* **In** *Little Red Riding Hood* **the girl meets a wolf. This wolf is very tricky. What trick does he play on Little Red Riding Hood?** *He pretends to be the grandmother to eat her.* **The little girl says, "My what big eyes you have!" and "My what big ears you have!" and "My what big arms you have!" Each time the wolf gives her a reason to believe he is the grandmother. What does he say?** *The better to see you, the better to hear you, the better to hug you.* **What conclusion does he want Little Red Riding Hood to believe?** *That he is her grandmother.* **Little Red Riding Hood continues to question because she has doubts. She doesn't believe that the reasons support the conclusion that it is her grandmother in the bed. However, she was too slow in deciding not to believe the argument, because the wolf jumped out of bed and ate her. Thank goodness for the woodcutter!**

- **In today's story we will meet another little girl who must go through a forest. She also will be confronted by an animal. This time the animal will be a fox and the girl will be named Flossie. As we read, we will be looking for whether there is anything the fox tries to con-**

vince Flossie of and, if there is, what it is and what reasons he offers. Read the story with students, enjoying the illustrations and the rich language. Allow students to immerse themselves in the story so as to appreciate the many and varied feelings of the fox and Flossie.

- **What is the task that Flossie has set out to do?** *She has to take a basket of eggs through the woods to the neighbors' farm.* **We know that the fox has been stealing eggs. We know that Flossie doesn't know what a fox looks like. But as she meets this animal, and he can't take his eyes off the eggs in her basket, she has to decide if the animal is who he says he is.**

- **Now let's make a statement that tells the conclusion the fox is trying to get Flossie to believe.** *He wants Flossie to believe that he is a fox.* **I will record the conclusion on a fresh graphic organizer.** Use a chart or transparency so it will be visible for the whole class. **When Flossie and the fox first meet, the fox gives no reasons at all to support his conclusion that he is a fox. Why do you think that is?** *He just thinks she should know that he is a fox. He is too busy looking at the eggs in her basket.* **Flossie tells Fox he must prove that he is a fox. She is asking him to provide reasons for her to believe him.**

- **What does Fox give as his first reason?** *That he is furry. He has thick, luxurious fur.* **I will record this reason on one of the reason pillars. Fox gives Flossie this reason to support his conclusion that he is a fox. Flossie heard the fox's reason. But what does she tell him?** *She says that he must be a rabbit because rabbits have thick, luxurious fur.* **What is Flossie telling the fox about this reason for thinking he is a fox? Is she telling him that it is a good reason or not a good reason for thinking he is a fox?** Most students recognize that she is telling him that it is not a good reason. If they are not sure ask them whether Flossie is convinced that he is a fox. They will say that she isn't. Then ask them what that shows about whether she thinks the reason should convince her. They will see that this means that she thinks that the reason is not good enough to convince her. **Flossie is telling Fox that he has not provided reasons that support the conclusion that he is a fox. Now we have an upset fox. He runs away, but is soon back with another reason to add to his first. What is his next reason?** *He has a long, pointed nose.* Record this reason on another pillar. **Now there are two reasons that the fox has given. Flossie is ready to decide whether this is a good reason. Does she think this is a good reason for accepting his conclusion that he is a fox?** *No, she says that he could be a rat because rats have long, pointed noses.*

- **So far Fox has not given reasons that Flossie thinks support his conclusion. Flossie skips away, but of course, they meet again soon. This time a large, orange cat joins them. Fox wants the cat to tell Flossie that he is a fox. He thinks that Flossie will believe the cat. What does the cat say?** *The cat says that it is a fox because it has sharp claws and yellow eyes.* **Again, we will record this reason on a pillar. How does Flossie evaluate the reasons? Does she think they support the conclusion that he is a fox?** *No, she says they are both cats.*

- **Let's stop for a minute and think about what kind of thinking Flossie is doing. Fox has given three reasons, but I am not sure that Flossie is thinking about all of the reasons together. Let's check back. Right now, at this point in the story, Flossie says they both could be cats. But I don't think all of the reasons support the conclusion that Fox is a cat. Which reason would not support Fox being a cat?** Allow students time to reread the reasons and discuss whether they support Fox being a cat. They should recognize that cats do not have long, pointed noses. **It seems that Flossie is looking at only the reason that Fox is offering each time they meet. Fox has not asked her to look at the reasons all together. Let's continue to examine the reasons, keeping in mind that Flossie seems to be considering only the new reason each time Fox returns.**

- **What is Fox's next reason?** *He says he has a bushy tail.* Record the reason on a pillar. **How does Flossie evaluate this reason?** *She doesn't think a bushy tail means he has to be a fox. He could be a squirrel.* **Fox is getting very frustrated. He wants to just promise that he is a fox. A promise is not a reason, so we can't write that on a pillar. A reason needs to provide some information that supports the conclusion. A promise does not do that. It only asks us to use our feelings or emotions to believe.**

- **By now Flossie has reached the other side of the woods, with Fox following right behind her. He is crying and pleads for one more chance to prove he is a fox. Flossie agrees to listen. What are his final reasons?** *He has sharp teeth and can run very fast.* Record these reasons on the reason pillars. **Do you know of any other animals that have sharp teeth and run exceedingly fast?** Students should be able to think of many animals that have those attributes. **Does Flossie evaluate the reasons and tell him again that they don't support the conclusion that he is a fox?** *No, she says she believes him now, but the dogs are coming to chase him away.*

- **Each time Flossie has only considered the reasons given at that moment, but this time, even though you know the reason does not support the conclusion, she agrees that he is a fox. Why does she agree now?** *Because the dogs are right there to chase the fox away. He can't get the eggs.* **Perhaps there was a point in the story that Flossie did believe the fox, but did not want to tell him. Why do you think that might have been the case?** POSSIBLE STUDENT RESPONSES: *Maybe she was convinced he was a fox but wanted to trick him. She wanted to get the fox to where the dog could chase him away so she made believe she wasn't convinced.*

- **So let's look at all the reasons that the fox gave together and evaluate them for ourselves. Would you be convinced that this was a fox for the reasons given?** Have students work with their partners and look over all of the reasons on the graphic organizer and evaluate whether together they support the conclusion that the animal is indeed a fox. When they have finished their discussion, they usually feel that the reasons together do support the conclusion. **I'm going to write "Good Reasons" under the diagram on the graphic organizer and check the conclusion to indicate that the reasons are good enough to support the conclusion.**

- **I am just now remembering that there is still another reason that was in the story. It was mentioned in the first few pages. Let's go back and check. Good readers often go back into a story to check on things. That helps them to understand the story and its characters better.** Read the first few pages of the story to the point where the fox introduces himself to Flossie. **What did Big Mama tell Flossie about the fox?** *She told her that the fox loved eggs.* **Would this be a good reason to add? Could Flossie tell if the fox loved eggs?** *The fox kept staring at the eggs, so he must have really wanted them.* **If we add this to the list of reasons would this make the reasons even better?** Most students say that it would. **So even when we have good reasons for something we might find out other things that make the reasons better.**

- **The story ends with a happy Flossie and a happy fox. Flossie got to complete the job of delivering the eggs, and even though he did not get the eggs, Fox finally convinced Flossie that he was a fox!**

THINKING ABOUT THINKING

- **Let's look back at the thinking we did. What did we do to find the reasons and conclusions?** *When we read the book, we thought about what the fox was trying to convince Flossie to believe. Then we looked for the reasons he offered Flossie to convince her that he was a fox.*

- Let's take a look at the thinking map again. We can look at the things we did to find the **reasons and conclusions in our story and see if we asked all of the questions on the thinking map.** Show the thinking map. Read each step and discuss, comparing how it matches the story. Point out to students that in this case the word "you" means Flossie. Also ask the students whether or not there were signal words that indicated what the reasons were. In this case there are not, but the fox makes it clear that he is giving Flossie reasons to believe that he is a fox.

- **What help was the graphic organizer in this lesson?** POSSIBLE STUDENT RESPONSES: *It was shaped to look like a tower. The reasons are supposed to hold up the conclusion. If they don't then the tower will fall down. That helped me to think about whether the reasons were good reasons. The graphic organizer shows us that we shouldn't believe a conclusion unless there are good reasons in the pillars to support it.*

APPLYING YOUR THINKING

Immediate Transfer

- Watch carefully the commercials that are on during one of your favorite television shows. Think about what the commercial is trying to convince you to do or believe. Are any reasons given? Are the reasons good? Do they support the conclusion? Use a reasons and conclusions think map and graphic organizer to help you with your thinking.

- In the book, *Noisy Nora,* what was Nora's conclusion? What reasons did she give to support her conclusion? Did her reasons support her conclusion? Use the reasons and conclusions thinking map and graphic organizer to help you.

Reinforcement Later

- In our studies of the Pilgrims we learned of the many difficulties they faced during their first year in the new land. What reasons did the Pilgrims have for inviting the Indians to the celebration of the first Thanksgiving? Did the reasons support the conclusion that the Indians belonged at this first feast? Use the thinking map and graphic organizer for reasons and conclusions to show why the Indians should be invited.

- In our health studies we have been told that frequent washing of hands helps to keep us healthy. What reasons are given to support this conclusion? Use the thinking map and graphic organizer for reasons and conclusions to determine if there are good reasons for washing our hands frequently.

- Although some insects seem to be a nuisance to us, there are insects that can be very helpful. Pick an insect that has been identified as helpful. What reasons would support the conclusion that we should not kill this insect whenever we find it? Use the thinking map and graphic organizer for reasons and conclusions to help you decide if the reasons are good and support the conclusion.

WRITING EXTENSION

(In grade 1 this could be done orally instead of having the students write.)

Ask the students to go back to one of the passages in which the fox tries to convince Flossie that he is a fox and rewrite it in two ways: first by adding signal words before the conclusion, and second by adding signal words after the conclusion.

It is November, and Thanksgiving is coming. The Pilgrims wanted to invite their friends the Indians to a feast. Pretend you are a Pilgrim boy or girl. Write a letter asking one of your Indian friends to come to the feast. Be sure to give the reasons that you think your Indian friend should come. Use the thinking map and a reasons and conclusions graphic organizer to plan your thoughts before you write.

We have learned in our health lessons that it is very important to wash our hands frequently. Write a note to an imaginary friend, and explain to them why they should wash their hands. Plan your note first using a reasons and conclusions thinking map and graphic organizer.

ART EXTENSION

In our study of insects we have read that some insects are helpful and should not be killed. Choose an insect that is helpful. Create a poster telling people not to kill this insect. Give reasons to support your conclusion. To plan your project, use the thinking map and graphic organizer for reasons and conclusions.

SUGGESTED SPECIAL NEEDS MODIFICATIONS

Frontloading: Prior to this lesson, some students may need multiple examples of drawing conclusions. "Concluding" requires the ability to infer something new from given information. Initially, the teacher may wish to think aloud conclusions which are based on data. Situations may range from curricular related items ("I notice a pattern in these words, I conclude the vowel has a long e because it has the vowel-consonant-silent e pattern") to daily situations (I notice a pattern of hurt feelings on the playground. I conclude that our class needs to discuss ways to solve problems."). As students state their own conclusions, they should be required to provide their reasons for the conclusions. Prior introduction and practice is beneficial if students are to be able to identify the conclusions and the reasons offered to support them .

For some students, understanding a *reason* for a conclusion may be difficult. Teachers may need to introduce these terms in the context of content area lessons and daily situations to provide students with prior practice. For example, in reading, students might be asked to discuss or list reasons for a character's actions. These can then be linked to the conclusions the character comes to. Similarly daily events can be used to highlight the relationship between the terms. "My conclusion is that we won't have outdoor recess. My reason is that it is raining."

Signal words may be a new concept to some students. This may require preteaching of the concept using everyday examples in which the signal word is highlighted and explained. For example, "It is chilly outside SO you should wear a jacket. 'So' tells me the reason I need a jacket." A list of the common signal words can be posted. Students may need multiple examples of these sentence types with the signal words in both the initial and medial position prior to this lesson.

Clarify: *Reasons* can also be referred to as *clues* or *evidence*.

Diversify: Due to the rich language and complexity of the story, students may benefit from hearing the story read aloud several times before they attempt to dissect it for reasons and conclusions.

The lesson itself could be guided over several sessions with the read aloud for enjoyment of the story occurring during one session and a rereading provided when the analysis stage is introduced. Similarly, students may benefit from segmenting the lesson with the Introduction in one session so that the concept of reason and conclusion can be more fully explained, and the Thinking Actively portion in a subsequent session after a brief review of the class examples of reasons and conclusions.

Some students may need additional guidance in stating ("breaking out") an argument based upon what is said in a text. The teacher may wish to talk through this process, guiding students' thinking through questions calling for support. This can be done in small groups or modelled with the large group.

Students who need help with their writing may respond orally or participate in a cooperative group in which a proficient writer serves as recorder. Oral interaction with these students can help them articulate what they have written. It is important that the thinking take precedence over the writing for these students.

Expand the Possibilities: Assessments of written responses may be based upon students' thinking first, and expressive skills second. Oral responses may also reveal thinking beyond students' ability to express themselves in writing.

ASSESSING STUDENT THINKING ABOUT REASONS AND CONCLUSIONS

Any of the transfer activities can be used as assessment tools. Be sure to look for evidence that students are identifying the conclusions they give, and that the reasons are supportive. If using reasons and conclusions from another source, have them evaluate the reasons and conclusions.

Sample Student Responses • Fox on the Loose!

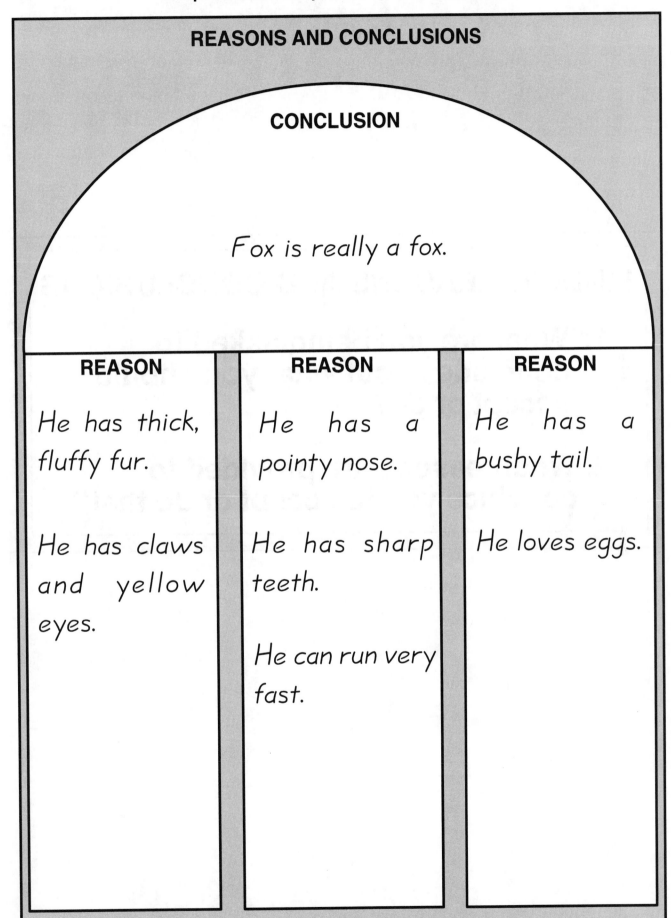

REASONS AND CONCLUSIONS

CONCLUSION

Fox is really a fox.

REASON	REASON	REASON
He has thick, fluffy fur. *He has claws and yellow eyes.*	*He has a pointy nose.* *He has sharp teeth.* *He can run very fast.*	*He has a bushy tail.* *He loves eggs.*

FINDING REASONS AND CONCLUSIONS

1. **What are you being asked to conclude about what you should accept or do?**

2. **What reasons are provided to convince you to accept or do that?**

REASONS AND CONCLUSIONS

CONCLUSION

REASON

REASON

REASON

CHAPTER 10
UNCOVERING ASSUMPTIONS

Infusing Uncovering Assumptions Skillfully into Language Arts

Helping students in grades 1 and 2 learn how to skillfully uncover assumptions that they and others make involves helping them learn to ask and carefully answer the following questions as they analyze their own and others' actions and beliefs.

In the assumptions lesson in this lesson book, this thinking map is used to guide your students' thinking explicitly as they engage with the lesson content.

UNCOVERING ASSUMPTIONS

1. What are we thinking about doing that might be based on an assumption?

2. What would you be assuming if you did that?

3. How can you find out whether the assumption is correct or incorrect?

---

figure 10.1

When students learn and use this strategy for uncovering assumptions, they first identify the action or belief that may be based on assumptions. Then they try to explain why the person did what he or she did, or believes what he or she believes, by identifying what that person might be taking for granted. This is especially true of others' actions and beliefs that we are inclined to ask, "Why did he (or she) do (or accept) that?" Then they can ask, of those ideas that they think the person really assumes, whether they are reasonable assumptions and how can they be checked out. An especially important way of asking this question is to ask, "What might the person have done at the time to check out his or her assumption if the person became aware that they were making an assumption?" This type of questioning is an important habit of mind for students to develop when they think about

whether they themselves are making any assumptions in considering what to do or believe.

In the lesson on uncovering assumptions, various supporting classroom strategies such as using a graphic organizer, engaging in cooperative thinking, thinking about thinking, and continued guided practice all supplement the use of the thinking map for uncovering assumptions. These classroom strategies enhance both the thinking skill that the students are learning and their mastery of the lesson content.

The key graphic organizer for uncovering assumptions is shown in figure 10.2.

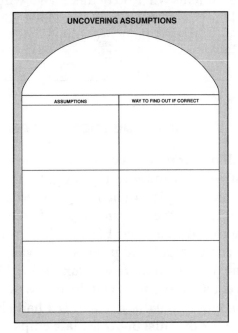

figure 10.2

This graphic organizer can be used to help students think about how the person could have checked out these assumptions if he or she was aware of their assumptions prior to their actions.

A reproducible blank graphic organizer is found at the end of this chapter.

For more in-depth information on teaching students how to uncover and evaluate assumptions, please refer to Chapter 9 in the book *Infusing the Teaching of Critical and Creative Thinking into Elementary Instruction*, by Robert Swartz and Sandra Parks. A computer disk containing the blank, reproducible graphic organizers used in this book is also available. Both book and disk are available through Critical Thinking Books & Software.

PETUNIA'S ASSUMPTIONS
PETUNIA

Language Arts   **Grades 1–2**

OBJECTIVES

CONTENT

Students will develop reading and listening skills as they learn to recognize details that support character development and the changes that occur in a character from the beginning to the end of a story.

THINKING SKILL/PROCESS

Students will learn to uncover assumptions by considering the actions that are based on those assumptions and by determining what those actions take for granted.

METHODS AND MATERIALS

CONTENT

The students will read or the teacher will read aloud the book *Petunia* by Roger Duvoisin. The class will discuss the story in large and small groups.

THINKING SKILL/PROCESS

Detecting reasons and conclusions is guided by structured questioning and by the use of a graphic organizer that highlights the conclusion and its supporting reasons for an argument.

LESSON

INTRODUCTION TO CONTENT AND THINKING SKILL/PROCESS

- In all of our daily lives we find times when what we thought would be is not what really is. Last week I promised my daughter that I would make a batch of her favorite cookies for her to share at a picnic she had planned. I was very busy with other things, so I left the baking until late in the evening. When I went to the cupboard to collect the things I would be putting into the cookies, I found that I was out of chocolate chips. I would not be able to make the cookies as I had promised. I was very disappointed. When I thought about what I had done, I realized there was something I believed that made me think I would be able to make the cookies. What do you think it was? POSSIBLE STUDENT RESPONSE: *You thought you had all of the ingredients but you didn't.* **If I had checked the supplies earlier, I could have gone to the store for the missing chocolate chips.**

- When I believe something that I haven't checked out, I am assuming something. When I am assuming something, I am making an *assumption*. Write the word "assumption" on the chalkboard or on a chart. **I want you to understand this word so that you will be able to use it. Let's use it with another example.**

- Suppose you were going to fly kites with your friend. When you went to get your kite from the closet, it wasn't there. What *assumptions* did you make? POSSIBLE STUDENT RESPONSES: *I assumed that I had put the kite away in the closet. I assumed that the kite was in the closet where I had put it.* **How did you feel when there was no kite in the closet?** I was disappointed and upset because I wanted to fly a kite. **That's how I felt when I wasn't able to bake the cookies I had promised to make.**

- When I thought more about the cookies, I realized that if I had known that I was assuming I had all the ingredients I needed, I could have checked out my assumption by looking in my cupboard. Then I would have gone to the store to buy what I needed. It is very common that people don't think about what they are assuming. If I had asked myself, "Am I making any assumptions about the cookies?" I might have become aware of what I was assuming when it was still early in the day. Then I would be able to get to the store. Suppose you asked yourself what you were assuming before it was time to go to the closet to get your kite. Then you would realize you were making an assumption and you could check out the assumption. That might give you time to find the kite before it was time to go to the park.

- Talk to a neighbor about a time when you made an assumption. Tell your partner what you should have done to avoid making the assumption. ANSWERS VARY.

- This is a thinking map with some questions to ask yourself whenever you think you might be making assumptions. Show the thinking map on a chart or the chalkboard and go over the questions on it. Relate some of the student's examples to the map. **The first question it asks us to consider is "What are we thinking about doing that might be based on an assumption?"** Then it asks "What would you be assuming if you did that?" After identifying our assumption, we need to think of a way to find out if the assumption is correct or incorrect. That is the third question, "How can you find out whether the assumption is correct or incorrect?"

> ## UNCOVERING ASSUMPTIONS
>
> 1. **What are we thinking about doing that might be based on an assumption?**
>
> 2. **What would you be assuming if you did that?**
>
> 3. **How can you find out whether the assumption is correct or incorrect?**

THINKING ACTIVELY

- Authors sometimes use assumptions in their writing. They have the characters make assumptions that affect the actions they take in the story. This sometimes makes the story funny or silly. In the book *Petunia*, by Roger Duvoisin, the animals make some assumptions. Today we will read about Petunia. As we read we will look for things that she does that may be based on assumptions and try to figure out what assumptions she makes. The other characters also make assumptions. Watch for those, too. See what actions they take. It's a silly story, and the assumptions made by the characters lead to silly actions. Read the story to the class, enjoying the silly antics of the animals.

- **Was Petunia really wise?** POSSIBLE STUDENT RESPONSE: *No, she thought carrying a book would make her wise.* **Petunia made an assumption that led to some problems for the other animals. What problems occurred for the other farm animals?** Students should share the things that happened to each of the farm animals. King, the rooster, was sad about his red comb; Ida, the hen, was mixed up about how many chicks she had; Noisy, the dog, got a burned nose; etc. **All of the animals had silly things happen to them because of the assumptions that they made. King was unable to shake his red comb for fear it would fall off. Ida declared that she would never be happy again because she had more than her own nine chicks to care for. Noisy the dog had a burned nose and some cuts and bruises from the fire that Petunia built to help him get unstuck from the hole in the ground. Petunia and all of the other animals made some assumptions. They could have used some help uncovering their assumptions. Maybe that would have prevented the things that happened in the story.**

- We can use this diagram to help us when someone is assuming something. Display the graphic organizer for uncovering assumptions on the overhead, the chalkboard, or a chart. **The space**

at the top asks us to identify what someone did, in this case what Petunia did. What did Petunia do all through the story? *She gave silly advice to all her friends.* **We'll record what Petunia did in the top section of the diagram.** Summarize students' responses into a statement to put on the graphic.

UNCOVERING ASSUMPTIONS

ASSUMPTIONS	WAY TO FIND OUT IF CORRECT

- **Now we need to think about what she was assuming. What was it that Petunia assumed? Let's look back to the text to find when Petunia makes her assumption.** Reread the pages where Petunia recalls seeing Bill with a book and then goes off with her own book. This section includes a statement that reveals what she was assuming: "If I take this Book with me and love it, I will be wise, too." If no one raises their hand when you come to this statement ask something like "Does this statement tell you anything about what she assumed?" When students recognize this as a statement of her assumption, record this in the first box under "assumptions." **Were there other things that Petunia assumed?** POSSIBLE STUDENT RESPONSE: *She assumed that she knew all the best answers and the ways to handle all the animals' problems.* These can be written in other boxes for assumptions.

- **Let's refer back to our thinking map to see what our next step should be.** As the class refers to the thinking map, touch the question as students identify the step. **We have recorded what actions Petunia took and what assumptions she made. These are the first two steps of the map. Now we are at the third question, "How can you find out whether the assumption is correct or incorrect?" Thinking about Petunia and her first assumption, was she correct in her assumption?** *No.* **What could she do to find out if carrying a book and loving it will make her wise?** Allow time for students to discuss this in small groups and then share their ideas with the large group. Record the responses in the spaces on the right side of the graphic organizer. POSSIBLE STUDENT RESPONSES: *She could open the book and see if it says the kinds of things she was saying. She could ask the farmer or Bill if it is true. She could ask someone what the book was and why it had words on the cover.*

- **How did Petunia find out that her assumption was incorrect?** Use a class discussion to help students think back to the events in the story. If they have problems identifying where she found out about her assumption, ask them to think about where in the story she finally found out what the book was. POSSIBLE STUDENT RESPONSES: *In the field there was a box of firecrackers. Petunia thought it was candy. When it exploded, the book fell open so that Petunia could see the words.* **This was a dangerous situation for Petunia and her friends. Opening a box of fireworks is a very dangerous thing for the animals to do. The assumption that she was wise and knew about the box could have seriously hurt someone. Because of her assumptions, Petunia could have caused a very real problem for her friends and herself. Although they were bumped and knocked, none were hurt badly in the book. In real life we know that it would be a very dangerous action to open the fireworks. But more important, we should now know that** sometimes *making assumptions* can cause something really dangerous to happen. That's one important reason to try to be aware of whether we are making any assumptions beforehand and to check them to see if they are correct at that time.

- **Let's think about the other animals in the story. They also made some assumptions, and they acted on those assumptions. We'll look at Ida the hen first. What did she do in the story?** POSSIBLE STUDENT RESPONSES: *She believed Petunia's statement that she had only six chicks and that six is more than nine. That meant she had too many chicks.* Record on a fresh copy of the uncovering assumptions graphic organizer transparency the actions of Ida the hen. **What was Ida's assumption about Petunia that made her believe this?** POSSIBLE STUDENT RESPONSES *Petunia must be wise.* Record the student response on the graphic. **Was her assumption correct?** *No.* **How could she find out if she was correct?** POSSIBLE STUDENT RESPONSES: *She could ask a person to help her count. She could think for herself about the chicks and whether they all look like her chicks. She could ask Petunia more questions to see if she really knows about counting.*

- **I'd like you and your partner to consider another animal from the story. Using a copy of the graphic organizer for uncovering assumptions, I want you to write in the top section what the animal did. Then write the assumption or assumptions they made in the boxes for assumptions. Finally, decide how the animal could find out if the assumption is correct. Write those things in the boxes on the right side of the page.** Allow time for students to work through the three steps of finding assumptions and recording their responses on their copies of the graphic. Be sure to keep one of the models of the completed graphic organizer up on display to help students remember how the graphic organizer is used. Then ask students to share. It works well to have all the groups that chose the same animal stand and share their answers together. This provides support for students.

- **At the end of the story, Petunia makes one final assumption. What is she going to do?** *She is going to learn to read.* **Let's put that statement on another graphic organizer.** Record the statement, "Petunia decides to learn to read." on the top of a new graphic organizer. **What assumption do you think she might be making?** POSSIBLE STUDENT RESPONSES: *She will be able to read. She will be wise if she learns to read so she can put wisdom in her head. She will be able to really help her friends if she can read and learn from books.* As students share, fill in the graphic organizer. **What can she do to find out if her assumption is correct?** POSSIBLE STUDENT RESPONSES: *She can try to learn to read and get help learning. She can ask someone who can read if reading makes them wise, or smart. She can learn to read and see what happens.* **Do you think that her last assumption is true?** Allow time for students to discuss this idea. **Can you relate this to your learning? Will learning to read help you become wise?** POSSIBLE STUDENT RESPONSES: *Yes, I can get smarter if I can read things.*

THINKING ABOUT THINKING

- **What do we call the kind of thinking we just did?** POSSIBLE STUDENT RESPONSES: *Uncovering assumptions. Finding assumptions.*

- **What questions did we ask as we did this kind of thinking?** POSSIBLE STUDENT RESPONSES: *What did Petunia or an animal do that night because of an assumption? What did she assume that made her do it? How could she find out if the assumption was correct?* Remind students of the thinking map and how their answers match the steps on the map.

- **How did we use the graphic organizer in this lesson?** POSSIBLE STUDENT RESPONSES: *We put down what the characters did, then we figured out what they were assuming. The other side was where we told how they could have checked things out first.* If students do not use the term, "uncovering assumptions," rephrase their response to include the term so that they learn to associate it with this thinking strategy.

- **Why is it a good idea to uncover assumptions?** POSSIBLE STUDENT RESPONSES: *This thinking helps us to not make silly mistakes. We can check out things before we do anything that would not be good. We can fix things so we don't make mistakes.*

APPLYING YOUR THINKING

Immediate Transfer

- In the book *The Terrible Thing That Happened at Our House*, the main character made some assumptions about the life she would have once her mother went to work. Use a graphic organizer to show what she did, the assumptions that she made, and what she could have done to find out if her assumptions were correct. Write a letter to her and tell her about your ideas.

- The skies are very cloudy. The wind is getting stronger. What assumptions are you making about the weather? How can you find out if your assumptions are correct? Use the uncovering assumptions thinking map and graphic organizer to help you with your thinking.

Reinforcement Later

- In our science lessons, we have begun studying which materials and objects sink and float. We have conducted a series of experiments to gather information about which objects sink and which float. What assumptions can we make as a result of our experiments? How could we find out if the assumptions are correct?

- In the fairy tale *The Emperor' New Clothes*, the characters make some assumptions. Use the thinking map and graphic organizer for uncovering assumptions to show how they could have uncovered their assumptions before the tricksters escaped.

WRITING EXTENSION

Use the information you have gained by uncovering Petunia's assumptions to write a poem about the goose. You may want to write a cinquain, or you may want to write a character poem. The graphic organizers will give you ideas to use in the poems you write.

SUGGESTED SPECIAL NEEDS MODIFICATIONS

<u>Frontload</u>: Understanding the concept of making assumptions can be difficult for some students. Time should be taken in discussing the meaning of "assumption" Pairing the language "taking for granted" with the term "assumption" may help students develop the concept. Examples from daily life should be used, such as," I didn't take an umbrella because I took for granted, or assumed, it wouldn't rain." With practice, students can become more aware of assumptions being made.

Similarly, the concept of "checking out" an assumption is a difficult for some students. Without mentioning assumptions, students might be given practice in developing plans for getting information to find out if some claim that is not obvious is true. Use concrete examples for this pre-lesson activity. For example, start with simple examples, like finding out whether someone who says "All Mrs. Jones' first graders are absent today" is right. Guide students in identifying the sorts of things they would do to check, such as listening for noise from Mrs. Jones' room or asking if there is a field trip. Gradually guide students in checking out assumptions, using teacher think aloud and guided discussion of daily events. ("How could I have checked out my assumption about the possibility of rain?")

Diversify: Partner work is often helpful to students who are not proficient writers. While both students can engage in the thinking, the more proficient writer can be the recorder, thereby reducing the task demands for the student who may struggle in this area.

Expand the Possibilities: Assessments of written responses may be based upon students' thinking first, and expressive skills second. Oral responses may also reveal thinking beyond students' ability to express themselves in writing.

ASSESSING STUDENT THINKING ABOUT ASSUMPTIONS

To assess the ability to uncover assumptions, have students listen to a story in which the characters make assumptions. Have students describe the steps they would take in identifying assumptions and checking to see if the assumption is correct. Use probing questions to help students show their thinking explicitly. The work they complete on the graphic organizer is also a tool in the assessment.

Sample Student Responses • Petunia's Assumptions

UNCOVERING ASSUMPTIONS

Petunia gave silly advice to all her friends.

ASSUMPTIONS	WAY TO FIND OUT IF CORRECT
If I carry this book and love it, I will be wise.	*Open the book. Ask the farmer or Bill if it was true. Look more carefully at the book because there are words on the cover.*
She knew all the best answers.	*Ask the animals if they thought her answers were good ones. Check with another animal to compare answers.*
She knew how to handle the animals' problems.	*To see if her advice worked, she could think about what happened when the animals followed it. Then she would need to think about why the advice she gave was not good.*

Sample Student Responses • Petunia's Assumptions

UNCOVERING ASSUMPTIONS

The animals ripped open the box of fireworks.

ASSUMPTIONS	WAY TO FIND OUT IF CORRECT
Petunia is wise.	Ask the farmer if Petunia is really wise.
The box is full of candy.	Go and get the farmer to check out the box.

UNCOVERING ASSUMPTIONS

Ida the Hen believed it when Petunia said that Ida had six chicks and that six chicks is more than nine.

ASSUMPTIONS	WAY TO FIND OUT IF CORRECT
Petunia is wise.	*She could ask Petunia how she got wise. She could check with the farmer to see if he thinks that Petunia is wise. She could ask Petunia more questions to see if she really is wise.*
She thought Petunia could count.	*She could ask a person to count her chicks and see if they get the same number as Petunia.*

Sample Student Responses • Petunia's Assumptions

UNCOVERING ASSUMPTIONS

King the Rooster quit shaking the comb on his head.

ASSUMPTIONS	WAY TO FIND OUT IF CORRECT
Petunia was wise.	Ask Petunia how she got so smart.
His comb was really stuck on by the farmer to tell the roosters from the hens.	Ask the farmer if that is really what he did.
His comb was made out of plastic.	Pinch the comb. If it is plastic, it won't hurt. If it is part of the rooster, it will hurt.

Sample Student Writing • Petunia's Assumptions

Cinquain poem

> Petunia
> Silly goose
> Gives bad advice
> Thinks she is wise
> Petunia

Character poem

> Petunia
> Silly, helpful,
> Friend of animals in the barnyard
> Who likes to be admired
> Who wants to help her friends
> Who really wants to be wise
> Who lives in the barnyard
> Silly Goose

UNCOVERING ASSUMPTIONS

1. What are we thinking about doing that might be based on an assumption?

2. What would you be assuming if you did that?

3. How can you find out whether the assumption is correct or incorrect?

UNCOVERING ASSUMPTIONS

ASSUMPTIONS	WAY TO FIND OUT IF CORRECT

CHAPTER 11
GENERATING POSSIBILITIES

Infusing Generating Possibilities Skillfully into Language Arts

Teaching students in grades 1 and 2 how to skillfully generate possibilities, whatever these possibilities are for (e.g., options in decision making, possible solutions in problem solving, possible uses of objects, possible causes of events), involves helping them learn to ask and carefully answer the following questions:

FINDING POSSIBILITIES

1. **Why do you want to find possibilities?**

2. **What possibilities can you think of?**

3. **What are some other types of possibilities?**

4. **What are some unusual possibilities?**

5. **How can you decide which is the best possibility?**

---

figure 11.1

This is what we call a "thinking map" for skillfully generating possibilities. In the lessons in this chapter, this thinking map is used to guide your students' thinking explicitly as they engage with the lesson content.

When students learn and use this strategy for generating possibilities, they will explicitly identify many varied and original ideas related to the task at hand. They will not do this simply by open brainstorming—brainstorming takes you only so far. They will also put the possibilities into categories. Students will then combine two categories so that they synthesize more original ideas. Finally, they will think about when such ideas might be feasible. This will prepare them to apply this creative-thinking skill to real decision-making and problem-solving tasks.

These lessons also supplement the use of this thinking map with various supporting classroom strategies, such as using graphic organizers, engaging in cooperative thinking, thinking

about thinking, and continued guided practice. These classroom strategies enhance both the thinking skill that the students are learning and their mastery of the lesson content.

The key graphic organizer for skillfully generating ideas is shown in figure 11.2.

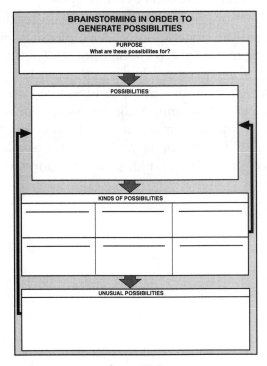

figure 11.2

Using this graphic organizer, students generate a large number of possibilities by open brainstorming. Students then classify the possibilities they have come up with into categories, while continuing to add new possibilities to the categories. These new possibilities recorded under the categories should also be recorded in the original "Possibilities" box and then underlined. Students then focus their attention on developing original ideas, which they write in the lower box and then transpose to the original list of possibilities at the top.

A second graphic organizer, shown in figure 11.3, aids in helping students develop original ideas. It helps them come up with ideas they most likely would never have come up with on their own had they simply engaged in open brainstorming. In this matrix, students record the categories that they have identified across the top and down the side. Students then combine possibilities where two categories intersect to get a new idea. This matrix is of great help in stimulating the development of original ideas that can then be written on the "Brainstorming In Order To Generate Possibilities" graphic organizer under "Unusual Possibilities" (figure 11.2). Reproducible blank graphic organizers are found at the end of each chapter.

For more in-depth information on teaching the skillful generation of ideas, please refer to Chapter 10 in the book *Infusing the Teaching of Critical and Creative Thinking into Elementary Instruction*, by Robert Swartz and Sandra Parks. A computer disk containing the blank, reproducible graphic organizers used in this book is also available. Both book and disk are available through Critical Thinking Books & Software.

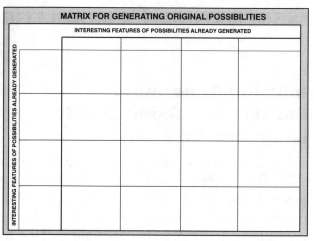

figure 11.3

LOTS AND LOTS OF PRESENTS
MR. RABBIT AND THE LOVELY PRESENT

Language Arts   **Grades 1–2**

OBJECTIVES

CONTENT	THINKING SKILL/PROCESS
Students will learn one way to create plots for a story.	Students will learn to generate possibilities skillfully in the context of solving a problem by brainstorming a variety of ideas and by combining ideas to generate new and original ones.

METHODS AND MATERIALS

CONTENT	THINKING SKILL/PROCESS
Students will read the book *Mr. Rabbit and the Lovely Present* by Charlotte Zolotow and then engage in a follow-up writing activity that will extend the story. Students will use their ideas to write a class book.	An explicit thinking map, graphic organizers, and structured questioning facilitate thinking strategies for generating possible uses for something. Collaborative learning enhances the thinking.

LESSON

INTRODUCTION TO CONTENT AND THINKING SKILL/PROCESS

• When you solve a problem by thinking of an unusual way to fix it, you are using *creative thinking*. Have you ever been a creative thinker when you had a problem to solve? A friend of mine had a problem. She needed to find a way to keep the raccoons from getting into her garbage cans. The latches that were designed to keep the raccoons out were defective, and she didn't have time to get a new can. She thought about some possibilities and then wrote them down. She could put a heavy brick on top of the cans, but the raccoons could just push it off. She thought some more, and looked around her garage for other things she could use. What she saw gave her an idea that worked. She took an old golf club and used it to connect the handles of the lid and the can. Sliding it all the way down created a lock that the raccoons would not be able to open. This worked great until she was able to get a new can.

• What she did was *creative problem solving*. She recognized that there was a problem, thought of a number of ways of solving it, thought about whether some of these solutions would work, and then figured out how to do it best. Her solution was a *creative* solution because she used something that is not normally used for this purpose. With your partner, describe a time when you used something in a new way to solve a problem. After a few minutes, ask three or four students to describe what they had done.

• Whenever you come up with new ideas, you are doing creative thinking. You do something new that works that you haven't thought of before. With your partner, explain what you thought about that helped you discover a new way to use something to solve your problem. Students often say that they didn't have what they needed, so they started thinking about other things they could use or other ways to solve the problem. Some students say that they pictured using another object (like the golf club) altered in a way that would solve the problem. If using the object didn't work, they considered another idea.

- All of our examples show how helpful it can be to think creatively. When we are being creative as we solve problems, we should try to think of many ways that the problem could be solved. Thinking of the different ways to solve a problem is called *generating possibilities*. Write the words "generating possibilities" on the chalkboard or on a flipchart. **To generate means to produce something, in this case, to produce a variety of possible ways to solve a problem.** When my friend was working to solve her problem with the raccoons and the garbage cans, she wandered around her garage looking for things that might help her to solve her problem. She saw bricks, tape, tools, clamps, pieces of wood, jump ropes, and golf clubs. After she generated this list of ideas of possible things she could do, she chose the one that she felt would best solve the problem of keeping the raccoons out of her garbage can. It was good to make a list of possible solutions because it made her think of all her possibilities.

- Why do you think that generating possibilities is a very important step in making decisions and solving problems? POSSIBLE STUDENT RESPONSES: *You want to make the best choice. You want to solve your problem in the best way.* In order to do this, you should learn to generate possibilities skillfully. Here are some questions on a thinking map. They will guide us to become skilled at this kind of thinking. Show the thinking map for generating possibilities on a chart or the chalkboard.

> **FINDING POSSIBILITIES**
>
> 1. Why do you want to find possibilities?
> 2. What possibilities can you think of?
> 3. What are some other types of possibilities?
> 4. What are some unusual possibilities?
> 5. How can you decide which is the best possibility?

The thinking map should be visible during the lesson. Go over the questions on the thinking map. Relate the questions to the previous examples. **This way of making a list or generating ideas is called "brainstorming." When you brainstorm, you try to think of as many ideas as you can about something. You don't try to decide whether these ideas will work at this point. You can do that later when you think about specific ideas. It is more important to get a lot of ideas. That's why we call these ideas *possibilities*.** It's possible that they are good ideas, but when we brainstorm, we haven't yet decided whether or not they are good ideas.

- Authors use the strategy of brainstorming to generate possibilities in order to help them write stories and poems. They try to look at topics in creative, unusual ways. As they work to develop the plots for their stories, they try to think of many possible things that could happen or be part of their story. All of these possibilities will help them create a story or poem that others will enjoy reading.

THINKING ACTIVELY

- In this lesson, we're going to see if we can take on the role of an author by generating a list of possible ideas to use in a story. The author that we will be working with today is Charlotte Zolotow. In her story, *Mr. Rabbit and the Lovely Present*, she uses a little girl and a rabbit as her characters. This book really shows how the author needed to generate possibilities as she created her story. We will be watching how Charlotte Zolotow uses lots of ideas to make her story interesting.

- **Now, let's look at the cover of our book.** Pass out the copies of the book, or if you will be reading to students, display the cover. **What do we know about the characters in our book from looking at the cover?** POSSIBLE STUDENT RESPONSES: *The rabbit acts like a person. He is sitting on a log like a person. The girl is not very old. I don't see any present. They look like they are talking.* **Your ideas are very good. The characters are talking about a problem that the little** girl has. **The rabbit is going to help her by generating ideas about choosing a present. There will be a pattern in the story. Watch for it as we read.** Read the story to the class or with the class. As students see the pattern of the story, they will begin to predict which presents the rabbit will suggest and which presents the girl will choose.

- **There were definite patterns that the author chose for this book about presents. Discuss the kinds of patterns that you noticed with your neighbor.** POSSIBLE STUDENT RESPONSES: *The girl always guided the rabbit's thinking by saying a color. The gifts chosen were all fruits. The rabbit always suggested a bird and the girl always said that her mother liked birds in trees. There were always gifts that were very unusual or silly.*

- **In order to write this story, Ms. Zolotow needed to generate a list of ideas for gifts. She wanted a list of many things that could be gifts for the little girl to give to her mother. The gifts that she chose for the story followed a specific pattern, but as she was making her list she probably tried to think of as many gifts as possible. When she had the list she could choose to use the ones she liked best. Do you remember what making a list or generating ideas is called?** Most students will identify it as brainstorming. If they don't remember easily, you can prompt them by telling them that the word that is used refers to a way they can use their brains. **What do you do when you brainstorm?** Once again, most students will respond that you try to think of as many ideas as you can about something. Some may also say that you don't try to decide whether these ideas will work at this point. But you may have to prompt them for this. You can ask something like "When you brainstorm ideas, do you try to decide whether they will work?" **So the author just let her mind go and came up with as many ideas as she could. Then as she planned and wrote her story, she picked the ideas that would work best.**

- **Today we will write a *sequel* to the story, *Mr. Rabbit and the Lovely Present*. A sequel is a new story that follows where another story stops. Our story will be about the little girl's birthday and the gifts that her family thinks about giving to her. We will need to develop a plot that tells about the family and their gift choices. It will need to have many ideas for gifts, just as Charlotte Zolotow needed many ideas for gifts to use in her story. As we learn this new way of thinking called generating possibilities we will brainstorm many ideas. To get ready for brainstorming, let's get the beginning of the story mapped out. That will help us focus on our task.**

- **Our purpose for brainstorming is to come up with a lot of ideas for a gift that will go to a little girl. The little girl in our story likes the color brown, so the gifts that her family gives to her must be that color. Who should be in the story besides the little girl and her mother?** POSSIBLE STUDENT RESPONSES: *the father, a brother and sister, a grandmother and a grandfather, a baby sister.* **We can include all of these family members in the story. We know that Charlotte Zolotow had her character unsure of what to give her mother. Should our characters be unsure or should they have many ideas?** The students will usually want the characters to be unsure. If someone doesn't come up with the idea of a helpful character like the rabbit, guide their thinking by thinking aloud about how the little girl made her decisions. Record the ideas on a chart for the class to refer to later in the lesson as they write their story. Be sure to include on the chart the importance of the gift being brown. **These ideas are a good frame for the beginning of the story. We are ready to get started on generating possibilities for the little girl's brown gifts.**

- **Our thinking map asks us to identify our purpose, why we want to find possibilities. The purpose of our thinking is to generate a list of gifts that are brown and are for the little girl.**

We can write that purpose in the first box on the graphic organizer for generating possibilities. On a chart or overhead transparency, display the Brainstorming In Order To Generate Possibilities graphic organizer. Write in the purpose box the phrase "a gift that is brown and is for a girl." **The second question asks what possibilities we can think of. Let's brainstorm in our groups. Each group will make a list of things that are brown and would make a good gift. Try to come up with five possibilities or more.** The groups should use paper or dry erase slates to make lists. After a few minutes, ask the students whether they are finding it easy or difficult to come up with more ideas. Many say that they can't think of any more beyond the ones that their group has already listed on the diagram. Ask the groups to report their ideas. As they report, write their ideas on the class graphic organizer in the section called "Possibilities." POSSIBLE STUDENT RESPONSES: *dog, shoes, wallet, chocolate, puppy, belt, desk, iced tea, hamster, football, chair, picture frame.*

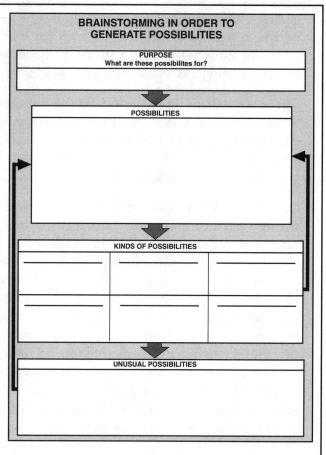

- **We have generated a good list by brainstorming, but this thinking strategy shows you a way to think of even more ideas. The third step of the thinking map asks us to think about other kinds of possibilities. The next box on the graphic organizer is labeled "Kinds of Possibilities." We can organize the ideas we have by looking for ways to group them. These groups are called categories. If we think about the categories for the ideas we have, we might be able to think of even more categories. The small lines are for writing the category label, or title, that tells why the things go together. Let's see, a dog, a puppy, and a hamster are animals, so lets label one category "animals."** Write "animals" on one of the lines. To help make the connection, the label and the words already on the graphic organizer that belong under the label can be color coded by underlining with the same color marker. **What other categories do you notice?** POSSIBLE STUDENT RESPONSES: *"clothes" since there are shoes and a belt, "toys" because there is a football, "house things" since some things go in a house, "food" because some things are food.* As you discuss and create labels with the students, be sure to make them broad rather than specific. This will help them to extend the brainstorming. Record the labels in the boxes, color coding them as you go along.

- **Now work with your groups again. This time try to think of more brown gifts that would fit in the categories we've created from our first list.** Allow time for working. When the students share with the group, be sure to have them identify the category for each item. Record the responses in the category boxes, then move them up into the top box and underline them. (Tell students that the underlined possibilities are ones that are newly generated.) POSSIBLE STUDENT RESPONSES: *(animal) cow, horse, mouse, squirrel, (toys) yo-yo, doll, blocks, (clothes) shirt, coat, pants, skirt, dress, (house) plate, pot, statue, basket, (food) bread, hamburger, steak, meatloaf, chocolate chip cookies.*

- **Did this thinking in terms of categories help you think of more brown gifts? Did anyone think of a new category?** Students usually agree that this helps a lot in generating new ideas. If a new category is suggested, add it to the graphic organizer and ask the students to brainstorm some possibilities that would fit there.

- **Let's look at our class graphic organizer for generating possibilities. We started out with a purpose, a gift that is brown and is for a girl, and listed some possibilities. Organizing our list into categories helped us to think of more ideas, and even more categories. The fourth question on the thinking map asks us to think of some unusual possibilities. Now we are going to flex our thinking in a new way with a different diagram. This diagram is called a matrix. It will help us to generate even more ideas.** Display the matrix on a transparency or a chart so it is easily viewed by everyone.

MATRIX FOR GENERATING ORIGINAL POSSIBILITIES

INTERESTING FEATURES OF POSSIBILITIES ALREADY GENERATED

INTERESTING FEATURES OF POSSIBILITIES ALREADY GENERATED

- **On the matrix we have room to put four of our categories.** Randomly choose four categories from the list the class has created and write them across and then again down the sides of the matrix. **This matrix is designed to help us combine categories so that we can come up with new possibilities. As we come up with new possibilities, we'll record them in the boxes where the categories meet. The matrix helps us come up with really creative ideas because we are putting together two types of things that don't usually go together.** Demonstrate how the matrix works by combining two categories to create a new idea. For example, by combining "animal" with "toy," someone could come up with a stuffed bear. Work with the whole class on using the matrix, so that students can hear each other think and work together on ideas. POSSIBLE STUDENT RESPONSES: *Combining animal with clothes—a hat rack shaped like a giraffe or horse pajamas; combining food with toy—Mr. Potato Head game or a brown pinata; combining toy with clothes—a doll outfit or a soccer shirt.*

- **We have now generated many more ideas for a gift that is brown. All of the ideas that we have generated give us lots of material with which to write our story. In the story of *Mr. Rabbit and the Lovely Present* there was just one person choosing gifts, and her gifts were different colors. The plot for our story is different from the one we read. We know that everyone in the little girl's family is going to get her brown gifts for her birthday. Charlotte Zolotow, the author of *Mr. Rabbit and the Lovely Present*, most definitely generated many possibilities for gifts just as we did. She chose to use the ones that she felt worked best in her story. She must have liked the idea of four colors, and she seemed to like to keep a pattern of gift categories with the final gift coming from the food category. She felt her story was best when she used this pattern. She let one of the characters be the thinker generating ideas for gifts, while the other character made the final choices. We will make choices from the many possibilities that we have generated. We may find a pattern that goes with all of the characters, or the pattern may change with each person. Perhaps we will chose one person to be the thinker, or perhaps we will have a new thinker as each gift is chosen.**

- **In the same way as Zolotow, we will choose the possibilities we want to use in our story, picking a pattern of gifts and following the pattern as we write. This answers the fifth ques-**

tion of the thinking map, "How can you decide which is the best possibility?" For us there will be a group of ideas that will be used as we create the events that make up the plot of the story we write. At this point in the lesson, follow the same procedure for writing a class story that we just discussed. As students do their prewriting activities, encourage them to revisit the graphic organizer for ideas that will help them develop the plot of their story. The story line may include one of the characters, perhaps the grandfather, being the person with the ideas just as the rabbit had many ideas for the little girl in the Zolotow story. Each family member could come to the grandfather asking advice and then choose one gift that would be good for them to give the little girl. The ending would be the party and the little girl's response to the gifts. Having the different family members pick gifts from the same or from different categories would both be good choices. The teacher should be the class secretary, writing the story map on a chart and then writing the class story on another chart or working on a computer that has large screen projection. The story should be illustrated by members of the class. This whole group story should be used as a model for independent stories written by students during another lesson. (See Writing Extension)

THINKING ABOUT THINKING

- **Here is the thinking map we looked at earlier. It shows the steps we took in generating possibilities for our story. Let's go through the steps as we remember the things we did to create a large list of brown presents.** Go through the five questions on the thinking map, asking students about the things they did in the lesson. Refer to the graphic organizers as the discussion focuses on each step.

- **Do you think this kind of thinking is helpful when you are writing?** POSSIBLE STUDENT RESPONSE: *Yes, it gives the writer lots of choices of what to put into the story.*

- **What helped you to keep on thinking of more ideas?** POSSIBLE STUDENT RESPONSE: *The categories helped first, and then the matrix gave more ideas.*

- **Is this a good way to generate ideas? Why or why not?** POSSIBLE STUDENT RESPONSES: *It gives us lots of ideas. It's a fun way to think. There are lots of ideas to choose from when you want to pick the best one.*

- **In this activity, you worked in groups. Is this a good way to do brainstorming or would you rather work on your own? Why?** Most students say that they like to work in groups because they get ideas from other students. If it comes up, identify this as "piggybacking." Some students may say that they would rather work alone.

- **The next time you have to generate possibilities, how will you do it? Will the diagrams we used help you? What will you do with them?** ANSWERS VARY.

APPLYING YOUR THINKING

Immediate Transfer

- **The class is getting ready for a party to celebrate the many books they have read. The party will be on the school playground. Generate a list of possible games and activities using the playground equipment. The thinking map and graphic organizers for generating possibilities will help you make this a very special party that everyone will enjoy!**

- **As a final project for our unit, you are going to create a play about weather. Brainstorm** different ways to make the sounds of weather. Use the thinking map and graphic organizers to help you in your work

- In the story *Little Bear's Trousers* by Jane Hissey, the characters find many uses for the trousers. Use the thinking map and graphic organizers to generate more uses for the trousers. Use the best ideas in another story about Little Bear.

Reinforcement Later

- We need to stay fit by exercising. Brainstorm a list of ways to get exercise when the weather is bad and you cannot go outside. Use the thinking map and graphic organizers for generating possibilities to help you. Choose the best ideas and share them by creating a book for the class.

- Read the book *The Big Orange Splot* by Daniel Manus Pinkwater. Pretend you live on the street with Mr. Plumbean. Draw a picture of the house of your dreams and write a story that tells about it. Before drawing and writing, brainstorm all the things that would be on and around your house.

WRITING EXTENSION

Have students use the generating possibilities thinking strategy with a new story, one involving some idea other than gifts, such as a contest, a homework project, a pet, or a trip. They should begin by choosing a topic, and then use the generating possibilities thinking map and graphic organizers to develop a plot that will be used in a story. This could be done as a whole class project to provide another model of the process before turning the task to small groups or individuals. Another format is to have the groups or individual students work through each of the steps of the strategy under the guidance of the teacher.

The ideas generated on the graphic organizer can be used to write another story involving gifts. The framework for the story and a story starter could be written as a class. The students would then work individually or in small groups to complete the story. Each group should have a copy of the graphic organizer to refer to as they write.

SUGGESTED SPECIAL NEEDS MODIFICATIONS

<u>Frontload:</u> Before learning the whole strategy for enhanced brainstorming, some students may need practice in simple brainstorming in which they concentrate on trying to generate ideas with fluency (quantity), flexibility (diversity), and originality (novelty). Students may brainstorm in the contexts of a subject area (all the words beginning with the letter "d") or everyday situations (all the games we can play at recess). The teacher should prompt students to direct thinking in a new way ("Those are all animals. Anyone have something different?"), reinforce novel ideas, yet instruct them to withhold making value judgments about others' responses.

Prior review with some students on sorting and categorizing items will be helpful. Teacher modelling by saying things like "These two items have (characteristic) in common, so they fall into the category (category)" can be very helpful. Sorting objects in mathematics class, for example, can be a common experience.

<u>Clarify</u>: Teacher guidance may be required in generating suitable category labels. This is crucial. Poorly formulated category labels (i.e. too general, vague, or similar to one another) will hinder the process of using the matrix to combine ideas. The teacher may need to paraphrase student responses to avoid ambiguities, such as, "things." A precise label is most helpful for using the matrix.

Diversify: Cooperative groups are effective in allowing all students to participate in the thinking. The proficient writer in the group can be the recorder, reducing the task demands of the less proficient writer.

Combining ideas using the matrix may take greater teacher guidance for some students. The teacher may choose to offer more teacher-led examples or to work more closely with some groups of students prior to assigning student-led group work.

Expand the Possibilities: Assessments of written responses may be based upon students' thinking first, and expressive skills second. Oral responses may also reveal thinking beyond students' ability to express themselves in writing.

ASSESSING STUDENT THINKING ABOUT POSSIBILITIES

To assess the ability to generate possibilities, select examples that challenge students to generate a wide range of ideas. Any of the transfer examples can serve as assessment items for written or oral responses. Developing multiple uses for common objects is a task that is often used to demonstrate this kind of thinking. Challenging problem-solving tasks in which you emphasize generating alternative solutions are also excellent vehicles for this type of assessment. Use the thinking map for generating possibilities as a guide to check that students are focusing their attention on the three basic factors for generating good ideas: fluency, flexibility, and originality.

Sample Student Responses • Lots and Lots of Presents!

BRAINSTORMING IN ORDER TO GENERATE POSSIBILITIES

PURPOSE
What are these possibilites for?

A gift that is brown and is for a girl

POSSIBILITIES

dinosaur toy	tree	bunny	owl	clipboard	pants	animal crackers
dog	shoes	chocolate	yo-yo	lunch box	skirt	fish-shaped French fries
puppy	bookshelf	muffins	doll	bread	dress	stuffed bear
shirt	belt	iced tea	blocks	hamburger	shorts	brown apron
hamster	bed	cow	box	beans	desk	brown lobster bib
goat	football	bear	tray	ice cream	cabinet	soccer shirt
wolf	wallet	horse	backpack	potato	couch	hat rack shaped like a giraffe
deer	desk	duck	cup holder	cupcake	rocking horse	rocking chair
butterfly	chair	mouse	bag	coconut	horse pajamas	
book	rock	bull	shelf	shirt		
frame	table	squirrel	drawer	coat		

KINDS OF POSSIBILITIES

Animals			Clothes			Food		
cow	duck	squirrel	shirt	hat	dress	bread	ice cream	coconut
bear	mouse	owl	shorts	pants		hamburger	potato	cereal
horse	bull		coat	skirt		beans	cupcake	

Toys			Holders			Furniture		
yo-yo			backpack	shelf	box	couch		
doll			tray	drawer	lunch box	desk		
blocks			cup holder	clipboard		cabinet		
			bag			rocking chair		

UNUSUAL POSSIBILITIES

rocking horse	hat rack shaped like a giraffe
horse pajamas	soccer shirt
brown apron	animal crackers
stuffed bear	fish-shaped French fries

Sample Student Responses • Lots of Presents!

MATRIX FOR GENERATING ORIGINAL POSSIBILITIES

INTERESTING FEATURES OF POSSIBILITIES ALREADY GENERATED

	Animal	Toy	Clothes	Food
Animal	✕	stuffed bear toy monkey	brown dogs on a dress brown rabbits on pajamas	animal crackers fish-shaped French fries
Toy	rocking horse wind-up chipmunk stuffed lion	✕	soccer shirt doll clothes	pinata
Clothes	horse pajamas lambs' wool coat	doll outfit Dad's pants for playing dress-up	✕	brown apron shirt with an ice cream cone on it
Food	chicken soup honey (from a bee)	Mr. Potato Head brown pinata	pants with an apple patch on the back pocket baby bib	✕

INTERESTING FEATURES OF POSSIBILITIES ALREADY GENERATED

FINDING POSSIBILITIES

1. Why do you want to find possibilities?

2. What possibilities can you think of?

3. What are some other types of possibilities?

4. What are some unusual possibilities?

5. How can you decide which is the best possibility?

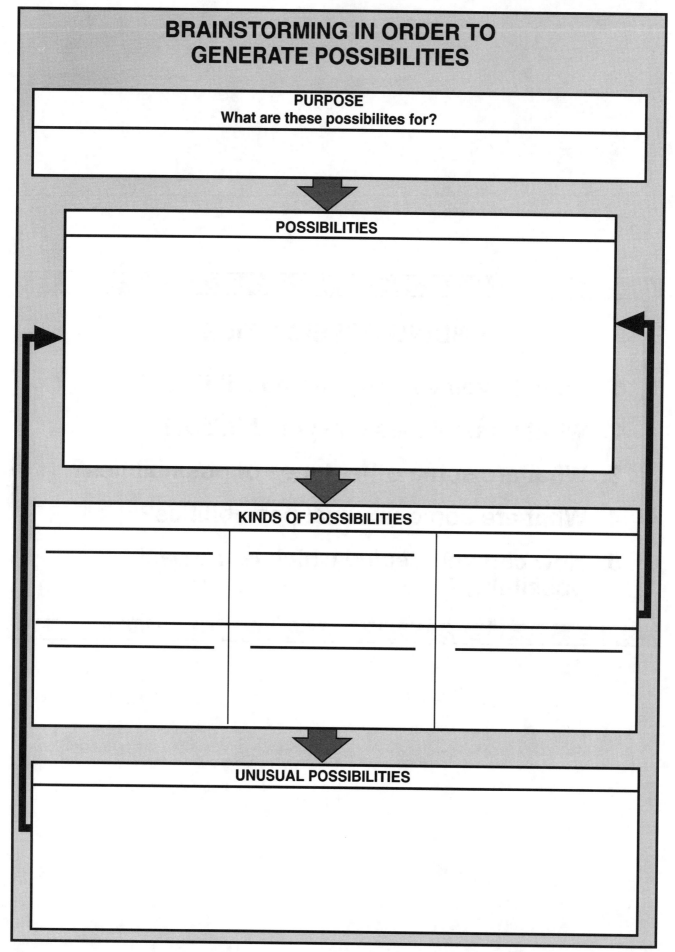

BRAINSTORMING IN ORDER TO GENERATE POSSIBILITIES

PURPOSE
What are these possibilites for?

POSSIBILITIES

KINDS OF POSSIBILITIES

UNUSUAL POSSIBILITIES

MATRIX FOR GENERATING ORIGINAL POSSIBILITIES

INTERESTING FEATURES OF POSSIBILITIES ALREADY GENERATED

INTERESTING FEATURES OF POSSIBILITIES ALREADY GENERATED

CHAPTER 12
CREATING METAPHORS

Infusing Skillfully Creating Metaphors into Language Arts

Teaching students how to skillfully create metaphors in grades 1 and 2 involves helping them learn to ask and carefully answer the following questions about possible metaphors before they commit themselves to one:

MAKING A METAPHOR

1. **What do I want to say with a metaphor?**

2. **What are some details about what I want to say?**

3. **What other things have the same characteristics?**

4. **Which of these things might make a good metaphor? What are some of its details?**

5. **Is it a good metaphor? Why?**

---

figure 12.1

This is what we call a "thinking map" for creating metaphors. In the lesson on creating metaphors in this chapter, this thinking map is used to guide your students' thinking explicitly as they engage with the lesson content.

When students learn and use this strategy for developing metaphors, they are engaging in a type of creative thinking informed by careful critical judgment about which possible metaphor best serves the purpose the metaphor is designed for. This means that students will not just come up with metaphors that pop into their heads and use them. Some of these may be very misleading and not communicate exactly what the students want to communicate. Rather, they articulate, first, what the metaphor is for and what they want to say with the metaphor. For example, they may want to write a poem about a president and stress his leadership and authority using a metaphor. Next, they make a list of things that manifest what they want to say about the president. They may come up with an orchestra conductor, a ship's captain, and a school principal. They then should make sure

that the details of each—the president as leader and the possible metaphors—match. They should think about whether there are any significant differences between the proposed metaphors and the president that might make the metaphor misleading. Finally, they can choose the best metaphor to say what they want to say.

The lesson on generating metaphors in this book also supplements the use of this thinking map with various supporting classroom strategies such as using a graphic organizer, engaging in cooperative thinking, thinking about thinking, and continued guided practice. These classroom strategies enhance both the thinking skill that the students are learning and their mastery of the lesson content.

The key graphic organizer for creating metaphors is in figure 12.2.

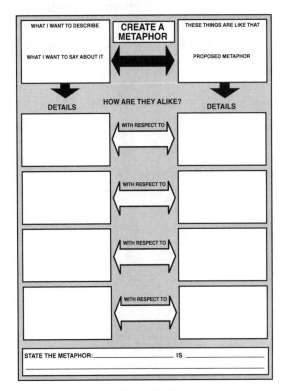

figure 12.2

This graphic organizer helps students record the answers they have to the questions on the thinking map by focusing them on exploring one possible metaphor in some depth.

The Suggested Metaphors web diagram in figure 12.3 helps students compare different metaphors. In the outer boxes, students write details about the metaphor that tell us what it is a metaphor for.

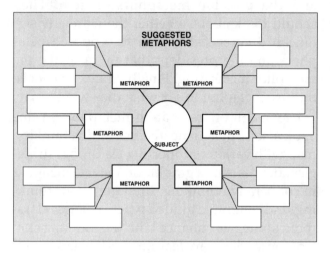

figure 12.3

When a number of students or student groups explore a variety of different possible metaphors for the same thing, they can compare their results. This can lead them to select what they think is the best choice, though there can be considerable variation in what students choose because of the variety of details that may serve some purposes but not others. If they disagree, they can explain in class why they chose what they did.

These completed graphic organizers can also do double duty, as you will find in the lessons in this book, by becoming pre-writing activities in creative extensions of the lessons. They can form the basis for writing both prose and poetry in which not only are the metaphors used, but a lot of the detail words that appear on the graphic organizer also appear to enrich and elaborate the force of the metaphor. Reproducible blank graphic organizers are found at the end of the chapter.

For more in-depth information on teaching skillful decision making, please refer to Chapter 11 in the book *Infusing the Teaching of Critical and Creative thinking into Elementary Instruction*, by Robert Swartz and Sandra Parks. A computer disk containing the blank, reproducible graphic organizers used in this book is also available. Both book and disk are available through Critical Thinking Books & Software.

WHAT IS IT LIKE TO BE IN A BLIZZARD?
TYLER TOAD AND THE THUNDER

Language Arts   **Grades 1–2**

OBJECTIVES

CONTENT

Students will learn how to analyze a figure of speech and to use metaphors in poetry and descriptive writing.

THINKING SKILL/PROCESS

Students will create metaphors effectively by performing the following steps: stating the ideas that the metaphor will convey, listing the characteristics of the thing being described, brainstorming other things which have important similarities, and selecting an item whose details will convey the idea well.

METHODS AND MATERIALS

CONTENT

The class will reread the story *Piggybook*, by Anthony Browne to learn about metaphors. They will then reread *Tyler Toad and the Thunder* by Robert L. Crowe and analyze the metaphors used in the story.

THINKING SKILL/PROCESS

Creating metaphors involves using structured questioning, graphic organizers, and a webbing diagram. Brainstorming is a vital element in the process as they think of possible metaphors and the details that express them.

LESSON

INTRODUCTION TO CONTENT AND THINKING SKILL/PROCESS

- Today we are going to look at the way that writers and speakers use one idea or thing to tell something important about another idea or thing. The term for describing this is "metaphor." Write the word "metaphor" on the chalkboard. Using a metaphor can help convey a particular idea about something. In the book *Piggybook*, by Anthony Browne, the author uses a metaphor to show how badly the boys and Mr. Piggot are behaving. He has the Piggot men turn into pigs to show that their behavior in their home is unacceptable. The metaphor states that the Piggot men are like pigs. Let's reread the story so we can analyze the way that a metaphor is used to help us understand the characters and their actions. We will look at the reasons that Mr. Piggot and the boys are like pigs in the ways they behave in their home. As the story is being read, stop to discuss the places where the Piggot family is being compared to pigs. The author/illustrator uses pictures to enrich the metaphor presented in the text. With students, track the appearance of the pigs in the illustrations and the development of the metaphor.

- The boys and Mr. Piggot behave so badly that Mrs. Piggot goes away for awhile, leaving them a simple note, "You are pigs." Other than the name of the family, the note is actually the first point where the metaphor appears in the story. Mrs. Piggot is saying that her husband and boys are pigs. Her statement identifies the metaphor.

- The author wants us to see that the boys and Mr. Piggot are behaving like pigs. Here is a graphic organizer for understanding metaphors. It will help us to organize our thinking about this metaphor. Show the graphic organizer for understanding metaphors on a chart or on an overhead transparency. It will show how certain things about pigs help us to understand more about the boys and Mr. Piggot. One side of the graphic will be used to write about the characters from our story, and the other side will be used to write about pigs. The center column will show how they are alike by comparing them according to certain characteristics. The characteristics are general things that can be found in both the characters and in pigs. We will identify these things as we study the metaphor.

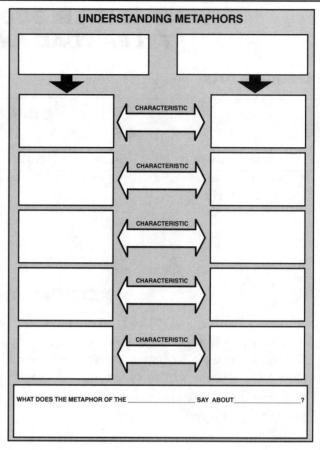

UNDERSTANDING METAPHORS

- There are certain things about pigs that help us to understand the boys and their father. **In what ways are the Piggot men like pigs?** As a group, discuss the ways that the characters are like pigs. Make a list on the chalkboard or on a chart. POSSIBLE STUDENT RESPONSES: *They act like pigs. They are slobs. They don't do chores. They yell at the mother to get them food. They just make messes and let her clean things up. They are lazy. They think they are the most important.* **There are general terms that we can use for these statements. It seems that you are saying that the actions of the characters are like pigs. "Actions" is a general characteristic label that can be placed on an arrow.** Write "Actions" on one of the arrows. **You mentioned the way that they speak to Mrs. Piggot. That is a sound. We can use "Sound" as another label for a characteristic.** Write "Sound" on another arrow. **In the story the Piggots became very dirty. The label we could use here is "Appearance." We'll write "Appearance" on another arrow. You also said that they are lazy and think they are very important. This is an attitude that they have. We can put "Attitude" on another arrow.**

- **The two sides of the graphic organizer can now be filled in with words that are used to show these characteristics in the two things, the Piggot men and pigs. Thinking back to the things we've stated that make us think the Piggot men are like pigs, what are some words that would describe these characteristics in the Piggots? For example, we said that they thought they were the most important and should be waited on. That is what's called an "attitude," so we'll put it in the box next to that characteristic.** For each characteristic, ask for student responses and write them in the boxes on the left side of the graphic organizer. POSSIBLE STUDENT RESPONSES: *Attitude (They think they are in charge.), Appearance (They have dirty clothes.), Sounds (They make sounds that aren't nice, like yelling and grunting and squealing.), Actions (They make big messes and don't clean up. They like to lie around).*

- **What are some words that we use to describe these characteristics of pigs? Thinking about a pig's "attitude," we could say that a pig wants a farmer to do everything for it. We can write that in the box by "attitude" on the pig side.** Record the students' details about pigs in the boxes on the right side of the graphic organizer. POSSIBLE STUDENT RESPONSES: *Attitude (They walk around looking important.), Appearance (They are all dirty from lying in the mud.), Sounds (They grunt and squeal.), Actions (They dig around in big mud holes.)*

- **The author chose to use pigs to describe Mr. Piggot and the boys. What do we understand about the characters from using this metaphor?** POSSIBLE STUDENT RESPONSES: *They are lazy.*

They think they are the most important. They are loud and bossy. They are behaving badly, not the way people should. They should not be so lazy. They should all work to do the jobs in their home. **You are right. There is definitely something we can learn from this metaphor. By creating the metaphor that the Piggot men are like pigs, the author is telling us that to sit around making messes while one person does all of the work in a home is the wrong way for people to behave. Animals may have a farmer to take care of them, but people should all help each other. Each member of a family is important.**

- **Let's look at some more examples of metaphors. That will give us time to understand and practice this new way of thinking. There are several metaphors in our next book.** *Tyler Toad and the Thunder,* **by Robert L. Crowe, is another story where metaphors are used to help explain things. In this book, the metaphors are used to try to help a character overcome his fear of thunder. Let's reread the story to remind ourselves of the metaphors that are in this book.** Read the story to students. Revisiting the story rather than using it in a "first read" situation is helpful to students as they look for the metaphors.

- **In the book, the animals tried to help Tyler overcome his fear of thunder by explaining it in a way that would not frighten him. There were several metaphors used to tell Tyler Toad about thunder and help him to get over his fears. Let's make a list of the metaphors that the animal friends used in explaining thunder.** On the chalkboard or a chart list the different metaphors from the story. The list should include: the Milky Way Patrol testing their cannons, the Sky Animals banging pots and pans, the big bass drum in the parade across the sky, and the Great Toad shaking a piece of tin up in the sky. **What was the author trying to say about thunder?** POSSIBLE STUDENT RESPONSES: *Thunder is a big sound but it won't hurt you. Thunder is a loud noise. It's a booming noise. It surprises us. It moves across the sky. It shakes things.* Record students' ideas on a nearby chart or board.

- **You have said that the author is telling about the sound of thunder, the force of thunder, the location of thunder, the safety of thunder, and the reaction of people to thunder. These are labels for the general characteristics we are thinking about when we think of thunder. We can put these things on another copy of the graphic organizer for understanding metaphors.** Write the words sound, force, location, safety, and people reaction on the arrows down the middle of the new copy of the graphic organizer for understanding metaphors.

- **Now let's put in some of the details about thunder. These words will go on the left side of the graphic organizer under the word "thunder." What are some words that we can use to describe these characteristics for thunder?** Record the responses for each similarity in the boxes on the left side of the graphic. POSSIBLE STUDENT RESPONSES: *Sound (big, loud, booming),Force (vibrates), Location (goes across the sky), Safety (won't hurt you), People reaction (startled).*

- **Let's consider one of the metaphors from the book to see how it is similar to thunder. We'll look at the big bass drum in the parade across the sky. What are some words to describe the characteristics down the center of the diagram and the way they relate to a big bass drum in the parade across the sky?** As before, fill the in boxes for each similarity on the right side of the graphic organizer. POSSIBLE STUDENT RESPONSES: *Sound (big, loud, booming), Force (vibrates), Location (goes across the sky), Safety (won't hurt you), People reaction (startled).*

- **What does this metaphor of the bass drum in parade across the sky say about thunder?** *It says that thunder is just a sound in the sky.*

- **Using a metaphor to tell something important about a person or thing that you want to describe can be very effective. To help a small toad understand thunder, his friends used a** variety of metaphors. To explain the bad behavior of a family, the mother used pigs. In both of these cases, the metaphor had important similarities to the person or thing being described.

- In this lesson I'm going to teach you how to make your own metaphors for things. We're not just going to look at metaphors that other people have made. To understand a metaphor, we have been looking at similarities between two things. That's part of what we do, but we have to do more to make our own metaphors. Here is a thinking map that tells us what is important to think about when we *create a metaphor.* Show on a chart or chalkboard the thinking map for making a metaphor. It should be visible during the les-

> **MAKING A METAPHOR**
>
> 1. What do I want to say with a metaphor?
> 2. What are some details about what I want to say?
> 3. What other things have the same characteristics?
> 4. Which of these things might make a good metaphor? What are some of its details?
> 5. Is it a good metaphor? Why?

son. Someone who is making a metaphor first needs to think about what he or she wants to say with it. The author of *Piggybook* wanted to show that it is very piggish to sit around and let one person in a family do all of the chores in the home. The second question on the thinking map asks about the details. What details should be pointed out? In our book, the characters were not working together around the house. They were letting one member do all of the work while they sat around and made messes. The third and fourth questions ask, "What other things have the same characteristics?" and "Which of these things might make a good metaphor?" Anthony Browne, the author of *Piggybook*, probably thought of a variety of things, and then decided that pigs had a lot in common with the characters he was thinking about. He probably looked at the things he knew about pigs and answered the last question, "Is it a good metaphor?" with a "Yes!"

He showed himself and the reader why it was a good metaphor as he wrote and published the book.

THINKING ACTIVELY

- In our studies of weather, we have learned about the many kinds of weather that occur. Our goal is to write our own metaphor to help someone understand blizzards, another type of weather. This could be a confusing or scary concept, and a metaphor can help someone better understand it.

- The graphic organizer for writing our own metaphor is slightly different from the one we have been using. Display the graphic organizer for creating a metaphor on an overhead transparency or chart. **Our topic, blizzard, needs to be written in the top part of the first box, under "What I want to describe." Underneath this area it asks us to think about "What I want to say about it." Think about the things you want to say about a blizzard. Write your ideas down on your slate. If indi-**

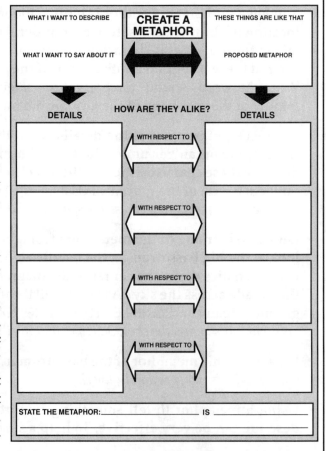

vidual dry erase boards are not available, use paper. Allow quiet think time. **Now share your ideas with your group.** Students should share in small groups. **As a large group we will record the things we want our metaphor to say about a blizzard on our graphic organizer.** Record the responses given in bottom portion of the first box. POSSIBLE STUDENT RESPONSES: *It is very cold. It is very snowy. It is very windy. It is very icy. It is very white. It is blinding.*

- **To describe a blizzard, the metaphor you pick must tell these important characteristics of a blizzard. We will write the labels for the type of characteristic on the arrows down the middle of our diagram. These characteristics must match between a blizzard and our metaphor. They are the idea bridges that carry the similarities back and forth. The things we have listed as characteristics would fit into the categories of "temperature" because blizzards are icy cold and snowy, "appearance" because they are very white, "motion" because they are windy, and "effect on vision" because blizzards are blinding.** Write the terms on the arrows down the middle of the graphic organizer.

- **I will assign each group one of the characteristics that we have written on the arrows. In your group write down all of the details you can think of that describe that characteristic of a blizzard. Writing down words that tell about the details of each characteristic helps us to imagine what this characteristic of a blizzard really seems like to you.** Assign one characteristic for each group and allow work time. When all have recorded their thoughts, share with the large group and record on the left side of the graphic organizer under "Details." POSSIBLE STUDENT RESPONSES: *(temperature) :cold, frigid, freezing, below zero, (appearance): snowy, cloudy, white, fluffy, big flakes, (motion): windy, sideways, rapid, falling, (effect on vision): blinding, confusing, need to squint.*

- **Now we are ready to think of a metaphor, something that we can say is like a blizzard. What other things have many of the same characteristics as the ones you have identified? With your group, brainstorm as many things as you can think of that have similar characteristics. Just as the author was in** *Tyler Toad and the Thunder,* **I want you to be creative in your thinking. What things might be good metaphors for a blizzard?** Allow small group work time. After sharing the results, choose six of the brainstormed ideas that various groups have suggested to record in the top portion of the right hand box on the graphic organizer under "These things are like that." POSSIBLE STUDENT RESPONSES: *a white unicorn stomping on the clouds, mice dropping ice cream crumbs from the clouds, dandruff from the Ice Man, bubble bath bubbles overflowing, a polar bear shaking off some of his fur, white paint dripping from the clouds.*

- **To continue our exploration of these possible metaphors, we will use a webbing diagram for suggested metaphors. On the web we can check out the ideas to see which ones have attributes, or things about it, that also could be said of a blizzard.** The possible ideas recorded on the Creating A Metaphor graphic organizer should also be written in the "Metaphor" boxes on the Suggested Metaphors webbing diagram. As a class, work together to record on the webbing diagram three things for each metaphor that the students believe describe both the metaphor and a blizzard. **If we think about a white unicorn stomping its feet on the clouds we can think of ways that this possible metaphor would explain a bliz-**

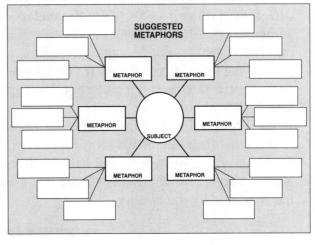

zard. **What details about a stomping unicorn would match a blizzard and help us to explain a blizzard to someone?** POSSIBLE STUDENT RESPONSES: *There can be lots of snow because the unicorn is stomping hard. The unicorn is white like the clouds and snow. It is sort of wild and a blizzard is a wild storm.* **Let's think about another possible metaphor. What details about dandruff from the Ice Man would match the details of a blizzard?** POSSIBLE STUDENT RESPONSES: *It is white like snow. It is flaky like snow. There can be lots of dandruff! It is cold because it is from the Ice Man.* Continue to work with the other possible metaphors generating details that would support the item being like a blizzard.

• **We have a large bank of ideas for a metaphor. Let's choose one of the ideas that you think best describes a blizzard. We should pick one that you think has the most important connections.** As a group decide which one will be used to test its similarities. **We will work down the right side of our graphic organizer to see how well the idea we have chosen matches the things we want to say about a blizzard.** As a class work down the right side of the graphic, recording the details of the suggested metaphor in the boxes next to each arrow. For example, if the class chose "mice dropping ice cream crumbs from the sky" as the metaphor, they would look for ways to match it to a blizzard's characteristics of temperature (It is cold and freezing.), appearance (Ice cream looks like big chunks of snow, so crumbs could be like snowflakes.), motion (It goes down and plops. There could be lots of mice dropping lots of ice cream.), and effect on vision (You can't see through ice cream, so it's blinding. People can get headaches from ice cream.).

• **The bottom box of our graphic organizer gives us a place to record the metaphor if we decide it is a good match. Do you think we have a good match between a blizzard and mice dropping ice cream crumbs from the clouds?** Students probably will like the metaphor that they have chosen. If there is a question about the match, allow class discussion to make alterations in the details that would more closely fit a blizzard.

• Thinking about whether the metaphor we choose is a good one to use is important. We want to be careful to use something that will help explain a blizzard and not confuse the idea. We should consider if there are any important differences that would make this metaphor about blizzards misleading. If we were working with the idea that a blizzard is like pieces of a white fence falling from the sky, a big difference would be the weight. A piece of fence weighs much more than snowflakes. If we said a metaphor for a blizzard could be little white butterflies swarming around it could also be misleading. Someone might think about spring when butterflies appear and not understand that a blizzard is a very cold storm. **What differences do you know of for the metaphors we have thought about? Would they mislead someone?** POSSIBLE STUDENT RESPONSE: *If people think about paint dripping they might not understand that there is so much snow it is very hard to see. It would have to be many buckets of paint dripping and making lots of drops all over.* **If you decide that the differences are too misleading and cannot be corrected, then it is not a good metaphor and we should return to our list of possibilities.** If time allows, other metaphors could be developed with the class, or small groups could work through the thinking with other possible metaphors. In later grades, the students will find on their thinking maps an additional question that addresses the possibility of misleading a person with a metaphor that has characteristics that would confuse someone's thinking. In grades 1 and 2, however, this should be addressed informally in a class discussion with thinking modeled by the teacher.

THINKING ABOUT THINKING

• **We will be using the metaphors we have created for a blizzard to do some writing, but we** need to look back at the thinking we've done first. **Let's think about the things we did to create a metaphor. What steps did we take?** As students go through the steps, revisit the thinking map to help them see the path they followed. Discuss each step.

- **Do you think this is a valuable way to think when you are trying to find one thing to describe another? Why or why not?** Students may feel that they like the organization of this plan. It helps them to see which thing is the best metaphor.

- **How does listing the characteristics of a blizzard help you to "see" the traits it shares with the metaphor?** POSSIBLE STUDENT RESPONSES: *Writing things down helps me to think of other things that I want to remember. When we write down the details, it makes it easier to decide on the best one.*

APPLYING YOUR THINKING

Immediate Transfer

- **Discuss with your partner how the metaphor in *Piggybook* helped you to understand why Mrs. Piggot was so upset. Now create a new metaphor for Mrs. Piggot. What is she like?** Use the thinking map and graphic organizers for creating a metaphor to help tell people what she is like.

- **You have had a wonderful day. You and your best friend spent the whole day together. Create a metaphor to describe how well you and your best friend get along.** The thinking map and graphic organizers for creating a metaphor will help you with your work. Draw a picture of you and your friend. Now draw a picture of your metaphor. Don't forget to write a caption explaining your pictures.

Reinforcement Later

- **In studying communities, we have learned about factories and the important role they play in our lives. Using our thinking map and graphic organizers, create a metaphor to explain the cooperation that is required in the process of assembly line work.** Use your metaphor in a report, written or orally presented. Include pictures to help show the metaphor.

- **We have learned about the life cycle of the butterfly. Use the thinking map and graphic organizers for creating a metaphor to create a metaphor for one of the stages.** Use your metaphor to create a story.

WRITING EXTENSION

When we record the details of a metaphor it helps us later as we write. The words we use for the details we have written on our graphic organizer can be included in our stories and poems about blizzards. Use the metaphor we created in our lesson to help explain a blizzard to someone who might be afraid of them. Our writing can be a story or a poem. To help with our prewriting, let's draw the metaphor. Then we can create a story or poem. In our writing we will want to be sure to use the words that we thought of to show the metaphor. They will help people who read our writing to see the metaphor as we do. Allow students to draw the metaphor the class created. Writing can be done individually or in pairs. A story map that includes a sequencing of events would be helpful to students who choose to write in prose form. If poetry is chosen, shape poems and triangle poems are good choices for metaphors at this age. Because of the different developmental levels of first and second grade students writing metaphor captions for pictures using sentence frames could also be an activity offered. (See writing templates in Appendix.)

SUGGESTED SPECIAL NEEDS MODIFICATIONS

<u>Frontload</u>: The concept of a metaphor in this lesson maybe abstract for some students. Therefore, students may benefit from examples of metaphors in order to understand their structure. It may be wise to start with similes and explicitly use the sentence frame "_____ is like _____ because" to aid students in articulating the connection. Begin by selecting common expressions , such as, "white as snow" or "green as grass" to discuss as a class.

Introducing the term "characteristic" would also be useful. Students may begin by describing a familiar story character or object. The teacher can label the attributes students list as "characteristics." The teacher may wish to provide "characteristics" and allow students to brainstorm objects that have those characteristics as the next step in understanding the term "characteristic."

<u>Diversify</u>: To assist some students in generating ideas, the teacher may wish to have students participate in a Think-Pair-Share activity. Working with a partner, students can discuss characteristics of thunder or blizzards, for example, prior to listing or responding in class.

Some students may also benefit from a greater degree of teacher modelling of additional examples prior to working in cooperative groups.

Cooperative groups are useful in reducing the task demands so that the less proficient writer may offer ideas while the recorder logs everyone's ideas for the group.

<u>Expand the Possibilities</u>: Assessments of written responses may be based upon students' thinking first, and expressive skills second. Oral responses may also reveal thinking beyond students' ability to express themselves in writing. Drawings may be used to convey the thinking behind the metaphor.

ASSESSING STUDENT THINKING ABOUT CREATING METAPHORS

The transfer activities provide good tools for assessing the students' ability to create metaphors. Students should be able to explain the steps they went through in creating a metaphor. Explicit questioning helps to determine if they are following the steps of the thinking map. This strategy can be assessed in a group format.

Sample Student Responses • Why Is This Happening?

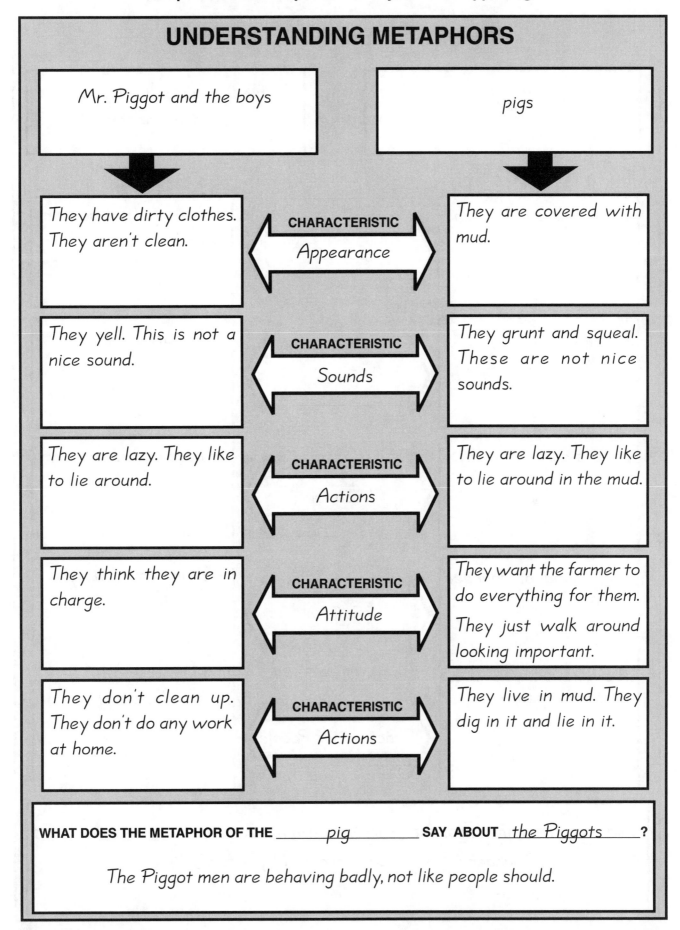

UNDERSTANDING METAPHORS

| Mr. Piggot and the boys | | pigs |

They have dirty clothes. They aren't clean.
CHARACTERISTIC *Appearance*
They are covered with mud.

They yell. This is not a nice sound.
CHARACTERISTIC *Sounds*
They grunt and squeal. These are not nice sounds.

They are lazy. They like to lie around.
CHARACTERISTIC *Actions*
They are lazy. They like to lie around in the mud.

They think they are in charge.
CHARACTERISTIC *Attitude*
They want the farmer to do everything for them. They just walk around looking important.

They don't clean up. They don't do any work at home.
CHARACTERISTIC *Actions*
They live in mud. They dig in it and lie in it.

WHAT DOES THE METAPHOR OF THE _____pig_____ **SAY ABOUT** _the Piggots_ **?**

The Piggot men are behaving badly, not like people should.

Sample Student Responses • Why Is This Happening?

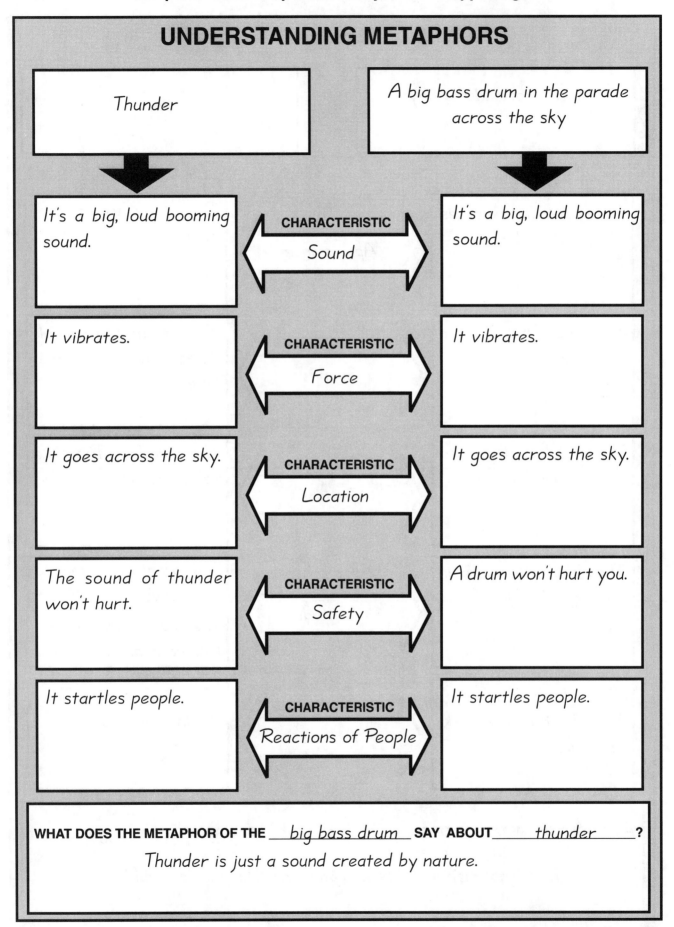

UNDERSTANDING METAPHORS

| Thunder | | A big bass drum in the parade across the sky |

| It's a big, loud booming sound. | **CHARACTERISTIC** Sound | It's a big, loud booming sound. |

| It vibrates. | **CHARACTERISTIC** Force | It vibrates. |

| It goes across the sky. | **CHARACTERISTIC** Location | It goes across the sky. |

| The sound of thunder won't hurt. | **CHARACTERISTIC** Safety | A drum won't hurt you. |

| It startles people. | **CHARACTERISTIC** Reactions of People | It startles people. |

WHAT DOES THE METAPHOR OF THE _big bass drum_ **SAY ABOUT** _thunder_ **?**
Thunder is just a sound created by nature.

Sample Student Responses • Why Is This Happening?

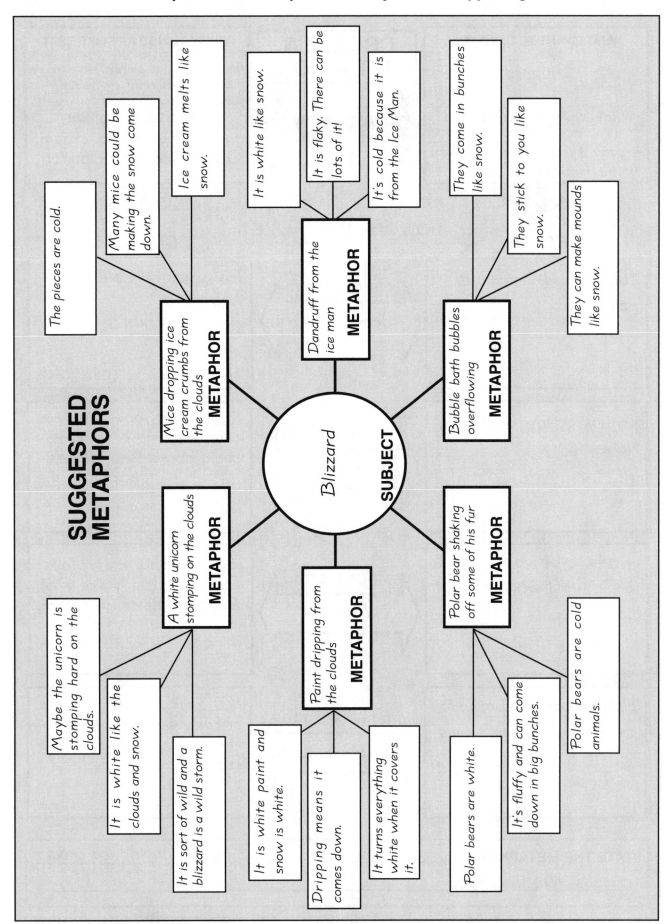

Sample Student Responses • Why Is This Happening?

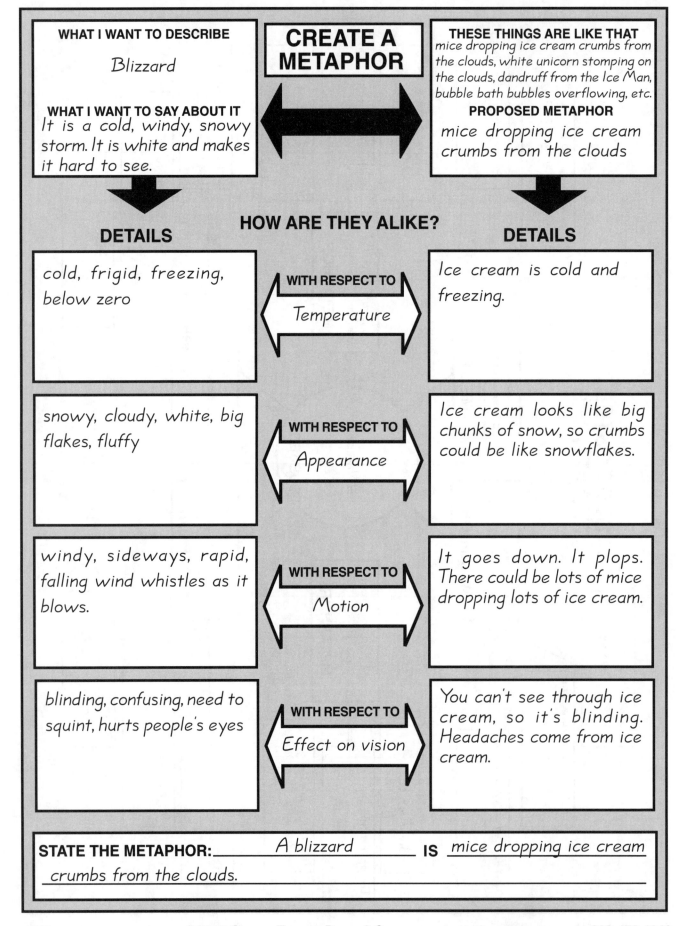

WHAT I WANT TO DESCRIBE

Blizzard

WHAT I WANT TO SAY ABOUT IT
It is a cold, windy, snowy storm. It is white and makes it hard to see.

CREATE A METAPHOR

THESE THINGS ARE LIKE THAT
mice dropping ice cream crumbs from the clouds, white unicorn stomping on the clouds, dandruff from the Ice Man, bubble bath bubbles overflowing, etc.

PROPOSED METAPHOR
mice dropping ice cream crumbs from the clouds

HOW ARE THEY ALIKE?

DETAILS

DETAILS

cold, frigid, freezing, below zero

WITH RESPECT TO
Temperature

Ice cream is cold and freezing.

snowy, cloudy, white, big flakes, fluffy

WITH RESPECT TO
Appearance

Ice cream looks like big chunks of snow, so crumbs could be like snowflakes.

windy, sideways, rapid, falling wind whistles as it blows.

WITH RESPECT TO
Motion

It goes down. It plops. There could be lots of mice dropping lots of ice cream.

blinding, confusing, need to squint, hurts people's eyes

WITH RESPECT TO
Effect on vision

You can't see through ice cream, so it's blinding. Headaches come from ice cream.

STATE THE METAPHOR: _____A blizzard_____ **IS** _mice dropping ice cream crumbs from the clouds._

Sample Student Writing • Why Is This Happening?

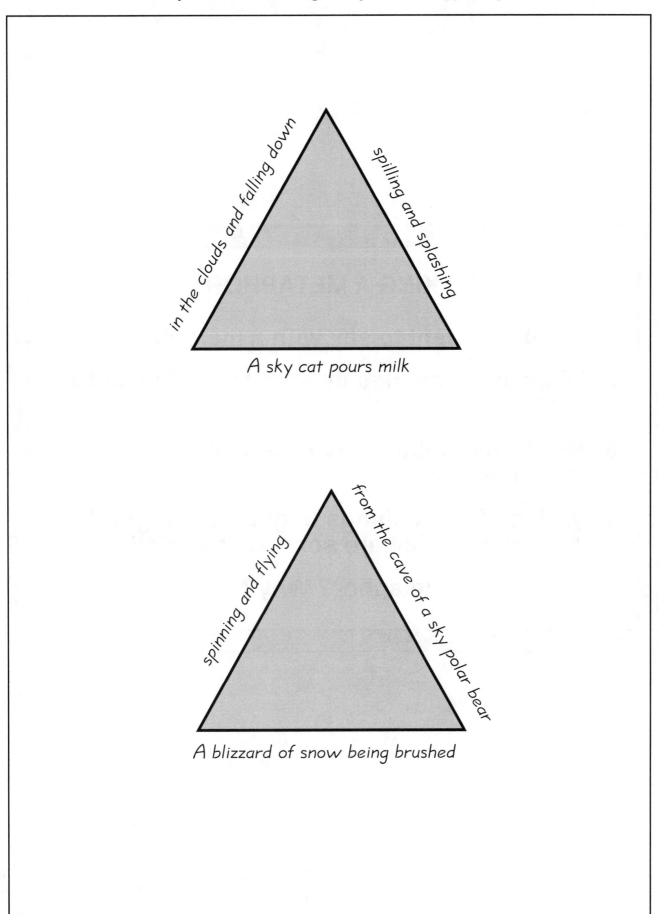

in the clouds and falling down / spilling and splashing

A sky cat pours milk

spinning and flying / from the cave of a sky polar bear

A blizzard of snow being brushed

MAKING A METAPHOR

1. What do I want to say with a metaphor?

2. What are some details about what I want to say?

3. What other things have the same characteristics?

4. Which of these things might make a good metaphor? What are some of its details?

5. Is it a good metaphor? Why?

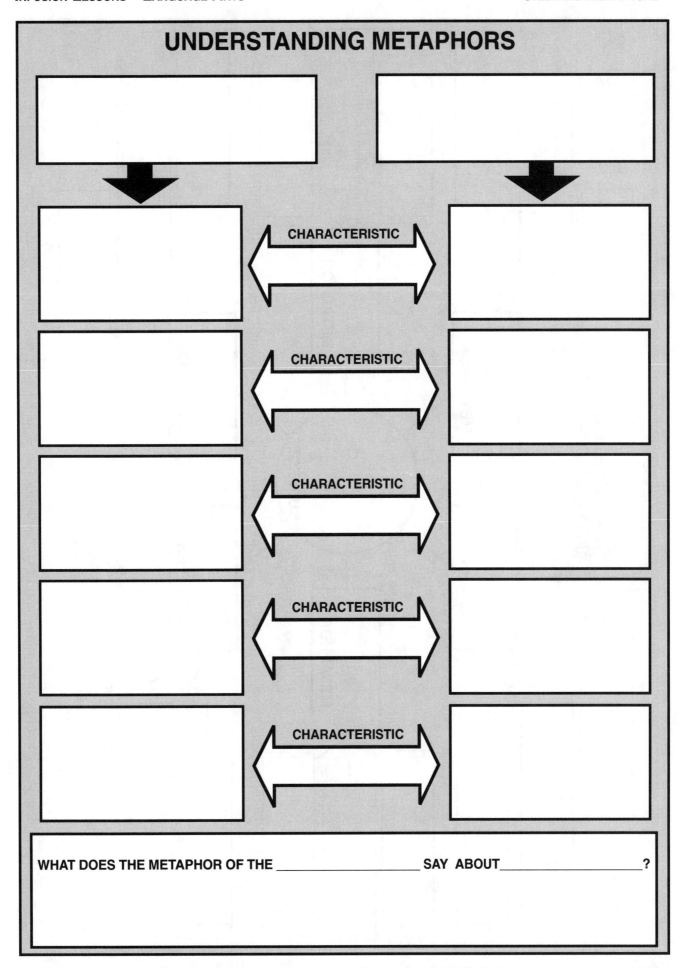

UNDERSTANDING METAPHORS

CHARACTERISTIC

CHARACTERISTIC

CHARACTERISTIC

CHARACTERISTIC

CHARACTERISTIC

WHAT DOES THE METAPHOR OF THE _____ SAY ABOUT_____?

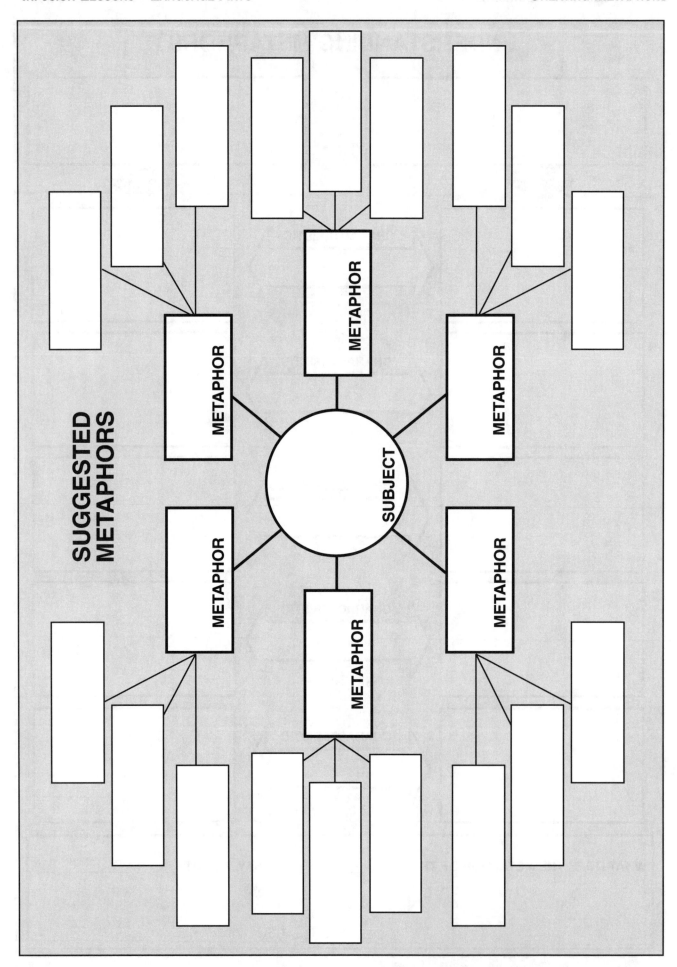

SUGGESTED METAPHORS

SUBJECT

METAPHOR

METAPHOR

METAPHOR

METAPHOR

METAPHOR

METAPHOR

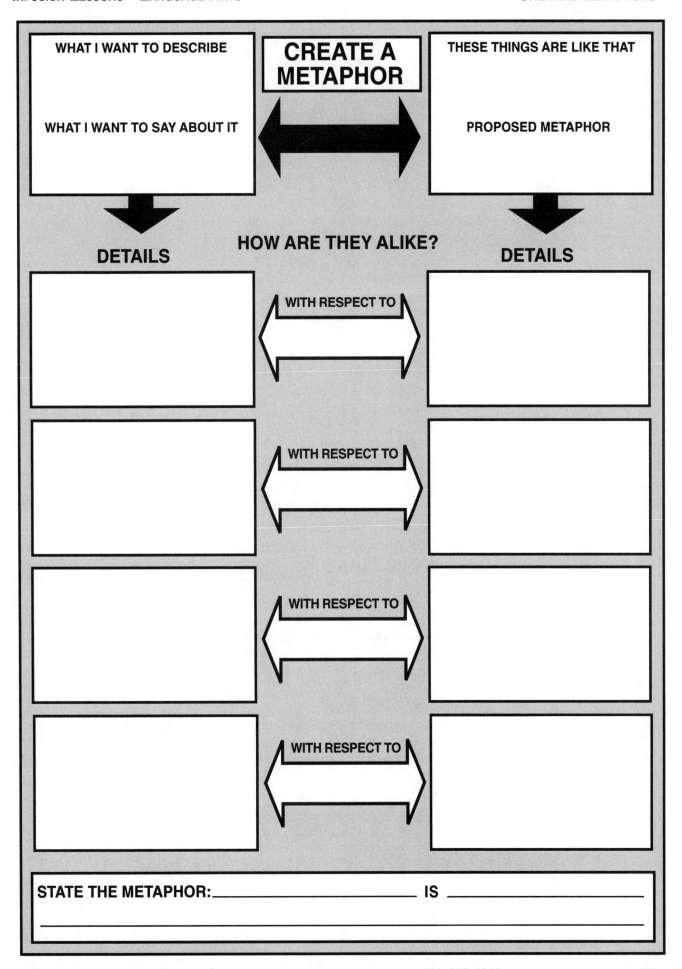

CHAPTER 13
RELIABLE SOURCES

Infusing Determining the Reliability of Sources into Language Arts

Teaching students to evaluate sources of information skillfully in grades 1 and 2 is an extremely important critical thinking skill that impacts on their use of information in all of the other types of thinking included in this book. It involves helping them learn to ask and carefully answer the following questions about a person as a source of information before they accept the information as reliable and accurate:

EVALUATING THE RELIABILITY OF A PERSON AS A SOURCE OF INFORMATION

1. Who is the source of the information being questioned?

2. What are the answers to these questions?
   a. Does the person know a lot about the subject?
   b. Do other people know and trust this person as a source of information?
   c. Does the person have something to gain by your accepting what he or she has to say?
   d. Did the person find out by his or her own investigation or get the information from someone else? If from someone else, is the other person reliable?
   e. Do others agree with this person?

3. Based on the answers to these questions, is the source reliable, unreliable, or uncertain?

---

figure 13.1

EVALUATING THE RELIABILITY OF WRITING AS A SOURCE OF INFORMATION

1. What is the source of the information?

2. What are the answers to these questions?
   a. The Writing
      What is the date of the writing?
      Is the writing fact or fiction?
      Do other people think the publication is a good one?
   b. The Author
      Is the person an expert on this topic?
      Has the person been wrong in the past?
      Does the person have a reason for wanting this information to be true?
   c. Agreement of Others
      Do others agree with the information from this source?

3. Based on the answers to these questions, is this source reliable, unreliable, or uncertain?

---

figure 13.2

If the source is a written source, use the thinking map shown in figure 13.2.

These are what we call "thinking maps" for skillfully determining the reliability of sources of information. In the lessons in this chapter, these thinking maps are used to guide your students' thinking explicitly as they engage with the lesson content.

When students learn and use this strategy for thinking about sources of information they don't just intuitively judge that a source of information is reliable or base their judgment on one factor, like expertise. Rather, they consider a range of factors that might affect the quality and accuracy of information they are getting, no one of which is definitive. However, consideration of all of them together can establish the likelihood that the information is reliable, unreliable, or, in many cases, cast doubt on the information and provide a basis for taking it as uncertain. Reproducible blank graphic organizers are found at the end of each chapter.

These lessons also supplement the use of this thinking map with various supporting classroom strategies such as using a graphic organizer, engaging in cooperative thinking, thinking about thinking, and continued guided practice. These classroom strategies enhance both the thinking skill that the students are learning and their mastery of the lesson content.

The key graphic organizer for determining the reliability of sources of information is in figure 13.3 (see following page). This graphic organizer helps students record important questions (see left-hand column) and the information they get from the questions (see right-hand column). Students then indicate, by using a "+," a "−," or a "?," whether the information they record is in favor, against, or uncertain with regard to the reliability of the source, and hence, the accuracy of the information.

For more in-depth information on teaching skillful determination of the reliability of sources of information, please refer to Chapter 12 in the

---

book *Infusing the Teaching of Critical and Creative Thinking into Elementary Instruction,* by Robert Swartz and Sandra Parks. A computer disk containing the blank, reproducible graphic organizers used in this book is also available. Both book and disk are available through Critical Thinking Books & Software.

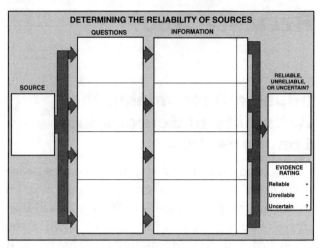

figure 13.3

WHO STOLE THE DIAMONDS?
CAM JANSEN AND THE MYSTERY OF THE STOLEN DIAMONDS

Language Arts   **Grades 1–2**

OBJECTIVES

CONTENT

Students will develop their reading comprehension skills as they identify relevant details that support the inferences they make from the text.

THINKING SKILL/PROCESS

Students will learn how to make judgments about the accuracy and reliability of sources of information based on the presence or absence of relevant factors.

METHODS AND MATERIALS

CONTENT

Students will have listened to (grade one) or read (grade two) the first three chapters of the book *Cam Jansen and the Mystery of the Stolen Diamonds* by David A. Adler. They will work in collaborative groups to share information from the story. Having read other books in the Cam Jansen series will be helpful in identifying the traits of the main character.

THINKING SKILL/PROCESS

Structured questioning is key to helping students identify the factors which influence the reliability of sources of information. Collaborative learning activities support students in their learning. A graphic organizer is used to help organize student thinking.

LESSON

INTRODUCTION TO CONTENT AND THINKING SKILL/PROCESS

• **We learn a lot by exploring and trying things ourselves. Do you remember what we learned about different kinds of leaves by looking at their shapes and pictures of the kinds of trees they came from? However, we cannot discover everything ourselves. We must rely on others to tell us things we need to know, like what it is like living in a different country or how to write a poem. These people are called our "sources of information."** Write "sources of information" on a chart or on the chalkboard. **Can you think of times when other people have been sources of information for you? Talk to a neighbor about people who have been sources of information for you.** Allow time for pair sharing, and then share with the class. Use probing questions to clarify and elaborate on answers. Record the answers under "sources of information." POSSIBLE STUDENT RESPONSES: *teacher, parents, firemen, policemen, doctor, dentist.*

• **Most of the time the information we get from others is correct. But sometimes it isn't. Perhaps one of your teachers told you that you would need your coat for recess, but when you got outside you found that it had warmed up so much that coats were not necessary. It is important to get good information when we have to depend on other sources. Can you think of a time when you got information from another person and it turned out to be wrong? Discuss this with your partner.** Allow share time, and again allow a few to share their examples with the whole class. As before, use probing questions to clarify and elaborate on the examples.

• **In order to get information that we can depend on, we should check the sources. We should try to find out if the sources are** *reliable.* **"Reliable" means that the source can be trusted to**

give information that is correct, or true. Sometimes what we find out about the source makes us wonder whether the information is correct. Write the word "reliable" on the chart or chalkboard next to the words "sources of information." **Let's think about a specific example. Suppose someone told you that the best backpack for carrying things to school was called the "A+ KidPack." You want to know that the information from this source is accurate because you are thinking about asking your parents to get you a backpack. You wonder if this is the kind of backpack you should ask them for. You are probably thinking about whether this person and the information can be trusted. What sort of things would you try to find out in asking whether this person is a reliable source? What questions would you try to get answers to? For example, when we are checking a source to see if it is reliable, wouldn't you want to find out if they know about the subject they are talking about? Wouldn't you want to find out if they know something about backpacks?** Students usually agree. On a chart, write "Reliable Sources of Information about Backpacks." Under this heading, write the question "Does the source know about backpacks?" Explain that the more a person knows, the more that person becomes an *expert* about backpacks. So if you answer that the person knows a lot about backpacks, or is an expert about them, that counts in favor of his or her reliability as a source. **What are some other questions you might ask? See if you can come up with two or three.** Allow time for sharing with a partner, then ask the teams to share one of their questions with the class. Record the questions suggested on the chalkboard or the chart under the first question. POSSIBLE STUDENT RESPONSES: *Did the person try the backpack himself or herself? Did the person try on a lot of backpacks before choosing this one? Did they hear about it in a commercial on television? Did they hear about it from a friend who has one? Did they read about it in the paper? Do they remember why it is a good backpack? Is the person trying to sell it to you? Do other people know and trust this person as a good source of information?*

- **Let's look at our questions. How would answers to these questions show whether the source could be trusted?** With the class, discuss the questions, elaborating on the information to be gained by asking each question. Explore different answers that would count in favor or against the accuracy of the information. For example, ask what they would think about the accuracy of the information if the source tried on the backpack and gave it a trial use. Most students would say that that counts in favor of the accuracy of the information. When they say that, you can tell them that if the source tried on the backpack and used it himself or herself, then we could say that he or she is a "primary source." Write the words "primary source" on the chalkboard. **A primary source is someone who got the information by seeing, hearing, feeling, tasting, or smelling. A secondary source is someone who got the information from someone else.** Write the words "secondary source" on the chalkboard. **What's better, a primary or a secondary source?** Most students agree that a primary source is better. **Why?** POSSIBLE STUDENT RESPONSES: *A primary source knows the backpack itself, but a secondary source doesn't. A secondary source doesn't know if the person they get the information from is telling the truth. A secondary source might make a mistake about what the other person tells them.* Put a check mark next to "primary source." **Does that mean that what a secondary source tells you is always wrong? Discuss this with your partner.** After a minute or two, ask for responses from the class. Most students realize that secondary sources could be correct, but that there is a greater chance the secondary source is wrong than the primary source. This would be a good place to tell them a story about rumors and how rumors really can distort the truth. You could even try a rumor game in the class.

- **Another question you identified is whether the person is trying to sell you an "A+ KidPack." What difference might that make?** POSSIBLE STUDENT RESPONSES: *They might just want you to buy it so they can make money.* **Who might such a person be?** Students usually identify salespeople or someone who is selling something in a yard sale. **Would such people always not be**

telling you the truth? Some students will say that they might be telling you the truth, but because they can make some money if you buy it, you can't be sure. However, other students will probably be more trusting of sales people, so encourage a discussion on this point. **Can you think of other examples like these where, because the person is trying to sell you something, you might wonder if they are giving you accurate information? Think about what you see on TV.** This prompt usually helps students identify television commercials as possible unreliable sources.

- **Now let's think about one final thing. Suppose someone else also says that the "A+ KidPack" is a really good pack. Would that help you to decide that the first person was a reliable source?** Give the students a few minutes to discuss this with a partner, then ask for some comments from the class. Most students recognize that the consenting opinions of two people are better than one. Guide the discussion to include the possible scenario of the second person getting his or her information from the first. Use questioning to bring them to the conclusion that if the second person got his or her information from the first, then this does not show that the first person is reliable. If they don't mention this important point, ask them what they would think if the new person got their information from the original source. They should then be able to see that this would not support the reliability of the original source.

- **Let me summarize what we've just said. When we use sources of information, we should think about the source. We want to know that we can believe the source. Here is a thinking map that contains the important questions that we should ask and try to answer before we accept that a source is reliable. It is based on what you identified as important questions to ask to see if the person who told you about the backpack is probably a reliable source.** Post the thinking map on the wall of the classroom or on a flipchart so that the students can refer to it during the lesson. **Sometimes these questions should even be asked about ourselves when we have to be our own reliable source! If you asked these questions and got good answers before believing the source, you are a good thinker.**

> ### EVALUATING THE RELIABILITY OF A PERSON AS A SOURCE OF INFORMATION
>
> 1. Who is the source of the information being questioned?
>
> 2. What are the answers to these questions?
>   a. Does the person know a lot about the subject?
>   b. Do other people know and trust this person as a source of information?
>   c. Does the person have something to gain by your accepting what he or she has to say?
>   d. Did the person find out by his or her own investigation or get the information from someone else? If from someone else, is the other person reliable?
>   e. Do others agree with this person?
>
> 3. Based on the answers to these questions, is the source reliable, unreliable, or uncertain?

THINKING ACTIVELY

- **We are going to think about the characters in the book we're reading,** *Cam Jansen and the Mystery of the Stolen Diamonds.* **So far, we've read and discussed the first three chapters. We know from what we've read about Cam Jansen that she usually gets involved in a mystery. What is the mystery that Cam is going to try to solve?** *She is trying to find the man who stole the diamonds from the jewelry store.* **Let's review what has happened in the story up to this point. Retell the first three chapters in your groups.** The students should include in their summaries the events of the first three chapters. Cam and her friend Eric are watching Eric's little brother at the mall. They are playing a memory game when they hear the jewelry store alarm go off. Cam jumps up on the bench where they are sitting and watches a man come out of the store and run through the mall knocking over several shoppers in his path. After the man leaves, a man and lady with a baby leave the store and go right out of the mall. Then two old ladies come out. They are very upset and sit down on the bench next to Cam and Eric. The police arrive and go into the store. Then they come out and ask for witnesses who may have seen the robber. They run to catch the man who ran from the store and Cam and Eric talk to the ladies about what happened when the store was robbed. They tell her about the man with the gun and how he took the diamonds: "He made the owner lay down on the floor. He made the ladies and the couple with the baby face the wall until he got away." When the police came back with the man who ran from the store, Cam recognized him as the man she saw running out of the store, but the ladies say he is not the man who stole the diamonds. The police let the man go and he goes out of the mall the same way the couple with the baby did. That makes Cam and Eric suspicious.

- **At this point in the story, there are several people who could be sources of information about who stole the diamonds. Who are the sources that may have information about the robber?** POSSIBLE STUDENT RESPONSES: *The ladies who were in the shop; Mr. Parker, the store owner; the people who were in front of the store when it happened; and Cam because she heard the alarm and she was watching the store.* Write the list of sources on a chart or the chalkboard under the heading "Sources."

- **We have a list of sources that need to be checked out. To be careful thinkers we should think about the questions we need to ask to check on each source's reliability in identifying the robber. I want you all to make believe that you are helping the police solve the mystery. Work in your groups to come up with two or three questions, the answers to which will help you decide who is the most reliable source. Use the thinking map for reliability of sources to guide you in deciding what questions to ask, but use words that make the questions fit the exact situation in this story. What questions would be helpful in picking out the reliable sources that the police should listen to as they work to solve this mystery?** Allow time for the groups to generate several questions. As they work, remind them to refer to the thinking map for reliable sources of information and to refine the questions to focus on the specific issue. When students have had time to make a list of questions, allow the groups to share their questions with the class, one question at a time. Record their questions on a chart, refining them to include the ideas in clear and simple language. Label the list "Questions to Help Find Reliable Sources for the Mystery of the Stolen Diamonds." From the list generated, circle the questions that the group feels will give the best idea of whether or not the source is reliable. POSSIBLE STUDENT RESPONSES: *Did the person see the robbery? Does the person have a reason for wanting you to believe they know who the robber is? Is the person known and trusted by others about remembering things? Does anyone else think the same thing?*

- **The sources we are considering are on our source list. Here is a graphic organizer that will help us in deciding how reliable they are.** Show the graphic organizer for reliability of sources using a transparency or a flipchart. A new graphic organizer will be needed for each of the four sources. **Now continue to make believe you are the police. You have used your police note pad to write down the possible witnesses. These are the sources that you will use to get information to solve the case. Using the questions we have generated, you will decide who are the most reliable sources and**

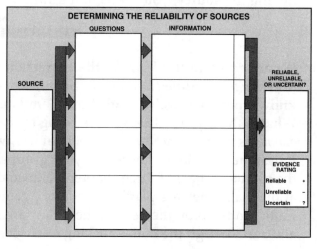

DETERMINING THE RELIABILITY OF SOURCES

QUESTIONS   INFORMATION

SOURCE

RELIABLE,
UNRELIABLE,
OR UNCERTAIN?

EVIDENCE
RATING

Reliable   +
Unreliable   −
Uncertain   ?

then you will listen to them carefully. Their information will help solve the case of the missing diamonds. We will record the name of the first source in the box marked "Source." We can begin with the ladies who came out of the store. The next section has boxes for us to put our questions from the thinking map. Record "Ladies in the jewelry store" in the source box and the questions from the thinking map in the boxes under "Questions."

- **Let's work together to check the reliability of the ladies in the jewelry store. The first question from our thinking map asks if they saw the robbery.** Read the question to the class. **What information do we have that we can record in the information box for this question?** Point out the information boxes on the graphic organizer where details that give information regarding the source and the questions will be recorded. **Discuss with your groups. What do we know that will help us answer this question?** The students will usually remember from the story that the ladies were in the store when it was robbed. They looked at the robber's face. Record this information in the box next to the first question. **Does this count for or against the ladies being reliable sources?** The student will agree that the information counts for the ladies being reliable. **We can put a plus sign in the small box next to our information to show that this supports the ladies being reliable.**

- **The second question asks if the ladies have anything to gain by the police believing they know who the robber is. What information do we have about this question?** The students usually come to the conclusion that the ladies have nothing to gain if the police believe they are reliable. They were scared by the robber pointing a gun at them and want the real robber to be caught. Record this information on the graphic organizer next to the second question. Ask if this supports the ladies being reliable. The students usually say it does and a plus sign can be recorded next to this information.

- **Let's continue with the third question.** Read the third question from the thinking map. **Are the ladies known and trusted by others?** As the students look in their books, they may say that there is nothing that says they are known and trusted. **Since there is nothing definite that lets us know if the ladies are known and trusted by others, we will put a question mark in the box to show that this makes it uncertain whether the ladies should be treated as reliable sources.**

- **Let's move on to the fourth question. Is there anyone else who agrees with who the ladies say stole the diamonds? What information do we have whether or not someone else agrees with the ladies?** The students usually recognize that Mr. Parker agrees with them. **Does this information support the ladies as reliable sources?** The students usually agree that it supports the ladies as reliable sources. A plus sign can be recorded next to the information.

- **Looking at our graphic organizer and the questions we have answered using our thinking map, what can we see from the information we have learned?** Go over the information on the graphic organizer, focusing students on the three supporting pieces of information and the one uncertain piece. The students will usually agree that the ladies are probably a reliable source. **If you think that the ladies are reliable sources, "reliable" can be written in the final box on the graphic organizer.** Do so. **Would you tell the police to listen to what the ladies have to say?** Students usually agree that they would advise the police to listen to the ladies.

- **Now let's think about the other sources. What about the shoppers, Mr. Parker and Cam Jansen? Are they reliable sources? I am going to give each group a graphic organizer. You will use it to decide if these other sources are reliable. I will assign one of these sources to your group. Each group will use our thinking map questions to decide if the source they are considering** is reliable. On your team's graphic organizer, record the source you are considering in the source box. Assign each group a source to investigate and allow time to record that source's name. In the next column, your group should record short versions of the questions from our thinking map, just as we did when we were considering the ladies in the jewelry store. Allow time for the questions to be recorded. Now your group should check back in the story for information that will help you answer each question so that you can decide if the source is likely to be reliable. Don't forget to record whether each piece of information would support or not support your source as reliable by writing a plus, a minus, or a question mark in the space for these signs in each box. Allow time for the groups to find information relating to the questions. Support students as they record the information and decide if it supports, does not support, or is uncertain. When all of the groups have completed their graphic organizers, share the results with the class. The usual response is that Mr. Parker is a reliable source while the shoppers outside the store are not reliable. They usually disagree about Cam because she is a good observer and has a good memory but didn't actually see what went on inside the store.

- It appears that the police would be wise to listen to Mr. Parker, the ladies, and possibly also Cam Jansen in solving the mystery of the stolen diamonds. However, Cam Jansen is not a good source for what went on inside the jewelry store when the diamonds were actually stolen. Now let's write down the information we think we can trust that we got from the sources we think are reliable. Work again with your partner and identify two pieces of information you think are accurate because the information comes from a reliable source. Give the students two or three minutes to discuss this together. Now tell me what you think is good, accurate information and who the source is. I am going to write it down like a good detective would. Ask for only one piece of information from any given team. As the information is presented, write it on the chalkboard or a flip chart under the heading "Accurate Information about the Mystery of the Stolen Diamonds." Make a column to the right of the information and put the heading "Source" over it. Write the source in the column next to the information as the students report. If a source cited by a team is a source that the students did not identify as reliable, remind the students that this is the place for information from reliable sources only.

- As we continue reading the story and new information becomes available, raise your hand if you think it should be added to the list. Only raise your hand if you think the source is a reliable source. Continue reading the story. When students raise their hands ask them for the information but also ask who the source is and why they think the source is reliable. Add it to the list only if the student agrees that the source is a reliable source. As more and more evidence accumulates, periodically stop and ask who, based on the information available, the students think stole the diamonds and why. Record their judgments under the heading "Who Stole the Diamonds" on the flip chart or on the chalkboard. Then, when the real culprit is revealed in the story, discuss what evidence it was that provided the clincher.

THINKING ABOUT THINKING

- **How did we figure out if our sources were reliable?** POSSIBLE STUDENT RESPONSES: *We asked questions about them and how they knew things. We thought about what would show that they were reliable sources. We used the questions on the thinking map we made.*

- **Why is it important to find out if a source is reliable?** POSSIBLE STUDENT RESPONSE: *If we listen to a source that isn't reliable, we won't get the right information.*

- **Do you think Cam was a good thinker about reliability of sources in this story? Why or why**

not? POSSIBLE STUDENT RESPONSES: *She was a good thinker because she considered the sources and looked for reasons why she should believe them. First she thought that the man running from the store was the robber. Then as more clues showed it wasn't him, she checked her reliability. She knew she wasn't in the store, so she could have been wrong at first. She was wrong and so she changed her mind.*

• **Was your thinking map helpful to you as you considered whether the characters were reliable sources? When would you want to have a thinking map for checking reliability of sources?** POSSIBLE STUDENT RESPONSES: *It would be good if I want to figure out what happened in a mystery I was reading. Everyone is telling my family which kind of dog to get for our pet. We could use it to figure out who really knows which one we should get.*

APPLYING YOUR THINKING

Immediate Transfer

• **Think about Jack in the story** *Jack and the Beanstalk.* **Was the man who traded him the beans for the cow a reliable source about beans? What questions should Jack have asked before he traded? Use your thinking map for checking the reliability of sources and a reliability of sources graphic organizer to show how Jack could have gotten more information before he traded for the beans.**

• **If you want to be a reliable source about the size of your desk, what things would you need to consider and do? What information would you want to have people know so that they would trust you?**

Reinforcement Later

• **Who would be a reliable source if you wanted to learn about how to care for a new pet? Why did you select that source? What questions did you ask before deciding?**

• **You must give a report on a city you have visited. What would you do to make sure that you are a reliable source when you share your information with the class? Use your thinking map for reliability of sources to make sure that you can be trusted to give accurate information about the city you visited.**

• **Suppose when you left school to go home someone you didn't know came up to you and said that your mother was sick and that you should get into his car. Use the thinking map for reliable sources to decide what you would want to find out first before you believed him and got into his car. How could you find out these things?** Encourage students to think of questions that they can ask people in the school. For example, "Does anyone know this person?"

THINKING SKILL EXTENSION

Using the skill of uncovering assumptions with the skill of checking the reliability of sources is often a good combination. Many times people assume that the sources of information they get are reliable. After students have identified who they think are reliable sources of information about who stole the diamonds, you can focus their attention on some of the characters in the mystery, for example the police. Ask them to uncover any assumptions they were making about sources of information they took to be reliable. Alternatively, you could design a lesson on reliable sources in which students first work to uncover any assumptions that the characters are making about who is a reliable source of information. Students then check out the reliability of the sources in question using the thinking map for this strategy.

Solving a mystery is an example of causal explanation. We are asking who caused the event in question, in this case the stealing of the diamonds. After students have identified reliable sources of information, you can shift them to the broader issue of who caused the event in question. Then have them identify possible causes (suspects) and gather all the evidence they can from these reliable sources to try to reach a conclusion about who the culprit is. Every time new evidence appears in the book as you read along, you can ask them to determine whether the source of this new evidence is reliable.

SUGGESTED SPECIAL NEEDS MODIFICATIONS

Frontload: Some students may need additional experiences with the concepts of "source" and "reliable." The term "source" could be used in multiple contexts in daily life. Students could be guided in brainstorming different types of sources (books, magazines, friends, scout leaders). Next they could be guided in reasons for selecting a source. "If you wanted to bake cookies, would you ask your grandmother or your little sister for information on baking cookies?" "What did you consider in making your choice?" "What other sources could you use?" "If a person tells you a story on the playground, what helps you decide whether or not to believe it?" "Would you rather believe someone who saw an accident happen or someone who heard about the accident from a friend?" "What is your reasoning?"

Similarly, the concept of "bias" which is implied in this lesson may require some prior discussion. Students' experiences with "bias" may have come in the form of a friend or sibling who attempted to persuade them to make a choice that could benefit the persuader. Discuss with students times when someone may have had a reason for suggesting a game, special treat, or activity because they had a special purpose for doing so beyond the reasons they stated. In this discussion, the motive need not be a negative one; it could simply demonstrate a person's preferences (like a favorite ice cream flavor).

Clarify: The term "reliable" may be unfamiliar to some students. It may be helpful to pair the term with phrases, such as, "count on to be true or right."

Diversify: As students are learning how to think through the steps in the reliability of sources strategy, the teacher may wish to model his/her thinking for choosing specific questions. Students who have difficulty in formulating questions would particularly benefit from this greater degree of guidance and modeling.

Expand The Possibilities: Assessment of written responses should be based upon students' thinking first, and expressive skills second. Oral responses may also reveal thinking beyond the students' ability to express themselves in writing.

ASSESSING STUDENT THINKING ABOUT RELIABLE SOURCES

To assess the ability to determine reliable sources, select examples that challenge students to use the questions from the class thinking map. The students should be able to justify believing or not believing that source. Any of the transfer examples can serve as assessment items for written or oral responses.

Sample Student Responses • Who Stole the Diamonds?

DETERMINING THE RELIABILITY OF SOURCES

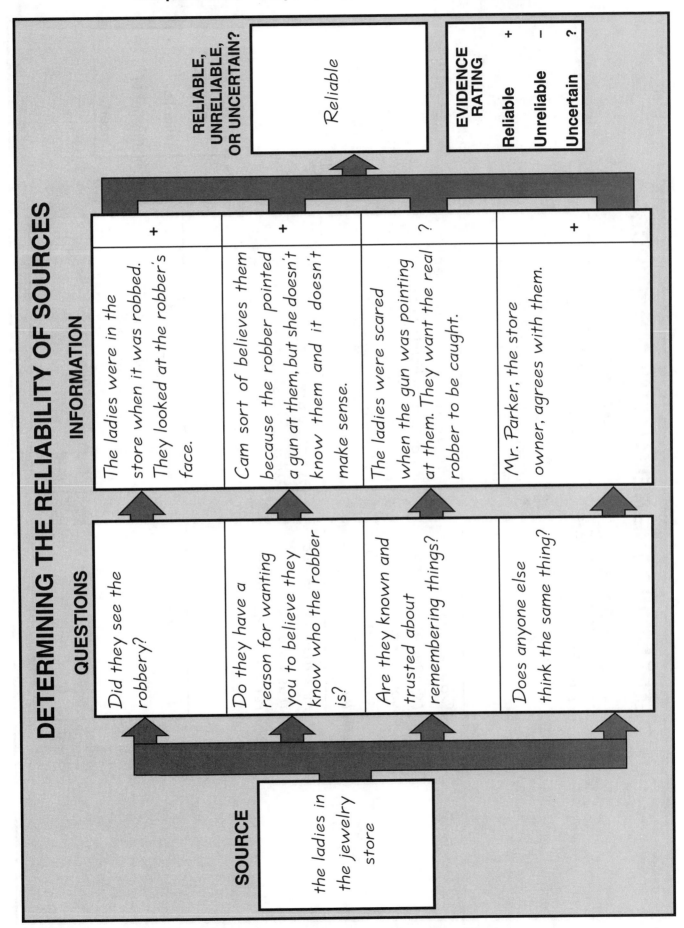

RELIABLE, UNRELIABLE, OR UNCERTAIN?

Reliable

EVIDENCE RATING

Reliable	+
Unreliable	–
Uncertain	?

INFORMATION

+ The ladies were in the store when it was robbed. They looked at the robber's face.

+ Cam sort of believes them because the robber pointed a gun at them, but she doesn't know them and it doesn't make sense.

? The ladies were scared when the gun was pointing at them. They want the real robber to be caught.

+ Mr. Parker, the store owner, agrees with them.

QUESTIONS

Did they see the robbery?

Do they have a reason for wanting you to believe they know who the robber is?

Are they known and trusted about remembering things?

Does anyone else think the same thing?

SOURCE

the ladies in the jewelry store

Sample Student Responses • Who Stole the Diamonds?

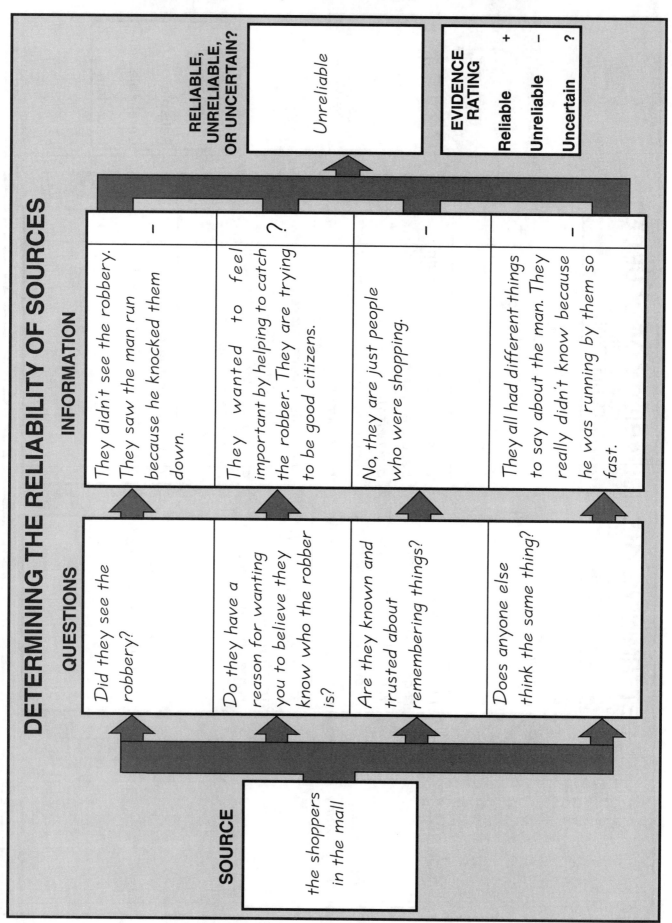

DETERMINING THE RELIABILITY OF SOURCES

RELIABLE, UNRELIABLE, OR UNCERTAIN?

Unreliable

EVIDENCE RATING	+	−	?
Reliable			
Unreliable			
Uncertain			

INFORMATION

	−
They didn't see the robbery. They saw the man run because he knocked them down.	

	?
They wanted to feel important by helping to catch the robber. They are trying to be good citizens.	

	−
No, they are just people who were shopping.	

	−
They all had different things to say about the man. They really didn't know because he was running by them so fast.	

QUESTIONS

Did they see the robbery?

Do they have a reason for wanting you to believe they know who the robber is?

Are they known and trusted about remembering things?

Does anyone else think the same thing?

SOURCE

the shoppers in the mall

Sample Student Responses • Who Stole the Diamonds?

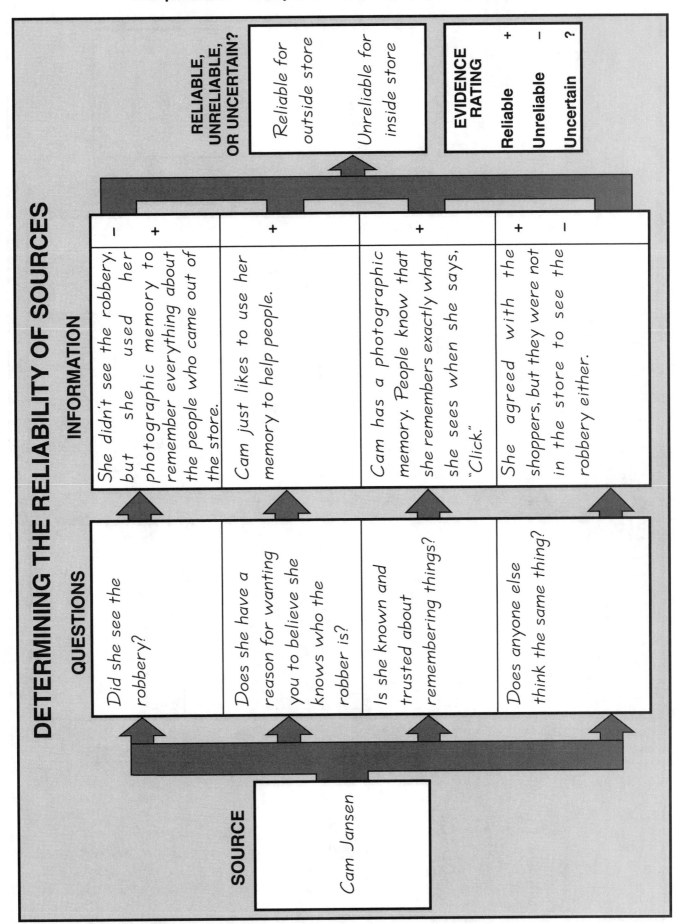

DETERMINING THE RELIABILITY OF SOURCES

RELIABLE, UNRELIABLE, OR UNCERTAIN?

Reliable for outside store

Unreliable for inside store

EVIDENCE RATING

Reliable	+
Unreliable	–
Uncertain	?

INFORMATION

–	+		
She didn't see the robbery, but she used her photographic memory to remember everything about the people who came out of the store.			

+			
Cam just likes to use her memory to help people.			

+			
Cam has a photographic memory. People know that she remembers exactly what she sees when she says, "Click."			

+	–
She agreed with the shoppers, but they were not in the store to see the robbery either.	

QUESTIONS

Did she see the robbery?

Does she have a reason for wanting you to believe she knows who the robber is?

Is she known and trusted about remembering things?

Does anyone else think the same thing?

SOURCE

Cam Jansen

Sample Student Responses • Who Stole the Diamonds?

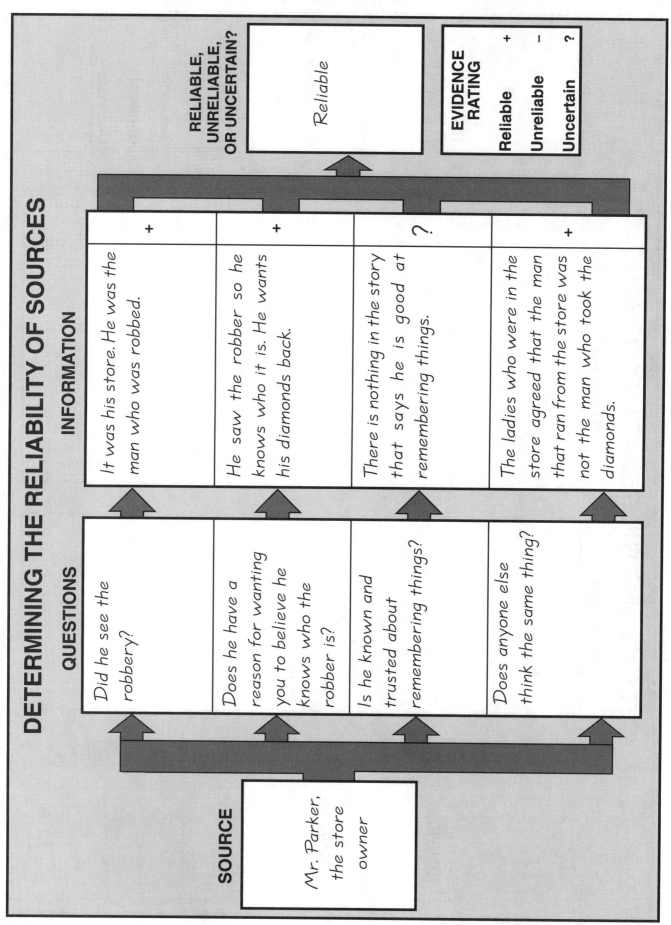

DETERMINING THE RELIABILITY OF SOURCES

RELIABLE, UNRELIABLE, OR UNCERTAIN?

Reliable

EVIDENCE RATING

Reliable	+
Unreliable	–
Uncertain	?

INFORMATION

+	+	?	+
It was his store. He was the man who was robbed.	He saw the robber so he knows who it is. He wants his diamonds back.	There is nothing in the story that says he is good at remembering things.	The ladies who were in the store agreed that the man that ran from the store was not the man who took the diamonds.

QUESTIONS

Did he see the robbery?	Does he have a reason for wanting you to believe he knows who the robber is?	Is he known and trusted about remembering things?	Does anyone else think the same thing?

SOURCE

Mr. Parker, the store owner

WHALES

Language Arts   Grades 1–2

OBJECTIVES

CONTENT

Students will learn how to gather information from a variety of sources and apply this information to whales and their unique characteristics as a water mammal.

THINKING SKILL/PROCESS

Students will learn how to make judgments about the accuracy and reliability of sources of information based on the presence or absence of relevant factors.

METHODS AND MATERIALS

CONTENT

The teacher will present a set of sources to compare and evaluate as possible sources of information about whales. Students will work cooperatively in pairs, small groups, and as a class to make decisions about where they will find reliable information.

THINKING SKILL/PROCESS

The lesson makes use of structured questioning and a graphic organizer to aid the students in identifying factors which influence the reliability and accuracy of sources of information. Collaborative learning enhances the thinking.

LESSON

INTRODUCTION TO CONTENT AND THINKING SKILL/PROCESS

- We can't discover everything for ourselves. Other people often tell us about things that we don't find out for ourselves. For example, we've been reading the book *Lon Po Po* in our reading sessions. We know that is what we are reading because we are here and we are doing it ourselves. But I have a friend who teaches in the next town and who also teaches at our same grade level. I wondered what she is reading with her students. I can't really go there during the day and see for myself because my job is to be here with you. So I asked her what they were reading and she told me. She said that they are also reading *Lon Po Po*. What a surprise! We compared how we were using *Lon Po Po* in our lessons and the learning that was happening with our classes. I told her how you liked it and what you were learning, and she told me the same things about her students. This example shows how I got information from my friend about what she was doing in her classroom. She was a "source of information" for me about information I could not get myself. Write the words "Sources of Information" on a chart or chalkboard. When I needed to find a book for us to use in class, I asked our school librarian. She was a source of information for me in finding the right book. Recently we had one of the local firemen come to share information with us about fire safety. He was a source of information for us about the ways that people can protect themselves against fire. Can you think of a time when other people have been sources of information for you, a time when someone told you something that helped you in some way? Talk to a neighbor about people who have been sources of information for you, and talk about what specific information they have given you. Allow time for pair sharing and then ask a few pairs to share with the group. Use probing questions to clarify and elaborate on answers. POSSIBLE STUDENT RESPONSES: *Teachers, parents, coaches: policemen, doctors, dentists, the crossing guard, the school principal.* EXAMPLES OF SPECIFIC INFORMATION VARY.

- **Often the information we get from others is correct. But sometimes it isn't. It is important to get good information when we have to depend on other sources. Can you think of a time when you got information from another person and it turned out to be wrong? Discuss this with your partner.** Allow share time, and again allow a few to share with the class. As before, use probing questions to clarify and elaborate on the examples. RESPONSES VARY.

- **We do not always get our information from talking to people. There are other ways to gather information. What are some other ways? Let's make a list of ways to gather information.** Use the chart or chalkboard to record the responses of the students. POSSIBLE STUDENT RESPONSES: Computers, the Internet, books, TV, magazines. **How are these sources of information different from people?** Students usually recognize that these are sources in which the information is recorded, usually written. You can help them with this idea if they are having difficulty by asking where the information appears and how it was found.

- **In order to get information that we can depend on from these sources, we should check the sources to see if they are reliable. That means that we can trust, or rely, on them to give us good information.** Write the word "Reliable" on the chart or chalkboard next to the words "Source of Information." **Sometimes what we find out about the source makes us wonder whether the information is reliable. For example, a number of years ago I decided that I wanted a pet. So I reached for the telephone book that lists businesses—"the yellow pages"— and looked up pet stores. There was one pet store listed in my town, so I went there. When I got there, there was an entirely different store at the address. I asked where the pet store was and the new shop owners told me that the pet store had moved two years ago to another location at the other end of town. Of course, I went there and got a nice little puppy, but I wondered why the book had given me the wrong information. When I went home, I noticed that I had picked up a yellow pages book that was five years old! That's when I learned to check the date of books I was using to get information to make sure that the information was not outdated.** Write the question "What is the date of the source?" on the chart or chalkboard under the words "Reliable Source of Information."

- **Now let's look at some information. I have something about bears that I would like to share with you.** A fictitious teacher-made example is used in this part of the lesson. It has been included as source material in this lesson. This example has many errors that students should be able to easily identify based on their experiences at national parks, zoos, watching television nature shows, and reading books. Pass out the sheet or display a transparency of the sheet for you and/or students to read. Allow time for students to respond. Ask them what they think about this information. Students will begin to point out the inaccuracies of the text. Encourage them to explain why they think these are inaccuracies. POSSIBLE STUDENT RESPONSES: *Bears can climb. I saw a bear climb on a show about bears on TV. I know that bears eat berries because I watched them eating berries when I was at the Smoky Mountain National Park. There are other kinds of bears. I saw them at the zoo. Lots of bears can swim. Polar bears are great swimmers. They live by the ocean and have a big tank at the zoo.*

- **It seems that you are questioning whether this is a reliable source. What questions would you want to ask about the source of information? First, let's think about questions about the piece of writing itself. We would want to find out the date it was written to make sure it was not out of date. What else might we want to find out? Work with your partner on this.** After a few minutes, ask for responses from the teams, getting only one from each. POSSIBLE STUDENT RESPONSES: *Maybe this doesn't come from a science book but from a make-believe story about bears. I'd want to find that out. I'd want to find out if the book you got this from was a book that didn't give good information. Maybe it had a lot of mistakes in it.* Make a list of the questions on the chart or on the chalkboard under the question about the date and put the heading, "Where the Information Appeared" above these questions. **Now let's try to come up with some questions about the person or persons who wrote this. What would you want to find out about the author as a source of information to decide whether they are a reliable source of information about bears?** After a few minutes, ask for responses from the teams, getting only one response from each. POSSIBLE STUDENT RESPONSES: *Does the author know about bears? Did the author find things out from a person who knows about bears, a bear expert? Did the author study bears to learn about them? Do other bear experts agree with what the author says about bears?* Make a list of these questions on the chart or on the chalkboard under the questions about where the information appeared and put the heading "The Author" above these questions. You will want to organize the questions to make an easy-to-follow thinking map for the class for later parts of the lesson. POSSIBLE THINK-

EVALUATING THE RELIABILITY OF WRITING AS A SOURCE OF INFORMATION
1. What is the source of the information?
2. What are the answers to these questions?

a. The Writing
    What is the date of the writing?
    Is the writing fact or fiction?
    Do other people think the publication is a good one?

b. The Author
    Is the person an expert on this topic?
    Has the person been wrong in the past?
    Does the person have a reason for wanting this information to be true?

c. Agreement of Others   Do others agree with the information from this source?
3. Based on the answers to these questions, is this source reliable, unreliable, or uncertain?

ING MAP QUESTIONS: *The Written Piece: Where does the information come from? When was it published? Do people trust the books from the publisher to give good information? The Author: Who is the author? Is the author an expert? How did the author get the information? Do other experts agree with the information? Some guided questioning may be needed to help students formulate the questions.* **Let me summarize some of the important things that you've just come up with. When we are checking the source to see if it is reliable, we want to find out about where it came from, whether it is supposed to be fact or fiction, for example. Because new things are being discovered continually, we also want to know that our source has the most up-to-date information. In addition, we would want to find out about the author(s) of the information. For example, do they know the subject: are they experts? We would also want to see if they were careful in getting their information to make sure that it was true: if they aren't experts, did they get it from experts? Finally, we want to know that the information from our source agrees with the information from other expert sources. So, if we can find out the *where*, the *when*, the *who*, and the *how* of the source of information, then we can tell if it is reliable.** Connect the four terms, where, when, who, and how with the questions, possibly writing the terms in boxes next to the matching questions. Later, this will provide a good visual prompt for students.

- **Now that we have a list of questions, we can check out this source.** Identify the list of questions on the thinking map for reliability of written sources of information. **There is no author or source listed, and we don't know where it appeared, or even if it appeared anywhere, so we cannot check for who the source was or where, how, or when the source obtained the information. But we do know that the information does not match the information we have gotten from others who are experts or from seeing things ourselves, such as the *National Wildlife* specials we've seen and the scientific books we've read. The conclusion that we seem to have made is that this is probably not a reliable source, though we might feel more sure of this if we had answers to the other questions as well.**

- **Let's use the questions you have and look for answers to see if the next source is one you would trust, one that is reliable. I have another article about bears to share with you.** Pass out the bears info #2 sheet or place a copy on the overhead for the class to read. This article is from a children's book and has the information about the source available. Read the article and discuss the various aspects of reliability. Do not offer any information about the source until asked. The class should be able to find the information that shows the source is reliable. Be sure to use the questions as you are checking reliability. Summarize, or have a child summarize the class decisions.

THINKING ACTIVELY

- We have created a good list of questions to use in checking the reliability of sources of information. This is our thinking map for determining whether a source is reliable. We will use that list now as we begin a new unit on whales. We are going to gather information from a variety of sources for our study. We are going to look at these sources to see if they are reliable. We will use the questions from our thinking map, the questions we developed, to check on their reliability.

- Before we begin our study, we should stop and think about whales. To do this in an organized manner, let's fill in a KWL chart. We will write down what we *know*, what we *want* to learn, and as we go through our study we'll record the things we've *learned*. Use a copy of the chart at the right to record the knowledge and the questions the students have about whales. The responses will vary.

WHAT I KNOW	WHAT I WANT TO KNOW	WHAT I'VE LEARNED

- **Where did you get your information about whales?** Student answers will vary. For example, some students may say that the information that they have came from their personal observations when they went to the oceanarium or to Sea World. Others may say that they saw a movie or a TV show about whales that gave them an opportunity to look at whales in action. Still others will say that they have gotten their information from books. Write a list of these sources on the chalkboard or on a flipchart under the heading "Sources of Information about Whales." **Does the information you have make you experts?** Students acknowledge that because they have not spent a lot of time studying whales with scientists, they would not say that they are experts. **Did you check your sources to make sure that they are reliable?** Most students also acknowledge that they haven't even checked their sources. They just assumed that they were reliable. **As we continue to gather information, we will see if there are other sources like those that you already mentioned, or even if there are new sources that we have not listed. As we seek information to answer our questions about whales from these sources, I want us to be careful to check the sources we are using to see if they are reliable. Let's see if we find anything in the sources that we think is reliable that shows that the information we have now is accurate. When we do this, we are** *confirming* **the accuracy of the information. We can use the questions our class developed for the thinking map to help us, and we will use a special graphic organizer to record our answers to these questions.**

- **Let's start by looking at some sources that I have collected. I have a variety of materials that we might use if the sources are reliable as we study whales.** Here is a list of the sources:

    1. *Dear Mr. Blueberry*, by Simon Jones
    2. *Whales for Kids*, by Tom Wolpert, Photographs by Flip Nicklin
    3. *I Wonder if I'll See a Whale*, by Frances Ward Weller, Illustrations by Ted Lewin
    4. *Free Willy* (the movie, on videotape), Directed by Simon Wincer, produced by Jennie Lew Tugend and Lauren Shuler-Donner, a Warner Brothers production
    5. *Baby Whales Drink Milk*, by Barbara Juster Esbensen, Illustrations by Lambert Davis

    If you can find these five resources, list them on the chalkboard or on a flipchart and show them to the students. If you cannot find them, get some that are comparable. For example, you could collect a variety of other sources on whales from *ZooBooks*, easy reader nonfiction books, Eyewitness books, articles from the Internet, library books, videos, and *National Geographic* magazines. Also make sure you include some fictional books that give some whale information but really are not the best sources in studying whales. Some preparation will be necessary to make the information accessible and understandable for students. You could utilize parent volunteers to tape record sections of the sources that you want for the study, but are too difficult for the students to read and comprehend. As the volunteers tape, encourage them to adapt the language to make it clear to a young child. The beginning of the tape should include documentation so students can make judgments about the reliability of the source the book is based upon. The book should be available as students listen to the tape so they can study any illustrations while listening. It is also good to encourage students to read captions. Even in complex pieces, the captions are frequently easy to understand and give good information. Nondamaging write-on tape can be used to change the language of any captions where advanced terms are used.

- **In order to check the reliability of these sources, we will break into groups of four. Each group will work on one of these sources. You will use this graphic organizer to check the reliability of the source you are working on.** Groups for this exercise should be planned to include strong readers who can support their group members by reading aloud. **To see how the graphic organizer works, I'm going to try one of these in front of the whole class first before we break into groups, and I'm going to think out loud as I use it. Listen to how I am thinking so that you can do the same when you work on your source in your group.**

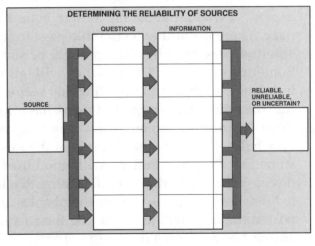

DETERMINING THE RELIABILITY OF SOURCES
QUESTIONS   INFORMATION
SOURCE
RELIABLE, UNRELIABLE, OR UNCERTAIN?

Show a transparency of the graphic organizer to the class. You should have already written the main question categories in the boxes under "Question." **Let's work on the book *Whales for Kids*. I will write the name of the source in the first box marked "Source."** Write the name of the book there and show it to the class. **On the diagram, I have written the name of one of the sources. I wrote the name of the book, author, and the photographer. As I look at the first question, "What is the *date* the information was published?" I think about where I can find that, and I remember that in a book the date usually appears on the page with the title or the very next page on the other side. So let's look there. What does it say?** Show the copyright page to some of the students and ask them if they can see the date. Some will recognize 1990 and will say that. Write "Date: 1990" in the box to the right of "what is the date this information was published?" **I've written "1990." What do you think—is that up to date enough? If it said 1890, that would be 100 years ago and it certainly would be out of date. So is 1990 good enough?** Most students agree that it is. **I agree too, so I'm going to put a plus sign in the little column to the right. That means that this information counts in favor of the source being reliable. It doesn't prove it, of course, because there might be a lot of other things that count against its being reliable.**

- **Now let's think about the second question: "Where does the information come from?" We want to know if this is a science book or if it is a story. If it is a story, what will go in the column on the right, a plus, a minus, or a question mark (which will indicate that it doesn't count for or against the reliability of the source)?** Most students agree that if it is a story then that would count against the reliability of the source. **So let's see, is there anything that indicates whether this is a story?** The students should recognize that the book is a factual piece of writing. The text and pictures are set up as a factual piece of writing about a science topic. **Our search has shown us that this is a science book. Will this count for or against its reliability?** The students will agree that it counts for the reliability and a plus sign should be placed in the small box next to the information.

- **The final question about the book is whether people trust books from this publisher to give them good information. On the page with the date the book was published are several sentences about the National Wildlife Federation.** Read the sentences describing the National Wildlife Federation to the group. **This group has sponsored the publication of this book. They are saying they agree with the information in the book. Is that support for the publisher?** *Yes.* **What should be put in the right-hand column?** Students usually say a plus sign should be placed in the column.

- **Now I will turn to the questions about the author. "Who is the author? Is the author an expert?" I wonder about the author. Is he a whale expert? The first place to look is the title page. There is nothing on the title page to say if he is an expert. If the author were an expert about whales, there would probably be some information about where he studied whales. Sometimes in books like this they will tell you a little about the source somewhere else, so let's look and see. The only thing that seems to give any clue is some information in the back that the publisher, Northword Press, has other books to use if adults need more information.** Read the information on the last page that provides a source for more in-depth information on whales. **Since the publisher is in the business of giving good information, could we assume that they hire authors with good information to write their books?** Allow for time to discuss this. The students should realize that it is a good assumption that the publisher is going to hire reliable sources to write their books, and that the National Wildlife Federation has supported the information by putting their name on the book. It is a good assumption that the author has gotten his information from good sources, but it is still unclear if he is an expert himself. In this case, since we are not sure, we can put a question mark to show that the answer to this question does not support whether the source is reliable or unreliable.

- **The second question about the author is about how the author got the information. In science, observation is often used as a way of collecting information. Scientists who study whales are able to go where the whales live and watch and learn about them. They see what the whales do, where they live, what they eat, and how they move. When they make these observations, they record them. If someone gets information by observation, we usually call that person a firsthand source. I am not sure if the author got the information firsthand. It doesn't say that the author studied whales firsthand. He may have, but it doesn't say. Now I** suppose I could write him a letter and ask him, but that would take time. For now, what should I put in the column next to "How did the author get his information about whales?" The students will say that you should put a question mark there. But wait. Here's something interesting. The photographer is also listed on the title page of the book. When I think about her, I realize that she must have gone directly to where the whales are and taken her pictures there. She is a firsthand source, and her pictures must show us what she saw. The photographer must have been where the whales are to take the photos, so I'm going to write that in the box next to the question about how the author got the information and give the photographer a "+."

- The last question asks if other experts agree with the source's information. There doesn't seem to be any mention of any other experts, so to find this out I will need to read the book and compare what it says to other sources we find. I will leave this box empty for now and put a question mark in the column on the right, but be ready to change this if, when I read other things, I find that other people who write about whales say the same things. Later in the lessons students will find that the material matches that of many experts; the question-mark can then be changed to a plus sign. Since the photographer has provided real whale pictures and the materials match other reliable sources, you should then indicate that this source will be counted as a reliable source as well. **Let me think, now. I have to say something in the last box. Can I say that the source is reliable or unreliable, or is this still uncertain? Well, there are no minuses, and there are some pluses, but there are also some question marks. And I can think of ways that the unanswered questions might be answered that might show that this source is unreliable. So until I find out, what I will say is that there is some reason for thinking this source is reliable, but we have to find out more to say that it is definitely reliable.** Later, of course, you will change what you say to an unqualified "reliable" and explain why to students.

- Each group will be given one of the other sources to check in the same way. Your group will look for information to tell if the source is reliable. The group will present their graphic organizer to the class to show the work they've done and to tell us if the source they have is one that should be used in our whale studies. It would be helpful to have the questions and source already recorded on the graphic organizers for the groups. Using chart-sized graphic organizers allows for the groups to share their work more easily. As the groups work, provide help with their search for support information. Remind them where they can get the kind of information they need in the books or films they are working on, but also show them how they can find out more about authors and their expertise.

- Now that you have determined which of these sources are likely to be reliable, let's use them to complete our KWL chart. In your groups, take a few minutes to share the sources that you think are reliable. Then I'm going to read some of your questions from the "I want to know" column. If you think your source gives information that answers these questions, raise your hand and tell the class what it says. Give the students a few minutes to look through the works that they think are reliable and then review each question in the "I want to know" column of their KWL chart, recording any information the students provide to answer these questions in the "I have learned" column. In future lessons, the groups should be rotated to allow students to gain information from many sources for their study of the whales.

- This lesson has shown us the importance of determining the reliability of the sources we use. What things did you learn as you checked your source? POSSIBLE STUDENT RESPONSES: *I learned that sometimes books look like great sources, but they are not written by experts, so I have to make sure the experts agree. I learned where to check for when a book was made. I found a book that was not really a good source. It was mostly just a story about a girl who liked whales. It is good that I had better sources to use.*

THINKING ABOUT THINKING

- **Let's take our thinking way back to the bear examples. We started talking about checking the reliability of sources with them. How did we get our thinking map?** POSSIBLE STUDENT RESPONSE: *We came up with questions we wanted to have answered about the sources because the sources seemed like maybe they weren't good.*

- **What are some sources that are important to think about to determine whether they are reliable in giving us accurate information?** Students usually identify the variety of sources mentioned in the lesson. If they fail to mention the Internet, remind them that it is a source of information as well.

- **What are some of the important things we thought about in deciding whether a source of information is reliable?** Students usually identify the three clusters of questions on the thinking map about the publication, about the author, and about corroboration. **Is there anything else you would want to add to the thinking map?** STUDENT RESPONSES VARY. Students sometimes bring up that people may lie because they want you to believe things that are not true. They suggest that you should also find out whether people think the source is a liar or has a reason for wanting to deceive you.

- **When you want to learn something next time, what steps will you take to make sure the information you get is good, accurate information?** Students should go back over the steps of the thinking map.

APPLYING YOUR THINKING

Immediate Transfer

- **You are ready to buy a new bike. What could you do to get information that will help you buy the best bike? What sources would be most likely to be reliable? Why?**

- **In the story *The Emperor's New Clothes*, the emperor and the people of the kingdom believed the two tricksters. What should they have done to avoid being tricked? What should the emperor think about as he sent the different people to check on the progress. How would he know that they were reliable?**

Reinforcement Later

- **You are going to be visiting the hospital as part of your study of communities. What information will be given to you? What will show the reliability of the source?**

- **Your class is learning about the life of George Washington. Since he is no longer alive, you will need to gather information from reliable sources. Visit the library to see the display of Washington materials they put out each February in honor of his birthday. Check the sources for reliability using the thinking map the class created during their study of whales. Tell the class about the materials in the library. Recommend to them the reliable sources and warn them about any unreliable sources you find. Be sure to explain why you felt the materials were reliable or unreliable.**

SUGGESTED SPECIAL NEEDS MODIFICATIONS

Frontload: Some students may need experience with the concepts of "source" and "reliability" prior to the lesson. The term "source" could be used in multiple contexts in daily life or in content material. Students could be guided into brainstorming types of sources (different types of books, textbooks, the Internet, friends, the television, or radio). Next, students could be guided in reasons for selecting a source. "If you wanted to bake cookies, would you ask Grandma or your little sister for information on baking cookies? What did you consider in making your choice? What other sources could you use?" "If a person tells you a story on the playground, what helps you decide whether or not to believe it?" Introducing these terms and concepts in relevant, everyday experiences builds understanding for the type of thinking required in the lesson.

For some students, particularly those with language impairments, formulating "wh" questions can be challenging. Teacher modeling may be needed throughout this process in addition to prior instruction in generating questions using the 5W's: who, what, when, where, and why.

When students are first learning how to determine the reliability of sources, some may benefit from a predeveloped list of questions.

Clarify: The term "reliable" may need further clarification for some students. Pair the term with phrases such as "count on to be true" and "depend on to be right or accurate." Students may discuss everyday examples of "reliable" sources of information that they trust for a specific reason (Mom's experience baking, the librarian's experience with books).

Diversify: As students are learning how to think through the steps in the reliability of sources strategy, the teacher may wish to model his/her reasons for choosing specific questions to ask about reliability. This may be especially helpful for students struggling with question formation and processing tasks. By thinking aloud, the teacher will be able to model for students the reasoning behind the sequence of steps in the strategy.

The number of questions to address may be reduced and highlighted for some students. If the actual writing of the questions is too cumbersome for the group, teacher-scribed sentences may reduce the taskload so that the focus can be on thinking.

In addition to the audiotapes recommended in this lesson sources such as videotapes or filmstrips may be used. Older students or parent volunteers may also be helpful in reading informational text to students.

Expand the Possibilities: Assessments of written responses may be based upon the students' thinking first, and expressive skills second. Oral responses may also reveal thinking beyond the students' ability to express themselves in writing.

ASSESSING STUDENT THINKING ABOUT RELIABLE SOURCES.

To assess students' ability to determine the reliability of sources, select examples that challenge them to use questions from the class thinking map. The students should be able to justify believing a source or not believing that source. Any of the transfer examples can serve as assessment items for written or oral responses.

Source Material • Bears #1

Bears are large, heavy mammals. They have strong legs, sharp claws, and thick, shaggy fur. American Indians called grizzly bears "the beasts that walked like people." Bears walk on the soles of their feet, and they can walk upright on their two back legs.

Bears are very clumsy and cannot climb. They must run away from enemies. When they are angry they run away, too. They have small ears and cannot hear very well. They can see and smell very well. This helps them find food.

Bears eat only animals. They do not like to eat plants. They hunt for their food in the daytime and sleep at night.

There are two main kinds of bears—the brown bear and the polar bear. Neither bear can swim, so they must be very careful when they are fishing.

Source Material • Bears #2

Grizzly bear, polar bear, and black bear are three kinds of bear that live in North America.

The grizzly bear is large and brown. Its thick fur is tipped with white. It has a humped back. Grizzly bears have long, sharp claws. They are good for digging.

Polar bears live in the Arctic. They have heavy white fur. They have a thick layer of fat. They stay warm in the ice and snow.

The black bear is the smallest bear in North America. It lives both in the west and the east. Black bears can be black or brown. Black bears have short claws that make them good tree climbers.

Bears can stand on their back legs like humans. Bears are omnivores like us. Omnivores eat all kinds of food. They like to eat meat and fish. They also like to eat berries, honey, moss, grass, leaves, roots, grubs, insects, nuts, and mushrooms.

Bears eat extra food in the fall. They sleep all winter in their dens. This is called hibernating.

Bear, E. K. Caldwell and Vic Warren, Scholastic Books, 1996. technical assistance by D.L. Birchfield

Sample Student Responses • Whales

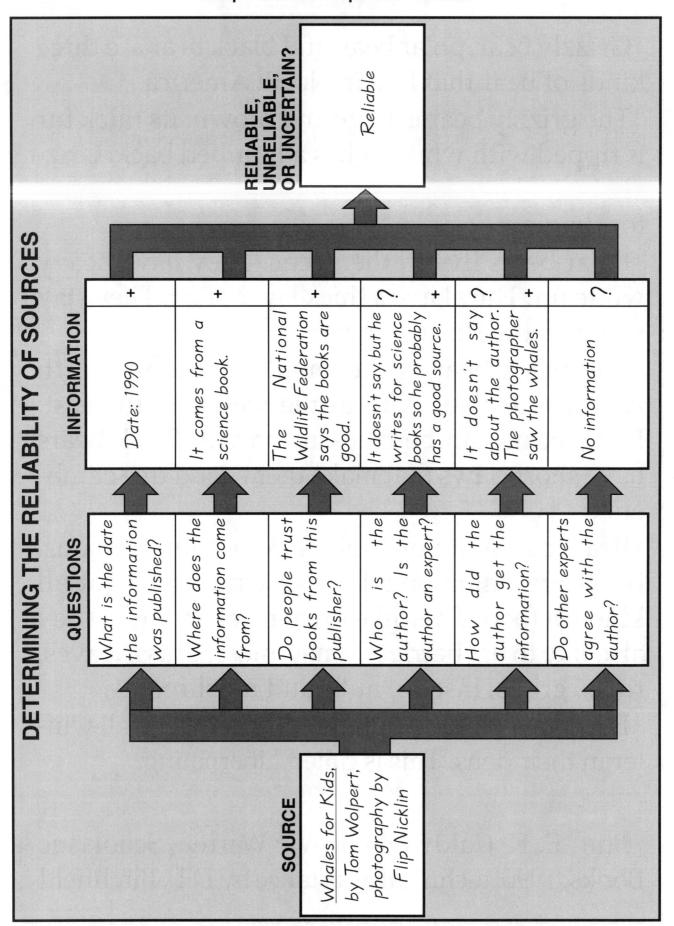

DETERMINING THE RELIABILITY OF SOURCES

RELIABLE, UNRELIABLE, OR UNCERTAIN?

Reliable

INFORMATION

+	Date: 1990
+	It comes from a science book.
+	The National Wildlife Federation says the books are good.
?	It doesn't say, but he writes for science books so he probably has a good source.
+	It doesn't say about the author. The photographer saw the whales.
?	No information

QUESTIONS

What is the date the information was published?

Where does the information come from?

Do people trust books from this publisher?

Who is the author? Is the author an expert?

How did the author get the information?

Do other experts agree with the author?

SOURCE

Whales for Kids, by Tom Wolpert, photography by Flip Nicklin

Sample Student Responses • Whales

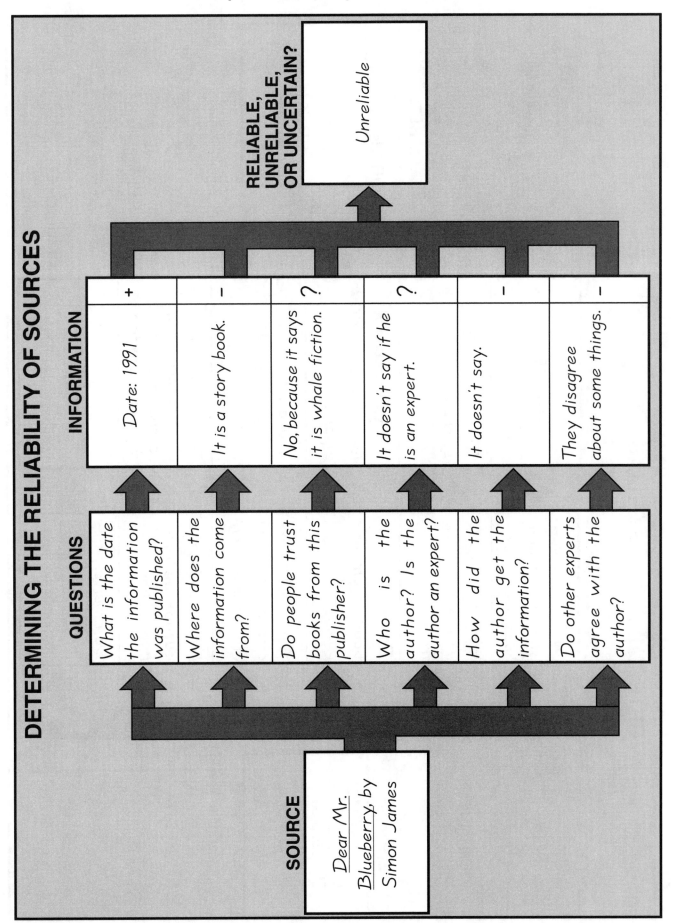

DETERMINING THE RELIABILITY OF SOURCES

RELIABLE, UNRELIABLE, OR UNCERTAIN?

Unreliable

INFORMATION

+	Date: 1991
–	It is a story book.
?	No, because it says it is whale fiction.
?	It doesn't say if he is an expert.
–	It doesn't say.
–	They disagree about some things.

QUESTIONS

- What is the date the information was published?
- Where does the information come from?
- Do people trust books from this publisher?
- Who is the author? Is the author an expert?
- How did the author get the information?
- Do other experts agree with the author?

SOURCE

Dear Mr. Blueberry, by Simon James

Sample Student Responses • Whales

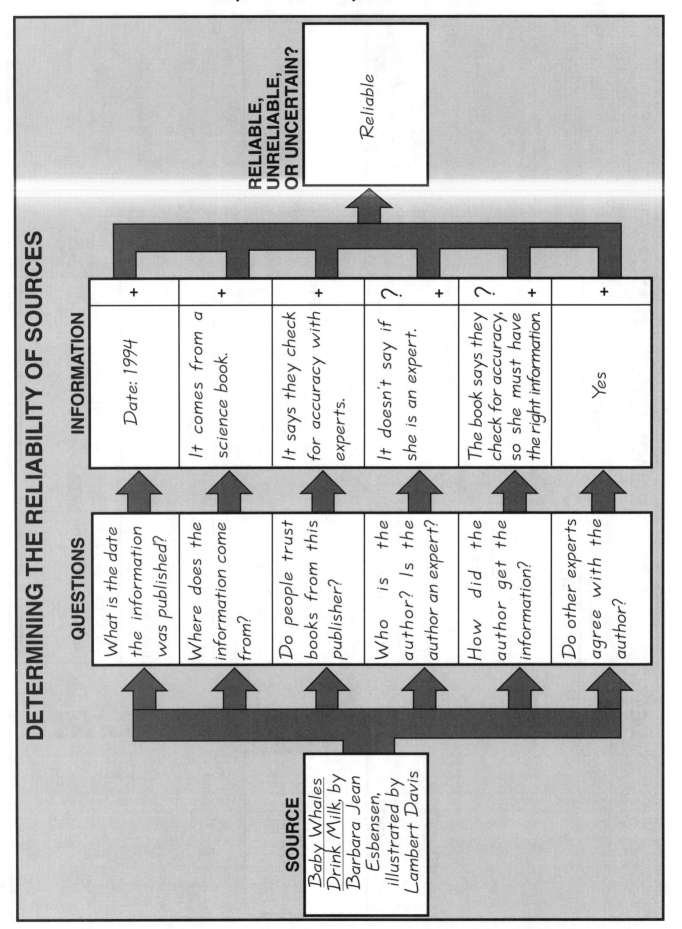

DETERMINING THE RELIABILITY OF SOURCES

RELIABLE, UNRELIABLE, OR UNCERTAIN?

Reliable

INFORMATION

+	Date: 1994
+	It comes from a science book.
+	It says they check for accuracy with experts.
?	It doesn't say if she is an expert.
+	
?	The book says they check for accuracy, so she must have the right information.
+	Yes

QUESTIONS

- What is the date the information was published?
- Where does the information come from?
- Do people trust books from this publisher?
- Who is the author? Is the author an expert?
- How did the author get the information?
- Do other experts agree with the author?

SOURCE

Baby Whales Drink Milk, by Barbara Jean Esbensen, illustrated by Lambert Davis

EVALUATING THE RELIABILITY OF A PERSON AS A SOURCE OF INFORMATION

1. Who is the source of the information being questioned?

2. What are the answers to these questions?

   a. Does the person know a lot about the subject?
   b. Do other people know and trust this person as a source of information?
   c. Does the person have something to gain by your accepting what he or she has to say?
   d. Did the person find out by his or her own investigation or get the information from someone else? If from someone else, is the other person reliable?
   e. Do others agree with this person?

3. Based on the answers to these questions, is the source reliable, unreliable, or uncertain?

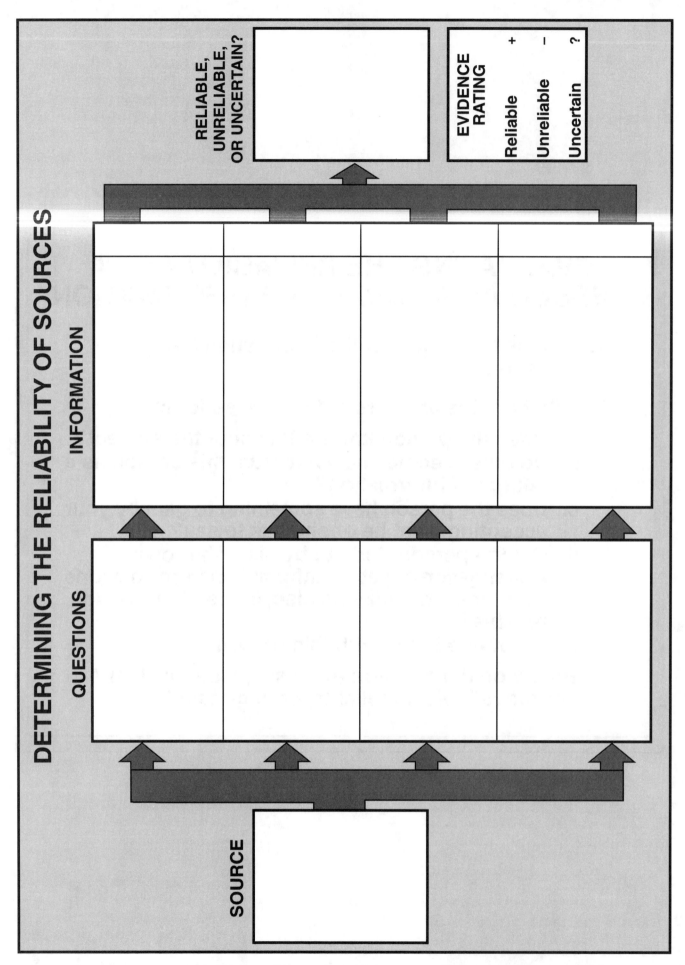

DETERMINING THE RELIABILITY OF SOURCES

RELIABLE, UNRELIABLE, OR UNCERTAIN?

EVIDENCE RATING

	+	–	?
Reliable			
Unreliable			
Uncertain			

INFORMATION

QUESTIONS

SOURCE

EVALUATING THE RELIABILITY OF WRITING AS A SOURCE OF INFORMATION

1. **What is the source of the information?**

2. **What are the answers to these questions?**

   a. **The Writing**

   What is the date of the writing?

   Is the writing fact or fiction?

   Do other people think the publication is a good one?

   b. **The Author**

   Is the person an expert on this topic?

   Has the person been wrong in the past?

   Does the person have a reason for wanting this information to be true?

   c. **Agreement of Others**

   Do others agree with the information from this source?

3. **Based on the answers to these questions, is this source reliable, unreliable, or uncertain?**

WHAT I KNOW	WHAT I WANT TO KNOW	WHAT I'VE LEARNED

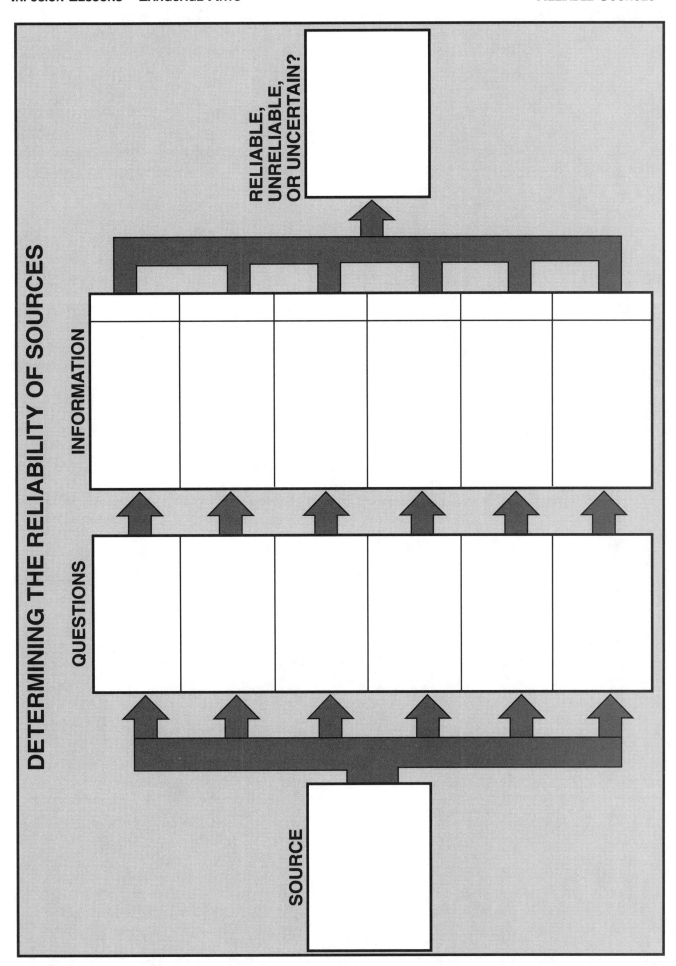

DETERMINING THE RELIABILITY OF SOURCES

RELIABLE, UNRELIABLE, OR UNCERTAIN?

INFORMATION

QUESTIONS

SOURCE

CHAPTER 14
CAUSAL EXPLANATION

Infusing Skillful Causal Explanation into Language Arts

Teaching students skillful causal explanation in grades 1 and 2 involves helping them learn to ask and carefully answer the following questions for circumstances in which they don't know what caused an event and they want to figure it out.

FINDING CAUSES

1. What are some possible causes?

2. What possible clues could you find?

3. What real clues do you have?

4. What do the clues show about the cause?

---

figure 14.1

This is what we call a "thinking map" for skillful causal explanation. In the lessons in this chapter, this thinking map is used to guide your students' thinking explicitly as they engage with the lesson content.

When students learn and use this strategy for thinking through and making good judgments about what caused something, they don't make hasty judgments about what caused something to happen—they don't just guess about a cause or base their judgment on a small amount of evidence. Rather, they take the time to do a careful investigation and make a judgment that they are confident is well supported. This means that they don't tackle the question "What caused this to happen?" without first considering a number of possible causes, determining what evidence they could find that would show whether any of these possible causes is likely to be the real cause, and then searching thoroughly for such evidence and judging what it shows about the possible causes. In skillful causal ex-

planation, students use their critical thinking in this way to figure out what the real cause of something is. In language arts the primary focus of lessons will be to help students do this through engagement with information they can get through their reading either about events described in the text or about the motivation of characters they read about.

These lessons also supplement the use of this thinking map with various supporting classroom strategies such as using graphic organizers, engaging in cooperative thinking, thinking about thinking, and continued guided practice. These classroom strategies enhance both the thinking skill that the students are learning and their mastery of the lesson content.

The key graphic organizer for skillful causal explanation is in figure 14.2.

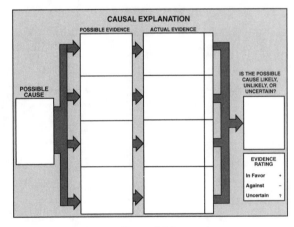

figure 14.2

This graphic organizer helps students focus on one from amongst a number of possible causes that they have already brainstormed and listed. They concentrate on recording what evidence they might find that would show that the possible cause they are considering is likely to be the real cause and on recording what they do actually find when they look for this evidence. Based on the actual evidence they record, they then make a judgment about the likelihood that this particular cause is the real cause. Reproducible blank organizers are found at the end of each chapter.

When a number of students or student groups explore a variety of different possible causes in this way, they can compare their results to select what they think is the best causal explanation based on the evidence. If they disagree they can debate the issue in class.

The Multiple Causes graphic organizer (14.3) is used to record the presence of a number of factors that all contribute to cause the effect, but no one in which, in itself, is sufficient to bring it about.

For more in-depth information on teaching skillful causal explanation, please refer to Chapter 13 in the book *Infusing the Teaching of Critical and Creative Thinking into Elementary Instruction*, by Robert Swartz and Sandra Parks. A computer disk containing the blank, reproducible graphic organizers that are in the lessons in this book is also available.

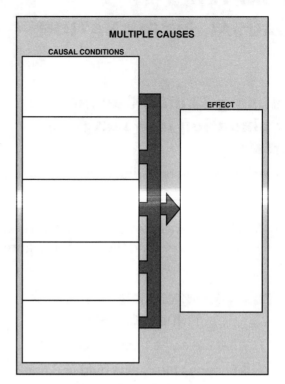

figure 14.3

WHY ALL THOSE STRIPES?
A BAD CASE OF STRIPES

Language Arts   **Grades 1–2**

OBJECTIVES

CONTENT

Students will develop comprehension skills for recognizing cause and effect relationships and identifying the moral of a story. Students will examine the speech and actions of the characters to find supportive evidence.

THINKING SKILL/PROCESS

Students will learn to consider possible causes and to look for evidence as they attempt to find what caused an event or situation.

METHODS AND MATERIALS

CONTENT

The story *A Bad Case of Stripes* by David Shannon will be read aloud to the students. The art and writing extension activities build on the thinking the students have done. Crayons, paper, and poster board are needed.

THINKING SKILL/PROCESS

In collaborative learning groups, students are guided by structured questioning to brainstorm possible causes and possible evidence. Students follow a thinking map of causal explanation.

LESSON

INTRODUCTION TO CONTENT AND THINKING SKILL/PROCESS

- Have you ever been puzzled because you didn't know why something happened? Last week my friend and I made plans to go to a movie. We were supposed to meet at the theater, but my friend did not come. I wondered where she was, and I tried to think of reasons why she hadn't come. **Think about a time when something happened and you wondered why it happened.** POSSIBLE STUDENT RESPONSES: *My best friend did not come to out to recess. I turned on the television set and it didn't work. My supply box was not in my desk.* **When you wonder why something is happening, you are trying to find out what** *caused* **it. Did you find out what caused some of the things you were wondering about?** POSSIBLE STUDENT RESPONSES: *My best friend needed to finish her work. The remote had a bad battery. I forgot to put my supply box away from the day before.* **My friend did not meet me because she was confused about which theater to go to. She went to the wrong one.**

- **When we answer the question "Why did that happen?" the name we use for what we find out is "cause." A cause is what makes something else happen. We usually call what happened the "effect" of the cause. When you go out in the rain you get wet. Going out in the rain is the cause, getting wet is the effect. If the cause wasn't there, then the effect wouldn't have happened.** Use an example that your own students have come up with here. The example used in this lesson has to do with the missing supply box. **For example, one example you gave me before was that your supply box was not in your desk. Is that an effect or a cause?** Usually students identify it as an effect. **If it is an effect, what is its cause?** Again, students usually readily identify forgetting to put the supply box away the day before as a cause. **So where would your supply box be if you** *hadn't* **forgotten to put it away the day before?** POSSIBLE STUDENT RESPONSE: *In my desk.* **So removing the cause means that the effect would not have happened. Work with your partner and make a list of three of four causes and effects that you know about.** STUDENT RESPONSES VARY.

• **Finding out the cause can help us in the future to try and prevent things we don't want to happen from happening again.** Use the same student example here. **I can be more careful from now on to put my supply box away so I can find it in my desk when I need it. If I know the cause of something, I can use that information to make good things happen too.** Use another student example here. **I can encourage my friend to finish her work so that we can play together at recess.**

• **It is important to find causes correctly. You need to think carefully about what makes something happen. A guess will not help you much. You should make sure that you have** *evidence***, or** *clues***, to show that what you think is the real cause is likely to be the one that** actually caused what happened. Have you ever thought one thing caused another thing, and then found out that it did not, that the real cause was a different cause? You may have thought of something that might be the cause, but as you investigated, there were clues to tell you that the cause was something else. Perhaps you thought the electric power was out at your house, causing the television set to not work. But looking for clues, you saw that the lights were on in the room. That is a clue that your idea of a possible cause is not likely. Why is that a clue? POSSIBLE STUDENT RESPONSE: *Lights use electricity just like televisions.* **In the case of the friend who was not at recess, what clues might have been there to find? Some might support the idea that the friend had to finish working, and others might show that staying in to finish work was not likely the cause for the friend to miss recess. What might you find out that would count one way or the other?** Ask the students to share some of their thoughts. POSSIBLE STUDENT RESPONSES: *The friend was playing during work time. The child went to the nurse before recess. The teacher asked the child to meet her at her desk before everyone lined up to go outside.*

• **Of course, if we want to know the cause, we should investigate to find all the evidence that is really there. In the case of meeting my friend at the movie, I thought that maybe she forgot the date. I thought that she would be at home if that were the case, so I called her house. I got no answer, so I thought that I needed to look for more clues to get at the cause of my missing friend. I knew that the show was playing at another theatre, so I decided to drive over to see if she was waiting at that one, and I found the real evidence. There she was, waiting for me!**

• **Today we will practice finding out what really causes things to happen. We will learn a way to check ourselves so that we don't make so many mistakes. Here is a thinking map for finding causes. It will help us in our thinking.** Show the thinking map on a flipchart. Go over the four questions, relating them to prior examples if necessary. (For example, you can identify my friend forgetting as a *possible cause* and her going to another theater as a *possible cause*. Then you can identify calling her house

> **FINDING CAUSES**
>
> 1. **What are some possible causes?**
>
> 2. **What possible clues could you find?**
>
> 3. **What real clues do you have?**
>
> 4. **What do the clues show about the cause?**

and finding her home as *possible evidence,* or clues, that you thought of to check out the first possible cause. Calling and getting no answer is *actual evidence,* or real clues, and you can identify it as evidence that counts against the first cause being likely. You can also identify seeing my friend at the other theatre as *actual evidence* that counts *in favor of the possible cause* that she got mixed up about which theater to go to. And, finally, you can explain that, based on this evidence, her getting mixed up rather than forgetting is the *likely cause*.)

THINKING ACTIVELY

- The story we are going to use for our lesson is titled *A Bad Case of Stripes*. The author is David Shannon. From the title and the cover we can see that the story is about a girl with a bad case of stripes. Do you wonder why she has stripes? As we read the story, pay close attention to what is happening. This will help us as we look for the cause of her stripes. Read the first part of the story, stopping at the bottom of the page where the principal has called and asked that Camilla not return to school.

- **What things have happened to Camilla?** Students will relate some of the events of the story. POSSIBLE STUDENT RESPONSES: *She couldn't decide what to wear to school and when she looked in the mirror she was all covered with stripes. They were lots of colors, like a rainbow. She had to miss the first day of school because of her stripes. She didn't feel sick but she looked like a rainbow. The doctor gave her ointment and sent her back to school. Everyone laughed at her at school, and when they said the pledge of allegiance she began to look like a flag. All of the kids yelled different things, and she turned into the colors of everything they yelled. The principal called her house and said that she had to stay home because she might be contagious.* **Camilla certainly wants to rid herself of the shapes and colors. Let's try to help her by looking for the causes that would explain why she has this bad case of stripes.**

- Our task is to find out what really caused Camilla to break out in stripes. Why did this happen? The first question on the thinking map asks us to think about possible causes. I'd like you to work in your groups to make a list of possible causes for Camilla's stripes. This is a brainstorming time, when we try to think of many possible reasons. Make a list of the reasons your group thinks of, and then we'll share and combine the ideas onto one big list. Write everything down that you think of. Remember, when we brainstorm we don't decide whether the ideas will work or not. All we want to do now is to come up with the ideas. We will decide whether they are good ideas later. Write "Possible Causes" on the board. After providing time for the groups to work, have them share their ideas with the class. Write the responses on the board. Encourage piggybacking as the students are sharing. (Piggybacking is using the idea of another student to come up with another idea. It is an important part of brainstorming.) POSSIBLE STUDENT RESPONSES: *She ate something. She has a virus. An alien is making it happen. She ate a box of crayons. She has an allergy to people's voices. It's magic. She is too worried about what other people think about her.*

- Each group will have one of the possible causes to explore. To decide whether your cause is a likely cause of Camilla's stripes, you need to act like a detective. Let's look at the thinking map for finding causes. A good detective does what you've done—he or she makes a list of possible suspects. He works with his list thinking of the possible evidence, or clues, he could find in the next part of the story that would prove each of the possibilities to be the real cause or show that it isn't. Then he goes out and looks for those clues. That's what we are going to do. In your groups your thinking should first focus on deciding what evidence you could find that would prove that the possibility you are considering is the real cause. What clues do you think would show that it is the right cause, or show that it isn't? Finding clues that show that the cause is not the real cause is also helpful because that eliminates some of our possibilities and gets us closer to the real reasons for Camilla's stripes. The paper your group will use to record the clues you think would be helpful looks like this. Show the class the graphic organizer for causal explanation on an overhead transparency or a flip chart. The groups will be sharing their findings, so having them work on chart-sized graphic organizers will make their work more visible to the others during share time. Explain how to record the group's possible cause in the box on the left-hand side of the graphic organizer (or write it yourself on the graphic organizer for the group as you pass out the papers). Then show the groups the column for possible evidence or possible clues. Explain that they should fill in as many boxes as they can by thinking of clues that would help show, one way or the other, whether their possible cause is likely. You may also want to mention that the next section, "actual evidence," will be filled in after we read more of the story and look to see if the possible evidence appears there. Move from group to group and help the students if they are having trouble by giving them an example of one piece of evidence they might find for their pos-

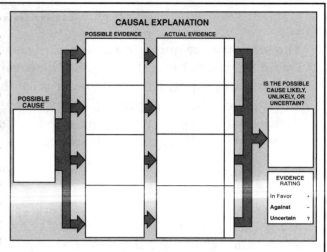

sible cause. Then ask them to fill in more like that. POSSIBLE STUDENT RESPONSES: *(Possible Cause: She ate something.) Possible Evidence: If they pump her stomach, they can find if there is anything that would make her be sick. (Possible Cause: She has a virus.) Possible Evidence: They can look down her throat and check her blood to see if she has a virus. (Possible Cause: An alien is making it happen.) Possible Evidence: They might find a spaceship parked in her yard. The aliens could be found in her closet. (Possible Cause: She ate a box of crayons.) Possible Evidence: There will be wrappers and a box in her room. (Possible Cause: She has an allergy to people's voices.) Possible Evidence: They can plug her ears to see if that makes the stripes and colors go away. If they take the plugs out and the stripes come back then it is probably the voices. (Possible Cause: It's magic.) Possible Evidence: A witch comes to cast a spell. Somebody says magic words or uses magical things. They find a magic hat and wand in Camilla's room. Camilla has been reading about magic. (Possible Cause: She is too worried about what other people think of her.) Possible Evidence: She can quit worrying and do what she wants. The stripes disappear when she does what she likes to do and come back when she does only what her friends like to do.*

- The things you have just listed are the possible evidence, or clues that you might find that would show whether or not your possible cause is the right cause. If you find these clues, then you have the likely cause as to why Camilla has a bad case of stripes. If you find just the opposite or no clues at all, you have evidence that that's not what caused her stripes. You have already answered the second question on the thinking map for finding causes, "What possible clues could you find?" Now we are ready for the third question, "What real clues do you have?" Finding the clues makes them real clues, or actual evidence. You should say that you know what caused Camilla's bad case of stripes only if you have actual evidence or clues to support it.

- We will try to find these clues in the story as we read the story. If you see or hear one of the things you thought would be a possible clue, then put a check mark next to it in the "Possible Evidence" box. If you find actual evidence that counts against the possible cause, put an "x" next to the box. Now, let's all listen and watch for evidence that will help us decide what the real cause of the stripes is. Pay attention to both the words and the pictures. Both can provide us with information about what caused this terrible thing to happen to Camilla. There may also be real evidence that we didn't expect to find. Watch for anything that can be used as evidence to show what caused Camilla's stripes. Read the entire story, repeating the beginning before continuing to the end. There is evidence in the beginning pages to support the real cause that students will now be ready to recognize. Take time to examine the illustrations and discuss the events that occur. What did you notice that would be evidence or a clue as to why Camilla has stripes? Give the students a few minutes in their groups to discuss any actual evidence in the story that they think is relevant to their possible cause. In second grade class-rooms, students should be able to fill in the real evidence boxes in their groups. If writing is a problem for a group, take on the role of recorder for them. At the first grade level, support for this task can be given by working through each group's evidence in a large group setting. Ask the groups to take turns coming to the front and discussing what they saw and heard. Tape their graphic organizer to the board so that the class can see as it is being completed. The teacher can take the role of recorder and write the real evidence on the graphic organizers as it is being identified and discussed. **If there is evidence found that is not in the possible evidence column, let's give it a box in the real evidence column anyway. It is still valid. It is just something that the we didn't think to suggest when we were considering possible evidence.** POSSIBLE STUDENT RESPONSES: *(Possible Cause: She ate something.) Actual Evidence: They didn't pump her stomach, so we don't know if she ate something to begin with. Sometimes she changed and got more stripes when she wasn't eating. The things that she ate to get better made her worse. The last thing she ate was the plate of lima beans. That cured her and she was back to normal. (Possible Cause: She has an allergy to people's voices.) Actual Evidence: She changed every time someone said something about her. Whatever people said made her change to match their words. Doctors can cure allergies and they couldn't cure Camilla. (Possible Cause: She had a virus.) Actual Evidence: None of the doctors could find any disease. Nothing any of the doctors tried worked. The little old lady came and told her to eat real lima beans and she was cured. Lima beans don't cure viruses. (Possible Cause: She ate a box of crayons.) Actual Evidence: It didn't show that she ever ate crayons. She also grew things like fuzzies and tails on her and that doesn't have anything to do with crayons.*

- **Now let's think about the real evidence that we have found. We want to decide if the real clues we have found support the possible cause, or show that it wasn't the real cause.** Read aloud each box of real evidence. Ask the class to evaluate the evidence, and mark it with a plus sign(+) or a minus sign (-) in the column to the right-hand side of the box to show whether the class feels it supports or does not support the possible cause. If there is no actual evidence corresponding to something in the possible evidence box write "no evidence" and put a "?" in the column and explain that this means there is no evidence one way or the other, so it makes the possible cause uncertain.

- **Our job now is to put all the clues together and decide if the possible cause we are investigating is likely, unlikely, or uncertain. If we have lots of pluses next to our real evidence, then we have lots of evidence to show that the possible cause is likely to be the real cause. If there are lots of minuses, then it is unlikely that our possible cause is the real one. If there are lots of question marks, then the possible cause is uncertain. Do you think that your group's possible cause is likely or unlikely to be the reason for her bad case of stripes, or is there not enough evidence to tell one way or the other?** The answers will vary from group to group. The group or groups with the likely cause(s) should say that it is likely to be the reason. As a class, write a summary statement saying what has been determined to be the cause(s) of the bad case of stripes. This statement can be written on the chalkboard or chart after the possible causes and under the heading "Likely Cause(s)." In this lesson, there may be two likely causes, one dealing with magic and the other dealing with the way that Camilla worries about other people's reactions to her. Here is the actual evidence that the students might gather: POSSIBLE STUDENT RESPONSES: *(Uncertain Cause: Magic)—Actual Evidence: A little lady comes at the end. It doesn't say for sure if she is a witch. The lady brings only lima beans. They didn't find a magic hat and wand in Camilla's room It doesn't say anything about Camilla reading about magic. (Likely Cause: Camilla's Worry About Other People's Reaction to Her)—Actual Evidence: She is very embarrassed about looking so unusual. She really wants lima beans, and that is something that she thought would make people laugh at her. The thing she wanted and wouldn't eat was what cured her. She turns into* *whatever anyone says. That is like people not doing what they want, only doing what other people want them to do.*

- **What lesson do you think we can learn from Camilla and her bad case of stripes?** POSSIBLE STUDENT RESPONSES: *That you should just be yourself and not worry all the time about what others think of you. Other people will like you for who you are, not who you pretend to be. It's O.K. for you to be different sometimes.* **Camilla was so worried about being different that she didn't allow herself to just be Camilla. She was always trying to be someone others would like. She even stopped eating her favorite food, lima beans, because she thought people would think she was weird. In the end Camilla didn't worry about making everyone like her, she quit worrying about what others thought. She even ate lots of lima beans! Our evidence shows that there was some magic involved in her stripes, but it also showed that Camilla should keep being herself and eating her favorite food so she will never have stripes again!**

THINKING ABOUT THINKING

- **Let's review the steps we took as we did this lesson. How did we go about finding the cause for Camilla's bad case of stripes?** Students should mention the terms possible causes, brainstorming, possible clues or evidence, and real evidence. Refer to the thinking map for finding causes to confirm their responses.

- **Think about the way that you played detective to find the cause of Camilla's stripes. Is this a good way to think when you are puzzled about something? Why?** POSSIBLE STUDENT RESPONSES: *Yes, it is a good way. Finding the real clues and finding the cause is better than not knowing or just guessing.*

- **Was the graphic organizer helpful as you played detective? How did it help you keep your thinking organized?** The students should be able to explain how the graphic organizer works in keeping track of the evidence and deciding if the evidence supports the possible cause.

APPLYING YOUR THINKING

Immediate Transfer

- **Suppose you found a baby bird in your backyard. What could have caused this bird to be in your yard? How could you find out? Use the thinking map and graphic organizers for causal explanation as you work on this puzzling situation.** For this thinking activity, a scenario should be created by the teacher including evidence that students could find to identify the real cause. The scenario should be based on local birds and a location familiar to the students so that they may use prior personal experiences in collecting evidence.

- **Suppose the team you are on has won every game this season. What could have caused this to happen? How could you find out? Use the finding causes thinking map and graphic organizers to help you discover what the causes of your team's success might likely have been.** For this thinking activity, a scenario should be created by the teacher including evidence that students could find to identify the real cause. The scenario should be based on a sport familiar to the students so that they may use prior personal experiences in collecting evidence.

- **The plants on the deck have all tipped over. What might have caused this to occur? How can you find out? Use the finding causes thinking map and graphic organizers to help you discover what the causes of this mess might likely have been.** For this thinking activity a scenario should be created by the teacher including evidence that students could find to identify the real cause. The scenario should be developed to include pertinent information (season, immediate surroundings, prior incidents, time of day, recent weather) and should have a location familiar to the students so that they may use prior personal experiences in collecting evidence.

Reinforcement Later

- **Several new families have moved into the neighborhood. What might cause people to want to move into our community? This is an interesting puzzle, so be a careful thinker. Use the finding causes thinking map and graphic organizer to get at the likely causes.** This thinking activity would be extremely effective if a real situation such as this exists in the area and the families are willing to cooperate. Using new families that move into the school attendance area will allow the students to use prior knowledge of their community and the parts of a community as well as their knowledge of families and economics to collect evidence.

- **In the book *Frog and Toad Are Friends* there is a chapter called "A Lost Button." Using the thinking map for causal explanation, think about what caused Toad to lose a button. Explain what you decide. Is there evidence to show this?**

- **What causes people to get cavities in their teeth? What evidence is there to support your answer? Use the Causal Explanation thinking map and graphic organizers to help you be a careful thinker. When you discover what the causes of cavities might likely have been, make a poster to let us know the likely causes of cavities.** For this thinking activity a scenario should be created by the teacher including evidence that students could find to identify the real cause. The scenario should be based on a hypothetical child the age of the students and should include information pertinent to dental health care, perhaps relayed to the child over a series of dental visits.

WRITING EXTENSION

Camilla has gone through a terrible ordeal. To be covered with stripes and all the other designs must have been very hard on her. Use the information that you recorded on your graphic organizer to write a persuasive letter to Camilla. Tell her the things she should do so that she never has to be striped again. The framework for writing persuasive paragraphs will help you to structure your letter. (See templates for persuasive letter writing in the Appendix.)

ART EXTENSION

I'd like you to imagine yourself with a bad case of the stripes. You have been so worried about being just like everyone else that you have been hiding some of the things that make you happy, that make you the person you are. What is the secret, favorite thing that you don't tell a lot of people? Would having or doing that cure your case of stripes? Here is an example for me: I like to play my radio very loudly and sing along with the songs. That is something that I don't tell everyone because it might make me different from them. They might think I am weird! I could imagine that the cure to my bad case of stripes would be singing along with the radio. Have students brainstorm a variety of things that they might like but that might not be popular among their friends. It could be food, books, activities, music, etc. **I'd like you to draw yourself with your bad case of stripes. Then I'd like you to write a caption to the picture that tells us what would cure your stripes. Trying to be just like your friends and not doing or having the thing that you like so much would be the cause of your bad case of stripes.**

ART/WRITING EXTENSION

Camilla needed to learn about being herself. She went through an awful case of stripes in order to learn that she should be herself. Use the ideas from the graphic organizer to design a poster that Camilla can hang in her room to remind her of the lessons she learned from her bad case of stripes. Your poster should have both words and pictures to make your message to her very clear.

SUGGESTED SPECIAL NEEDS MODIFICATIONS

<u>Frontload</u>: Causal explanation lessons presuppose that students are able to identify cause and effect relationships. Some students may need assistance in cause and effect thinking. Use examples in daily lessons and everyday situations to help illustrate the concept. It may be important to do this with examples in which both the cause and effect are known. Under headings list the cause and effect links: rain—wet; forgotten lunch—hungry; unfinished work—work time during recess.

Causal explanation lessons present situations in which an effect is known but the cause isn't. Students have to think through the question, "What was the cause?" Students may benefit from brief brainstorming sessions in which they list all the "reasons" or causes for a known event (effect). "What could be all the reasons Bob was late for school?" This provides students with practice in generating possible causes. It is important to label these ideas as "possible causes" in order for students to become familiar with the terms.

"Evidence" may also be defined in prior settings in the same way. Provide examples in which students may use their prior knowledge of the concept of "clues," like the fingerprints on a stolen bicycle being evidence that Mr. X took Mr. Y's bicycle, or the fact that the food that Jimmy ate was spoiled being evidence that his eating that food, rather than having some stomach flu, caused his stomach ache.

Students will need many examples of possible versus actual evidence when they are first learning the causal explanation strategy. Use classroom examples as models when appropriate to explain this distinction.

<u>Diversify</u>: For some students, a greater degree of teacher guidance may be required. Rather than allowing groups to generate possible evidence, the teacher may wish to more directly guide this process as a whole group activity.

This lesson can be broken into segments over several days to accommodate all the steps.

The number of possible causes some students are asked to generate or to examine can be limited.

Special needs students are often aided by working in cooperative groups, especially if the students are trained to include all group members in the discussion and if the tasks are divided relative to each student's strengths. For example, a skillful note taker can honor everyone's ideas and reduce the writing task for some. Establish an atmosphere in which all answers are accepted during the process of brainstorming.

<u>Expand the Possibilities</u>: Assessments of written responses may be based upon students' thinking first, and expressive skills second. Oral responses may also reveal thinking beyond students' ability to express themselves in writing.

ASSESSING STUDENT THINKING ABOUT POSSIBILITIES

To assess the skill of causal explanation, ask students questions like the immediate transfer questions. Additionally, if there is a situation in the classroom where causal reasoning could easily be used, have students process the situation and use causal reasoning to think through the situation as they search for a cause. Encourage students to use the terms of the strategy, and use questioning to determine if they are using the steps of the thinking map.

Sample Student Responses • Why All Those Stripes?

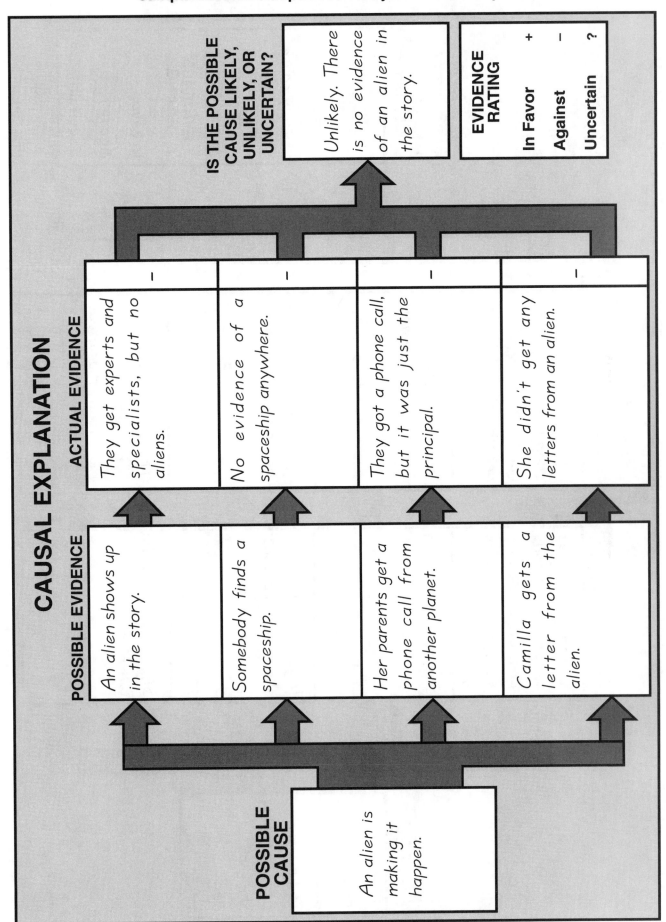

CAUSAL EXPLANATION

IS THE POSSIBLE CAUSE LIKELY, UNLIKELY, OR UNCERTAIN?

Unlikely. There is no evidence of an alien in the story.

EVIDENCE RATING

In Favor	+
Against	–
Uncertain	?

ACTUAL EVIDENCE

–	They get experts and specialists, but no aliens.
–	No evidence of a spaceship anywhere.
–	They got a phone call, but it was just the principal.
–	She didn't get any letters from an alien.

POSSIBLE EVIDENCE

An alien shows up in the story.

Somebody finds a spaceship.

Her parents get a phone call from another planet.

Camilla gets a letter from the alien.

POSSIBLE CAUSE

An alien is making it happen.

Sample Student Responses • Why All Those Stripes?

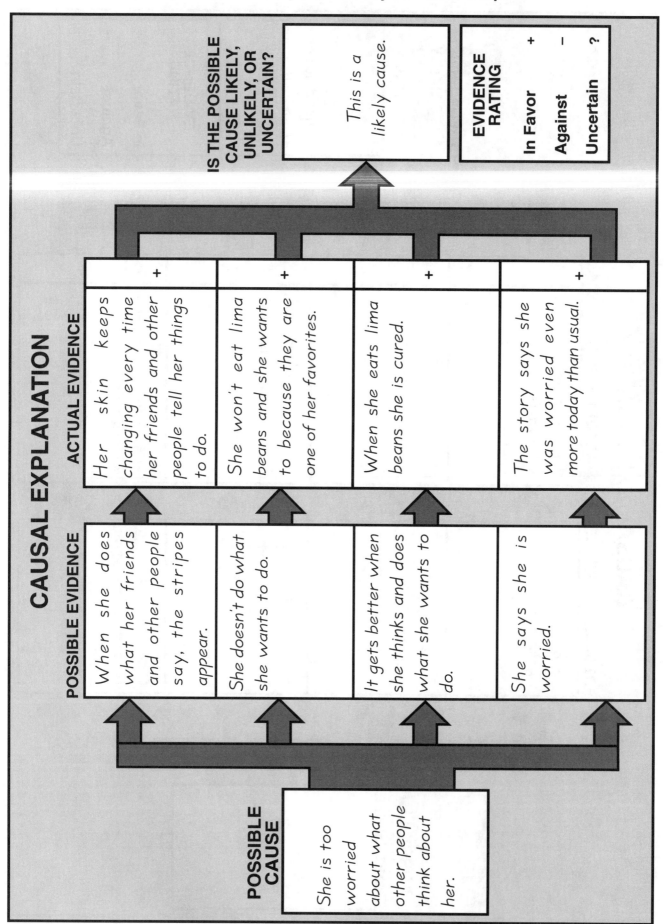

CAUSAL EXPLANATION

IS THE POSSIBLE CAUSE LIKELY, UNLIKELY, OR UNCERTAIN?

This is a likely cause.

EVIDENCE RATING

In Favor	+
Against	–
Uncertain	?

ACTUAL EVIDENCE

Her skin keeps changing every time her friends and other people tell her things to do.

She won't eat lima beans and she wants to because they are one of her favorites.

When she eats lima beans she is cured.

The story says she was worried even more today than usual.

POSSIBLE EVIDENCE

When she does what her friends and other people say, the stripes appear.

She doesn't do what she wants to do.

It gets better when she thinks and does what she wants to do.

She says she is worried.

POSSIBLE CAUSE

She is too worried about what other people think about her.

Sample Student Responses • Why All Those Stripes?

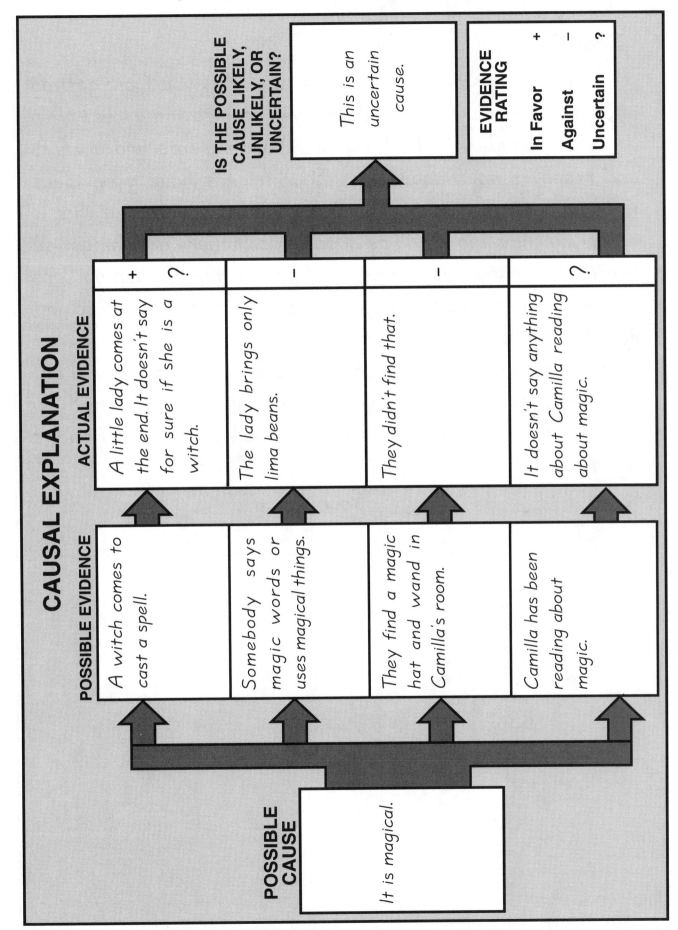

IS THE POSSIBLE CAUSE LIKELY, UNLIKELY, OR UNCERTAIN?

This is an uncertain cause.

EVIDENCE RATING

In Favor   +
Against   –
Uncertain   ?

CAUSAL EXPLANATION

ACTUAL EVIDENCE

+ ?	A little lady comes at the end. It doesn't say for sure if she is a witch.
–	The lady brings only lima beans.
–	They didn't find that.
?	It doesn't say anything about Camilla reading about magic.

POSSIBLE EVIDENCE

A witch comes to cast a spell.

Somebody says magic words or uses magical things.

They find a magic hat and wand in Camilla's room.

Camilla has been reading about magic.

POSSIBLE CAUSE

It is magical.

Sample Student Responses • Why All Those Stripes?

Dear Camilla,

    I have some ideas for you that will stop you from getting any more stripes. You should always listen to others but then do what you think is best for you. Your parents and doctors and teachers have good ideas. Your friends have good ideas too. You have to think about what they say and then if that is what you think too it will be good to do. If there are things you like that your friends say are silly just do them when you are not with your friends. Eating lima beans is good for you so just eat them when it is only your family eating with you. Don't take them to school for lunch! They don't have to see you eat them. It is important to be your own thinker and do what you like so don't give up on your favorite things even if others don't agree.

          Your friend,

_____

WHY IS THIS HAPPENING TO ME?
ALEXANDER AND THE TERRIBLE, HORRIBLE, NO GOOD, VERY BAD DAY

Language Arts   **Grades 1–2**

OBJECTIVES

CONTENT

Students will develop comprehension skills as they identify cause and effect relationships and then transfer their knowledge of cause and effect to a writing project. Students will learn how the speech and actions of the main character can be examined to find supportive evidence.

THINKING SKILL/PROCESS

Students will learn to consider possible causes and to look for evidence as they attempt to find what caused an event or situation.

METHODS AND MATERIALS

CONTENT

The story *Alexander and the Terrible, Horrible, No Good, Very Bad Day* by Judith Viorst is read aloud or read by the students.

THINKING SKILL/PROCESS

In collaborative learning groups, students are guided by structured questioning to brainstorm possible causes and possible evidence. Students follow a thinking map of causal explanation.

LESSON

INTRODUCTION TO CONTENT AND THINKING SKILL/PROCESS

- Have you ever been puzzled, not knowing why something happened? Last week I was talking to my friend on the phone and all of a sudden we lost our connection. I couldn't call her back because my phone had no dial tone. Think about a time when something happened and you wondered why it happened. POSSIBLE STUDENT RESPONSES: *The school bus was late. I opened up my lunch, and it wasn't mine. My dog was jumping and barking at the window.* When you wonder why something is happening, you are trying to find out what *caused* it. Did you find out what caused some of the things you were wondering about? POSSIBLE STUDENT RESPONSES: *The school bus broke, and they had to send a different one. I got my sister's lunch box by accident. There was a new dog in the neighborhood.* I found out that my friend and I lost our phone connection because a construction worker accidentally cut the phone lines.

- The name we use for what we found out when we asked and answered the question "Why did that happen?" is "causes." Write the word "Cause" on the chalkboard or on a chart. Finding out the cause can help us in the future to try and prevent things we don't want to happen from happening again. Use a student sample here from your own classroom. The example used here is the student response about the lunch box. For example, if you know that the cause for confusing your lunch box and your sister's was that they look alike, you could mark your lunch box with your name so you don't get the wrong lunch next time. Also, if I know the cause of something, I can use that information to make good things happen. Again, use a student sample from your own classroom. You can check right away when your dog is barking again to see if the new dog is out in its yard. Then you can take your dog out to meet and get used to the new dog.

- It is important to find causes correctly. If you get the cause wrong and try to prevent the same thing from happening again, it might still happen because you didn't find the *real* cause. Many people just guess about what the cause is. But if you don't know what the cause of something is and you want to find out, you need to think much more carefully. For example, my neighbor's car didn't work the other day, and he thought it had a dead battery. So he bought a new battery. But when he put the battery in, he found out that his car still did not start! He had the wrong cause. My neighbor just guessed that it was the battery. What do you think he should have done instead to make sure it was the battery? POSSIBLE STUDENT RESPONSES: *Checked the battery to make sure it was dead. Turned the radio on.* When you do things like that you are getting *evidence* to make sure that it is the battery that is causing the problem. Write the word "Evidence" on the chalkboard or on a chart under the word "Cause" and make an arrow between them pointing from "Evidence" to "Cause." Does anyone know another word for evidence? Usually someone in class will say that when we get evidence we get clues. If not, tell the students that getting evidence is like what a detective does in trying to solve a crime. That usually brings out the word "Clues." If that fails, tell the students that "Clues" is another word for evidence. Write that word next to the word "Evidence." So what would happen if the radio played? Students usually respond that they could tell that it probably isn't the battery. And if the radio didn't play? Students usually respond that that shows it probably is the battery. So what you find out about the radio can be *evidence* for or against the battery being the cause of the car not starting, or a *clue* about why it didn't start. Is it important to try to get evidence or to look for clues when you are trying to find the cause? Most students agree that it is. Why? POSSIBLE STUDENT RESPONSES: *Then you can make sure that you've got the right cause. You won't just be guessing. You can get it right. You can make sure that the battery is not the wrong cause.*

- Let me summarize what you've been saying. When you try to find out what caused something, you should make sure that you have evidence, or clues, that show that the cause you are thinking about is or is not likely to be the one that actually caused what happened.

- When I lost the phone connection with my friend, I thought at first that my friend had accidently hung up the phone. What clue do you think I had to find to realize that it was not my friend hanging up? Allow students time to think and then share their ideas. POSSIBLE STUDENT RESPONSES: *The telephone made no noise. You tried to call your friend back but the phone was not working.* Have you ever thought one thing caused another thing, and then found clues that it did not, that it was a different cause? You may have thought of something that might be the cause, but as you investigated, there were clues to tell you that the cause was something else. Perhaps when your bus did not arrive to pick you up, you thought there was no school, but then you saw another bus drive down a different street. That would be a clue that school was open. Your idea that there was no school was not likely. In the case of the dog jumping and barking at the window, you may have thought that the mailman was delivering the mail. When you thought some more, you realized that it was much too early for the mail to be delivered. That was a clue that made you think that your idea was not likely to be the cause of the dog's barking. Work with your partner and describe a time when something like that happened to you. After a few minutes ask for two or three examples. STUDENT ANSWERS VARY.

- Of course, if we want to know the cause, and we've rejected one idea, we should think about other possible causes and investigate further to find what clues are there so that we can see which of these possible causes is likely to be the right cause. Today we will practice finding out what really causes things to happen. We will learn a way to check ourselves so that we don't make so many mistakes. Here is a thinking map for finding causes. It will help us in our thinking. Show the thinking map on a chart. Go over the four questions, relating them to prior examples if necessary.

> **FINDING CAUSES**
>
> 1. **What are some possible causes?**
> 2. **What possible clues could you find?**
> 3. **What real clues do you have?**
> 4. **What do the clues show about the cause?**

THINKING ACTIVELY

- **The story we are going to use for our lesson is one written by Judith Viorst. The title is** *Alexander and the Terrible, Horrible, No Good, Very Bad Day.* **This story tells us of one miserable day in the life of a boy named Alexander. I'm sure many of you are familiar with some of the problems that Alexander has. Everyone has bad days, but I hope that none of us has days like the one in this book. As we read the story, pay close attention to what is happening. This will help us as we look for the causes of Alexander's bad day after we are finished.** Pass out the books to students, or gather them close for the read aloud. Read the story. If it is a read aloud, be sure to involve students in the story by asking them to join you for the repeated parts of the story, "I'm having a terrible, horrible, no good, very bad day," and Alexander's inclusion of the continent Australia in his responses to the events of the day.

- **What events were part of Alexander's terrible, horrible, no good, very bad day?** Students will relate some of the events of the story. POSSIBLE STUDENT RESPONSES: *He went to sleep with gum in his mouth, and it got gum in his hair. He didn't get anything in his cereal box and his brothers did. He got in trouble at school. His best friend said he was only his third best friend. He didn't get the shoes he wanted. He was the only one to have a cavity when they went to the dentist. He made a mess at his dad's office. There were lima beans for dinner, and he hates lima beans.* **There were a lot of things in his day that would make anyone groan and complain. But we are going to investigate to find the cause of the whole day being such a bad day for him. When we read the story, we wonder why he was having such a bad day. There were so many things that went wrong! We will think of some possible causes for the awful day that he had, then we will look for clues that will be evidence to use in deciding what the cause actually was. Alexander did not stop to find the cause of his miserable day. Let's try to help him prevent this kind of a day from happening again.**

- **You will be working in groups to think of possible causes first, as it is stated on the thinking map. I'd like you to make a list of possible causes for Alexander's horrible day. This is a brainstorming time, when we try to think of many possible causes. We have read the story, so keep the events of the story and Alexander's actions and feelings in mind as you make your list. Certainly you may look back into the story if it helps you to think. Make a list of the possible causes your group thinks of, and then we'll share and combine the ideas onto one list. And remember, when we do brainstorming like this we don't think about whether the idea is a good idea yet. Our purpose is to get as many possible causes as we can.** Write "Possible Causes" on the chalkboard or on a chart. After providing time for the groups to work and record their ideas on dry erase slates or paper, have them share their ideas with the class. Write the responses under the heading. POSSIBLE STUDENT RESPONSES: *It was bad luck. He was not paying attention, He was not following directions. He was not planning ahead. He just expected everything to go wrong. He was in a grouchy mood.*

- **We are ready for the next step of our thinking map, finding possible clues for the causes we have listed. Each group will get to pick a possible cause to work on. To see whether or not your cause is likely to be the real cause, you need to act like a detective, and think of the**

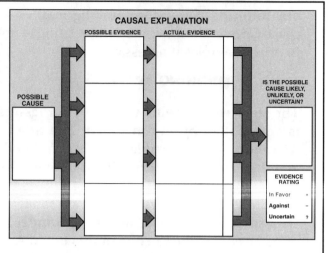

possible evidence, or clues, you could find that would prove this to be the real cause. If your group has the right cause, what evidence will be necessary to prove it? If your group has the wrong cause, what evidence, or clues, do you think you might find that would show that? The paper your group will use to record the clues you think would be helpful to find looks like this. Show the class the graphic organizer for causal explanation. Explain how to record the possible cause they are exploring by writing one possible cause in the possible cause box on a transparency or large chart of the graphic organizer, and/or write it on their graphic organizers as you pass out the papers. Then show the groups the column for possible evidence or clues. Students should fill in as many boxes as they can for specific evidence that might show, one way or the other, whether their possible cause is likely. Providing a chart-sized copy of the graphic organizer for each group will make sharing work easier later in the lesson. POSSIBLE STUDENT RESPONSES: (*Possible Cause: He was not paying attention*) *Possible Evidence: Maybe we could ask his family and his teacher to tell us what they saw. They may have seen him playing with a toy or looking at something else.* (*Possible Cause: He was in a grouchy mood*) *Possible Evidence: Other people could tell about the things they heard him say and saw him do that were grouchy things. Maybe his mother could tell us why he was grouchy.*

- The things you have just listed are the possible evidence, or clues. If you find these clues, then you can say that your cause is a likely cause of why Alexander had the terrible, horrible, no good, very bad day. If they aren't there, then that counts against your possible cause. Finding the clues makes them real clues, or actual evidence. You should always have an *open mind* when you look for clues and if the clues show that the cause isn't likely, you should be ready to say that. You should say that you know what caused Alexander to have his bad day only if you have evidence or clues to support it. This is the third step on our thinking map.

- Now look in the story. See if you can find the possible evidence we've written on the graphic organizer. Look at the words and the pictures. Both can provide us with information about what caused this terrible day. Is there anything that looks like evidence for your possible cause? If there is some real evidence in the story that matches the evidence you listed as a possible clue, we will write it in the next column. This is the one labeled "Actual Evidence." This real evidence will be written next to the possible evidence it matches. We will do the same thing if there is evidence in the story that counts against your possible cause. Help the students to fill in the real evidence boxes in their groups. Then ask each group to report to the class. An alternate plan is to do this as a whole group activity, with the groups taking turns coming to the front. Tape their graphic organizer to the board so that the whole class can see it as it is being completed. Match the real evidence to the possible evidence box where they listed that item. If there is evidence found that is not in the possible evidence column, give it a box in the real evidence column anyway. It is still valid. It is just something that the students didn't think to suggest when they were considering possible evidence. POSSIBLE STUDENT RESPONSES: (*Possible Cause: He was in a grouchy mood*): *Actual Evidence: He never smiles, he just frowns or has his mouth open, yelling. He is always complaining. He yells with his mouth wide open. He says bad things to people. He isn't nice to the people around him. He holds his head with his hand. He looks down a lot. He pouts.* Follow the next steps for each graphic organizer.

- **Let's think about our real evidence now as it appears on your graphic organizers. We want to decide if the real clues we have found support the possible cause. This will answer the final question on the thinking map, "What do the clues show about the cause?"** Read aloud each box of real evidence. Evaluate the evidence as a class, and mark it with a plus sign(+) or a minus sign (-) to show whether the class feels it supports or does not support the possible cause.

- **Our job now is to decide if the possible cause we are investigating is likely, unlikely, or uncertain. If we have lots of pluses next to our real evidence, then we have lots of evidence to show that the possible cause is the real cause. If there are lots of minuses, then it is unlikely that our possible cause is the real one. Do you think that this possible cause was likely or unlikely to be the real cause of Alexander's bad day?** The answers will vary from group to group. The group (or groups) with the cause(s) that they judge to be likely should say that it is likely to be the reason for Alexander's bad day. As a class, write a summary statement to put in the final box of each graphic organizer. Most students identify a likely cause of Alexander's terrible day to be his attitude. Once he had one thing go wrong, he expected everything to go wrong. Another likely cause of his bad day, one that students usually find support for, is the way that he reacted to the events of his day. He was always negative in his responses, so being grouchy is a possible cause for which the students often find evidence.

THINKING ABOUT THINKING

- **Let's review the steps we took as we did this lesson. How did we go about finding the cause for Alexander's bad day?** Students should mention the terms possible causes, brainstorming, possible clues or evidence, and real evidence. Refer to the thinking map for finding causes to confirm their responses.

- **Think about the way that you played detective to find the cause of Alexander's bad day. Is this a good way to think when you are puzzled about something? Why?** POSSIBLE STUDENT RESPONSES: *Yes, it is a good way. Finding the real clues and finding the cause is better than not knowing or just guessing.*

- **Was the graphic organizer helpful as you played detective? How did it help you keep your thinking organized?** The students should be able to explain how the graphic organizer works in keeping track of the evidence and deciding if the evidence supports the possible cause.

- **Think about a time when you might want to use this kind of thinking. It might be when something happens at home, or perhaps at school. What will you do to find the most likely cause?** Students should include the steps from the lesson and thinking map in their responses.

APPLYING YOUR THINKING

Immediate Transfer

- **Suppose you couldn't find your backpack at the end of the day. Why do you think this might have happened? How could you find out? Use a graphic organizer and the thinking map for causal explanation to help you think of some possible causes and the evidence you would need.** For this thinking activity, a scenario should be created by the teacher including evidence that the students could find to identify the likely cause. The scenario should include details that are specific to your actual school setting.

- Suppose the flowers in your yard are all trampled. What could have caused this to happen? How could you find out? Use the causal explanation thinking map and graphic organizer to help you as you do your thinking. For this thinking activity, a scenario should be created by the teacher including evidence that the students could find to identify the likely cause. The scenario should include details that are specific to a typical local yard.

Reinforcement Later

- There is a large group of people standing in line at the grocery store. What do you think has caused this to happen? What information might you need in order to find the cause? Record your work on a causal explanation graphic organizer. The causal explanation thinking map will guide you in your thinking. For this thinking activity, a scenario based on a local grocery store should be created by the teacher including evidence that the students could find to identify the likely cause.

- Choose a city near you. Think about what caused it to grow up where it is located? What can you find out about its beginning that will give you clues about why the settlers chose that location? Record your work on a Causal Explanation graphic organizer. The Causal Explanation thinking map will guide you in your thinking.

WRITING EXTENSION

If Alexander had tried to be more positive in the things he did during the day, do you think that he would have had a better day? Pick one of the things that happened during Alexander's day. Rewrite that part, showing what would have happened if Alexander had been less negative and complaining and more cooperative, trying to get along. Your story will show that if Alexander eliminated the cause of his bad day, it would not have been the awful day it was. To plan your story, you will each have a graphic organizer that shows how causes have an effect on the way that things happen. Allow time for students to discuss, write, and illustrate these new scenarios. Some students will want to use the multiple causes graphic organizer while others will be more comfortable using a single cause graphic organizer. The finished copies should be shared, and could be displayed along with the class summary statement from the graphic. (See writing templates in the Appendix for examples.)

SUGGESTED SPECIAL NEEDS MODIFICATIONS

<u>Frontload:</u> Causal explanation lessons presuppose that students are able to identify cause and effect relationships. Some students may need assistance in cause and effect thinking. Use examples in daily lessons and everyday situations to help illustrate the concept. It may be important to do this with examples in which both the cause and effect are known. Under headings list the cause and effect links: rain—wet; forgotten lunch—hungry; unfinished work—work time during recess.

Causal explanation lessons present situations in which an effect is known but the cause isn't. Students have to think through the question, "What was the cause?" Students may benefit from brief brainstorming sessions in which they list all the "reasons" or causes for a known event (effect). "What could be all the reasons Bob was late for school?" This provides students with practice in generating possible causes. It is important to label these ideas as "possible causes" in order for students to become familiar with the terms.

"Evidence" may also be defined in prior settings in the same way. Provide examples in which students may use their prior knowledge of the concept of "clues," like the fingerprints on a stolen bicycle being evidence that Mr. X took Mr. Y's bicycle, or the fact that the food that Jimmy ate was spoiled being evidence that his eating that food, rather than having some stomach flu, caused his stomach ache.

Students will need many examples of possible versus actual evidence when they are first learning the causal explanation strategy. Use classroom examples as models when appropriate to explain this distinction.

Diversify: For some students, a greater degree of teacher guidance may be required. Rather than allowing groups to generate possible evidence, the teacher may wish to more directly guide this process as a whole-group activity.

This lesson can be broken into segments over several days to accommodate all the steps.

The number of possible causes some students are asked to generate or to examine can be limited.

Special needs students are often aided by working in cooperative groups, especially if the students are trained to include all group members in the discussion and if the tasks are divided relative to each student's strengths. For example, a skillful note taker can honor everyone's ideas and reduce the writing task for some. Establish an atmosphere in which all answers are accepted during the process of brainstorming.

Expand the Possibilities: Assessments of written responses may be based upon students' thinking first, and expressive skills second. Oral responses may also reveal thinking beyond students' ability to express themselves in writing.

ASSESSING STUDENT THINKING ABOUT POSSIBILITIES

To assess the skill of causal explanation, ask students questions like the immediate transfer questions. Additionally, if there is a situation in the classroom where causal reasoning could easily be used, have students process the situation and use causal reasoning to think through the situation as they search for a cause. Encourage the terms of the strategy, and use questioning to determine if they are using the steps of the thinking map.

Sample Student Responses • Why Is This Happening?

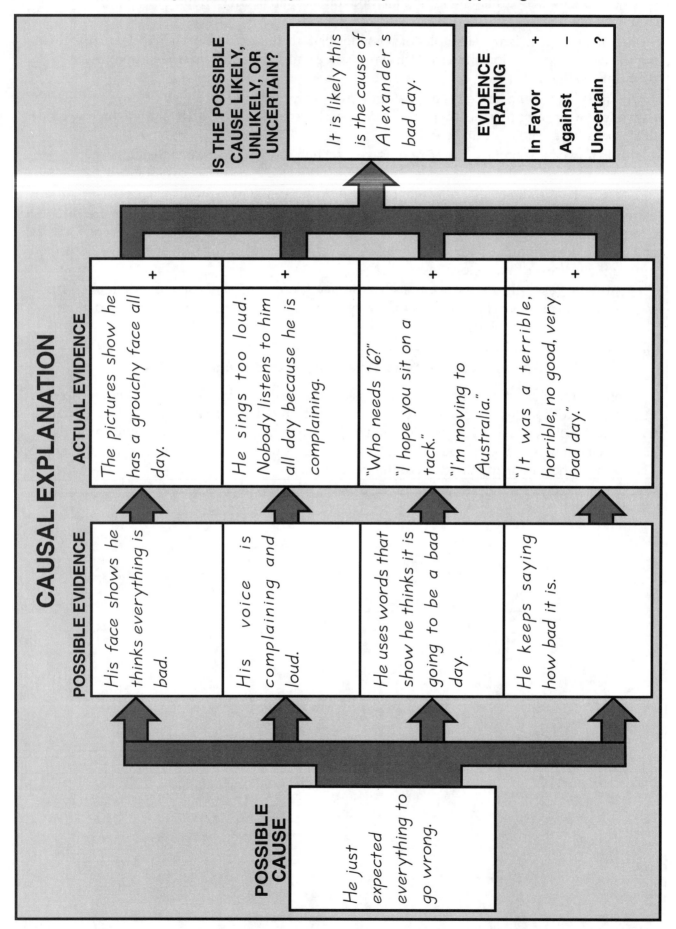

CAUSAL EXPLANATION

IS THE POSSIBLE CAUSE LIKELY, UNLIKELY, OR UNCERTAIN?

It is likely this is the cause of Alexander's bad day.

EVIDENCE RATING

In Favor	+
Against	−
Uncertain	?

ACTUAL EVIDENCE

+ The pictures show he has a grouchy face all day.

+ He sings too loud. Nobody listens to him all day because he is complaining.

+ "Who needs 16?" "I hope you sit on a tack." "I'm moving to Australia."

+ "It was a terrible, horrible, no good, very bad day."

POSSIBLE EVIDENCE

His face shows he thinks everything is bad.

His voice is complaining and loud.

He uses words that show he thinks it is going to be a bad day.

He keeps saying how bad it is.

POSSIBLE CAUSE

He just expected everything to go wrong.

FINDING CAUSES

1. What are some possible causes?

2. What possible clues could you find?

3. What real clues do you have?

4. What do the clues show about the cause?

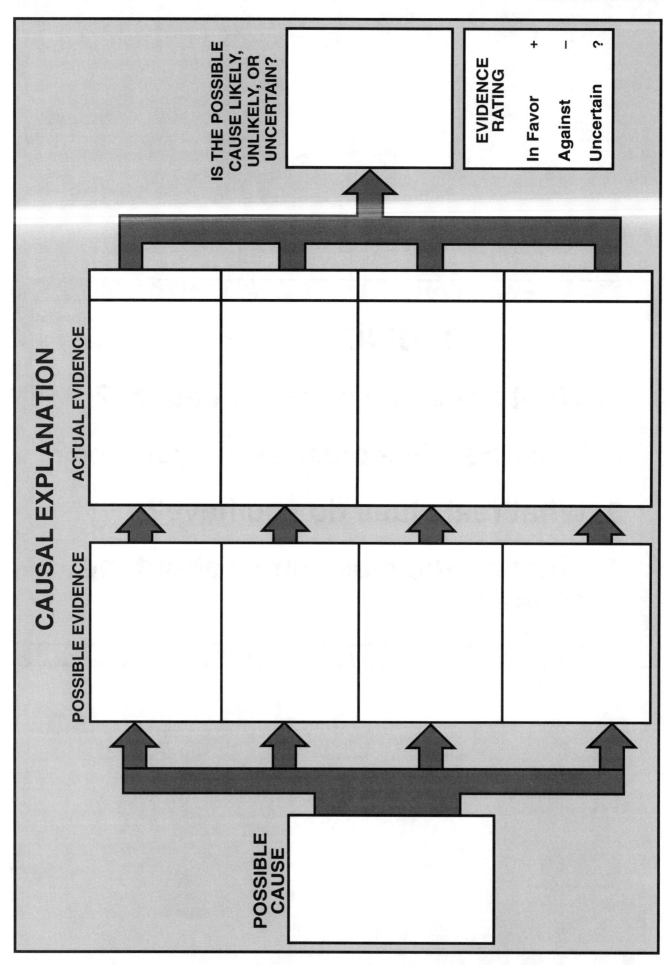

CAUSAL EXPLANATION

IS THE POSSIBLE CAUSE LIKELY, UNLIKELY, OR UNCERTAIN?

EVIDENCE RATING

In Favor	+
Against	−
Uncertain	?

ACTUAL EVIDENCE

POSSIBLE EVIDENCE

POSSIBLE CAUSE

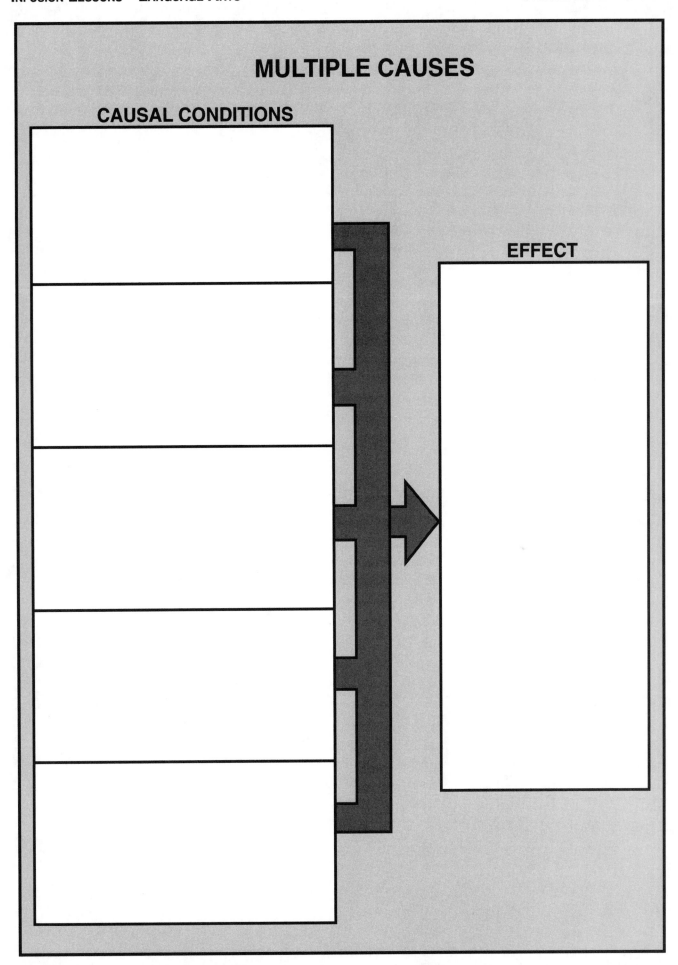

CHAPTER 15
PREDICTION

Infusing Skillful Prediction into Language Arts

Teaching students skillful prediction in grades 1 and 2 involves helping them learn to ask and carefully answer the following questions about the inferences they make about the future before they accept them as likely to happen:

This is what we call a "thinking map" for skillful prediction. In the lessons in this chapter, this thinking map is used to guide your students' thinking explicitly as they engage with the lesson content.

SKILLFUL PREDICTION

1. **What might happen?**

2. **What clues do you have for thinking it might happen?**

3. **Based on the clues, how likely is it that it will happen?**

---

figure 15.1

When students learn and use this strategy for determining how likely is a prediction they make, they avoid just guessing what will happen in the future and learn to base the predictions they make on evidence. They make tentative predictions and identify information on which they have based their predictions. They then make judgments about how likely these predictions are based on this information. When they think skillfully in this way about their predictions, they are exercising their critical thinking in judging whether the predictions they make are likely to happen. While someone might assume that a character in a novel will respond to a situation in a certain way, it isn't until this judgment is grounded in actual evidence, that one should be confident that the character will probably act that way.

In these lessons, using a graphic organizer, engaging in cooperative thinking, thinking about thinking, and continued guided practice supplement the use of this thinking map for skillful

prediction. These classroom strategies enhance both the development of the thinking skill that the students are learning and their mastery of the lesson content.

The key graphic organizer for skillful prediction is in figure 15.2.

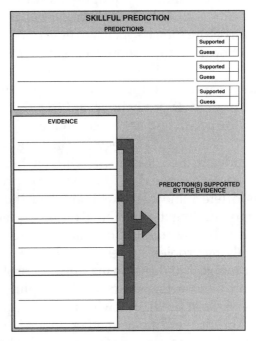

figure 15.2

This graphic organizer helps students record predictions, then note the evidence for or against these predictions, and last judge whether the predictions are guesses or are supported, given the evidence. So, if they thought that a character in a novel would confront danger rather than back down from it, they would go over the text again to cite evidence that is relevant to this prediction. For example, they may record that the character faced danger a number of times and did not back away from it. They would record this information in the "Evidence" column on the graphic organizer. In the last box, they would indicate that the character will probably face danger again. Then they would check off the "Supported" box in the box where they stated the prediction. If they found no evidence, or not enough strong evidence, they would check off the "Guess" box and not write the prediction

---

in the last box. Instead, they would write a different prediction that is supported by the evidence. Reproducible blank graphic organizers are found at the end of each chapter.

In many present language arts texts, prediction activities are included, but they usually involve asking students to make predictions about what will happen and then look ahead to see if their predictions are correct. This fosters guessing and does not help students learn how to make discriminating judgments about how likely things that they think might happen really are before they happen. So these traditional prediction activities should be supplemented by the steps in skillful prediction to help students learn to attend to actual evidence that is relevant to their predictions and to judge how likely the prediction are based on the evidence.

There is a second strategy for prediction that is included in these lessons. It builds on the same basic idea—the need for evidence for predictions to determine their likelihood—but the context is predicting the likelihood of consequences of things that we might do in making decisions and solving problems. In essence, this is a way to fine-tune skillful decision making and problem solving by concentrating on developing students' skills at predicting what might happen if a person adopted one or another option in decision making, or one or another possible solution in problem solving.

On the right is the thinking map for predicting the consequences of options (figure 15.3) followed by the graphic organizer (figure 15.4).

This graphic organizer, when completed, can do double duty, just as the graphic organizers for decision making and problem solving can. It, too, can become a pre-writing activity for writing extensions of prediction lessons. A writing template for predicting the consequences of options is included in the Appendix to this book. It can help students transition from the graphic

PREDICTING THE CONSEQUENCES OF OPTIONS

1. What consequences might result from this option?

2. Does each consequence count for or against choosing this option?

3. What evidence is there that the consequence will or won't happen?

4. Based on the evidence, how likely is each consequence?

5. Based on the likelihood of the consequences, is it wise to choose this option?

figure 15.3

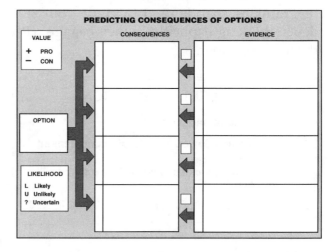

figure 15.4

organizer to well-organized expository writing about the consequences of options.

For more in-depth information on teaching skillful prediction, please refer to Chapter 14 in the book *Infusing the Teaching of Critical and Creative Thinking into Elementary Instruction,* by Robert Swartz and Sandra Parks. A computer disk containing the blank, reproducible graphic organizers used in this book is also available. Both book and disk are available through Critical Thinking Books & Software.

DREAMS
THE SWEETEST FIG

Language Arts

Grades 1–2

OBJECTIVES

CONTENT

Students will develop skills at listening for details in a story read orally.

THINKING SKILL/PROCESS

Students will develop skills at predicting outcomes by considering possible evidence and then gathering real evidence to support the likelihood of the predicted outcome.

METHODS AND MATERIALS

CONTENT

Students will listen to the book *The Sweetest Fig* by Chris Van Allsburg.

THINKING SKILL/PROCESS

Students will be guided by a thinking map for predicting based on evidence and a graphic organizer to record the evidence for the predictions that they make. They will also work in teams to identify evidence in the story that is read to them.

LESSON

INTRODUCTION TO CONTENT AND THINKING SKILL/PROCESS

- **When we wake up in the morning, we open our eyes and begin to think about what we expect to happen during the day. When we do that, we are doing what is called "predicting." Predicting is thinking ahead and coming up with ideas about what we think will happen at a later time before they happen.** Write the words "predict" and "prediction" on the chalkboard.

- **At this time of the year we might hear that summer is ending and fall is beginning. Can you predict some of the things that will happen as the seasons change? Draw some things that you predict will occur during the fall season.** If this lesson is used at another time of year, the upcoming season should be substituted. It is very acceptable to use illustrations that students have made for other activities instead of making new drawings for this lesson introduction. Allow a few minutes work time for students to draw the things they predict will happen during the fall. Encourage them to share ideas with each other as they draw. The teacher should include the words "predict" and "prediction." Students usually draw trees with yellow, red, or brown leaves falling, leaves on the ground, students with coats on, and sometimes pumpkins. **Now let's share in small groups.** Allow time for the students to share. **Why did you predict that those things would occur in the fall?** POSSIBLE STUDENT RESPONSES: *It always gets cooler in the fall. We go to the pumpkin farm in the fall. Halloween is in the fall. The leaves always change colors in the fall.* **We can make these predictions about what will happen because we have experienced fall before. Our memory of past fall seasons provides us with good *clues* about what will happen next fall. These clues are often called *evidence* because they show us what predictions will probably happen.** Write the words "clue" and "evidence" on the chalkboard with the other terms.

- **Today you went to Music.** (Name the special class that the students went to, and include the teacher's name.) **Before you left the classroom, did you predict some of the things you would do in Music? Share with a neighbor the things you expected to happen, the things you predicted.** Allow time for sharing with a neighbor, then have several share with the group. **Now share with your neighbor what clues or evidence from the past you had that made you pretty sure those predictions would happen.** STUDENT RESPONSES VARY. Usually students mention things that have happened in the past, especially on a regular basis; for example, every time they have music, the teacher asks them to start the class with a song they have learned, so they predict that that's what's going to happen this time.

- What do you think you can do if you don't have any evidence about whether a prediction is probably going to come true? Suppose that your neighbors get a puppy. You have never seen a puppy like it before. You are wondering what the puppy will look like when it is grown up. Will it be big or small? Will it have long hair or short curly hair? You could make some guesses, but if you want to do some skillful prediction, you would look for evidence. Where could you find evidence that would help you predict what the puppy will look like? Students usually say they would ask the owner what kind of dog it is and what it will look like when it grows up. They also should be guided to recognize the use of books as sources for evidence.

- **Let me summarize what we have learned so far about predictions. To decide whether a prediction we are making is a good prediction, we should first consider what we already know. Sometimes information or knowledge that we already have provides us with evidence or clues that can show what things are** *probably,* **or likely, to happen. But sometimes you have to get evidence from someone else or from a book. When you were predicting the things that would happen in the fall, you used the experiences you have had with other fall seasons to help you think about the things that would probably happen this coming fall. When you were thinking about predicting what the puppy would look like, you said you would get evidence from the owner and books about puppies. If you find evidence to support your prediction, you can say it will probably be right. It is likely to happen just as you predict. If there isn't evidence that says your prediction is probably going to come true, then you shouldn't think that your prediction will probably happen. To be a careful predictor we need to find evidence to show that what we think will happen** *probably* **will happen.** Write "probably" on the board with the other terms.

- **Help me with some other examples. This morning when I got into my car I saw that the gas gauge was almost on "Empty." I predicted that I would probably run out of gas very soon, so I stopped at the gas station and filled up the tank with gas. How did seeing "empty" on my gas gauge help me?** POSSIBLE STUDENT RESPONSES: *It was a clue that you'd run out of gas soon. You know about the car that when it says "empty" that means you have no more gas. Maybe you ran out of gas another time.* **Our predictions can help us to avoid trouble in this way. If I had never seen "empty" on my gas gauge before and didn't know what it meant, I would probably not have predicted that my car would run out of gas, and I might have gotten stuck somewhere with no gas! Can you think of times when your past experience has helped you predict things so that you can avoid trouble or harm?** POSSIBLE STUDENT RESPONSES: *When I cross the street and see a car coming, I predict that if I keep going I will get hurt, so I wait for the car to pass. I know that I'll get very cold and could get sick if I don't wear my coat when I go out in the winter, and I don't want that to happen, so I put my coat on. I know that when I am at school I have to do my work during work time or I will not be ready to have recess with the class.*

- **Sometimes people don't make predictions based on good evidence. Often people just guess** what will happen, and if you ask them why they can't tell you. I heard someone say at the beginning of the baseball season that he thought his baseball team would win the championship for our town. When I asked him why, he said, "Well, I just think so!" I thought to myself, that man is just guessing—maybe wishing—that the team he plays on will win, but he really doesn't have any evidence that they will. **What should this person say instead of what he actually said?** Students usually recognize that if there is no evidence then this person shouldn't feel so sure that their prediction will happen, and should say things like "I am not sure who will win the championship," or "I hope that my team wins the championship, but I really don't know who will."

- **There are also situations in which people make predictions based on *some* evidence, but there's more that shows that what they predict probably won't happen. If you say that you think it will be nice weather tomorrow because it's nice today, is that enough evidence to make a good prediction?** Students usually agree that the weather can change from day to day and you need to know more before you can predict the weather well. **That's why we have to be careful and make sure that if we think a prediction is a good one—if we think it is probably going to happen—we have *good* evidence. That's critical thinking also.**

- *Skillful* prediction involves thinking carefully about what might happen, then noting what evidence there is for or against the prediction, and deciding how likely the prediction is based on all the evidence. Here is a thinking map to help us remember what things we should think about as we predict. Show the thinking map for prediction on a chart, an overhead transparency, or on the

> **SKILLFUL PREDICTION**
>
> 1. What might happen?
> 2. What clues do you have for thinking it might happen?
> 3. Based on the clues, how likely is it that it will happen?

chalkboard. It should be displayed where the students can refer to it during the lesson. Go over the questions, using the prior examples.

THINKING ACTIVELY

- **When we read, one of the things we always do is to predict what the characters will do as we read along. It's important to make sure that we are not just guessing when we make these predictions. We should make sure that we make skillful predictions. What does that involve?** POSSIBLE STUDENT RESPONSES: *We need evidence that shows that our predictions will probably happen. The predictions we make should be based on evidence.* **When you make predictions during reading, the evidence you use is from the part of the book that you've read so far and also from things that you already know. If I ask you why you think a prediction you make as you read a story will probably happen, how will you answer that question?** POSSIBLE STUDENT RESPONSES: *I will tell you things that I've already read in the story and other things that I remember that make me think that my prediction will probably happen.*

- **Today we are going to work with a story about a dentist and his dog. The dentist is named Monsieur Bibot and his dog is named Marcel. They live in Paris, France. The word "Monsieur" in French means "Mister." In the story Monsieur Bibot is just called Bibot for short. The story is called *The Sweetest Fig* and it was written by Chris Van Allsburg.** Share the cover of the book with the students. It shows Bibot holding a fig with his mouth open as if he is about to eat it. **Notice that on the cover Bibot is holding a fruit. It is a fig.** You may want to show your students a picture of a fig and/or a fig tree and tell them that figs are often dried and sold that way in stores in the United States. **When you look at the cover, is there anything you can** predict about the story? **I'm going to use this graphic organizer for prediction to record your predictions.** POSSIBLE STUDENT RE-SPONSES: *Bibot has figs for dessert when he has dinner in the story. Bibot will eat a lot of figs. Bibot will eat a fig in the story.* Students typically respond with some things that are not supported by what is on the cover. For example, they may say that Bibot will eat a lot of figs or that Bibot has figs for desert when he has dinner. Using an overhead transparency of the graphic organizer for prediction, write what they say in boxes under the label "Predictions." Cover up the right side starting with the evidence boxes, leaving only the column on the left labelled "Predictions." **Now let's think about what you saw in the picture that made you predict what you did. What is in the picture? I'm going to use this graphic organizer for prediction again to record what is actually there in the picture that you used to make your predictions.** Uncover the rest of the graphic organizer for prediction. As the students respond, write

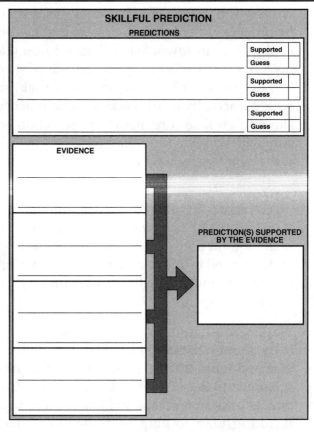

the evidence in the evidence boxes. POSSIBLE STUDENT RESPONSES: *Bibot is holding a fig, his mouth is open, he has a knife in his other hand.* **What do you know about people who look the way Bibot looks in the picture?** POSSIBLE STUDENT RESPONSES: *That's what people look like when they are going to eat what they have in their hand. When you use a knife, you cut something, and people cut things just before they eat them.* Also enter this information in the evidence boxes. **So when you put this information together in our evidence boxes, is it enough to support the idea that Bibot will probably eat the fig?** Students typically recognize that this is a good prediction based on what is in the picture. **Does it support the idea that Bibot will eat a lot of figs?** Students recognize that this is only one fig and that there is nothing else in the picture that tells us that he will eat any more figs. **Each of the prediction boxes has a place where we can show by marking an "x" if the prediction is supported by the picture or if it is a guess.** Based on the students' thinking and discussion, put an x next to "supported" or "guess" for each prediction. The supported predictions should be written in the box on the graphic organizer for Predictions Supported by the Evidence. Remind them that even though the prediction that he will eat a fig is supported, we can't tell anything from the cover about when he does it and why he does it.

- **What does this make you wonder about? What questions come into your minds when you think about the cover in this way?** POSSIBLE STUDENT RESPONSES: *Why is Bibot going to eat this fig? What will the fig taste like? Is something going to happen to Bibot when he eats this fig?*

- **Now let me read you the story.** Read up to the point where Bibot eats a fig before he goes to bed. Up to this point in the story we are told that Bibot is very harsh with his little dog, Marcel—he hits him with a newspaper if he gets up on the furniture, etc. We are also told that Bibot reluctantly lets a woman into his dentist's office to have a tooth pulled who doesn't have an appointment, pulls her bad tooth, and then kicks her out without giving her pain medicine when she pays him with two ripe figs rather than money. She says "These figs are very special...They can make your dreams come true." Bibot thinks she is crazy, but eats one of the figs just before going to bed. **What is happening in the book now?** POSSIBLE STUDENT RESPONSE: *Bibot is eating a fig.* **So what do you think about your predictions now?** Students are quick to say that the prediction that he would eat a fig was correct, while some of the other predictions were not. **When you say that Bibot is eating a fig now, is that still a prediction?** POSSIBLE STUDENT RESPONSES: *No, because we can see that he is. No, because it isn't in the future anymore.* **So the important thing about making a prediction isn't so much waiting to see if it will happen, but to make sure that you have good evidence for it when you make it. Then you can feel pretty sure it will happen, like in this case. That kind of thinking is a great help when you are reading. Careful prediction helps you follow a story much better than if you guess about what will happen all the time.**

- **Now I'm going to continue reading.** Students will listen as you read to them about when Bibot went out with his dog, who he dragged down the stairs instead of carrying him, and how he was shocked to find that he was dressed only in his underwear! He remembered that he had a dream the night before in which he was in the same spot and dressed only in his underwear. Then he remembered the rest of the dream. He had dreamed that the Eiffel Tower (explain to students what the Eiffel Tower is) had drooped over like it was rubber. He looked out and sure enough, the Eiffel Tower was drooping, just like in his dream, as if it were made of rubber. Stop at this point. **Isn't that amazing! What Bibot dreamed came true! Do you think you could have predicted that was going to happen earlier in the story?** Students typically recognize that they had no way of knowing about Bibot's underwear or the Eiffel tower, but they often remember what the woman said—that the figs will make your dreams come true. Some of them will say that they could have predicted that whatever Bibot dreamed after he ate the fig would come true, though they often say that they are not sure because Bibot thinks she might be crazy. If they do not say this, help them formulate this prediction by asking them whether or not they could have predicted it and why. Then read the next paragraph in the story: "Bibot understood now that the old woman with the figs had told him the truth. He would not waste the second fig." **What do you think that Bibot is predicting?** POSSIBLE STUDENT RESPONSES: *If he eats the second fig, what he dreams that night will also come true. His dreams will come true.* **And what is his evidence?** POSSIBLE STUDENT RESPONSES: *His evidence is that he ate the first fig and then he had a weird dream and it came true.* **So what do you think might happen in the story next?** POSSIBLE STUDENT RESPONSES: *Bibot will eat the second fig and dream about nice things and get them. Bibot will eat the second fig -and dream that he is a millionaire. What Bibot dreams about will come true after he eats the second fig.* **I'm going to write these on a new blank graphic organizer for predicting.** Put a second transparency for prediction on the overhead projector and write these predictions in the "Predictions" boxes. **Now let's do the same thing we did before. Which of these predictions is supported by what is in the story so far and which are just guesses?** Students usually recognize that there is no evidence so far that he will dream about nice things and that you can't control your dreams. If they don't mention these points, ask them directly (e.g., Do you think you can force yourself to dream only nice things when you go to bed?"). They recognize that the most you can say is that he will eat the second fig and what he dreams about will come true. Write the evidence from the story that the students come up with and sort out the guesses from the predictions that are well supported. Write these into the new graphic organizer in exactly the same way that you entered their predictions on the earlier graphic organizer based on the cover.

- **Let's see what happens next in the story.** Begin reading about how Bibot tried to get himself to dream only good dreams in which nice things happened to him, and how he succeeded to the point where he was ready to eat the next fig. Then he took out the fig and put it on the table on a dish. To help focus the students' attention, pause before reading the next page which describes Marcel, the dog, putting his front paws on the table while Bibot's back is turned and eating the fig off the plate! Then read the next page and stop. It describes Bibot getting very angry and chasing Marcel around the apartment till Marcel hides under the bed and Bibot threatens to teach him a lesson tomorrow. Then Bibot goes to sleep. **Now what do you think might happen? Work together with your partners and make some predictions. Your groups will have a graphic organizer to record your predictions.** Give the students blank copies of the prediction graphic organizer. POSSIBLE STUDENT RESPONSES: *Marcel will become rich. Bibot will never become rich. Bibot will beat Marcel. Marcel's dreams will come true.* **Now use your copy of the graphic organizer to write what evidence you have in the story about what will happen and indicate which predictions are supported by the evidence.** POSSIBLE STUDENT RESPONSES: *Evidence: Bibot's dream came true after he ate one of the figs. Marcel ate the second fig. Bibot says he'll teach Marcel a lesson tomorrow. Bibot hasn't been nice to Marcel in the past.* Most students also recognize that there is no evidence that Marcel will become rich because we don't know about his dreams, and the evidence that Bibot will beat Marcel tomorrow may not be very good depending on what Marcel dreams (he could dream that he was far away from Bibot), so these are guesses. Usually students will say that the evidence supports the prediction that what Marcel dreams will come true, but they don't know what Marcel will dream. Write "What Marcel dreams will come true" in the box for supported predictions.

- **Now let's finish the story.** Read the rest of the story. It tells how when Bibot woke up the next morning he was confused because he found himself under his bed, not on it. He was looking at his own face staring back at him from the floor on the side of the bed and saying "Come to Marcel!" When Bibot tried to get away from Marcel's grasp, he found that he couldn't yell but only bark! Show students the picture. **What has happened?** Most students realize that Marcel has become Bibot and Bibot has become Marcel. **Why do you think that happened?** Students quickly realize that Marcel, when he was a dog, must have dreamed that he was Bibot and Bibot was Marcel so that he could treat Bibot the way Bibot was treating him. If they do not grasp this, ask them direct questions to elicit the response. **Work with your partners once more and discuss whether there was any evidence in the story that might have supported this prediction.** Students recognize that there was some evidence in the way that Bibot treated Marcel, but not enough to make a prediction that they were sure of. Still, some students say that they might have been able to guess that was going to happen if they thought about it. Explain to the students how writers sometimes give you a little bit of evidence to make you wonder what will happen, but not enough to make a real prediction you feel sure about, and then they surprise you. Ask students how many were surprised by the ending. Usually, most students say that they were surprised.

THINKING ABOUT THINKING

- **In this activity, we made predictions about what would probably happen as we read a story. What steps did we follow as we did this?** The students should go through the steps of the thinking map.

- **At the beginning of the lesson we talked about making predictions everyday. How is the predicting we did in this lesson alike and different from the way you usually make predictions?** ANSWERS VARY. The students may say they don't always think about the clues that will support what they predict, but some will be able to give examples of times when they did think about things that would help them predict.

- **Do you think finding evidence to support our predictions helps? How?** POSSIBLE STUDENT

RESPONSES: *It helps me to decide which predictions are probably going to happen. I can tell when I am just guessing.*

- **Were the thinking map and graphic organizer for prediction helpful in your thinking?** Most students say that they were helpful because they made them think about the evidence for their predictions.

- **Next time you make predictions about what will happen, what will you do?** POSSIBLE STUDENT RESPONSES: *I'm going to make sure I have evidence. I'm going to ask myself whether I'm just guessing or have good evidence.*

Immediate Transfer

- **You have been reading books about Amelia Bedelia. Are there any things you can predict about the main character and the way she handles situations around the Rogers' household? What evidence supports your prediction?**

- **What do you think would happen if we did not recycle? Why? What evidence would show that your prediction was likely to occur?**

- **Read a new story. Part way through, stop and consider what the main character will do. What evidence is there that supports your prediction? Read the rest of the story. Did you predict correctly? Was there any new evidence that caused you to change your predictions as you read further?**

Reinforcement Later

- **Predict what will happen when a variety of common things are placed near a magnet. Explain your predictions. Test the predictions.**

- **In our study of plants, we have learned about the things necessary for a plant to grow. What predictions did you make as the plants in the window grew? What evidence did you have? Did you change any of your predictions as you kept track of the amount of daily growth?**

- **Predict what would happen if you could bring your own toys to recess. Explain your prediction. What evidence would support your prediction? Plan one day to bring your own toys. What real evidence did you find? Did it support your prediction?**

- **It is your birthday. What will happen today? What evidence would support your prediction? Do you have any real evidence to support your prediction?**

SUGGESTED SPECIAL NEEDS MODIFICATIONS

<u>Frontload:</u> Students may benefit from practicing finding "evidence" in situations prior to the lesson. Model this by discussing everyday events, such as, "The fact that every Friday in the past we've had fish in the cafeteria is a <u>pattern</u> that gives me <u>evidence</u> to <u>predict</u> that this Friday we will also have fish. This <u>evidence counts in favor</u> of the prediction, and makes it likely we'll have fish again." Similarly, pointing out situations in which the evidence isn't present to support a "prediction" may help students make the distinction between "likely" and "less likely" predictions. "Suzy thinks that we may have extra recess today. Let's see if we have any evidence, or clues, that might support that. Sometimes our thinking is a wish or a guess. Skillful predictors use evidence!"

<u>Clarify:</u> Pairing the terms "evidence" and "clue" or "likely" and "probably" may clarify the terms for students. In order to avoid confusion, it is important to refrain from using the terms

"predict" and "guess" as if they were synonyms. Predictions use evidence. Guesses may not use evidence.

Expand the Possibilities: Assessments of written responses may be based upon students' thinking first, and expressive skills second. Oral responses may also reveal thinking beyond students' ability to express themselves in writing.

ASSESSING STUDENT THINKING ABOUT PREDICTING

To assess how skillfully students predict using evidence that supports their predictions, present a situation in which it is not obvious what will happen but there are clues. Ask the students to make predictions about what will happen and then sort out the ones that are supported by the evidence and the ones that are just guesses. Depending on the skills of the students, the assessment can take a written or oral form.

Sample Student Responses • Dreams

SKILLFUL PREDICTION

PREDICTIONS

Bibot has figs for dessert.

Supported	
Guess	X

Bibot will eat a lot of figs.

Supported	
Guess	X

Bibot will eat a fig in the story.

Supported	X
Guess	

EVIDENCE

Bibot is holding a fig and his mouth is open. That is what people look like when they are going to eat what they have in their hand.

Bibot has a knife in his hand. The fig looks like it has been cut.

When you use a knife, you cut things with it.

People cut things before they eat them.

PREDICTION(S) SUPPORTED BY THE EVIDENCE

Bibot will eat a fig in the story.

Sample Student Responses • The Sweetest Fig

SKILLFUL PREDICTION
PREDICTIONS

Marcel will become rich.

Supported	
Guess	X

Bibot will beat Marcel.

Supported	
Guess	X

What Marcel dreams will come true.

Supported	X
Guess	

EVIDENCE

Bibot's dream came true when he

ate the first fig.

Bibot says he will teach Marcel a

lesson tomorrow.

Bibot hasn't been nice to Marcel

in the past.

Marcel ate the second fig.

PREDICTION(S) SUPPORTED BY THE EVIDENCE

What Marcel dreams will come true.

TO HELP OR NOT TO HELP?
DR. DESOTO

Language Arts

Grades 1–2

OBJECTIVES

CONTENT

Students will learn how to interpret character traits and motives by analyzing details about a character's actions and what the character says.

THINKING SKILL/PROCESS

Students will develop skill at predicting outcomes by considering possible evidence and then gathering real evidence to support the likelihood of the predicted outcome.

METHODS AND MATERIALS

CONTENT

Students will listen to or read the book *Dr. DeSoto* by William Steig. This lesson presupposes that students have engaged in lessons on skillful decision making.

THINKING SKILL/PROCESS

Predicting consequences will be guided by structured questioning and a graphic organizer that focuses their thinking on skillful prediction. The lesson will involve collaborative learning to increase student involvement and support the students as they learn a new skill.

LESSON

INTRODUCTION TO CONTENT AND THINKING SKILL/PROCESS

- Today, let's start by thinking about an example of a scary situation that a friend told me a second grader found himself in one day. He was playing at the park and he noticed storm clouds in the sky. The wind was picking up and he could see that a storm was coming. Then he heard thunder and saw lightning near the clouds. His house was about six blocks from the park, and he had ridden his bike. What details do you know that would help you figure out what probably scared this boy? POSSIBLE STUDENT RESPONSES: *He is at the park with his bike. He sees that a storm is coming. His house is six blocks from the park.*

- What type of skillful thinking does this boy have to do? Most students recognize that he has to do skillful decision making. When we do skillful decision making, what are some of the important things we should think about? Ask students from the class to mention one important thing he should think about. POSSIBLE STUDENT RESPONSES: *He should think about different things that he could do. He should make sure he thinks about the consequences of his choices so that he doesn't do something that would be dangerous. He should make sure he thinks about the pros and cons of his choices.* In the decision making strategy, we need to consider options that may have some pros and cons. Thinking ahead to the possible consequences of the options uses a special kind of thinking called "prediction." We should try to predict the consequences of the options so that we do not choose an option with a lot of cons. Write the words "predict" and "prediction" on the chalkboard.

- The boy my friend told me about first thought quickly of some things that he might do, like some of you suggested. He was trying to do skillful decision making. What do you think some of his options were? POSSIBLE STUDENT RESPONSES: *He could ride his bike home right away.*

He could go to a friend's house that might be closer. He could go into a park shelter. He could call his mom and dad. Record the options shared on the chalkboard or a chart under the label "What He Might Do—Options."

- As he was thinking, he could see the storm was coming very quickly. He realized that the consequences of some of his options were risky, and some were helpful. I'm going to use the words "risks" and "benefits" for these cons and pros. For example, if he tried to ride his bike home and beat the storm, he predicted that he would be taking the risk of being out on his bike in a thunderstorm. He knew from his science classes at school that lightning was a danger and that it was possible that he would be struck by lightning. He could also skid on the wet road. The benefit he predicted was that he would get home with his family and out of the storm pretty quickly.

- There is something else that is very important in skillful decision making, and that is going to be the main thinking focus of this lesson. Before we let a risk or a benefit determine our decision, we should try to figure out how *likely* our prediction of the risk or benefit is. Sometimes our fear makes us think that something bad is going to happen and it really isn't. Sometimes our hope makes us predict that something good is going to happen and it really isn't. For example, you may worry that you are going to miss the school bus in the morning, and so you rush to get to the bus stop. But then you might have to wait five minutes for the bus, and you might realize that you really didn't have to worry that you'd miss the bus. Is there some way that you could have thought about it and figured out that you probably wouldn't miss the bus and that you didn't have to worry? What if every time you go to the bus stop in the morning, the bus is five minutes late? If you remembered that, what would that show about the prediction that you would miss the bus if you weren't there on time? Most students recognize that that would show that the bus probably would be five minutes late again this morning, and that you didn't have to worry about being late. If they don't, ask about this directly by asking whether this shows that the bus would probably be late again this morning. Once this is established, identify facts like, the bus has been late in the past, as *evidence* for the likelihood that it will be late again. **To think carefully about how likely your prediction of the consequence of missing the bus is, then, it is important to find evidence one way or another that shows how likely it is.**

- Now let's return to the boy in the park with a thunderstorm coming. How likely is it that he will be hurt or injured in riding his bike home in the storm? Most students will agree that it is a dangerous thing to ride a bike six blocks in a lightning storm. The boy agreed with this. He used evidence that he had about the consequences of riding a bike in a thunderstorm. The evidence came from prior knowledge about thunderstorms, lightning, and the effects of lightning on people, and how easy it was to skid on a bicycle on a very wet road.

- Let's think about another option. If he chose the option of taking cover in the park shelter, what might the consequences be? POSSIBLE STUDENT RESPONSES: *He would be safe from lightning, but he would be taking the risk of worrying his parents.* Is this risk as great a danger as the risk of being struck by lightning? *No, his parents might worry, but nobody would probably be hurt or killed by lightning.* Why? Students can usually articulate that when you are sheltered you don't get wet from the rain and if lightning strikes, it will strike the shelter and not you.

- In predicting the consequences of this new option, the boy also predicted that his parents would be worried and that they would come looking for him in the car. He then thought about how likely this was. He remembered that in the past they worried when he was not home when he said he would be, and they often came looking for him when they worried.

They knew that he was at the park, and he remembered the conversation his family had recently about storms and safety. His parents had told him that riding his bike in a storm was a dangerous thing to do. They agreed with the information he knew from his science classes. He knew that in situations when there were storms his parents would check to make sure that all members of the family were safe. He also remembered that once his mother had come looking for him in the car because he had not noticed that it was getting dark. She did not want him riding his bike home in the dark so she came to get him. What should this evidence tell the boy about how likely it was that his parents would come looking for him? Students recognize that this evidence makes the prediction highly likely. If they are not vocal about this, you might ask, "How many think this makes the prediction unlikely? Likely?" and get a show of hands. Usually there is unanimity that the evidence makes the prediction likely.

- In making his decision the boy considered the options, and used evidence to predict the consequences of the options. He recognized which options had risks that were important and should not be ignored as he made his decision. Of these two options, which do you think the boy should have chosen? Talk to your neighbor about what you think would be the best option. Allow time for discussion, then discuss the responses as a whole group. The usual response is to wait for his parents to come for him.

- In this situation, the boy agreed with you. He decided to wait in the shelter, safe from the storm. A few minutes later, his father pulled up in the car and gave him a safe ride home. The boy was a careful thinker. He used good predicting skills to help him make the best decision. No one was put in a risky situation by choosing the wrong option. The boy was able to make the choice by predicting the things that would happen based on evidence he had about the situation.

- Skillful prediction is important when a decision needs to be made. Here is a thinking map to help us remember what things we should think about as we predict the consequences of an option. Show the thinking map for predicting the consequences of options on a chart, an overhead transparency, or on the chalkboard. It should be displayed where the students can refer to it during the lesson. Go over the five questions, using prior examples. **The first question asks us what consequences might result from this option. When we thought about the consequences of waiting** in the shelter at the park our list included the parents worrying, the parents looking for him at home, and the parents coming to find him at the park.

> ## PREDICTING THE CONSEQUENCES OF OPTIONS
>
> 1. What consequences might result from this option?
> 2. Does each consequence count for or against choosing this option?
> 3. What evidence is there that the consequence will or won't happen?
> 4. Based on the evidence, how likely is each consequence?
> 5. Based on the likelihood of the consequences, is it wise to choose this option?

- The second question asks us to decide if the consequence is a pro and counts for choosing the option or if it is a con and counts against choosing the option. Getting struck by lightning while riding home on a bike would most definitely be a con and count against choosing that option.

- The third question asks, What evidence is there that the consequence will or won't happen? Predicting the consequence of an option asks us to base our predictions on the evidence that an option probably will or won't happen. The evidence is the information or knowledge that shows things are likely or unlikely to happen. When you were predicting the things that would happen to the boy in the storm, you used the evidence you had about the situation to think about the things that would happen. We knew that his science classes had taught him about lightning, we knew that he had had family discussions about storm safety, and we knew that he had been rescued by his parents in other dangerous situations.

• The fourth question asks us to evaluate the consequence based on the evidence. Is it likely or unlikely to happen, or in a case where there is no evidence, is it uncertain whether it will happen? The boy based his decision to stay in the shelter on the evidence that showed it was likely he would be safe from the lightning and be rescued by his parents.

• The fifth question will be answered when all of the consequences have been considered using the thinking we have done with the first four questions. This question pulls everything together as it asks us to decide if it is wise to choose this option.

• Today we are going to practice predicting the consequences of options by thinking about a decision that must be made by a character in a book. We will use this strategy for thinking to help us evaluate the decision made by the character. We will put ourselves in his situation and try to avoid taking risks by being careful thinkers. Being aware of the benefits and risks that may occur will help us avoid making decisions that would put the character in dangerous situations.

THINKING ACTIVELY

• The story we are going to work on today is about a dentist, an animal dentist. This dentist is a mouse and his name is Dr. DeSoto. The book *Dr. DeSoto* was written by William Steig. Share the cover of the book with the students. From the cover we can see that Dr. DeSoto has all the tools necessary to take care of animals, at least animals that would fit into his chair. He does occasionally take care of other animals, ones who are larger. For those he has special tools. **Can you think of some animals that would require special tools?** POSSIBLE STUDENT RESPONSES: *bears, elephants, wolves, horses, cows.* There are some decisions that are made in this story by Dr. DeSoto. The decisions will involve some danger. As we read the beginning of the book, I want you to think about the choices Dr. DeSoto could make and the consequences that are likely to result. Look for evidence, clues that show that these consequences might actually happen. Give students their copies of the book or begin reading aloud the story to students. It is about what happens when a fox with a toothache comes to Dr. DeSoto. The story should be read and discussed up to the page showing the DeSotos in their bed worrying about the fox and what they should do. There is a point where Mrs. DeSoto encourages her husband to help the fox, based only on her feelings of empathy for the fox's pain. This should be acknowledged during the reading and then referred to in the next section of the lesson. Stopping after the words "'But we must do something to protect ourselves,' said his wife." is very effective. The pages are not numbered, so getting students to stop at the appropriate spot is easily done by marking the place with a small post-it sticker. A paper clip also can be used to discourage students from continuing to read past the stopping point.

• **What danger is Dr. DeSoto facing?** Students will recognize that the danger is the threat of being eaten by the fox. **What details from the story lead you to believe that?** POSSIBLE STUDENT RESPONSES: *The dentist told the fox he could not treat him and to read his sign. It said, "Cats and other dangerous animals not accepted for treatment." The fox almost ate Dr. DeSoto while he was pulling the tooth. They had to gas him and put in a pole that held his mouth open. The gas made him dream about eating mice. The fox thought about eating the mice when the job was done.*

• **What might Dr. DeSoto do in this situation?** Record ideas from the class on the chalkboard or a chart. Group the responses into two sections, one giving ideas about treating the fox and one giving ideas about not treating the fox. POSSIBLE STUDENT RESPONSES: *He could tell the fox to go to another dentist. He could treat the fox and be careful not to be eaten. He could just close the window and pretend to be gone until the fox leaves. He could give the fox something to make him sleep for a long time so that he could fix the tooth and then escape.* **It appears that there are really two major choices that the dentist has, letting the fox into his office and finishing the job or not letting him back into the office. The last page we read had a clue about the choice Dr. DeSoto would make. Can you find the clue?** The students will find the statement made by Dr. DeSoto, "Once I start a job I finish it. My father was the same way."

- **Let's look at one of the options, letting the fox back into the office and finishing the job. We will try to decide if this is a wise thing to do or if it is not so wise. I am going to record this option on a graphic organizer for predicting the consequences of options.** Show a copy of the graphic organizer on a transparency or chart. Record the option in the box on the graphic organizer. **The first question on our thinking map asks us to think about the consequences that will result from this option. In your groups, make a list of all the consequences you can think of that might happen if Dr. DeSoto lets the fox back into his office.**

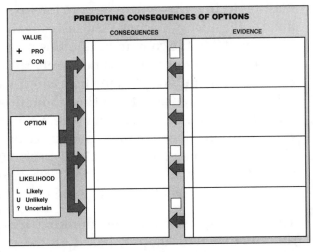

Allow time for students to think and list consequences of the option. Support the groups as needed during this activity. Some may need help with the recording, while others may need help recognizing consequences as things that happen because the dentist allowed the fox back into the office. When sharing with the whole class, ask each group to give one consequence until all groups have shared. Then ask for any other consequences not mentioned. Record these on the chalkboard, combining or refining ideas as necessary. This list will be used on the graphic organizer in the next section of the lesson. POSSIBLE STUDENT RESPONSES: *The mice will protect themselves and not be harmed by the fox. The fox will gobble up the mice as soon as they finish the job. The fox will decide to be a nice fox and not eat the mice. Fox will hurt them.*

- **Our next step is to think about whether each of the consequences is a pro or a con. Would the consequence count for or against choosing the option? In your groups, I'd like you to think about our list of consequences and decide if they are pros or cons.** Allow time for the groups to discuss the consequences and whether they are for or against choosing the option. With the class, share the results of the discussions and mark each consequence with a plus (for pro) or a minus (for con).

- **Now let's think whether or not the consequences are likely that Dr. DeSoto will let the fox in and finish the job he started. We will write the first consequence in this top box in the section labeled "Consequences" and mark it with a plus sign because it would count in favor of the mice choosing this option.** Record the first consequence, "They will protect themselves and will not be harmed at all by the fox," in the top box. **Our graphic organizer will help us keep our ideas clear in our minds as we think about the decision the DeSotos are making. The third question on the thinking map asks us to find evidence, or clues, that our consequence will happen. Look back in the story and see if there is evidence that they will protect themselves.** Allow time for students to search back in the text. If the story is being read aloud, the teacher may reread the beginning of the book to assist students. In this case, students should be reminded to listen carefully and then be given time to record evidence after the reading.

- **Did you find any evidence that shows that the mice are likely to protect themselves or that they are not likely to protect themselves? Let's hear one piece of such evidence.** POSSIBLE STUDENT RESPONSES: *They have lots of tools they can use to protect themselves.* **I will record this evidence in the evidence box next to our first consequence.** Record the first piece of evidence in the evidence box on the graphic organizer. **Does the fact that they have many tools that will help them protect themselves against the fox count toward this being a likely consequence or an unlikely consequence?** Most students will say that this supports the likelihood of the mice protecting themselves against the fox. **To show that this evidence supports the likelihood of the mice protecting themselves against the fox, we can mark it with an "L" for "likely."** Mark an "L" in the column next to this piece of evidence on the graphic organizer. **If it were evidence that showed it was not likely that the mice would protect themselves, we would put a "U" for "unlikely" in the box, and if we were unsure of the results we would put a "?" What other evidence did you find about this consequence?** Record each piece of evidence in the evidence box for this consequence. For each piece of evidence, ask if it supports or does not support the likelihood of the consequence by marking an "L," "U," or "?" in the box in front of the evidence statement. POSSIBLE STUDENT RESPONSES: *They have lots of tools that they can use to protect themselves (L). Dr. and Mrs. DeSoto are smart (L). The fox dreamt that he was eating the mice (U). The fox is big and the mice are small (U).*

- **The fourth question on the thinking map asks us to decide how likely it is that the consequence will happen, based on the evidence we collected. When we look at all the evidence for the first consequence, is it likely, unlikely, or uncertain that the mice will protect themselves?** The students should see that some of the evidence points to the likelihood of the mice protecting themselves, but that there is some evidence that they couldn't protect themselves. **Since there is evidence that this could be a likely or an unlikely consequence, we will mark it with a "?" That means it is uncertain if the consequence will happen.**

- **Let's go on to another consequence. We said a consequence of the mice letting the fox back into the office and finishing the job would be that the fox would decide to be a nice fox and not eat the mice. This would be a pro, a result that would make us want to choose the option. With your group, look back into the story and make a list of evidence, or clues, that shows this is likely or unlikely to happen. As you find evidence, discuss with your group whether the evidence shows the consequence is likely, unlikely, or uncertain to happen if the option is chosen by Dr. DeSoto and his wife.** Allow the groups to make lists of evidence, supporting them as needed. Make sure that students are discussing the evidence and whether it shows that the consequence is likely, unlikely, or uncertain. When the groups have completed this task, record the evidence as before. POSSIBLE STUDENT RESPONSES: *Mrs. DeSoto said, "Why should he harm us? We're helping him" (L). The fox is very polite (U). The fox keeps thinking about eating them (L). The fox dreamt he was eating the mice (U). Dr. Desoto says foxes are "wicked creatures."* After the evidence has been recorded and each piece has been marked to show if it supports (L) or does not support (U), the class should again address the third question on the thinking map.

- **We have found evidence that relates to this consequence, and we have marked whether it shows the consequence is likely or unlikely to happen. That answers the third question, "What evidence is there that the consequence will or won't happen?" What should we say in response to the fourth question, "Based on the evidence, how likely is this consequence?"** As a class, discuss the responses and the likelihood of the consequence. In this case, the class should conclude this consequence to be unlikely to occur.

- **Just as we worked on the first two consequences, we will now continue with the third and the fourth.** Continue to work in the same pattern for the first two consequences. POSSIBLE STUDENT RESPONSES: <u>Fox will gobble up Dr. Desoto and his wife</u>. *Dr. DeSoto says foxes are too dangerous to treat (L). The mice are smart (U). They protected themselves the first time (L). The fox said the mice were "tasty morsels" (U). The fox tried to eat them once, so he'll try again (U).* The class will say that this is an unlikely consequence or that it is uncertain based on all the evidence. POSSIBLE STUDENT RESPONSES: <u>Fox will hurt them.</u> *The DeSotos have tools to protect themselves (U). The mice are smart (U). The fox is bigger than the mice (L). The fox wants to eat Dr. and Mrs. DeSoto (L).*

- **In the final step of the thinking map, we want to consider whether this option is one we would advise the mice to choose. Should they let the fox in and finish the job? Let's consider the evidence and what it says about the consequences.** The students should recognize that they judged many of the consequences "uncertain" in their likelihood to occur. This presents a very teachable moment for the author's craft. Discuss with students why the author would like the option of letting the fox in to be one filled with uncertain consequences. If students don't recognize this as a deliberate ploy to make the story more exciting, work with them through guided questioning to reach this conclusion. **It seems the author has tried to create a puzzle within the story. We have found evidence that leaves us uncertain in predicting what will happen if the mice choose the option of letting the fox in and finishing the job. Based on the pros and cons and the likelihood of the consequences, can we say that this option is a wise one for the mice to choose?** POSSIBLE STUDENT RESPONSES: *It has risks, but the mice are smart and they will handle the fox. Dr. DeSoto said that he always finishes a job, so he will choose this option but he will have to be very careful. It could turn out to be a very dangerous thing for the mice to do.* **This uncertainty really makes a story fun to read! The suspense of not knowing if Dr. DeSoto and his wife will or won't be eaten keeps us involved in the plot of the story and wanting to read to discover what will happen.**

- **As we continue to read the story, think about the characters: Dr. DeSoto and his wife, and the fox. Did this activity help you learn more about them how they would handle difficult situations? We will see how well we made our predictions about the choices they would make as we finish the story.** At this point, the story should be finished. **We have finished the story, and the mice did, in fact, outfox the fox. Did the fox behave as you predicted he would?** *Yes.* **What did you learn about the fox that helped you to predict the way that he would behave?** POSSIBLE STUDENT RESPONSES: *He kept thinking about eating the mice, just like he did in the beginning of the book. He didn't like pain at all so I knew he would want the secret formula that stops all toothaches. The fox would have eaten the mice if they hadn't glued his mouth shut.* **Did Dr. DeSoto and his wife behave in the way that you thought they would?** *Yes.* **What did you know that helped you predict the things they would do?** POSSIBLE STUDENT RESPONSES: *They were always thinking about what would happen and how to make sure they were safe. They said they had a plan to trick the fox. They had things they could use to keep the fox from eating them. They were good thinkers! They thought about the best plan and made it work. They used things they had to help the fox, but they didn't really hurt him.*

THINKING ABOUT THINKING

- **What do we call the thinking that we did today?** The students should be able to recognize the thinking as predicting the consequences of options.

- **In this activity, we considered the characters and tried to predict the consequences of the options that they had. What steps did we follow as we made our predictions?** The students should go through the steps of the thinking map.

- **Why is this a good way to think about the consequences of options when you have to make a decision?** POSSIBLE STUDENT RESPONSES: *It is good to predict what will happen with each option before you choose the one that is best. Then you won't do something dangerous.*

- **Were the thinking map and graphic organizer for predicting the consequences of options helpful in your thinking?** ANSWERS VARY. Usually students point out how the questions on the thinking map helped them remember what they should think about and the graphic organizer was a good place to write the evidence so they could remember.

Immediate Transfer

- In the story *Peter Rabbit,* Peter made a decision that involved great risk. Use the thinking map and graphic organizer for predicting the consequences of options to learn more about Peter and the kind of rabbit he was.

- In the story "Jack and the Beanstalk," Jack made a lot of decisions that involved great risk. Use the thinking map and graphic organizer for predicting the consequences of options to learn more about Jack and the kind of person he was.

- Consider this situation: The school has eliminated all playground toys and has announced that toys from home may now be brought for use during recess. Use the graphic organizer and thinking map for predicting the consequences of options to determine the likely the results of this new option. What would be ways to eliminate any problems you predict will occur?

Reinforcement Later

- Had Goldilocks predicted the consequences of entering the cottage of the three bears, she may have made a different choice. Certainly, entering a strange home is a risky thing to do! Use the thinking map for predicting the consequences of options to help her think through the options. You may find that you learn something about Goldilocks. Do you like her? Why or why not?

- Suppose that there is trouble brewing in your group. You have a big important project to complete and one of the group members is not behaving. Consider the options for the group. Predict the consequences of the options using the thinking map and graphic organizer for predicting the consequences of options. What will be the best option for your group to choose in this very serious situation?

WRITING EXTENSION

I want you to consider the fox and the way that he left Dr. DeSoto's office. Things did not work out as he thought they would. The fox is probably thinking of how he could still come back and eat the mice. Consider what might happen if the fox returns to Dr. DeSoto's office after the glue wears off. Use a graphic organizer for predicting the consequences of options as a prewriting map for a letter to Mr. Fox advising him of the consequences that may occur if he comes back and tries to have a mice dinner. This activity could be done individually, in small groups, or as a blend of these. It could be supported by having the class fill in a new graphic organizer that would consider this new scenario. Students could then write letters to the fox. For students who struggle with writing, provide a tape recorder to tape messages that can be sent as letters to the fox. Both groups would use the graphic organizer as a map for their work.

SUGGESTED SPECIAL NEEDS MODIFICATIONS

<u>Frontload</u>: The notion of prediction in this lesson may differ from the sort of prediction students are accustomed to using. In reading, for example, students may be accustomed to using a given set of clues (title, illustrations, etc.,) to predict story events. In this lesson, students must anticipate consequences of actions that have not yet taken place. To do this, they must rely on prior knowledge and text clues, or "evidence," as well as form a judgment. To prepare students for this type of complex thinking prior to this lesson, the teacher may use several examples from daily life. For example, the teacher may lead a discussion or think aloud about the consequences of choices in bringing a type of birthday treat, selecting a recess game, deciding on which task to do first, or planning a class event. In presenting these examples, the teacher should also model ways to determine the likelihood of a consequence. "Likelihood" can sometimes be expressed as a pattern, such as, "Every Friday we have had pizza in the cafeteria and students have said it was good. It is likely that a pizza party for our class next Friday would be enjoyable." Often students equate "consequences" with a negative result. It is important that the teacher model positive consequences of actions and decisions, as well negative consequences.

<u>Diversify</u>: Special needs students are often aided by working in cooperative groups, especially if students are trained in the skill to include all group members in the discussion and if the tasks are divided relative to each student's strengths. For example, a skillful note taker can honor everyone's ideas and reduce the writing task for some.

<u>Expand the Possibilities</u>: Assessments of written responses may be based upon students' thinking first, and expressive skills second. Oral responses may also reveal thinking beyond students' ability to express themselves in writing.

ASSESSING STUDENT THINKING ABOUT PREDICTING CONSEQUENCES

To assess how skillfully students predict the likelihood of consequences in a decision-making context, present a decision-making problem that involves a situation that is risky or serious in nature. Provide the thinking map and graphic organizers for predicting the consequences of options. Observe and question the students as they work through the steps of the strategy. Depending on the skills of the students, the assessment can take a written or oral form. Students should explain their response to the final question on the thinking map, telling why it is or is not wise to choose the option.

Sample Student Responses • To Help or Not to Help?

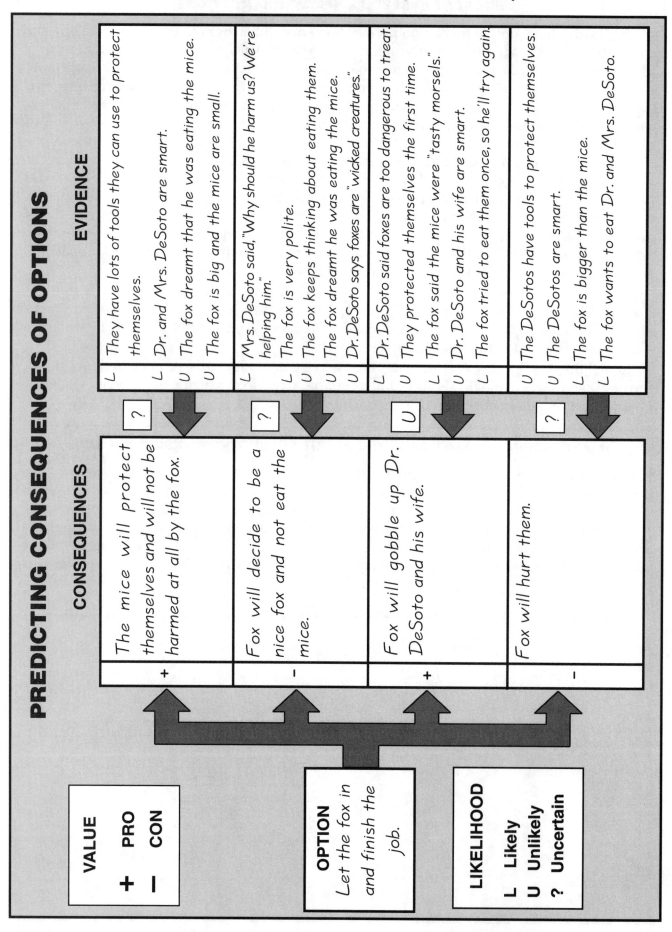

PREDICTING CONSEQUENCES OF OPTIONS

EVIDENCE

?
- L They have lots of tools they can use to protect themselves.
- L Dr. and Mrs. DeSoto are smart.
- U The fox dreamt that he was eating the mice.
- U The fox is big and the mice are small.

?
- L Mrs. DeSoto said, "Why should he harm us? We're helping him."
- L The fox is very polite.
- U The fox keeps thinking about eating them.
- U The fox dreamt he was eating the mice.
- U Dr. DeSoto says foxes are "wicked creatures."

U
- L Dr. DeSoto said foxes are too dangerous to treat.
- U They protected themselves the first time.
- L The fox said the mice were "tasty morsels."
- U Dr. DeSoto and his wife are smart.
- L The fox tried to eat them once, so he'll try again.

?
- U The DeSotos have tools to protect themselves.
- U The DeSotos are smart.
- L The fox is bigger than the mice.
- L The fox wants to eat Dr. and Mrs. DeSoto.

CONSEQUENCES

+ The mice will protect themselves and will not be harmed at all by the fox.

– Fox will decide to be a nice fox and not eat the mice.

+ Fox will gobble up Dr. DeSoto and his wife.

– Fox will hurt them.

VALUE

+ PRO

– CON

+

–

OPTION
Let the fox in and finish the job.

LIKELIHOOD

L Likely
U Unlikely
? Uncertain

Sample Student Letter • To Help or Not to Help?

Dear Fox,

We think that you are planning to sneak back into Dr. DeSoto's to eat the mice. That is not a good idea. You are not thinking about the consequences. If you go back and try to sneak in the mice will see you because they look out their window. They have lots of things they can use to trick you again. They probably already have a trick ready for you. If you do get in, there will be another patient. Everyone likes Dr. DeSoto so they will help him to escape. They will save Mrs. DeSoto, too. It is not a good idea for you to go back. Just give it up!

Sincerely,

_____

SKILLFUL PREDICTION

1. What might happen?

2. What clues do you have for thinking it might happen?

3. Based on the clues, how likely is it that it will happen?

PREDICTING THE CONSEQUENCES OF OPTIONS

1. What consequences might result from this option?

2. Does each consequence count for or against choosing this option?

3. What evidence is there that the consequence will or won't happen?

4. Based on the evidence, how likely is each consequence?

5. Based on the likelihood of the consequences, is it wise to choose this option?

SKILLFUL PREDICTION
PREDICTIONS

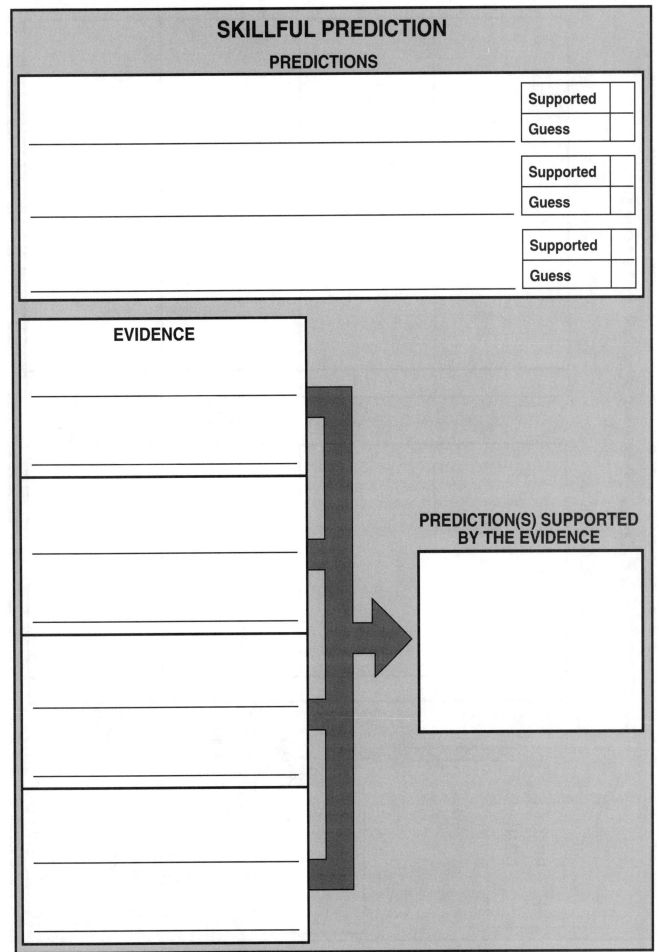

Supported	
Guess	

Supported	
Guess	

Supported	
Guess	

EVIDENCE

**PREDICTION(S) SUPPORTED
BY THE EVIDENCE**

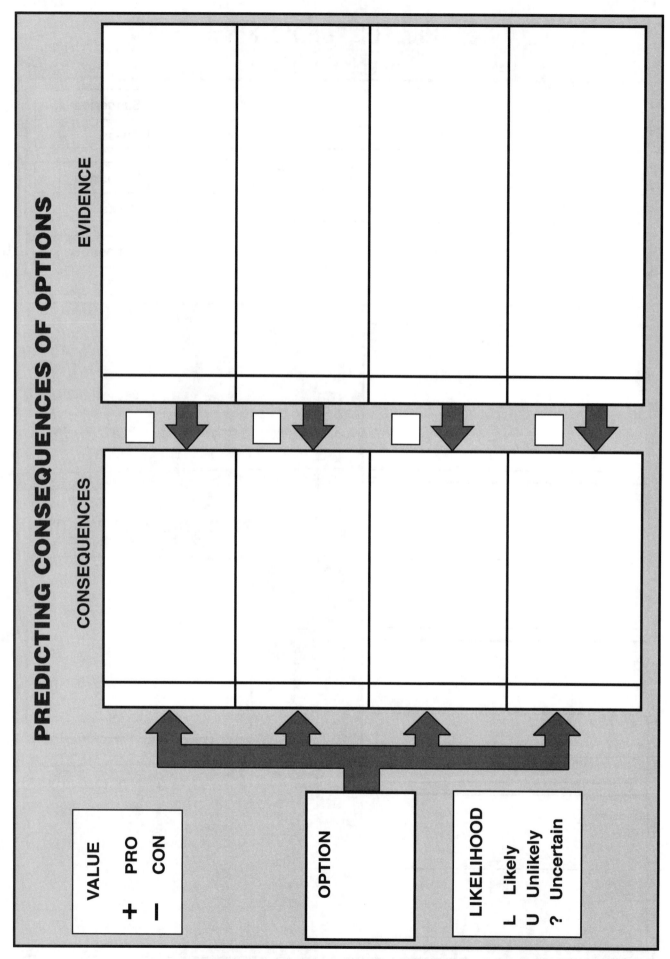

CHAPTER 16
GENERALIZATION

Infusing Skillful Generalization into Language Arts

Teaching students skillful generalization in grades 1 and 2 involves helping them learn to analyze and assess information based on generalizations that someone else or they themselves have made. Students analyze by asking and carefully answering the following questions before accepting generalizations:

SKILLFUL GENERALIZATION

1. What generalization is suggested?

2. What sample is being used to support the generalization?

3. Is the sample being used large enough?

4. Is the sample being used like the whole group?

5. Is the generalization well supported by the sample?

6. If not, what additional information is needed to support the generalization?

---

figure 16.1

In the lessons in this chapter, this thinking map is used to guide your students' thinking explicitly as they engage with the lesson content.

When students learn and use this strategy for thinking about their generalizations, they focus their attention not so much on the generalizations themselves but rather on the information on which the generalizations are based. Usually, generalizations like "Dr. Seuss stories are all fantasies" are based on a sampling of what the generalizations are about, in this case some of Dr. Seuss' stories. In most cases of generalizations, even though they are about all things of a certain sort, a person cannot sample all of the items. In skillful generalization, students are asked to identify the sample that the generalization in question is based on and to determine whether it is strong enough to make the generalization reasonable. Once again, an inference is involved, this time from "Some..." to "All...." Sometimes

this is a good inference, sometimes not. Students have to think about whether the sample is large enough and whether it is representative enough of the whole group. If so, then the generalization is well supported; if not, then it is not. In developing this skill, students can easily identify cases in which people make hasty generalizations, and they can learn to avoid these themselves. Moreover, they learn that biases and prejudices are sometimes rooted in faulty generalizations from skewed samples.

The lesson on generalization in this book also supplements the use of this thinking map with various supporting classroom strategies such as using a graphic organizer, engaging in cooperative thinking, thinking about thinking, and continued guided practice. These classroom strategies enhance both the thinking skill that the students are learning and their mastery of the lesson content.

The key graphic organizer for skillful generalization is in figure 16.2.

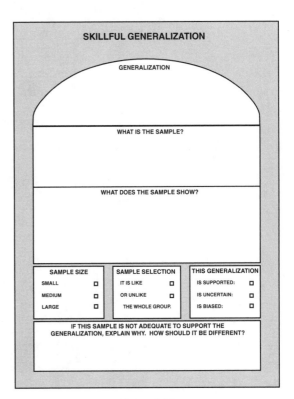

figure 16.2

This graphic organizer helps students record what the generalization is, what sample it is based on, what the sample shows, and then to assess whether the sample is too small or too nonrepresentative. But it also gives students a place to design a better sampling technique that would provide support for the generalization. Reproducible blank graphic organizers are found at the end of each chapter.

For more in-depth information on teaching skillful generalization, please refer to Chapter 15 in the book *Infusing the Teaching of Critical and Creative Thinking into Elementary Instruction*, by Robert Swartz and Sandra Parks. A computer disk containing the blank, reproducible graphic organizers used in this book is also available. Both book and disk are available through Critical Thinking Books & Software.

VOWEL SOUNDS

Language Arts   **Grades 1–2**

OBJECTIVES

CONTENT	**THINKING SKILL/PROCESS**
Students will identify the sounds made by the vowels and the generalizations made about these letters.	Students will learn to evaluate generalizations and develop samples that would provide support for an accurate generalization.

METHODS AND MATERIALS

CONTENT	**THINKING SKILL/PROCESS**
Students will search in written material for a variety of words containing a specific vowel letter and/or sound. They then examine the vowel sound within the words to see if particular patterns, or generalizations, arise. Last, students look for support for their generalizations in other written material.	An explicit thinking map, graphic organizers, and structured questioning emphasize a thinking strategy for well-founded generalization. Collaborative learning enhances the learning.

LESSON

INTRODUCTION TO CONTENT AND THINKING SKILL/PROCESS

- **Last week my friend tried a sandwich at the new sandwich shop near her home. She really liked it, so she told her friends that the sandwiches at this shop were great. Do you think this was a good way to decide that the sandwiches at this shop are great?** Some students will say that this was a good way to decide, but most of the students will disagree, saying that the shop may have only one or two good sandwiches, and the rest are not very good. They may point out that she should know more about the other sandwiches first. **Trying just one sandwich probably isn't a good way to decide that all the sandwiches at the shop are great.**

- **What you've been doing is discussing a** *generalization.* Write the word "generalization" on the chalkboard or on a chart. **A generalization is a statement that says something that is true of** *all* **things of a certain sort. When my friend said that the sandwiches in the shop were great, she meant that** *all* **the sandwiches at the shop were great. "All the sandwiches at the shop are great" is the generalization we've been discussing. With your group, list three more generalizations.** Have the students work together in groups of three or four. Write six to ten of their generalizations on the board, asking for only one generalization per group. POSSIBLE STUDENT RESPONSES: *All the students in the school are nice. All candy is sweet. All balls can bounce. All backpacks have straps. All desks have legs.*

- **Think about this for a minute. How can we find out whether a generalization is one that we can accept? Sometimes generalizations are not right. If I said that all the students in this school had brown hair would that be right?** *No.* **So if someone said that to you, how could you find out if it was right?** Students often suggest the obvious answer, that you look at all the students in the school to see if anyone doesn't have brown hair. **Sometimes we can look at everything in a group if it's small enough and easy to find, but you can't always do that. For example, if my friend tried to check out all of the sandwiches in order to tell whether her** generalization is a good one, what would she have to do, and could she actually do it? Most students recognize that that means she would have to eat all of the sandwiches, and they realize that she couldn't do that. **Can you think of some generalizations you can't check out by simply looking? Think about some of the generalizations you have already identified. Are there some that wouldn't work by simply looking? Talk to your partner and try to come up with at least two generalizations that wouldn't work.** After a few minutes, ask for one example per group that volunteers. POSSIBLE STUDENT RESPONSES: *All candy is sweet. All balls can bounce. All backpacks have straps. All desks have legs. All teachers are women. All school buses are yellow.*

• **Let's think about the sandwich shop again. What specifically could my friend do in order to be able to tell us something about all the sandwiches? She can't try them all, and trying one isn't enough. What could she do?** Ask for volunteers from the class to respond. POSSIBLE STUDENT RESPONSES: *Go back to the shop and try different sandwiches every time. Order a bunch of sandwiches and ask her friends to come and eat them. She could eat a sampling. She could eat some of them, maybe one of each kind, but she couldn't do that all at once.* If no student comes up with the idea of eating a sample of each kind, suggest this idea to the class. **So maybe she could** *sample* **some of them and get an idea about what they are like. Maybe we can tell that our generalizations are probably good ones if we check out a smaller** *sample*—only *some* **of the sandwiches, but not all of them, are like the different kinds of sandwiches that the sandwich shop makes. A good sample includes a good variety from the group. That is important. Picking only ham sandwiches would not tell about all the other kinds.**

• **In this lesson, we are going to try out these ideas and see if we can make some good generalizations. To help us, let's use this thinking map for skillful generalizations. It includes the ideas we have just came up with about the kind of sample that can help us generalize.** Show the thinking map to the group. Use a chart-sized copy posted on the wall or a flip chart, or write it on the board, so that it will be visible to students throughout the lesson. With students, go over the questions on the map, referring to the example of the sandwich shop. **This thinking map will help us to make sure that the generalizations we work with are based on good samples and therefore are probably good generalizations.**

SKILLFUL GENERALIZATION

1. What generalization is suggested?

2. What sample is being used to support the generalization?

3. Is the sample being used large enough?

4. Is the sample being used like the whole group?

5. Is the generalization well supported by the sample?

6. If not, what additional information is needed to support the generalization?

THINKING ACTIVELY

• We often make generalizations in our lives. **In science, when we study weather, it is not necessary for us to study every cloud in the sky. We look at samples of the clouds and the kinds of weather produced by each kind of cloud. We can then make generalizations about the different kinds of weather that are caused by different clouds. In math, we estimate by making a generalization about the amount of space one set fills. One set of ten teddy bear counters fills one fourth of the container, so four sets, or 40 teddy bears would be needed to fill the container.** Draw a diagram of this on the board. **Today we are going to look at the way that generalizations are used in learning how to say letter sounds in words.**

• Let's think about vowels. In our reading, we have learned that vowels make different sounds. Today we are going to look at a group of words to see what sound specific vowels make. We will try to figure out when they make these sounds. To begin our lesson, we will collect some words. You will be working in groups again. Each group will be assigned a vowel and each person will be given paper on which to record the words that use the vowel. The recording sheet should be divided into boxes in which students can record the words they find. Have the students write the vowel for their group in the first box. Depending on the level of the group, you may want to stipulate the size of the words. They will need to be able to read the words they write. Because these sheets will be shared in their group, they should use markers and neat printing so that their work can be read by everyone. **Using any of the books in the classroom, I want you to fill your sheet with words that include your vowel. There may be other vowels in the word, that's fine. Try to find words that have the vowel in different places in the words, at the beginning, in the middle, or at the end. For instance, if you are in the "e" group, don't pick all of the words that have an "e" at the end. Find words where the "e" is in other places in the word, and write these different words in the boxes. We want as many different words as possible, so you will need to check with your group each time you find a word to make sure that no one else has already written that word on their sheet. When everyone in your group has filled his or her sheets, you can cut out the word boxes and put the words together in your own stack. This will be your word bank, the collection of words with the vowel you are working with.** As the sheets are filled and cut, ask the students to begin reading the words, listening for the sounds of the vowels. This should take no more than five minutes.

• Each group has created a large group of words. As we look at these words, think about the sounds of the vowels. We know that there are words with short vowel sounds and words with long vowel sounds. I'd like each student to read his or her list of words to their group. As the words are being read, divide them into two groups, those with a long vowel sound and those with a short vowel sound. Then think about these questions: What do you notice about the words with a long vowel sound in them? Are there any clues that let a reader know that the vowel will be long in that kind of word? What do you notice about the words with a short vowel sound in them? Is there a pattern in the words that gives you a clue that the vowel will be short? Are there any words in which the vowel you are looking at does not make a sound? What do you see about the placement of the silent vowel? Are there words in which the vowel is not long or short? Do you notice any patterns in these words? Allow time for discussion after each of these questions, first in the small groups and then as a class. Some groups will need support and guidance from the teacher. Monitor the groups closely, watching for a group that would be a good group to use for modeling. POSSIBLE STUDENT RESPONSES: *If an "o" is in the middle of two consonants, it will be a*

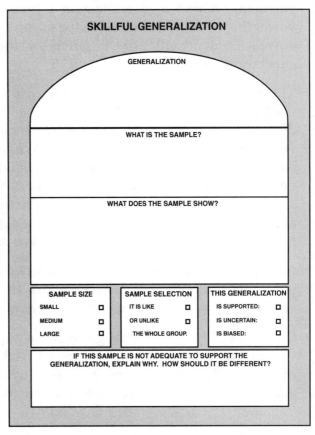

SKILLFUL GENERALIZATION

GENERALIZATION

WHAT IS THE SAMPLE?

WHAT DOES THE SAMPLE SHOW?

SAMPLE SIZE		SAMPLE SELECTION		THIS GENERALIZATION	
SMALL	☐	IT IS LIKE	☐	IS SUPPORTED:	☐
MEDIUM	☐	OR UNLIKE	☐	IS UNCERTAIN:	☐
LARGE	☐	THE WHOLE GROUP.	☐	IS BIASED:	☐

IF THIS SAMPLE IS NOT ADEQUATE TO SUPPORT THE GENERALIZATION, EXPLAIN WHY. HOW SHOULD IT BE DIFFERENT?

short sound. If an "i" is after an "a" it will be silent. When an "a" has a "y" after it, the vowel sound is long.

- **What kinds of statements are you making about the vowel sounds?** Usually students will recognize that they are making generalizations about vowels. If they don't, ask them if what they are doing is like what your friend did in the sandwich shop and then prompt them to identify what they are doing as generalizing. **I'd like each of the groups to pick one generalization to share with the class. I am giving each group a graphic organizer.** The graphic organizers should be on transparencies or on chart paper so that they can be shared with the other groups later in the lesson. **Follow the thinking map for skillful generalization as you use the graphic organizer.** Make sure the thinking map is visible to the whole class. **What is the first thing that we will write on the graphic organizer?** Students recognize that they should write the generalization on the "dome" of the graphic organizer. If they have difficulty, tell them that there is a place at the top for the generalization you have picked. To model this, call on one of the groups to share their generalization, supporting them by repeating the questions about the things they noticed about the words. For example, they may find a consonant-vowel-consonant pattern. Here is a possible exchange between students and teacher: **What did you notice about one of the vowels in your words?** *We have a big group of words that all have short "i" sounds.* **Are there any other things that you have noticed about these words?** *The words all have three letters with "i" in the middle, and the other two letters are consonants.* **What is your generalization from this information?** *We think that if there is a consonant, then an "i," then another consonant, the "i" will always make the short "i" sound.*

- **Look back at the words to make sure that the generalization fits the words that you are using. If the generalization is about a vowel that is short, for example, you should make sure that all the words you use have that short vowel sound in them. This is the group of words that you base your generalization on, so all the words in the group should be like the words you mention in your generalization. If there are words in your group that do not have a short vowel they would not belong in the group you use to make your generalization about short vowels.** Students will need to group together the words they are using for their particular generalization.

- **The next box on your graphic organizer is for you to describe the group of words that you used to make your generalization. Do you remember what this group is called?** Most students will remember that this is called the sample group. If they don't, tell them. **In this box, write about the sample you collected. Where did you get your words?** *We found them in the books in our room.* **So I think we can all say that the words came from our books. What else can you say about this sample?** POSSIBLE STUDENT RESPONSE: *The ones that made the sound that we are checking went into this group.* **Write the vowel sound that you wrote the generalization about. For example, you could say that the sample is all the words that have a short "i" sound that are from the books in the room.** Allow students time to write.

- **Now you should write what you've learned about the sample in the next box. For example, you could write that you discovered that the words in the sample are all ones in which the vowel "i" appears between two consonants.** Allow students time to write.

- **Do you think you have enough words to support the generalization you've made? Perhaps you have a generalization about long vowel "a," but your group only has ten words with a long "a" in them. Is this enough, or do you need to get a bigger sample? Talk together in your groups and check the boxes you think are the right ones to check about whether the sample**

you used is good enough to make this a good generalization. If you think you need more words, explain that in the bottom box. If the students feel that they should find more words, provide them with some guidance before sending them to look for more words. They need to concentrate on looking for words with the same pattern to see if they confirm the generalization or not. Those groups who feel confident that they can support their generalization can choose another generalization to explore. Allow plenty of time for students to explore the words and test their generalizations. As an extra challenge, have them include their own names in the word bank.

- **It is time for us to share the work we have done. Each group will have a chance to show the class the generalization they have been exploring. If the people in the group feel that they need to look at more words, I will be their secretary and record their ideas about how to make the sample better on the bottom part of their graphic organizer. As each group reports, we will look at the thinking map for generalizations to make sure we are answering all of the important questions to ask when we think about generalizations.** Using the overhead transparencies or chart copies of the graphic organizer for skillful generalization, have each group share the following information: the vowel they examined, the generalization they made about that vowel, the sample that was used, and the results shown by the sample. This will fill in the top boxes of the graphic organizer. As needed, support the groups in the recording process. The bottom of the graphic is the assessment piece for their generalization. Students should discuss with their group and the class what they have found and determine if the generalization is supported, is questionable, or is not supported. POSSIBLE STUDENT RESPONSE: *Our generalization was, "<u>When an 'e' is at the end of a word that is bigger than three letters, it is silent.</u>" We looked in our favorite books to get lots of words. The ones we used all had "e" at the end. We listened to the sounds that the "e" made to see if it was silent. All of the words had a silent "e" at the end. The sample is large and has many words, but they all came from just a few books in our library, and the generalization is about every word in English that ends in "e." Maybe we need to look at things other than books, like letters and signs. Our generalization was "<u>Short words with an 'i' in the middle have a short 'i' sound.</u>" We found some words like this in the books we looked in, and all of the words we found had a short "i" sound, but we think we need to get more to make sure we are right.*

- **How will the work we've done with vowels and generalizations help us as we read and write?** POSSIBLE STUDENT RESPONSE: *When we come to a new word, we will know which sound will probably be the sound that the vowel makes. It makes it easier if you know what the sound is going to be because of the letters that are in the word.* **We did find some words that did not fit the generalization. If the generalization is true for many words, is it good to think about it as we learn to read new words?** POSSIBLE STUDENT RESPONSE: *Yes, because we can try the sound that the letter probably makes first. If it doesn't make sense, we will know that there must be another sound it makes. We shouldn't just trust the generalization if it doesn't make sense in the word. We can try other sounds then. When it makes sense and makes a word, we will know we have the right sound.* **Although we have found some times when a generalization is not true for vowels, there are many generalizations that give us clues about the sounds the letters probably make. The letter "o" has certain sounds that we know it makes. The letter "a" has other sounds that we know it makes. If we know the generalizations about the different sounds that the letter "o" or the letter "a" makes, we will be able to use those sounds to help us pronounce new words.**

THINKING ABOUT THINKING

- **What do we call this kind of thinking?** *Generalization.*

- **What questions were important to answer as you did this kind of thinking?** POSSIBLE STUDENT RESPONSE: *What generalization are we making? How big is the sample? Is there a good variety in the sample? Is the sample like the whole group?* Students should include the questions from the thinking map.

- **Is it good to support generalizations? Why?** Students should recognize that they want to rely on only generalizations that they know are probably true. If they don't recognize this, ask them what would happen if they relied on a generalization that was false. Go back to the sandwich shop example to support this.

- **One thing that you found out is that you usually can't check up on a generalization by sampling all of the things that it covers. If a friend asked you what the best way was to check up on the generalization you made about words and vowel sounds, what would you advise him or her?** POSSIBLE STUDENT RESPONSE: *If we couldn't check all the words in the world, we could check a group—that is the sample. If we picked only ten words, the sample would not be big enough. If we tried to use 10,000 words, the sample would be too big.*

- **Was the thinking map helpful as you made the generalizations?** Most students say that the thinking map is a good guide to tell them what they need to do.

APPLYING YOUR THINKING

Immediate Transfer

- **Find the list of school rules in the handbook. Write some generalizations about the reasons for the school rules and how they are made. Use the thinking map and graphic organizer for skillful generalizations to help you with your thinking.**

- **Think about the birthday parties that you have been to and the things that you did there. Are there any generalizations you could make? What would you need to do to make a skillful generalization?**

Reinforcement Later

- **Collect weather information for your town for a month. What generalizations can you make about weather for that month? How many days would need to be in your sample? Which days would you choose? What other questions would you need to think about?**

- **We have been talking to many of the senior citizens we know. Are there any generalizations we can make about the way things were when they were in first grade? Use the thinking map and graphic organizer for skillful generalizations to help you with your thinking.**

SUGGESTED SPECIAL NEEDS MODIFICATIONS

<u>Frontload:</u> Some students may need help distinguishing between the concepts of "all" and "some." It requires a preciseness in thinking and expressing oneself. Concrete examples may be useful in highlighting this distinction. Students may arrange books by attributes, such as, "all reading books" or "all picture books." Then the students can be lead into a discussion which introduces the concept of "some" using the frame, "All these are picture books. Some have blue covers, some are square, and some are rectangle. But all the books are picture books." This process can be used in sorting and discussing other objects.

Similarly, the idea of a sample being like or unlike the total population can be used with concrete objects. Given a set of objects, like a set of gloves, what might the set tell us about "all" gloves? Are these gloves different in some ways from other gloves (work gloves, gardening gloves, sport gloves)?

Streamline: The expectations for some students can be streamlined by preselecting a few vowel patterns on which students will work. For example, the teacher may have materials which feature only the specific vowel patterns being reinforced and allow students to generate their generalizations based on samples of these patterns.

Diversify: The task load for students for whom fine motor tasks are challenging can be reduced by allowing students to select and sort word cards, rather than print and cut words copied from books. Another option is to pair students with a partner proficient in fine motor skills who can serve as the group's recorder. Oral interaction with these students can help them articulate their understanding. It is important that the thinking take precedence over the writing for these students.

Some students may benefit from a greater degree of teacher guidance. The teacher may wish to provide an additional teacher guided model of the process of making generalizations about a vowel pattern before asking students to generate their own on other patterns.

Special needs students are often aided by working in cooperative groups. Establish an atmosphere in which all answers are initially accepted in such groups. Additional time may be needed for the students to complete the graphic organizer.

Expand the Possibilities: Assessments of written responses may be based upon student's thinking first, and expressive skills second. Oral responses may also reveal thinking beyond students' ability to express themselves in writing.

ASSESSING STUDENT THINKING ABOUT GENERALIZATIONS

Ask the students to think about a generalization they've heard. A list could be made of generalizations suggested by the group. Allow the students to choose a generalization and support it or explain how the support should be improved. They should use the ideas from the thinking map in their explanation.

Sample Student Responses • Vowel Sounds

SKILLFUL GENERALIZATION

GENERALIZATION

When an "e" is at the end of a word bigger than two letters, it is silent.

WHAT IS THE SAMPLE?

We looked in our favorite books and made a list of 25 words with more than two letters and "e" at the end.

WHAT DOES THE SAMPLE SHOW?

The words all had a silent "e" sound at the end.

SAMPLE SIZE		SAMPLE SELECTION		THIS GENERALIZATION	
SMALL	☐	IT IS LIKE	☐	IS SUPPORTED:	☐
MEDIUM	☐	OR UNLIKE	☒	IS UNCERTAIN:	☒
LARGE	☒	THE WHOLE GROUP.		IS BIASED:	☐

IF THIS SAMPLE IS NOT ADEQUATE TO SUPPORT THE GENERALIZATION, EXPLAIN WHY. HOW SHOULD IT BE DIFFERENT?

We need to look at more words not just from books but from letters and signs.

SKILLFUL GENERALIZATION

1. **What generalization is suggested?**

2. **What sample is being used to support the generalization?**

3. **Is the sample being used large enough?**

4. **Is the sample being used like the whole group?**

5. **Is the generalization well supported by the sample?**

6. **If not, what additional information is needed to support the generalization?**

SKILLFUL GENERALIZATION

GENERALIZATION

WHAT IS THE SAMPLE?

WHAT DOES THE SAMPLE SHOW?

SAMPLE SIZE		SAMPLE SELECTION		THIS GENERALIZATION	
SMALL	☐	IT IS LIKE	☐	IS SUPPORTED:	☐
MEDIUM	☐	OR UNLIKE	☐	IS UNCERTAIN:	☐
LARGE	☐	THE WHOLE GROUP.		IS BIASED:	☐

IF THIS SAMPLE IS NOT ADEQUATE TO SUPPORT THE GENERALIZATION, EXPLAIN WHY. HOW SHOULD IT BE DIFFERENT?

CHAPTER 17
REASONING BY ANALOGY

Infusing Skillful Reasoning by Analogy into Language Arts

Teaching students skillful reasoning by analogy in grades 1 and 2 involves helping them learn how to use analogies to infer conclusions about other things that they cannot determine the truth of directly. They can also do so by asking and carefully answering the following questions about these analogies:

REASONING BY ANALOGY

1. **What is similar to the object?**

2. **How are they similar?**

3. **What do the things I know about B help me to understand more about A?**

4. **Are there any important differences which stand in the way of the conclusion?**

---

figure 17.1

This is the thinking map for skillful reasoning by analogy. In the lesson in this chapter, this thinking map is used to guide your students' thinking explicitly as they engage with the lesson content.

When students learn and use this strategy for thinking about what they can learn about something by studying something else that is analogous, they have to make sure that the two things are sufficiently alike, but they also have to make sure that there aren't any differences between the two things that stand in the way of drawing certain kinds of conclusions about the first thing based on the analogy. Many people draw conclusions based on analogies simply because of the similarities without attending to possible differences that may be significant.

This lesson also supplements the use of this thinking map with various supporting classroom strategies such as using a graphic organizer, engaging in cooperative thinking, thinking about thinking, and continued guided practice. These classroom strategies enhance both the thinking skill that the students are learning and their mastery of the lesson content.

The key graphic organizer for skillful reasoning by analogy is in figure 17.2.

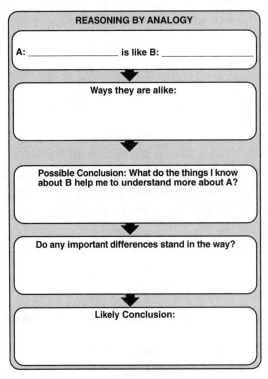

figure 17.2

This graphic organizer helps students record relevant similarities that make the analogy, which is written at the top of the diagram, seem like a good one. They then write tentative conclusions about the first object that are suggested by the analogy and record whether or not there are differences that make a difference in accepting the tentative conclusions. If not, then the tentative conclusions are affirmed as good conclusions to draw; if so, they are not. Reproducible blank graphic organizers are found at the end of each chapter.

For more in-depth information on teaching skillful decision making, please refer to Chapter 16 in the book *Infusing the Teaching of Critical and Creative Thinking into Elementary Instruction*, by Robert Swartz and Sandra Parks. A computer disk containing the blank, reproducible graphic organizers used in this book is also available. Both book and disk are available through Critical Thinking Books & Software.

HOW DOES THAT BEAK WORK?

Language Arts   **Grades 1–2**

OBJECTIVES

CONTENT	THINKING SKILL/PROCESS
Students will learn that a bird's beak is used as a tool in much the same ways as common hand tools are used.	Students will learn what an analogy is, how to specify the ways in which analogous things are similar, and to determine whether ideas suggested by an analogy are accurate by noting any important differences.

METHODS AND MATERIALS

CONTENT	THINKING SKILL/PROCESS
Students will work together in pairs to read nonfiction material about different types of birds. They will use a variety of hand tools to help them think about the ways that birds use their beaks.	Structured questioning, the use of a graphic organizer, and a thinking map guide the students through reasoning by analogy. Collaborative groups support the students in their learning.

LESSON

INTRODUCTION TO CONTENT AND THINKING SKILL/PROCESS

- When we were learning about dinosaurs, we wanted to understand the ways that they behaved, but because they were on our earth so long ago, we needed to compare them to things that we knew more about. As we studied *Tyrannosaurus Rex*'s teeth, we learned that scientists compared them to very sharp steak knives. How did this help you to understand T. Rex's teeth and the way the dinosaur used them for eating? POSSIBLE STUDENT RESPONSES: *I knew that steak knives have jagged edges to make it easier to cut meat. Since T. Rex is a meat eater, his teeth must have worked like a knife to eat meat because they had edges like a steak knife.* **We could make a conclusion about the eating behaviors of this dinosaur by comparing his teeth to something familiar to us. We know how it helps to have a sharp knife for cutting meat, and we know that the jagged edges make cutting the meat easier. Since the dinosaur fossils show us that the T. Rex's teeth were sharp with jagged edges and very similar to steak knives, scientists can make the conclusion that this probably was a dinosaur that used its teeth to cut meat in a manner similar to the way a steak knife cuts through meat. What the scientists were doing was using a special comparison to explain something. This special comparison is called an "analogy" and the thinking that scientists have done with this comparison is called "reasoning by analogy."** Write the words "reasoning by analogy" on the chalkboard or a chart. **To make an analogy, we must find things that are alike in important ways. Then using those important similarities, we can reason that what is true about something we know about is likely to be true about the other thing.**

- **To help you understand this way of thinking, I want you to try to do some reasoning by analogy yourself.** (This analogy assumes that the students have had previous lessons on germs and their spread as part of their health curriculum. If they have not, it could be used but would need more details about germs to help support the analogy.) **Let's pretend we are doctors and nurses who are concerned by the many absences in the local schools. We want to help chil-**

dren understand more about the ways that germs can be spread. **One of our group of health professionals has developed an analogy that should help children understand more about the way that germs are spread. She wants us to compare wet sand to germs on our hands. This is the experiment recommended to demonstrate the analogy.** Show students the materials for the experiment. **I have bowls of water, sand, and crackers. These will be used to demonstrate the analogy that will help the children understand more about the problem of germs being spread.** Have several volunteers come up to the front demonstration area. One child should dip his hands in the water and then in the sand. **What do you notice about our volunteer's hand right now?** POSSIBLE STUDENT RESPONSE: *He has sand stuck all over his hands.* **The sand on our volunteer's hand is similar to germs that can be stuck on our hands. This is the analogy we are going to use to understand more about germs. This experiment compares wet sand stuck on a person's hands to germs. Now I'd like our volunteer to pass out crackers to the rest of our volunteers. What do you notice about the crackers that he is passing out to the others?** POSSIBLE STUDENT RESPONSES: There *is sand stuck on the crackers. The sand came off of his hands.* **What will this analogy teach the students at the local schools about germs?** POSSIBLE STUDENT RESPONSES: *They will see that germs can stick to their hands and then be passed on to other people by the things that they touch.* **Will this analogy help students understand how they can spread germs?** POSSIBLE STUDENT RESPONSES: *Yes. I don't want to eat crackers with sand all over them, and I don't want to eat crackers with germs on them either.* **What should we have our "germ-spreader" do to show how to get rid of the sand, or the germs, on his hands?** POSSIBLE STUDENT RESPONSES: *He should wash his hands carefully with soap and water. Then the sand will be gone, just like the germs.* **The experiment will help the children reach a conclusion, a statement of something they have learned, by making an analogy between the two things. In your groups, talk about the conclusion they will reach.** The students usually quickly come to the conclusion that washing your hands carefully with soap and water will help prevent the spread of germs. **They will be able to <u>reason</u> from the <u>analogy</u> that they should wash their hands to help prevent the spread of germs. The conclusion is based on your reasoning by analogy.**

- **We do have to be careful in using reasoning by analogy. Sometimes there are important differences between two things that make it wrong to accept a conclusion about one based on knowledge about the other. For example, think for a minute about animals with shells. What animals would fit into this group?** POSSIBLE STUDENT RESPONSES: *turtles, lobsters, oysters, snails.* **Some people have made the analogy between the shells of these animals and houses. In houses, one can usually find rooms and furniture. Can we conclude that there are rooms and furniture inside the shells of these animals?** Students usually say no. **Why?** Students usually respond that the shells are really parts of the animal and are not buildings like houses are. **That's an example of an important difference that shows that you can't make the conclusion from the analogy. So it's always worth thinking about whether there are important differences between the things that are analogous before you accept a conclusion.**

- **Here is a thinking map that will help us as we use reasoning by analogy in our learning.** On a chart or the chalkboard, show the reasoning by analogy thinking map. **There are four questions we can work through as we do this kind of thinking. First, we should look for important similarities between the thing we want to learn about and something else. What can we think about that may help us understand more about that thing we want to learn**

REASONING BY ANALOGY

1. **What is similar to the object?**
2. **How are they similar?**
3. **How do the things I know about B help me to understand more about A?**
4. **Are there any important differences which stand in the way of the conclusion?**

about? In the case of the dinosaur's teeth it was the steak knife. Second, we need to identify the ways that they are similar. We did that with the teeth and the knife, finding several important ways that they were alike. The third question asks us to think about what things we know about B, or the steak knife in our example, that will help us to understand more about A, the dinosaur's teeth. We thought about the way that the knife is used to cut meat. That could lead to a conclusion. Before we actually make the conclusion, we must be sure there are no important differences that would stand in the way of our conclusion. We can make the conclusion because the teeth of the dinosaur really are like the knives we use for cutting steak. In this analogy, there were no important differences that would stand in the way. Finally, we must decide what conclusion we can make based on the analogy. For the dinosaur analogy, we said that the dinosaur used its teeth to cut the meat of its prey when it ate. Go back to the sand analogy, fitting the thinking map questions to the example to further model the process.

• Today we will be reasoning by analogy to understand more about the ways that birds' beaks are designed by nature to help them survive. To understand how this happens, we can look for things that are similar to beaks in important ways. Comparing birds' beaks to something that we already know about that is similar to beaks in important ways will help us to understand more about the ways birds use their beaks and how their beaks help them to survive.

THINKING ACTIVELY

• Reasoning by analogy can be very helpful to us in understanding animals and the ways they survive. Comparing things about animals to things we know and understand in our world can help us make conclusions. We are able to see why two items are similar. From the comparison we can go on to the very important final step, reaching a new understanding about the animals based on the comparison, the analogy, that we have made. That is the conclusion, that new thing we know because of our comparison. On the chalkboard under "Reasoning by Analogy" write "analogy (arrow pointing to) understanding (arrow pointing to) conclusion." In our work today, we will be reading nonfiction material about birds' beaks. We will work with analogies to help us make conclusions about how birds use their beaks. We do not have a collection of live birds here for our studies, but using analogies will help us learn and make conclusions about beaks by comparing them to things we do know.

• All of us have seen a variety of birds in a variety of settings. We know and recognize many different kinds of birds. One of the ways that we recognize birds is by their beaks. They can be very different. In your groups, talk about some of the beaks that you have seen. Allow time for students to discuss some of the beaks of birds they know in small groups and then share their thoughts with the group. POSSIBLE STUDENT RESPONSES: *Hummingbirds have long pointed beaks. Eagles have a hook on their beak. Toucans have big striped beaks. Some birds have really big beaks, and others have really small beaks. My canary has a real small beak. Ducks have a flat beak.*

• What are birds' beaks for? *They use them for eating.* Of course you are right, birds use their beaks to eat. We all know that eating is necessary in order for living things to survive, so the way that a bird uses its beak must be important. If it isn't able to eat, it will die. We are going to look at two kinds of bird beaks today. We will also be looking at some tools that you might have in your homes. We will be searching for a tool that might be similar to the bird beaks. I am going to give you some information about each kind of bird beak. I also will give you some objects that might be good to use in making analogies to the beaks. Your job will be to read about the bird beaks. You will look at the tools to find one that has similarities to the beak you have read about. That task goes along with the first question on our thinking map. Then, as question two asks you to do, you will decide how they are similar. That will lead you to question three, deciding what you can learn from the analogy. "What do the things you know about B help you to understand more about A?" That is where we start the important part of reasoning by analogy, coming to a conclusion from comparing the two things. But before we can actually make the conclusion we need to think about the two things, checking for any important differences that would stand in the way of the conclusion we want to make. I will be doing some think-alouds to model the process for the first beak. For the second beak you will be in charge of the thinking.

- **Our first beak belongs to a bird you all know, the flamingo. It is very interesting to watch a flamingo eat.** It would be helpful to to show a short video clip of a flamingo eating. A picture of a flamingo eating would also be a good teaching tool to use here. **Here is some information I would like you to read about the flamingo.** Display the information about flamingo eating habits found at the end of this lesson on a chart or as a handout to the group to read. Read the information to the students or have them read it by themselves, depending on their skill level. **The information we have tells us something about the way that flamingos eat, but I would like to understand more about how the flamingo's beak works. We cannot actually have a flamingo here, and even if we did, we would not be able to actually go into its mouth to see how it works, but we can try to find something that we can compare to the beak. This will help us understand more about how a flamingo's beak helps it to survive. Our first step on our thinking map asks us to find something that is similar to the flamingo's beak. I have brought some tools for us to look at. Let's see if we can match one of these with the beak of a flamingo to help us understand more about how it works.** Show the students a variety of tools that may be compared to bird beaks. Tools should include a straw, a nutcracker, a slotted spoon, an awl, a grapefruit spoon, and tweezers. The students should be allowed to manipulate the tools to determine the ways they are used. Simulated bird food like water, gummy worms, celery chunks, unshelled nuts, and small fruits can be used to help students as they manipulate the tools. Guide the students by questioning to make the connection between a slotted spoon and the flamingo's beak. **Looking at these tools, did you find one that you think might be used to make an analogy to the flamingo's beak?** Students should identify the slotted spoon as being similar to the beak of the flamingo.

- **We can use this graphic organizer to help us keep our ideas clear as we are use reasoning by analogy.** Show the students the graphic organizer for reasoning by analogy. **The analogy we are considering is between the flamingo's beak and a slotted spoon. The words "a flamingo's beak" belong on the "A" side of the first box because that is the object we are trying to understand more about, and the words "a slotted spoon" belong on the 'B" side of the box because that is the object we are going to use to help us reach a new un-**

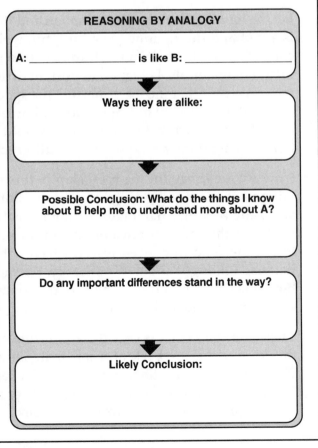

REASONING BY ANALOGY

A: _____ is like B: _____

↓

Ways they are alike:

↓

Possible Conclusion: What do the things I know about B help me to understand more about A?

↓

Do any important differences stand in the way?

↓

Likely Conclusion:

derstanding about flamingo beaks. Now our top box reads, "A flamingo's beak is like a slotted spoon."

• It is time for us to move to the second step in our thinking map. How are they similar? I want to try to think of ways they are similar that are important to making this analogy. I remember that the article we read said that the flamingo eats with its head upside down in the water. If I turn a picture of a flamingo upside down its beak looks like a spoon. That is a way they are alike. I can record my idea in the next box on the graphic organizer. In the box labelled "Ways they are alike" write the sentence, "They have the same shape." The article also said they have slits that let the water out. Slotted spoons have slits, too. That is another way they are alike. I'll record that, too. Write the sentence, "They have slits."

• The third step on our thinking map tells us to think about what we know about slotted spoons that can help us understand flamingo beaks. It says, "What do the things I know about B, a slotted spoon, help me to understand more about A, a flamingo's beak? Refer to the top box of the graphic organizer to help the students see the connection between the letters and the two objects. Let's think about that. The article says that the flamingo opens and closes its beak very quickly so that the water is pushed out some slits and the food stays inside. Hold up the slotted spoon. Dip it into water that has celery floating. The water will drain out of the spoon and the celery will stay in. I can see that the water goes out the holes in the spoon and the celery stays in the spoon. It can't get out the holes. I think that I can say that flamingo beaks have slots to let the water go out and that they have only food left in their beaks like a slotted spoon only has the food left in it. I can write that idea in the next box. Write the sentence in the box. This is a tentative conclusion until possible differences are checked out. I think this may be a conclusion that I can make from my analogy, but first I need to check for any differences that may stand in the way of this thinking. That is the fourth step on the thinking map.

• Let me look again at the slotted spoon and the picture of the flamingo. I know that the spoon is a tool and the flamingo is a bird, but wait. The analogy is about the flamingo's beak. It could be called a tool for the bird to eat, so that is not really a difference. They are made of different materials. Is that an important difference? A discussion should lead the students to the agreement that the materials that the spoon and the beak are made of does not change the way that they work. The important similarities are the ways these two things are shaped and used. I don't see any differences that would change that comparison, so we can write a sentence saying there are no important differences in the next box.

• Now we are ready for the final step in this thinking strategy. What can we learn about flamingo beaks by comparing them to the slotted spoon? Our analogy has helped me understand the way that flamingos are able to eat. They gather water plants and animals in their mouth as they are underwater. Then they push the water out through holes until all that is left is the food they need to eat. I have a better understanding of the way flamingos eat because I thought about this analogy. We can record these ideas in the "Likely Conclusion" box. It is likely that this is the way that flamingos' beaks help them eat. Record the conclusion from the think-aloud on the graphic organizer.

• The flamingo's beak is very different from our next beak. We are now going to practice this thinking using the beak of a cardinal. Show pictures of a cardinal and, if possible, a short video of a cardinal eating. Here is an article on the cardinal and the way that it uses its beak. Display the article at the end of this lesson for students to read or for you to read to them. Allow time for processing of the information. Look at the thinking map and the first question. Where do we begin with our thinking? POSSIBLE STUDENT RESPONSES: *We need to find something that is similar to the cardinal's beak.* **What did we use when we were thinking about the flamingo?** POSSIBLE STUDENT RESPONSES: *We looked at the tools to see which one would make a good analogy.* **Right! Let's look at the tools again.** Allow time for students to explore the tools and find the tool that is similar to the cardinal beak. Guided questioning should lead them to the nutcracker.

- **We have chosen the nutcracker to use in our analogy. Let's begin a new graphic organizer.** The graphic organizer for flamingo beaks could be hung to the side for reference during the next section of the lesson. **Since we want to learn more about the cardinal's beak, we will write that in the "A" section. We are comparing it to the nutcracker so that will be written in the "B" section.** Fill in the top section of the graphic organizer. **What is the next step in this strategy of reasoning by analogy?** POSSIBLE STUDENT RESPONSES: *We have to find ways they are similar.* **Work in your groups to discuss the important ways that nutcrackers and cardinal beaks are alike.** After small groups discuss, have students share their ideas with the class. The ideas should then be recorded in the second box on the graphic organizer. POSSIBLE STUDENT RESPONSES: *They are very thick and strong. They have a top and a bottom part that squeeze together.*

- **The third step on the thinking map asks us to think about what we know about nutcrackers that will help us understand more about cardinal beaks.** Refer to the thinking map and the third question. **Talk in your groups about what you know about nutcrackers that might help you understand more about cardinal beaks.** Allow time for discussion and then move to group sharing. Record the group's ideas in the third box of the graphic organizer after the sharing time. POSSIBLE STUDENT RESPONSE: *They can crack open nuts when they squeeze together.*

- **Are there any differences that might stand in the way of using this analogy? That is the fourth question. Before we can decide on a likely conclusion we must be sure there is nothing that would mean our conclusion is unlikely. What differences do you notice about the cardinal's beak and a nutcracker?** POSSIBLE STUDENT RESPONSES: *They are not made of the same things. The nutcracker is not part of a live animal.* **They are not made of the same things. That is a difference we should consider. If the cardinal's beak were not made of a strong material would it be able to crack nutshells?** *No.* **Do we know if the beak is strong and hard or soft and weak?** *We read that the beak is strong.* **Yes. It was in the article that we read that the cardinal's beak is strong. So the fact that it is a different material than the nutcracker is not an important difference. They are both strong enough to crack nuts. What about the idea that a nutcracker is not part of a live animal. Is that an important difference? Talk in your groups and decide.** Students will generally realize that the beak and the nutcracker are both tools, even though the beak is part of an animal's body. **We can record our thinking in the fourth box, the one for considering differences.** Record that there are no important differences even though they are made of different materials and one is connected to an animal.

- **The final step in our reasoning by analogy is to use our analogy to come to a conclusion. What can we say is a likely conclusion from the analogy we have made?** With the class, discuss the things they have said, guiding them to a likely conclusion about cardinal beaks. POSSIBLE STUDENT RESPONSES: *The cardinal's very strong beak can crack open nuts by squeezing the top and bottom together.*

THINKING ABOUT THINKING

- **What do we call the thinking we did?** *Reasoning by analogy.*

- **What steps did you follow to do this type of thinking? What did you do first, second, etc.?** POSSIBLE STUDENT RESPONSES: *I thought about the two things, cardinal beaks and nutcrackers. Then*

I thought of the ways that they are alike. That was making the analogy. At the end, I thought about what our analogy showed me about cardinal beaks that I didn't know. It is supposed to teach me something new. And I made sure that there were no differences that would make the conclusion wrong.

- **Were the thinking map and the graphic organizer helpful to you in practicing reasoning by analogy?** The children usually respond that the map and organizer were easy to use. They make the thinking easier.

- **Is reasoning by analogy a good way to learn new things?** Most students say that it is but only when we can't find those things out directly, like in the case of the dinosaurs or things we can't open up to see inside.

APPLYING YOUR THINKING

Immediate Transfer

- We have studied our teeth and the ways that we use them. Use the thinking map and graphic organizer for reasoning by analogy to explain how the different teeth in your mouth are used like different tools. What conclusions can you draw about your teeth from what you know about those tools? Draw pictures of these tools if it will help you to better understand how teeth work.

- You've been studying how the systems work in your body. Some people say that the heart is like a pump. Use the thinking map for and a graphic organizer reasoning by analogy to explore this analogy and to draw some interesting conclusions about the heart. Illustrate your analogy.

- In our science lessons, we have learned about different kinds of rocks and minerals. Your teacher has a chart comparing rocks to cookies. It says that igneous rocks are like wafer cookies, metamorphic rocks are like chocolate chip cookies, and sedimentary rocks are like sandwich cookies. Use the thinking map and graphic organizer for reasoning by analogy to help you come to a conclusion that tells what new understanding you have about the ways these rocks are formed.

Reinforcement Later

- What analogy can be made to help people understand the problem of pollution? Work in groups to go through the steps of reasoning by analogy. Write a story about why your analogy is a good one or, use your analogy to give an oral report on pollution.

- What analogy can help us understand the feelings of a new student in our class? Does your analogy suggest any things that could be done to help a new student feel comfortable? Use your analogy to make a poster for the room.

CONTENT EXTENSION

The other household tools used in the lessons could be used to explore other beaks with the reasoning by analogy strategy for thinking. The teacher should use available sources to gather information about beaks, translating the information into readable passages for the level of the students. Then, using the tools, the thinking map, and the graphic organizer, the students would develop an analogy and come to a conclusion about other bird beaks. The tools included would be good to use in the following analogies: straw—hummingbird beak, tweezers—robin beak, awl—woodpecker, a grapefruit spoon—a parrot (Note that a parrot's beak is a combination of sharp scoop for fruit eating and nutcracker for seed eating.)

SUGGESTED SPECIAL NEEDS MODIFICATIONS

Frontload: The concept of "analogy" may require preteaching for some students. Simple, quick discussions of "How is a_____like a ____?" using familiar objects may be helpful. The frame "a___is like a____because ____" adds the reason for the comparison. The term "analogy" can be used simultaneously in these discussions. As the lesson suggests, allowing students to manipulate objects often assists in their generating the analogy.

Prior to this lesson, some students may need multiple experiences with drawing conclusions. "Concluding" requires the ability to infer something new from given information. Initially, the teacher may wish to think aloud illustrating conclusions which are based on data. Situations may range from curricular related items ("I notice a pattern in these words. I conclude this word must be a noun because it is a place and the names of places are nouns.") to daily situations (I notice a pattern of hurt feelings on the playground. I conclude that our class needs to discuss ways to solve problems."). As students state their own conclusions, they should be required to provide their reasons for conclusions.

Diversify: To develop the background knowledge necessary for the content information in this lesson, students may benefit from access to information through nonfiction read alouds by the teacher or adult volunteer, partner reading, books on tape, videos, or filmstrips.

Expand the Possibilities: Assessments of written responses may be based upon students' thinking first, and expressive skills second. Oral responses may also reveal thinking beyond students' ability to express themselves in writing. Student drawings which illustrate and label the similarities may be useful in assessing the students' understanding, while reducing the demands of written expression.

ASSESSING STUDENT THINKING ABOUT POSSIBILITIES

Any of the application items can be used as assessment tools to demonstrate the students' understanding of the strategy and their ability to use reasoning by analogy. They should be able to explain analogies, recognize the similarities, and note if there are differences that may cause a problem. They should be able to tell what conclusion comes from the analogy.

The flamingo eats underwater plants and animals. It lives near water where it can find the food it needs to survive. This bird has a way of eating that is very different from most other birds. The flamingo eats with its head upside down. Its beak is designed to gather food from the water. There are thin slits on the top section. With its head upside down, the flamingo puts its beak into the water. It opens and closes its beak very quickly to gather its food, which it then swallows.

Bird beaks serve as more than mouths for swallowing the food they need to survive. Because birds are unable to hold their food with their wings they have adapted their beaks in ways that allow them to prepare their food for eating. Cardinal beaks are an example of one way birds use their beaks to prepare and then eat their food. The cardinal's diet includes a variety of seeds and nuts. Its beak is short and cone-shaped. It is very strong at its base, the place where it is connected to the body. Great force can be made against food when it is placed at the base of the cardinal's beak.

Sample Student Responses • Vowel Sounds

REASONING BY ANALOGY

A: _A flamingo beak_ **is like B:** _a slotted spoon._

Ways they are alike:

They are shaped the same.

They scoop things up in the water.

They have openings in them.

Possible Conclusion: What do the things I know about B help me to understand more about A?

They let the water go out. Then they only have food left in them.

Do any important differences stand in the way?

There are no important differences. Even though they are made of different materials, that doesn't change how they work.

Likely Conclusion:

It is likely that when flamingos gather food in their beaks from the water, the water goes out through holes until all that is left is the food.

Sample Student Responses • Vowel Sounds

REASONING BY ANALOGY

A: *A cardinal beak* **is like B:** *a nutcracker*

▼

Ways they are alike:

They are very thick and strong.

They have a top and a bottom part that squeeze together.

▼

Possible Conclusion: What do the things I know about B help me to understand more about A?

They can crack open nuts when they squeeze together.

▼

Do any important differences stand in the way?

There are no important differences. Even though they are made of different materials, the beak is hard enough to crack nuts.

▼

Likely Conclusion:

The cardinal's very strong beak can crack open nuts by squeezing the top and bottom parts together.

REASONING BY ANALOGY

1. What is similar to the object?

2. How are they similar?

3. How do the things I know about B help me to understand more about A?

4. Are there any important differences which stand in the way of the conclusion?

REASONING BY ANALOGY

A: _____ is like B: _____

Ways they are alike:

Possible Conclusion: What do the things I know about B help me to understand more about A?

Do any important differences stand in the way?

Likely Conclusion:

CHAPTER 18
CONDITIONAL REASONING

Infusing Skillful Conditional Reasoning into Language Arts

Teaching students in grades 1 and 2 to engage in valid conditional reasoning involves helping them learn to ask and carefully answer the following questions about conclusions that can be drawn from "If.....,then......" statements and other information before they endorse any particular conclusion:

```
CONDITIONAL REASONING

1. What topic are you trying to learn more about?

2. Write an "if...then" statement about something
   you know about the topic.

3. Do you know anything more about either part
   of the "if...then" statement?

4. What conclusion can be drawn by combining
   your "if...then" statement with this new
   information?

5. Does your thinking follow the patterns of valid
   or invalid reasoning?
```

figure 18.1

In the lessons in this chapter, this "thinking map" for conditional reasoning is used to guide your students' thinking explicitly as they engage with the lesson content.

When students learn and use this strategy for conditional reasoning, they first formulate "If.....,then......' statements that they know about a given topic (like "If you put a snowball on your desk, then it will melt") and then ask what other information they have about the component statements in this conditional statement. ("The ball is made out of snow. Snow melts when it gets warm.") They then consider what conclusion they might draw from these pieces of information and the conditional by testing whether it follows logically from the given information. This critical thinking skill is a deductive reasoning skill, the only one in this book. Some conclusions follow from the information the students start with, some do not, and students learn how to discriminate using this type of deductive inference.

These lessons also supplement the use of this thinking map with various supporting classroom strategies such as using a graphic organizer, engaging in cooperative thinking, thinking about thinking, and continued guided practice. These classroom strategies enhance both the thinking skill that the students are learning and their mastery of the lesson content.

The key graphic organizer for conditional reasoning is in figure 18.2.

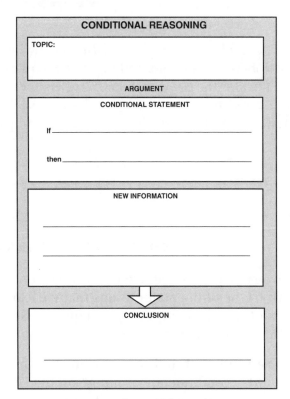

figure 18.2

This graphic organizer helps students record the conditional statement and the additional piece of information related to one or another of the components of the conditional. Reproducible blank graphic organizers are found at the end of each chapter.

For more in-depth information on teaching conditional reasoning, please refer to Chapter 17 in the book *Infusing the Teaching of Critical and Creative Thinking into Elementary Instruction*, by Robert Swartz and Sandra Parks. A computer disk containing the blank, reproducible graphic organizers used in this book is also available. Both book and disk are available through Critical Thinking Books & Software.

THE TALKING EGGS

Language Arts   **Grades 1–2**

OBJECTIVES

CONTENT

Students will develop their listening comprehension skills as they analyze the thinking of the characters and how their actions impact their rewards.

THINKING SKILL/PROCESS

Students will learn to combine information that is conditional in character (information expressed by "if...then" statements) with other relevant information to draw conclusions.

METHODS AND MATERIALS

CONTENT

The teacher will read aloud *The Talking Eggs* by Robert D. SanSouci and direct the students to listen for the conversations of the characters and the actions taken by the characters. The story will be discussed in collaborative groups.

THINKING SKILL/PROCESS

Students will be guided to engage in conditional reasoning by structured questioning and a graphic organizer. They will work together in collaborative groups and as a class investigate the validity of conditional statements and to create conditional statements based on information from the story.

LESSON

INTRODUCTION TO CONTENT AND THINKING SKILL/PROCESS

- Every year in school we study fire safety. We learn the things to do to be safe when there is a fire. One of the major things that we learn is if the fire alarm sounds, then everyone should exit the building quickly and quietly. So on the day when the fire alarm sounds, you know that we must all exit the building.

- The kind of thinking we do in this situation is called "conditional reasoning." Write the words "conditional reasoning" on the chalkboard. You will be developing a list of terms for students and referring back to this list, so it should be written where it can be viewed during the lesson. **We put two ideas together and we drew a conclusion from them. The first of these ideas was the conditional statement.**

  If the fire alarm sounds, then we should exit the building.
  Then you discovered that the fire alarm was sounding.
  The conclusion you drew was We should exit the building.

- If someone did not know the first statement, the conditional statement, that if the fire alarm sounds, you must leave the building, then that person would not know what to do if they heard the fire alarm sound. It was in putting the two ideas together that you were able to draw a conclusion. By doing this you were able to proceed to a safe spot. You drew a conclusion from things you already knew. This is "conditional reasoning." On the chalkboard write the terms "conditional statement," "new information," and "conclusion." To help the students remember what a conditional statement is, you might want to tell them that it is the "if...then statement." These words could be written after conditional statement. To help them with the term conclusion, you could write the words "what you now know."

- Here is another example from our studies of animals. We have studied the different animal groups. We know that birds are the only animals with feathers. If you are presented with a new animal, one you are not familiar with, and you see that it has feathers on its body, then you will say that it must be a bird. The conditional statement you have is

    If the animal has feathers, then it is a bird.
    The new information you have is: The animal has feathers.
    The conclusion that you can draw from knowing this information is:
    The animal is a bird.

    Point to the terms on the chalkboard as they are used to help students make the connection and understand the language.

- Can you think of another example in which you came to know something by conditional reasoning? Allow the students time to think, then ask the students to discuss their example with another student and to write down the examples. (The written portion depends on the level of the group.) Have two or three students tell the class about their examples. Write them on the board in the same form as the example. ANSWERS VARY.

- There is a pattern that conditional reasoning follows. It can help us check our reasoning. It looks like this. Show the conditional reasoning chart at left in a larger form.

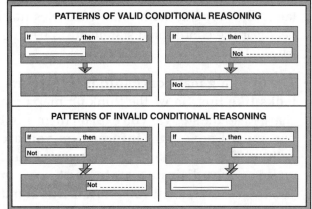

- Let's take one of the samples we have written on the board and fit it into the pattern. Use one of the student's conditional statements to demonstrate the pattern. Involve students in filling in the sections, and discussing the relationship of the statement, the new information, and the conclusion drawn. When working with the new information, use the sentence frame, "If I can find out ___ I will be able to conclude ___."

- We want to be careful when we do this kind of thinking, as we do in all our thinking because mistakes can be made if we are careless. Earlier I reminded you that we all know that if a fire alarm sounds, then we should leave the building. Suppose someone tells you that everyone in the school left the building this afternoon. Can you conclude that the fire alarm sounded? Ask for a show of hands from students who think you can conclude this. Some students will probably raise their hands. On a copy of the patterns of conditional reasoning chart, write the following conditional statement and new information in the bottom right frame. "If the fire alarm sounds, everyone must exit the building," and "Everyone exited the building." Follow this with the conclusion, "The fire alarm must have sounded." Well, let's think about this. Could there have been other reasons why people left the building? What other reasons could there have been for the people to have left the building? POSSIBLE STUDENT RESPONSES: *Everyone may have left the building because there was something special going on outside, like a parade or field days. Maybe it was the end of the school day.* So the conclusion that a fire alarm sounded does not necessarily follow from the information you started with. It might not have sounded at all. There could have been something else that happened.

- When the conclusion doesn't follow from the given information, the reasoning is called "invalid." We mark this reasoning invalid by putting a slash mark over the arrow pointing to the conclusion. This means that you can't definitely accept the conclusion as true based on the information you are given because something else might have happened. Mark a slash through the arrow.

- On the other hand, when you can draw a conclusion that follows from the information you start with, like in the first example, the reasoning can be called "valid." That means that given the information you start with, the conclusion must definitely be true. There can't be any other possibility. Think about it. If it is true that if an animal has feathers, it is a bird and this animal before you has feathers, it *must* be a bird. There could be no other possibility. Write the term "valid" on the chalkboard. After it, add the words "Must be true because of the starting information." In this case, we do not put a slash through the arrow on the chart. **So when the information you start with is definitely true, then the conclusion must be true. That makes this a very special type of reasoning. The information and the conditional statement can <u>prove</u> that the conclusion is definitely correct. But you should remember that you can say this only after you are satisfied that the information you start with is true and the reasoning is valid.** Use an example like "If something has feathers, then it is a fish," which you can identify as a conditional statement that is not true, to show the students that if you start with a conditional statement that is not true, you might end up drawing a conclusion that is false. Go over this with other examples until you are sure that the students understand the need for the conditional statement to be true in order to be able to say that the conclusion is true.

- **The thinking map for conditional reasoning looks like this.** Show the thinking map on a chart. Read the steps as you explain them. **First you must know what information you are getting.** Read question #1. **Then you should write a conditional statement, or an "if...then..." statement you know is true about the topic.** Read question #2. **Question 3 asks you if there is any new information you have that goes along with the first, the conditional statement.** Read question #3. **That new information can be thought about together with the conditional statement and you can draw a conclusion.** Read question #4. **Finally, you should think carefully about the information and your thinking to check for valid reasoning.** Read question #5.

> ## CONDITIONAL REASONING
>
> 1. What topic are you trying to learn more about?
>
> 2. Write an "if...then" statement about something you know about the topic.
>
> 3. Do you know anything more about either part of the "if...then" statement?
>
> 4. What conclusion can be drawn by combining your "if...then" statement with this new information?
>
> 5. Does your thinking follow the patterns of valid or invalid reasoning?

THINKING ACTIVELY

- Today we are going to practice conditional reasoning. The book we will read in this lesson is titled *The Talking Eggs* by Robert D. SanSouci. This story is a version of a Creole folktale originally told in Louisiana many, many years ago. It seems to match some fairy tales from places such as France. It may have been brought to the United States by French people who came to settle in a new land. Let's read the book. As we read, we can watch to see if the characters do any conditional reasoning in their thinking. Read the story, taking time for students to really understand and discuss the events and the characters reactions.

- This certainly is an unusual story filled with unusual things! And yet, the characters may have reminded you of characters from fairytales you have read. In your groups, talk about the characters of this story. **What characters did they remind you of from other stories?** POSSIBLE STUDENT RESPONSES: *Blanche was like Cinderella. She had to do all of the work around the house. She had a wicked mother like Cinderella's stepmother. She only had one wicked sister, but she was like the stepsisters in Cinderella. The old woman was sort of like the fairy godmother except she did bad things to the sister. The fairy godmother didn't do that. Blanche didn't get a prince to marry in this story.*

- **Good thinking! You made some good connections to another story. There definitely are similarities, but there are also differences. Of course the setting is different. There were no castles in** *The Talking Eggs,* **only a poor farm and woods where the girls met the old woman. Blanche did all of the housework like Cinderella, but no one got to go to a ball and meet a prince. Let's discuss the plot of this story. What were the events of the story that led to Blanche meeting the old woman and going to her house?** The students should retell the events of the story leading to the old woman taking Blanche back to her cottage in the woods. Blanche got sent to the well for water. She meets the old woman at the well and stops to give her a drink. When she gets home her sister Rose throws the water out because she thinks it is too warm to drink. The mother and Rose scold and hit Blanche until she runs away. When she is in the woods crying, the old woman finds her and takes her home.

- **As the events of the story take place, the characters' actions reveal some situations where conditional reasoning was needed. When the old woman took Blanche back to her cottage, she asked Blanche to make some promises. These promises are based on conditional reasoning. What did the old woman say to Blanche when she took her back to her cottage?** POSSIBLE STUDENT RESPONSE: *She said that Blanche had to promise not to laugh and then she would deserve supper and a clean bed.* The class could find and reread this section of the story. **Can we write this as a conditional statement that the old woman considers as they get to her home?** Students usually recognize this as the conditional statement, "If Blanche doesn't laugh then she'll deserve supper and a clean bed." If they have trouble with this, give them the sentence frame "If_____then_____" and ask them to fill it in according to what the old woman says. When they have identified the conditional statement show them a transparency of the graphic organizer for conditional reasoning. You have filled in "Getting a nice supper and a clean bed" as the topic. Now you

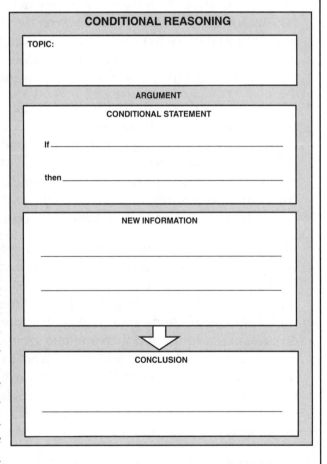

should write the conditional statement. Explain how the graphic organizer parallels the thinking map for conditional reasoning. **When the old woman watches to see what Blanche does, what new information does she get? What should we write?** POSSIBLE STUDENT RESPONSE: *Blanche doesn't laugh at all the strange things she sees.* Write the students' response in the new information box. **What conclusion can the old woman draw as a result of this new information?** POSSIBLE STUDENT RESPONSE: *Blanche deserves supper and a clean bed.* **Do we know from the story that this happened?** *Yes.*

- **We need to be sure that this conditional reasoning is valid. Does the conclusion follow from the information she started with?** Walk through the patterns of valid conditional reasoning to show that the argument is valid.

- **Now let's look at the thinking that the old woman did the next morning as she sent Blanche home. She talked to Blanche about the talking eggs and a pleasant surprise. What conditional statement was the old woman thinking about at this point?** For this second conditional reasoning statement, ask students to talk in their groups and then share with the class. The first was done with a whole group to model, and now they should start practicing with the support of their group. The conditional statement that the old woman was thinking as she sent Blanche home is, "If Blanche throws the plain talking eggs over her left shoulder, then she will deserve a pleasant surprise." Fill this in a new blank graphic organizer for conditional reasoning in which you write "The Talking Eggs" as the topic. If the students are having difficulty, give them the sentence frame for a conditional statement (above) and ask them to fill it in. **We now know what the old woman is thinking. She thinks, "If Blanche throws the plain talking eggs over her left shoulder, then she will deserve a pleasant surprise." What do we need to know next about her conditional reasoning?** Students readily say that we now need to know what new information appears in the story. **So we need to know what Blanche did. What did she do?** POSSIBLE STUDENT RESPONSE: *She threw the plain talking eggs over her left shoulder.* **If this is the new information, what conclusion can the old woman draw?** POSSIBLE STUDENT RESPONSE: *That Blanche deserves a pleasant surprise.* **Does the story confirm that this happens?** *Yes.* Walk students through the patterns of valid reasoning again. This is another valid argument.

- **We have looked at two situations with the old woman and Blanche. When Rose came into the picture, the old woman was not thinking the same things. She knew the kind of girl Rose was from the things that Blanche had said. Now Rose was coming to get the same riches that Blanche had received. Because of the differences in the two girls' attitudes and behaviors, the old woman changes her conditional reasoning. We don't hear the old woman's conditional reasoning in what she says, but we can figure out her argument based on the things that happened to Rose when she came to visit.**

- **When Rose went to the cottage, the old woman made the same statement, "If you don't laugh, then you'll get supper and a clean bed." What did Rose do when she saw the strange things at the old woman's home?** POSSIBLE STUDENT RESPONSE: *She laughed at everything.* **Thinking about the story, talk in your groups. What do you think the old woman was really thinking? Begin your conditional reasoning statement with, "If Rose laughs,..."** Allow time for discussion in groups and then a whole group discussion to create the second part (the consequent) of the statement. POSSIBLE STUDENT RESPONSE: *If Rose laughs, then she will not get a good supper and a good night's rest.* **What is the new information?** *Rose laughs at everything.* Write all of this on a new graphic organizer. **What conclusion can we draw based on this information?** POSSIBLE STUDENT RESPONSE: *That Rose will not get a good supper and a good night's sleep.* Discuss the validity of this argument with the students in the same way. It, too, is valid.

- **When we consider the events of the following morning, again we see that the old woman is going to change her conditional statement. Work in your groups to see if you can create a conditional reasoning statement for the way that the old woman is thinking at this point in the story.** Support the groups as they attempt to create a conditional reasoning statement for the old woman's thinking. POSSIBLE STUDENT RESPONSE: *If Rose takes the jeweled talking eggs and throws them over her right shoulder, then she deserves to have awful things come out to chase her.* **You have composed a conditional reasoning statement that the old woman is probably thinking. What is the new information presented in the story?** POSSIBLE STUDENT RESPONSE: *Rose takes* *the talking jeweled eggs and throws them over her right shoulder.* **Go back to your groups and create a conclusion by combining the information in the conditional statement with this information.** POSSIBLE STUDENT RESPONSE: *Rose deserves to have awful things come out of the eggs.* **Is this good conditional reasoning? Does the conclusion follow from the information she started with?** Walk through the patterns of valid conditional reasoning to show that the statement is valid.

- **The conditional reasoning that the old woman does is valid when she deals with Blanche and Rose. Her thinking follows the patterns of valid reasoning as stated at the beginning of the lesson. Which of the girls listened and followed the same line of reasoning in her thinking as the old woman?** Encourage the use of the language of conditional reasoning as students discuss and respond. POSSIBLE STUDENT RESPONSES: *Blanche did. She always did what she was told, so she thought (reasoned) that the same things would occur. Rose did not pay any attention to what the old woman was saying. She just wanted to take everything that was good without doing what the old woman asked her to do. She did not think (was not drawing the conclusion) that she would have awful things happen to her.*

THINKING ABOUT THINKING

- **Let's think about the thinking we did with conditional reasoning. What steps did we take in using conditional reasoning?** POSSIBLE STUDENT RESPONSE: *We thought about what the topic was, then we made an "if...then..." statement with the things we knew. The new information we found was compared to the "if...then..." statement to make a conclusion. The whole thing had to match the patterns of the right thinking if it was valid.* Refer the students to a copy of the thinking map for conditional reasoning and discuss whether what they have said coincides with what is on the thinking map.

- **Is this kind of thinking important for you to know? Why?** The students often see this as important in solving a puzzle. There are lots of times when they can use conditional reasoning to get an answer they don't yet know. They can use the patterns to prove that they have concluded the right answer.

APPLYING YOUR THINKING

Immediate Transfer

- **Suppose your friend wanted a new bike. (S)he needs to save his (her) allowance for five months in order to have enough money to pay for it. What would be the conditional statement you could make about this information? What new information would you need to go with your conditional statement so that you can draw the conclusion that you have enough money to pay for the new bike? Create a story that would show the conditional reasoning you used in this situation.**

- **The characters in the fairy tale *Rumpelstiltskin* use conditional reasoning in their thinking several times during the story. Use a thinking map and the graphic organizer for conditional reasoning to help you identify and check the validity of their thinking.**

Reinforcement Later

- **Use conditional reasoning to create some posters for giving advice on how to dress for different kinds of weather.**

• We have been studying plants and the things they need to grow. Use conditional reasoning to predict what will happen to plants that do not get any water. The thinking map and graphic organizer for conditional reasoning will help you.

SUGGESTED SPECIAL NEEDS MODIFICATIONS

Frontload: This lesson contains sophisticated language as well as abstract reasoning. It will be important that the terms "conditional" and "valid" are fully defined prior to the lesson. Conditionals can be introduced as "If...then..." statements. Several simple if...then statements should be explored. These should relate to the students' everyday lives. "Valid" can be explained as being "definitely true."

Similarly, examples from everyday school situations can be used to introduce students to the forms of conditional arguments. "If you are sick, then you will be absent from school. Joe is absent today. Joe is sick." Discuss other reasons for being absent to demonstrate that the conditional argument is not valid, then identify the pattern. Simple examples like this will familiarize students with the lines of reasoning involved, so that they can better recognize them in more abstract situations.

Streamline: For some students, the expectation (at least in the initial lessons on this skill), may be to develop greater skill at stating reasons and identifying the conclusion of conditional arguments. This may require significant teacher guidance through paraphrasing and questioning.

Clarify: Simplify the vocabulary by coupling terms with a synonym or providing alternatives which capture the meaning, for example, "valid" is "always correct," "conditional" is "if...then... statement."

Diversify: Special needs students are often aided by working in cooperative groups, especially if the students are trained in the skills to include all group members in the discussion and if the tasks are divided relative to each student's strengths. For example, a skillful notetaker can honor everyone's ideas and reduce the writing task for some. Establish an atmosphere in which all answers are initially accepted in such groups. Think-pair-share helps students generate ideas and hear clear models.

Expand the Possibilities: Assessments of written responses may be based upon students' thinking first, and expressive skills second. Oral responses may also reveal thinking beyond students' ability to express themselves in writing.

ASSESSING STUDENT THINKING ABOUT CONDITIONAL REASONING

To assess students' conditional reasoning skills, use any of the transfer activities or a real life situation in the classroom. Meeting with individuals or small groups will allow you to assess their skill as they compose an oral or written argument on the topic using the language of the strategy.

CONDITIONAL REASONING

TOPIC: *supper and a nice bed*

ARGUMENT

CONDITIONAL STATEMENT

If *Blanche doesn't laugh*

then *she will deserve supper and a clean bed.*

NEW INFORMATION

Blanche doesn't laugh at all the strange things she sees.

∨

CONCLUSION

Blanche deserves supper and a clean bed.

Sample Student Responses • The Talking Eggs

CONDITIONAL REASONING

TOPIC: *the talking eggs*

ARGUMENT

CONDITIONAL STATEMENT

If *Blanche throws plain talking eggs over her left shoulder*

then *she will deserve a surprise.*

NEW INFORMATION

She threw the plain talking eggs over her left shoulder.

CONCLUSION

Blanche deserves a pleasant surprise.

CONDITIONAL REASONING

TOPIC: *laughing, supper, and a bed*

ARGUMENT

CONDITIONAL STATEMENT

If *Rose laughs*

then *she'll get a bad supper and a terrible night's sleep.*

NEW INFORMATION

Rose laughs.

∨

CONCLUSION

Rose will get a terrible supper and a bad night's rest.

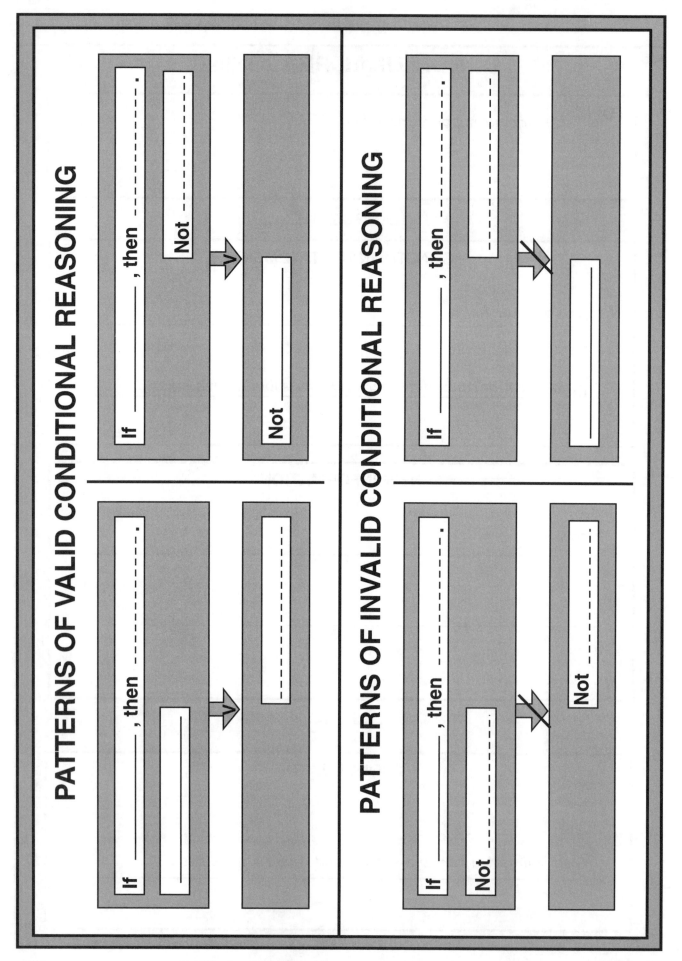

PATTERNS OF VALID CONDITIONAL REASONING

PATTERNS OF INVALID CONDITIONAL REASONING

CONDITIONAL REASONING

1. **What topic are you trying to learn more about?**

2. **Write an "if...then" statement about something you know about the topic.**

3. **Do you know anything more about either part of the "if...then" statement?**

4. **What conclusion can be drawn by combining your "if...then" statement with this new information?**

5. **Does your thinking follow the patterns of valid or invalid reasoning?**

CONDITIONAL REASONING

TOPIC:

ARGUMENT

CONDITIONAL STATEMENT

If _____

then _____

NEW INFORMATION

_____

_____

CONCLUSION

_____

APPENDIX

INFUSION LESSON PLAN EXPLANATION

LESSON TITLE
STORY TITLE (if appropriate)

Subject   **Grade Level**

OBJECTIVES

CONTENT
Statement of content objectives from curriculum guide or text outline.

THINKING SKILL/PROCESS
Description of the thinking skill/process the students will learn.

METHODS AND MATERIALS

CONTENT
Use of instructional methods to teach the content effectively

Expository methods	Discourse/Socratic
Inquiry methods	dialog
Cooperative learning	Integrated arts
Graphic organizers	Directed observation
Advance organizers	Advance organizers
Higher order questions	Higher order questions
Specialized software	
Using Manipulatives	

THINKING SKILL/PROCESS
Use of instructional methods to teach the thinking process effectively

Structured questioning strategies

Specialized graphic organizers

Collaborative learning, including Think/Pair/Share

Direct or inductive explanation of thinking processes

Learner-generated cognitive maps (diagrams and pictures)

LESSON

INTRODUCTION TO CONTENT AND THINKING SKILL/PROCESS

• Teacher's comments to introduce the content objectives. The lesson instruction should activate students' prior knowledge of the content and establish its relevance and importance.

• Teacher's comments to introduce the thinking process and its significance. The lesson introduction should activate students' prior experience with the thinking skill/process, preview the thinking skill/process, and demonstrate the value and usefulness of performing the thinking skillfully. The introduction serves as an anticipatory set for the thinking process and should confirm the benefits of its skillful use.

THINKING ACTIVELY

• Active thinking involving verbal prompts and graphic maps

• The main activity of the lesson interweaves the explicit thinking skill/process with the content. This is what makes the content lesson an infused lesson. Students are guided through the thinking activity by verbal prompts (e.g., questions) in the language of the thinking skill/process and by graphic organizers.

THINKING ABOUT THINKING

- Distancing activities that help students think about the thinking process.

- Students are asked direct questions about their thinking. The metacognition map guides the composition of these question. Students reflect about what kind of thinking they did, how they did it, and how effective it was.

APPLYING THINKING

- Transfer activities that involve student-prompted use of the skill in other examples.

- There are two broad categories of transfer activities: (1) near or far activities that immediately follow the substance of the lesson and (2) reinforcement later in the school year. Both types of transfer involve less teacher prompting of the thinking process than in the Thinking Actively component of the lesson.

Immediate Transfer

- Near Transfer: Application of the process within the same class session or soon afterward to content similar to that of the initial infusion lesson. Decrease teacher prompting of the thinking.

- Far Transfer: Application of the process within the same class session or soon afterward to content different from that of the initial infusion lesson. Decrease teacher prompting of the thinking.

Reinforcement Later

- Application of the process later in the school year to content different from that of the infusion lesson. Decrease teacher prompting of the thinking.

OPTIONAL EXTENSION ACTIVITIES
(Can occur at any time during the lesson)

REINFORCING OTHER THINKING SKILLS AND PROCESSES: Working on additional thinking skills/processed from previous infusion lessons which can play a role in this lesson.

RESEARCH EXTENSION: Gathering additional information which may be useful in researching a conclusion or an interpretation in this lesson.

USE OF SPECIALIZED ASSIGNMENTS TO REINFORCE THE THINKING: Assigning written or oral tasks or projects which may further illustrate students's thinking about the content in this lesson.

ASSESSING STUDENT THINKING

Extended written or oral assignment of performance assessments of the effective use of the thinking skill or process.

INFUSION LESSON PLAN

TITLE:

SUBJECT: **GRADE:**

INFUSION LESSONS
Introduction
Thinking Actively
Thinking about Thinking
Applying your Thinking

OBJECTIVES

CONTENT   THINKING SKILL/PROCESS

METHODS AND MATERIALS

CONTENT   THINKING SKILL/PROCESS

LESSON

INTRODUCTION TO CONTENT AND THINKING SKILL/PROCESS

INTRODUCING THE THINKING

1. Importance of the thinking.
2. How do you do the thinking?
3. Importance of the content.

THINKING ACTIVELY

THINKING ABOUT THINKING

THINKING ABOUT THINKING

1. Kind of thinking?

2. How did you do it?

3. Is it effective?

APPLYING THINKING

Immediate Transfer

APPLYING YOUR THINKING
1. Immediate Transfer
a. Near Transfer
b. Far Transfer
2. Reinforcement Later

Reinforcement Later

**OPTIONAL EXTENSION ACTIVITIES
(CAN OCCUR AT ANY TIME DURING THE LESSON)**

ASSESSING STUDENT THINKING

WRITING TEMPLATES

When students are confronted with the idea of writing ideas down on paper, their first frightening thought is "How do I begin?" and "What do I put down on my paper?" This is especially true in the first and second grades when students are developing hand-eye coordination necessary for writing as well as the basics of word, sentence, and paragraph construction. The writing templates included in this appendix will help students write and organize their thoughts. By using the templates, their writing will come more quickly and become much easier for them.

What we include in this appendix are tools that you can use in your classrooms to help students translate the thinking they do in the Infusion lessons into organized and informative writing that reflects this thinking. Hence, these templates should be used in the later months of grade 1 and throughout grade 2 when you feel that students have mastered enough of the mechanics of writing to be able to organize what they write. Each of the writing templates included is a suggested framework. Some templates are connected explicitly with certain types of thinking, e.g., persuasive writing and decision making/problem solving, while some have much broader applications. Each of the templates included is used in at least one of the lessons in this book.

The writing templates included in this appendix, we should add, will not inhibit or interfere with the students' creative flow of words. Since writing is a form of communication and a life long skill, it is important for students' writing to have structure and purpose in order to be understood; within this structure there is ample room for creative expression.

When a student uses a writing template, he or she translates good thinking into good writing in steps. The first step in this process is careful and critical thinking. The completed graphic organizer is a visual showing of the student's thinking which, in turn, serves as a prewrite planner. This prewrite planner helps to answer the question: "What do I put down on my paper?" The next step in the process is to provide the students with guidance in answering the question: "How and where do I put these ideas down on paper?" That, of course, will depend on the purpose of the writing. When that is determined, the type of writing and appropriate template will serve the purpose. It is *your* job to specify the purpose of the writing and the type of writing students should do to achieve this purpose. *Their job* is to follow the template. This may mean that (e.g., in the first grade) you may want to *read the template out loud* to guide the students. If you judge that their reading skills are adequate, then you can give it to them and have them read it.

Lessons that include writing extensions that call for the use of these templates also include writing samples from students who have used the templates.

Writing templates can be used for other thinking skills lessons that you may wish to develop yourself.

Some suggestions to guide the use of the templates in the 1st and 2nd grades

1) Each student should *always* have his/ her own template even if you read it out loud.

2) As you go over the template with the class, tie its parts to the parts of the graphic organizer so students can transfer their thinking more easily.

3) Students should write their names and date due at the top.

4) When another student proofreads the draft of the writing, they can use the template as a guide to make suggestions.

5) Students may always elaborate more than what is required by the template.

6) Remember to modify according to the IEPs of special needs students. This may be done by writing the individual modifications on the templates of those students requiring them.

7) Have students turn in their completed template draft and graphic organizer with the final copy of their writing.

8) The templates may also be used to aid in assessment of student work. Suggestions:

   a) Assess whether the students know the main idea, details, and topic sentences from the sentences they choose to use in their writing.

   b) Place the template side by side with the final draft of the writing.

   c) Write assessment comments about the writing on the completed templates.

   d) Students may use the corrected template to revise their writing.

   e) If you use a portfolio system in your classroom, students may wish to include the template with pieces of writing they place in their portfolios.

Special note on writing persuasive prose related to decision making and problem solving

When first- and second-grade students engage in a writing extension based on the strategies of decision making and problem solving, it is more developmentally appropriate to ask them to describe one option for a decision and one solution for a problem. It will be far too overwhelming for students to compare, contrast, and then evaluate a number of options or solutions within a piece of writing, and at the same time learn the format for persuasive writing.

At the same time, first- and second-grade students can still learn and practice thinking about more than one option when they choose the best option or the best solution among a series of options or solutions as they discuss the pros and cons that they have recorded on their graphic organizers. Once a best option or solution has been chosen, it can then be the topic of their persuasive writing.

You can help students make this transition from their thinking to their writing by explicit modeling of planning and drafting a persuasive paragraph for students while eliciting their ideas about the pros and cons of the specific option or solution they have chosen to recommend. These ideas should come directly from their completed graphic organizer. See the persuasive writing templates for decision making/predicting the consequences of options and problem solving that follow these comments.

Student Writing Samples

Many student writing samples are included in this book. When they are included, there is always a writing extension towards the end of the lesson explaining the writing task. In many cases, a writing task includes the use of a writing template. The writing templates in this Appendix are designed so that you can photocopy them and give one to each student. They include lines for students to write individual sentences. Individual sentences are components of the overall writing. Each template that students write on can be viewed as the first draft of their writing. Students should then be asked to transpose the sentences from the template to another piece of paper, which will become their final writing. The writing samples that appear at the end of the lessons are final writings and are based on the use of these templates.

STORY STARTERS—USED IN CONJUNCTION WITH NARRATIVE WRITING

Story starters are very helpful for young writers because they provide a framework in which the student can place the ideas generated and recorded on the graphic organizers. Decision making, problem solving, and generating possibilities are all thinking strategies that lend themselves to story writing. A story starter is written by the teacher or by the group, using the template for narrative writing. It includes a place for character introductions, identification of setting, and may include the introduction of the problem. The students are able to move quickly into the events that develop the story and the solution that brings closure to the problem. The graphic organizer is used as a map to help the students with the information they will include in their writing. It should be available to them as they are writing and should be referred to in the writing discussion.

CLASS NARRATIVE STORY WRITING

The writing of class stories allows the students to be supported in a task that may still be difficult for them. The modeling provided nurtures the writing development as the students work with the teacher to map a story and then put it in print. Once written, it can be divided into pages that students illustrate for a class book. A modification of this type of writing strategy is used in the generating possibilities strategy. In that lesson, the beginning is written as a class. The possibilities are then used with a sentence frame with each idea chosen receiving its own page. These are completed individually by the students along with illustrations. An ending is then written as a class.

STORY MAPS

The basic frame of a story map allows a place for students to write or draw the important ideas in the beginning, middle, and end of a story. This can be accomplished on a folded piece of legal-sized paper. The front section should have the title and the author, the inside-left section should be labeled "Beginning," the inside-right section should be labeled "Middle," and the back section should be labeled "Ending."

There are a variety of ways to story map. Story maps can be used as a final project for certain activities or certain students. They can also be used to take the information gathered from the thinking map and translate it into a form that guides students in their story writing.

EXPOSITORY WRITING FRAMES

Providing paragraph frames can be a helpful tool for students. This allows students to drop their ideas into sentences that are partially written and arranged in a logical sequence for a paragraph. The focus for the student can be directed to the thinking that has occurred in the Infusion lesson.

SENTENCE FRAMES

For certain writing activities, especially in the first grade, the use of sentence frames can be a way of supporting the students in expressing the ideas gathered through an Infusion lesson. These can be given to students on a page that allows for illustration to further express their ideas. The responses should be based on information from the graphic organizers completed in the lesson.

PICTURE CAPTIONS

Illustrating ideas and writing captions allows students to share their thoughts and knowledge with a combination of drawing and printed text. The key to this type of response is detail in both the illustration and the caption. Students should take time to make sure that they express their ideas in a way that others will understand.

- Think about what it is that you have learned and will be sharing.
- Draw the picture that will show your ideas. Be sure to make a picture that includes enough details to show your ideas.
- Write a caption for your picture. It can be one, two, or three sentences long. The sentences must be clear and tell about the main details of your picture.

Using a mobile to display caption writing is very effective. Have the students make a series of pictures about the topic and write captions for the pictures. Write a title for the set of pictures and captions. Put everything together on a mobile with each picture and its caption hanging together on a string.

NARRATIVE PARAGRAPH WRITING TEMPLATE

This template is to be used with the completed graphic organizer for decision making, problem solving, or creating a metaphor.

NARRATIVE PARAGRAPH

- Sentence 1: Write a topic sentence for your paragraph. It should tell the main idea.

1) _____

_____

- Sentences 2–4: Write about the details of the main idea. They elaborate (tell more about) the main idea.

2) _____

_____

3) _____

_____

4) _____

_____

- Sentence 5: This is the clincher sentence. It wraps up everything in the paragraph with a concluding thought.

5) _____

_____

STORY BOXES: A WRITING TEMPLATE FOR USE WITH DECISION-MAKING OR PROBLEM-SOLVING GRAPHIC ORGANIZERS

Used in sets of four, eight, or more, story boxes provide a quick place to draw the events of the story or jot down the ideas for the events of the story in sequence. The first one or two boxes are filled with the beginning of the story. The next two–four boxes are filled with the middle events of the story. The last box or boxes are filled with the problem solution and ending. They can be used with the problem-solving or decision-making graphic organizers to show other solutions or options.

STORY BOXES

- Boxes 1–2: Show the beginning of the story. Be sure to include the setting, characters, and beginning action.

- Boxes 3–6: Fill these boxes with the events that show the events of the story. There should be details that clearly tell the problem in the story and what the characters do because of the problem.

- Boxes 7–8: Show the way that the problem is solved and the way that the story ends.

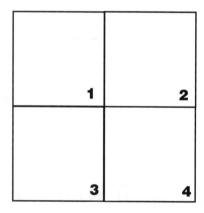

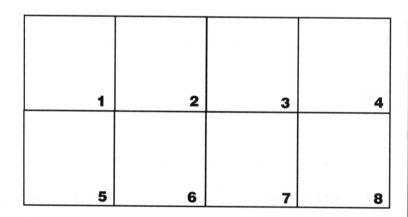

2

4

1

3

6

8

5

7

PERSUASIVE PARAGRAPH WRITING TEMPLATE

This template uses as a prewriting map the completed graphic organizers from any of the following thinking strategy lessons: problem solving, decision making, or uncovering assumptions.

PERSUASIVE PARAGRAPH

- Sentence 1: Tell the main idea of the paragraph. This is the thought or action you are trying to convince someone to believe or to do.

1) _____

_____

- Sentences 2–4: Tell the reasons that support your thought or action.

2) _____

_____

3) _____

_____

4) _____

_____

- Sentence 5: This is the clincher sentence. Restate your main idea so that the reader will be convinced to believe it or take the action.

5) _____

_____

EXPOSITORY PARAGRAPH WRITING TEMPLATE

This template can be used with completed graphic organizers from lessons on comparing and contrasting, uncovering assumptions, parts/whole relationships, or classification.

EXPOSITORY PARAGRAPH

- Sentence 1: Tell the main idea of the paragraph, what it is you will be describing.

1) _____

_____

- Sentences 2–4 : These are the supporting sentences. Give the details and describe your subject. Use different beginnings for your sentences so that they are interesting to read.

2) _____

_____

3) _____

_____

4) _____

_____

- Sentence 5: Write a clincher sentence that restates the topic sentence.

5) _____

_____

OPEN COMPARE/ CONTRAST EXPOSITORY WRITING TEMPLATE

This template is to be used with the open compare/contrast graphic organizer.

OPEN COMPARE/ CONTRAST

- Sentence 1: State the names of the two things being compared and contrasted in a sentence that tells the reader that there are ways the two things are alike and different. This is your topic sentence.

1) _____

_____

- Sentences 2–4: These should be the sentences telling about some important ways that the two things are alike. Make sure that you give details about the similarities.

2) _____

_____

3) _____

_____

4) _____

_____

- Sentences 5–7: These should be sentences telling about some important ways that the two things are different. Make sure that you give details about the differences.

5) _____

_____

6) _____

_____

7) _____

_____

- Sentence 8: This is your last sentence. It should tell something important about the conclusions that were made about the similarities and differences.

8) _____

_____

POETRY WRITING TEMPLATES

ACROSTIC POEM

This writing activity uses the completed graphic organizer as a springboard for ideas relating to the characters, settings, topics, or situations presented in the thinking lesson. It can be used with a variety of thinking strategies, including the following: problem solving, comparing and contrasting, parts/whole relationships, uncovering assumptions, and reasons and conclusions.

The poem can take several forms but the key to its formation is in the first letter that begins each line. It is usually unrhymed. Another style of this poem puts the letters down the side as above but the student creates phrases that begin with each of the letters and relates important ideas about the subject.

ACROSTIC POEM

- Choose the word that will be the subject of your poem. Write it down the side of a piece of paper.

- Brainstorm a list of words that begin with each of the letters. Try for words that may be helpful in telling the ideas about the subject. Use a box sheet for your brainstorming. Each box has one of the letters from the subject word.

- Think about the subject. Play with the words to put them into your poem in a way that describes the subject. Add extra words to the ends of lines if they help to make your thought clearer to the reader.

ACROSTIC POEM

- Choose the word that will be the subject of your poem. Write it down here. _____

- Think about the subject and the things that are important to say.

- Put together groups of words (phrases) that begin with each letter of the word. These phrases will describe an important thought about the subject. For example, let's use the word, "dog."

Dashes after the cat next door

Offers his paw for me to shake

Goes with me to the park to play ball

_____

_____

_____

_____

_____

_____

DEFINITION POEM

This poetry form begins with a question, "What is (subject)?" as the first line, answers the question in the body of the poem, and concludes with the phrase, "That's (subject)!"

DEFINITION POEM

- Think about the subject that you are explaining in your poem.

- Complete the sentence frame, "What is _____?" This is your first line.

- Brainstorm a list of things that tell important things about the subject and will help the reader understand it.

- Choose the ones that are your favorites and really tell about the subject. Write each one on its own line under your question from above.

- Finish the poem with the line, "That's _____!"

CHARACTER POEM

This poem asks students to use the knowledge they have gained about a character to create a poem that summarizes their important characteristics. It works well with the graphic organizers used in uncovering assumptions, comparing/contrasting, and generating possibilities. The lines of the poem can be adjusted or deleted to fit the character being described.

CHARACTER POEM

Line one—name

1) _____

Line two—three describing words

2) _____

Line three—relative or friend of

3) _____

Line four—who likes

4) _____

Line five—who wants

5) _____

Line six—who really

6) _____

Line seven—resident of

7) _____

Line eight—synonym

8) _____

BIBLIOGRAPHY

Adler, David A. *Cam Jansen and the Mystery of the Stolen Diamonds*. New York: Penguin Books, 1991.

Brett, Jan. *Town Mouse Country Mouse*. New York: Putnam and Grosset Group, 1994.

Browne, Anthony. *Piggybook*. New York: Dragonfly Books, 1986.

Cannon, Janell. *Stellaluna*. San Diego, CA: Harcourt Brace, 1993.

Crowe, Robert L. *Tyler Toad and the Thunder*. New York: E.P. Dutton, 1980.

Duvoisin, Roger. *Petunia*. New York: Alfred A. Knopf, Inc., 1950.

Esbense, Barbara Juster. *Baby Whales Drink Milk*. New York: HarperCollins Children's Books, 1993

Havill, Juanita. *Jamaica's Find*. Boston: Houghton Mifflin Company, 1986.

Hoberman, Mary Ann. *A House Is a House for Me*. New York: Viking Penguin, Inc., 1978.

Jones, Simon. *Dear Mr. Blueberry*. New York: Macmillan Publishing Company, 1991.

Lobel, Arnold. *Fables*. New York: Harper and Row Publishers, Inc., 1980.

McCloskey, Robert. *Make Way for Ducklings*. New York: Penguin Books, 1969.

McKissack, Patricia C. *Flossie and the Fox*. New York: Penguin Books, 1986.

SanSouci, Robert, D. *The Talking Eggs*. New York: Penguin Putnam Inc., 1989.

Stanley, Diane. *Rumpelstiltskin's Daughter*. New York: Morrow Junior Books, 1997.

Steig, William. *Dr. DeSoto*. Farrar, New York: Straus and Giroux Publishers, 1982.

Shannon, David. *A Bad Case of Stripes*. New York: Scholastic Books, Inc., 1998.

Van Allsburg, Chris. *The Sweetest Fig*. Boston: Houghton Mifflin Company, 1993.

Viorst, Judith. *Alexander and the Terrible, Horrible, No Good, Very Bad Day*. New York: Alladin Books, Macmillan Publishing Company, 1972.

Warner Brothers Productions. *Free Willy* (the movie on videotape). Directed by Simon Wincer. Produced by Jennie Lew Tugend and Lauren Shuler-Donner.

Weller, Frances Ward. *I Wonder if I'll See a Whale*. New York: Putnam Publishing Group, The., 1998.

Wolpert, Tom. *Whales for Kids*. Minnetonka, MN: Creative Publishing International, 1991.

Young, Ed. *Lon Po Po*. New York: Putnam and Grosset Group, 1989.

Young, Ed. *Seven Blind Mice*. New York: Putnam and Grosset Book Group, 1992.

Zolotow, Charlotte. *Mr. Rabbit and the Lovely Present*. New York: HarperCollins Publishers, 1990.

INDEX